Jesus as witnessed
by the disciple he loved

A commentary on the gospel of John

Alan Asay

Foreword by Murray Stein

Q

First Published in Great Britain in 2024

7 Grape Lane, Petergate, York YO1 7HU
Tel: +44 (0)1904 635967
Email: info@quacks.info
Website: radiusonline.info

Quacks Books is an imprint of Radius Publishing Ltd

A CIP catalogue record for this book is
available from the British Library.

ISBN: 978-1-912728-81-7

Set on a page size of 210mm x 297mm printed by offset lithography on an eighty gsm
chosen for its sustainability.

Acknowledgements

I am very grateful to Fiona Morgan, Geoffrey Durham and Murray Stein for their advice and encouragement, and most grateful to Martin Stone for introducing me to Jung and helping me become a person who could write this book.

Contents

Foreword by Murray Stein.. 7

Preface 10

Why bother at all with such an old book?...................................12

Why John? Why Jesus?...15

   Traditional Christian views of Christ..16

   Quaker experience of Christ and the inward Light 17

   Jung's view of God's relationship with humanity................... 20

The disciple Jesus loved and the development of his gospel............................ 29

   Origination with the Beloved Disciple...................................... 29

   Who was the Beloved Disciple? 31

   The manuscript tradition 32

The historical setting of John... 34

   Judean culture around Jesus' time... 36

   Is John antisemitic? 38

The life and death of Jesus... 46

   "What canst thou say?"... 46

   The literal/historical and the spiritual/archetypal................. 47

   Prologue (1:1-18) 49

     Meaning and resonance 50

   A spiritual community begins (1:19-51)................................... 56

     Meaning and resonance 57

   Wedding at Cana (2:1-12) 60

     Meaning and resonance 60

     Reflection... 62

       Whose wedding was it?..62

   Clearing the Temple at Passover (2:12-25) 63

     Meaning and resonance 63

     Reflections 65

       "My Father's house" (2:16)..65

       "But he was speaking of the temple of his body" (2:21): Who tells us this? 66

   Birth out of water and spirit (3:1-21)....................................... 68

     Meaning and resonance 68

     Reflections 70

       Nicodemus from "among the Pharisees" (3:1)..................70

       "born out of water and spirit" (3:5) 73

       "For God so loved the World that he gave his Unique Son" (3:16).......................75

"those who do not Trust are condemned already" 78

John the Baptist and a man "from above" (3:22-36) 79

   Meaning and resonance 80

   Reflection...81

      "God is True" (3:33).. 81

Samaritan woman at Jacob's Well (4:1-42) 85

   Meaning and resonance 87

   Reflections 90

      "No greater than our father Jacob" (4:12): Supplanting the supplanter............. 90

      "True worshippers will worship the Father in spirit and Truth" (4:23)............. 95

To Galilee; an official's son healed (4:43-54) 98

   Meaning and resonance 99

   Reflection... 99

      "Unless you see Signs and miracles, you will not Trust" (4:48)............99

A healing on the Sabbath and its aftermath (chapter 5) 102

   Meaning and resonance 103

   Reflection...105

      "You have never heard his voice or seen his image" (5:37) 105

Bread of life (chapter 6)... 108

   Meaning and resonance 110

   Reflections 113

      "No one can come to me unless the Father ... draws him" (6:44) 113

      "the bread that I will give for the Life of the World" (6:51) 116

Jesus at the Festival of Booths, part 1 (chapter 7)......................... 119

   Meaning and resonance 120

   Reflections 122

      "You are not also from Galilee, are you?" (7:52) 122

Jesus at the Festival of Booths, part 2 (chapter 8) 123

   Meaning and resonance 125

   Reflections 128

      "the Truth shall set you free" (8:32) 128

      "your father the devil" (8:44) 129

The man born blind healed on the Sabbath (chapter 9).............................132

   Meaning and resonance 133

   Reflections 134

      "who did Wrong, this man or his parents, that he was born blind?" (9:2) 134

      "excluded from synagogues" (9:22, also 12:42, 16:2) 137

The good shepherd (chapter 10)..139

   Meaning and resonance 140

   Reflection...142

      "My sheep know my voice" (10:4) 142

Jesus raises Lazarus (11:1-44) 144

   Meaning and resonance 146

Caiaphas and the plot to kill Jesus (11:45-55) 148

   Meaning and resonance 148

   Reflection...149

      "better for you that one person die for the people" (11:50) 149

The Hour comes (chapter 12)..154

   Meaning and resonance 156

   Reflection...162

      "Glorify your name" (12:27) 162

The Last Supper (chapter 13) 165

   Meaning and resonance 166

   Reflection...169

      "I, your lord and teacher, washed your feet" (13:14) 169

Words before leaving (chapter 14)...171

   Meaning and resonance 173

   Reflection...173

      "If you Love me, you will keep my commandments" (14:15).............173

Jesus is arrested and interrogated (18:1-27) 175

   Meaning and resonance 175

Jesus before Pilate (18:28-19:16)..177

   Meaning and resonance 178

   Reflection...179

      "We have no king but Caesar" (19:15) 179

Jesus is crucified (19:17-37) 181

   Meaning and resonance 182

   Reflections 187

      The cross (19:17, 19, 25, 31) 187

      "Woman, there is your son." (19:26) 190

Burying the body of Jesus (19:38-42)...191

   Meaning and resonance 191

Resurrection morning (20:1-18)..192

   Meaning and resonance 193

Reflection 194

    "Rise again from the dead" (20:9) 194

Appearances to disciples (20:19-29) 196

    Meaning and resonance 197

    Reflection 198

    "Blessed are those who don't see and yet Trust." (20:29)................................ 198

Original ending of John 201

    Meaning and resonance 201

Epilogue 201

Breakfast by the sea (21:1-15) 201

    Meaning and resonance 202

Jesus, Peter, and the Beloved Disciple (21:15-25)................................... 203

    Meaning and resonance 203

    Reflection 204

    "Peter felt hurt that he said to him a third time, 'Do you love me?'" (21:17) 204

The final words of Jesus (John 15-17) 209

"I am the vine" (15:1-17) 209

    Meaning and resonance 209

    Reflections 210

    "I am the vine; you are the branches." (15:5) 210

    "You are my friends if you do what I command you" (15:14)............................215

The World's hatred (15:18-16:4) 220

    Meaning and resonance 221

Jesus will go, the Counsellor will come (16:4-15) 221

    Meaning and resonance 222

    Reflection 222

    "Unless I go away, the Counsellor will not come to you." (16:7)....................... 222

Sorrow will turn to joy (16:16-33) 226

    Meaning and resonance 226

Jesus speaking with his Father (17:1-26) 227

    Meaning and resonance 228

    Reflection 229

    "that they may be one just as we are one, I in them and you in me" (17:22) 229

John's key words... 234

    Counsellor.. 235

    Darkness 236

    Father 236

Hour...237

I am..238

Jews 239

Know, Recognise, Realise 241

Life, Live..243

Light..244

Love...245

Recognise 245

Remain..245

Rescue, Rescuer...247

Sign 247

Testify, Testimony...252

Trust 252

Truth, True 254

Unique Son 255

Very truly I tell you 255

Witness, Testimony, Testify 256

World..256

Wrong, Wrongdoing, Wrongfulness 258

Concepts not found in John 260

Opposites in John and Jung 263

What happened afterwards 270

Fate of the community that wrote John..............270

The apocalypse of Carl Jung 276

The remedy for individuals....................................281

Collective prospects: shards and hopes 282

Bibliography 287

Appendix...293

The woman (and text) caught in adultery (John 7:53-8:11) 293

Meaning and resonance 293

Index..295

Foreword

Growing up in the home of a Baptist pastor my early life was infused with Bible verses, and of them all committed to memory in my childhood the one that stands out above all others is John 3:16: "For God so loved the world, that he gave his only begotten Son, that whosoever believeth in him shall not perish, but have everlasting life." I quote the King James Version because that was our Bible. The message contained in these few words is timeless and contains the essence of John's Gospel.

Who is this "only begotten Son"? This is a mystery. John refers to him as "the Word" (Logos): "In the beginning was the Word, and the Word was with God, and the Word was God" (John 1:1). This is John's introduction to the main character in his narrative, namely Jesus Christ. To say that the reference here is simply to a man named Jesus who lived at a certain time and in a particular place is insufficient. This figure is a symbol, and symbols express something largely unconscious and in need of further elaboration in consciousness.

Beginning with people like the beloved disciple, John, Christian thinkers have been busy with the task of interpreting this symbol for over twenty centuries, and the work is still ongoing. In fact, it is begun over and over again in every generation precisely because it is such an inexhaustible and timeless symbol. In the 20th Century, the great Swiss Protestant theologian, Karl Barth, spent his entire life reflecting on this symbol and then writing about it as the central theme in his massive work, *Church Dogmatics*. The equally great Swiss Protestant psychologist, Carl Gustav Jung, also worked persistently at interpreting this symbol in many of his writings, especially in the late works such as "The Spirit Mercurius" (CW 13) and *Aion* (CW 9/ii). And now in this new commentary placed before us by Alan Asay, we have a contemporary reflection on the meaning of this symbol in which the author combines religious, scholarly and psychological methods to bring the meaning of John's narrative about the mystery of the Word made flesh into modern consciousness. Hermeneutical work on John's Gospel is without doubt a labor that will continue indefinitely through the Ages. Symbols such as the one John presents in his narrative about "the only begotten Son of God," Jesus Christ, are absolutely inexhaustible.

The type of narrative presented in the Gospel of John is of events historical but more importantly symbolic. Symbol is presented as history and history as symbol. The two levels are intertwined. The historical man, Jesus of Nazareth, who walked along the shores of the Sea of Galilee with his disciples has been transformed in this narrative into the symbolic Jesus Christ, the "only begotten Son," the eternal Word. He is presented as man, but he is also God. As he declares: "I and the Father are One." As symbols do, Jesus represents something beyond thought or words, namely God who is here shown as active in history at a particular time and place.

This Gospel has a dreamlike quality, therefore. There are humans in the story, and there is a God-man in the story. They meet and communicate, but they are not made of the same stuff. Jesus has a ghostly quality in this Gospel, unlike his pre-resurrection life as depicted in the three Synoptic Gospels. As the unconscious speaks to us in symbols in our dreams, so the Fourth Gospel speaks to us in symbols as though it were a dream.

The problem is how to interpret symbolic communications like this. For that we need a Joseph or a Daniel, the great biblical dream interpreters who brought the meaning of dreams home to the life and times of the dreamers. Obviously, this dream had great meaning for John, the dreamer, and his times. On the assumption that symbols of John's Gospel retain relevance even for us, what does this figure named Jesus Christ mean for us today? That is the hermeneutical question, and this is the daunting challenge Alan Asay has taken up in this meticulously researched and detailed commentary.

There is no question that this text is subversive. It challenges what Jung called "the spirit of the times." This is the dominant worldly ideology of any particular age or culture. In Jesus' time, it was represented by the priestly caste in control of the Temple in Jerusalem. Everyone fears them, but Jesus confronts them again and again with "a way, a truth and a light" that is spiritually beyond their reach and threatens their power. "My kingdom is not of this world," Jesus declares, and he speaks of another spirit, a "spirit of the depths" in Jung's words. Some people hear his message and respond; many do not. This too is a mystery. Why some and not all?

As John's Gospel is presented in the New Testament, the script for this drama has been written by God in eternity and not created by humans in time acting out of their various specific motivations. God is the author of the narrative as is frequently mentioned in the text. The fate of Jesus and its precise timing are given by the Father, not by humans. Hence, all the actors in the story, both the good and the evil, are enacting God's will. Thus there is no blame to be assigned to those who attack or betray Jesus. They too are enacting a script written by a hand above their heads. They are important actors in the drama that unfolds in the play, and without them there would be no tension. The tension builds to a climax, the crucifixion and resurrection, which embodies the great revelation of Christ's meaning for the world. This is therefore not a moralistic tale from which we are to derive lessons for living an ethical life. It is rather a portrait of God's "only begotten Son" bringing good news to all sentient beings – God loves you! And beyond that: God is making you immortal like his only begotten Son, and you will not die! Jesus Christ has entered the temporal world from eternity with a mission, namely to transform its destiny from death, the normal end of all material creation due to entropy and the laws of nature, to eternal life in the Holy City revealed in the 22nd chapter of John's Revelation. History is a Divine Comedy, not a Greek or Shakespearean tragedy. Goethe understood this when he concluded his life's work with the redemption of Faust. This is John's vision. Our destiny is to arrive at a "new heaven and a new earth" where there is "no more sea" (i.e., evil and death).

I come back to John 3:16 – οὕτως γὰρ ἠγάπησεν ὁ θεὸς τὸν κόσμον, ὥστε τὸν υἱὸν τὸν μονογενῆ ἔδωκεν, ἵνα πᾶς ὁ πιστεύων εἰς αὐτὸν μὴ ἀπόληται ἀλλ᾽ ἔχῃ ζωὴν αἰώνιον.

> Yes, God loved the world so much
> that he gave the only Son,

that everyone who believes in him may not perish
but may have eternal life.[1]

Raymond Brown, the translator, comments on the word "loved" in this passage: "The aorist implies a supreme act of love... Notice that in 1 John the love is oriented toward Christians ("we") while in John iii 16 God loves the world... The verb here is agapan... a perfect example of agapan expressing itself in action, for vs. 16 refers to God's love expressing itself in the Incarnation and the death of the Son."[2] God's action is agapan, love.

To my mind, a successful Jungian analysis is one that uncovers this source of love and total acceptance within. John found it in his discipleship and relationship with Jesus of Nazareth. Patients in analysis may find it in the therapeutic relationship or in experiences in dreams and active imagination. And deep reading of texts like the Gospel of John may open the way to the Source as well.

This most impressive scholarly work by Alan Asay will assist deep readers of John's narrative to re-discover the timeless realities beyond the words of translation on a page of paper, and thereby to perform what M.-L. von Franz describes as "progressively transforming 'ancient, eternal truths' into more highly differentiated conscious patterns of realization."[3]

Murray Stein, Goldiwil, July 2023

---

[1] Translation by Raymond E Brown, *The Gospel of John, The Anchor Bible*, Vol. 1, p. 129.

[2] *Ibid.* p. 133.

[3] M.L. von Franz, *Number and Time*, pp. 302-03.

Preface

Mary L. Coloe prefaced her brilliant study of John with her translation of John 15:4, where Jesus says:

> Make your home in me, as I make mine in you.

Then, with remarkable candour, she explained why she has devoted much of her life to the study of John:

> These words have been the basis of my own ongoing spiritual journey from long before I professed religious vows. The quotation expresses for me the sense I have of the wonder and mystery of God's dwelling within me.[4]

Her words describe my experience as well, though I have professed no vows. No other gospel emphasises as much that the Holy Spirit must be a part of our lives so that Jesus lives on in us. I eventually became a Quaker because Quakers take the Holy Spirit very seriously.

Some parts of John still mystify me, but I have learned to sit with those in hopes that experience and growing in the Spirit will bring greater insight. Sometimes my patience has been rewarded. I follow and recommend William Taber's method:

> I began to read the Bible in what I sometimes call the Quaker way—that is, reading with both the analytical mind and the intuitive mind, leaving plenty of space for the Holy Spirit. On the one hand, Biblical scholarship and all the light science can provide; on the other hand, savoring and resting in the meaning, pausing from time to time to stare off into space...[5]

Another thing I value about Mary Coloe's work is that she is not afraid to write in the first person, rather than adopt a false air of detachment and disinterest like many scholars. She is no less a scholar for being honest with us about where she is coming from. Carl Jung, another major influence on me, began his monumental spiritual essay, *Answer to Job*, with this observation:

> In what follows, I shall attempt ... a "coming to terms" with certain religious traditions and ideas. Since I shall be dealing with numinous[6] factors, my feeling is challenged quite as much as my intellect. I cannot, therefore, write in a coolly objective manner, but must allow my emotional subjectivity to speak if I want to describe what I feel when I read certain books of the Bible.[7]

---

[4] Coloe, *God Dwells with Us*, page vii.

[5] Quoted in Pacific Yearly Meeting, *Faith and Practice*, no. 62 (page 83).

[6] Jung used terms like 'numinous' for the concepts he discovered in his psychological enquiries. A glossary of Jungian terms is found at http://www.jungpage.org/learn/jung-lexicon. Isaac Penington advised to give attention to the numinous, whether positive or negative: "Mind and watch to that which quickens and enlivens the soul towards God, and watch against that which flats and deadens it." *Works,* vol. 4, page 410.

[7] Jung, *Answer to Job* in *Collected Works*, volume 11, paragraph 559. Compete references to works cited in brief like *Answer to Job* are found in the Bibliography near the end of this book.

I must add, for honesty's sake, that I can't claim to be a biblical scholar myself. A good scholar of John will know over a dozen languages, most of them ancient, and will have studied a great many ancient texts.[8] Becoming a scholar of John takes an entire career, but I spent mine elsewhere. I also cannot claim to be an expert on Jung or analytical psychology, expertise that also takes a lifetime to develop.[9] However, I have over my lifetime had an interest in John and have often been struck by intriguing similarities between Quakerism, Jung, and John. I can point out a few of those and leave many others untouched for the better qualified to consider exploring.

Capitalised words (words not ordinarily capitalised) in This Typeface appear in "John's key words" below.

---

[8] Charlesworth, *Jesus as Mirrored in John*, page 275. "The sheer volume of secondary literature on John's Gospel makes it impossible for any single person to have read everything in every relevant language", Reinhartz, *Cast out of the Covenant*, page ix.

[9] Jung spent most of his time in his late years writing to save Christianity. In *Jung's Treatment of Christianity*, Murray Stein explains that Jung's late writing was analysing Christianity psychologically. It takes an analyst to understand an analysis, but I am not an analyst. I include material from Jung, not because I entirely understand it, but in a sense because I don't. As with John, it is a case of sitting with a mystery and perhaps it will unfold, probably into a paradox. I have found Jung enormously helpful in my own spiritual life, and his fresh look at Christianity breathes profound new life into it. However, I do not claim that he approved of Quakerism, or even knew much about it, although he had encountered two Quakers (see "better for you" (John 11) below). I just note some interesting similarities but I imply no endorsement of my view by Jung.

Why bother at all with such an old book?

As the first Quaker George Fox walked through Cumbria in 1652, he came to the home of Margaret Fell, wife of a judge and manager of an estate in the market town of Ulverston. Margaret and George soon became acquainted, and he accompanied her to her parish church a day later, where he stood up and spoke. That day his subject was one obscure to Friends now, the Jew outward and inward (Romans 2:28-29). Friends in the early days looked and behaved peculiarly, as Jews also did. Fox's point was that outward characteristics do not make a someone a Jew; instead it is the heart and mind of the person that make him a Jew, or make a Christian a Christian, for that matter.

Margaret stood up in her pew in wonderment as George went on to rebuke those whose understanding of the scriptures lacked the illumination of the Spirit that produced them.[1] Margaret later wrote of the experience:

> This opened me so, that it cut me to the heart. ... Then I cried bitterly in my spirit to the Lord, "We are all thieves; we are all thieves; we have taken the scriptures in words, and know nothing of them in ourselves."[2]

Our Friend Margaret would have little reason to accuse most of her present spiritual descendants of such thievery now. We have repented by ignoring the Bible, a thing she never did. There is, however, an alternative. We can try to understand the Bible, with the Spirit as our guide, as George had advised. He himself was steeped in the Bible, as Margaret Fell, Isaac Penington and many early Friends also were. Biblical phrases give their words a deep resonance.[3]

This book is meant to help particularly Quakers toward greater understanding of the Bible, but it is also meant only for the willing. Although Friends have long considered the Bible an important source of wisdom, we have never believed that knowledge of the Bible is essential to spiritual development.[4] Nor is Christianity the only way.

If willing, then please note that Bible study is not like reading a contemporary novel. The Bible comes with impediments to comprehension in that it is from a different time, culture, and place, and it was written in languages that relatively few people now understand. Yet its remoteness is also its greatest benefit: it lets

---

[1] Isabella Ross, *Margaret Fell: Mother of Quakerism* pp. 8-12 (York: William Sessions Book Trust, 1984).

[2] *Ibid.* Jung avoided about the same thing during his visit to India. "I studiously avoided all so-called 'holy men.' I did so because I had to make do with my own truth, not accept from others what I could not attain on my own. I would have felt it as a theft had I attempted to learn from the holy men and to accept their truth for myself." *Memories, Dreams, Reflections*, page 305.

[3] Michael Birkel shows how that resonance derives from scripture in *Engaging Scripture: Reading the Bible with Early Friends* (Richmond, Indiana: 2005) pages 2-11.

[4] The Bible is not essential to spiritual fulfilment, but the inner Light is, because from it alone a person can learn all that is necessary for spiritual fulfilment. Patricia Williams, *Quakerism: A Theology for our Time* pages 94-97. Melvin Keiser explains, "A true Christian [is] not someone who professes the name of Christ but someone who is a 'new creation' by the creativity of the divine Spirit, 'feeling the thing...though they never heard the outward ... name Christ.'" "Felt Reality in Practical Living", p. 203.

us escape the mindset and echo chambers of ourselves and our time and culture.[5] Knowledge and study can close much of the circumstantial gap between then and now, although it is important not to get carried away with them. Understanding the Bible is not an entirely intellectual exercise.

Carl Jung saw the excessive rationality of our time as worsening humanity's disconnect from the unconscious mind.[6] He devoted much of his energy late in his life toward reviving Christianity, which he believed had become so obsessed with the rational that it had lost its connection with the inward soul, where individuation (self realisation) occurs, if it ever does.

> In an outward form of religion where all the emphasis is on the outward figure (hence where we are dealing with a more or less complete projection[7]) the self[8] is identical with externalised ideas but remains unconscious as a psychic factor. When an unconscious content is replaced by a projected image to that extent, it is cut off from all participation in and influence on the conscious mind. Hence it largely forfeits its own life, because prevented from exerting the formative influence on consciousness natural to it; what is more, it remains in its original form—unchanged.... At a certain point it develops a tendency to regress to lower and more archaic levels. It may easily happen, therefore, that a Christian who believes in all the sacred figures is still undeveloped and unchanged in his inmost soul because he is "all God outside" and does not experience him in the soul. His deciding motives, his ruling interests and impulses, do not

---

[5] Brian Drayton wrote of Quakers:

> We are as liable as any people in history to fall prey to idolatry, and a habit of honest encounter with scripture is one way to combat this tendency.

> By idolatry, of course, I do not mean the obvious, old-fashioned paganism of offering worship to images of god or gods, but giving in to our tendency to mistake the human for the divine, the façade for the substance, and in short, to worship gods of our own making, who bear an eerie resemblance to ourselves. We thus are all too prone to shape a religion for ourselves, that is unchallenging and comfy, and we bow down to an image in a mirror.

On Living with a Concern for Gospel Ministry, p. 69 (Philadelphia: Quaker Press of Friends General Conference, 2006).

[6] *Collected Works*, volume 11, paragraph 443.

[7] Projection is a psychological action in which contents of the unconscious are encountered—not in the mind, where they actually reside—but in the outward environment where we live in a consciousness shared in varying degrees with all of humanity. The good and bad elements of the unconscious both get projected, so it can result in seeing others as hostile or bad, or nice, when really it is not the other person but our own fear, distaste, need, desire or other repressed feeling.

> During the process of treatment the dialectical discussion leads to a meeting between the patient and his shadow, that dark half of the psyche which we invariably get rid of by means of projection either by burdening our neighbours—in a wider or narrower sense— with all the faults that we obviously have ourselves, or by casting our sins upon a divine mediator with the aid of [contrition] or [attribution].

C.G. Jung, *Psychology and Alchemy,* in *Collected Works*, volume 12, paragraph 36.

[8] The self is "an archetypal image of man's fullest potential and the unity of the personality as a whole." Andrew Samuels, Bani Shorter and Fred Plaut, *A Critical Dictionary of Jungian Analysis*, page 135 (London: Routledge, 1986). The self appears in the image of God if we are open to its appearance.

spring from the sphere of Christianity but from the unconscious and undeveloped psyche, which is as pagan and archaic as ever. Not the individual alone but the sum total of individual lives in a nation proves the truth of this contention. The great events of our world as planned and executed by man do not breathe the spirit of Christianity but rather unadorned paganism.[9]

Jung's point is remarkably like George Fox's in that both call for spiritual life to look inward. In contrast, modern biblical scholarship aims to be evidence based and focuses on factual aspects such as history and the meaning of words, with minimal scope for inspiration with all its suspect subjectivity. It is a question of balance though; seeking to ascertain facts from the available evidence can make a contribution to understanding, particularly in understanding words and circumstances. If we remain open to the Spirit within, we have the benefits of both.

Joel Bean was one of the first Friends in California. His life as a Friend was plagued by the division among American Friends. Like Britain Yearly Meeting, he retained our traditional openness *and* our roots in Christianity:

> Our society [Quakerism] has had opportunity to learn, by sorrowful lessons, the danger of exalting too exclusively the Christ within, on the one hand, and Christ without, on the other. We have need ever to guard alike against that refined and emasculated spirituality, which undervalues the Bible and the outward means of grace, and even the incarnation and sacrifice of the Son of God, and that no less fatal outwardness and superficiality which would substitute profession, and prescription, and ritual, for saving faith and all the soul-renewing and life-transforming verities of Christian experi-ence, realized through the imparted energy of the Spirit of Christ within.
>
> Joel Bean, 1880[10]

---

[9] C.G. Jung, "Introduction to the religious and psychological problems of alchemy", in *Psychology and Alchemy, Collected Works*, volume 12, paragraph 12.

[10] Quoted in Pacific Yearly Meeting, *Faith and Practice*, no. 59 (page 82). Joel Bean and his family suffered first-hand the terrible division in Quakerism in the USA.

Why John? Why Jesus?

> [A person] is never helped in his suffering by what he thinks
> of himself; only suprahuman, revealed truth lifts him out of
> his distress.

Carl Jung[1]

John itself states its purpose and the rationale for the selection of the material in it:

> So Jesus performed many other signs in the presence of his
> disciples that have not been written in this book. These things
> have been written so that you might Trust that Jesus is the
> Christ and the son of God, and by that Trust may have Life in
> his name.

John 20:30-31

"Christ" is not a name but a title. It is the Greek equivalent of the Hebrew word "messiah", and both words mean "anointed". Anointing (smearing oil on someone) is what was done in ancient Israel to make someone king. Samuel anointed Saul in 1 Samuel 10 and David in 1 Samuel 16.

Jews traditionally see the Messiah as a mainly political leader, like David, who saves his people. However, for traditional Christians, the saving is more religious than political (see below). Quakers see "Christ" as an inward and transforming power, with many synonyms. Isaac Penington:

> It would be better for you to learn his name by experiencing
> his virtue and power in your heart. Yet, if you can receive it,
> this is his name: the Light, the Light of the World. ....

> Only by receiving him as the light do we come to know his
> other names. He is the life, the righteousness, the power, the
> wisdom, the peace, etc., but he is all of these in the light, and
> in the light we learn and receive them all.[2]

Lacking words that adequately describe all aspects of experiencing the divine, Quakers use incomplete single attributes such as 'Light' to stand for the many-faceted divinity experienced. The name is often a metaphor such as light or seed, words with levels of meaning.[3] Although Isaac Penington's writing leaves no doubt of his sweet tooth for words, he repeatedly declared that words failed to describe his inward experience adequately, even though they were also

---

[1] *Collected Works*, volume 11, paragraph 531 (1932).

[2] *The Scattered Sheep Sought After*, in *Works*, volume 1, pages 123-24.

[3] Melvin Keiser explains:

> The language of early Friends is rife with metaphors because they can bear people into
> unsayable depths. Metaphors interrelate aspects of felt reality beyond concepts'
> boundaries, integrating places in ourselves, awakening passions for new ways of being,
> and shaking our worldview. When they reach into ineffable depths, metaphors function
> symbolically: expressing a hidden dimension through an everyday level. "Christ is a rock,"
> Isaac said believers use this as an idea who are "without knowledge of the mystery... My
> meaning is, they have a notion of Christ to be the rock...but never come livingly to feel him
> the rock...inwardly laid in their hearts."

"Felt Reality in Practical Living", p. 202. See also Keiser, *Seeds of Silence*, pages 5-19, 179-194.

all he had to express it. "My spirit hasteneth from words ... [to] sink in spirit into the feeling of the life itself ... and cease striving to ... comprehend."[4] "Wait to feel the thing itself which the words speak of, and to be united by the living Spirit to that, and then thou hast a knowledge from the nature of the thing itself; and this is more deep and inward than all the knowledge that can be had from words concerning the thing."[5]

John is written in words, but for the purpose of bringing about enough Trust in Jesus for the Trusting to have Life (John 21:30), which Quakers say comes through the direct experience of God rather than the study of words about God; it "arises out of daily experience 'by a process of looking for signals of transcendence'."[6] However, for most Christians, the phrase, "Jesus is the Christ" from John 20:31 has a different significance that is worth noting, if only because Jung assumes this version in his writing about Christianity.

Traditional Christian views of Christ

In traditional Christian theology, humanity needs saving because of Adam and Eve. Our spiritual history is essentially angular in structure; it has start and end states and a turning point in the middle:

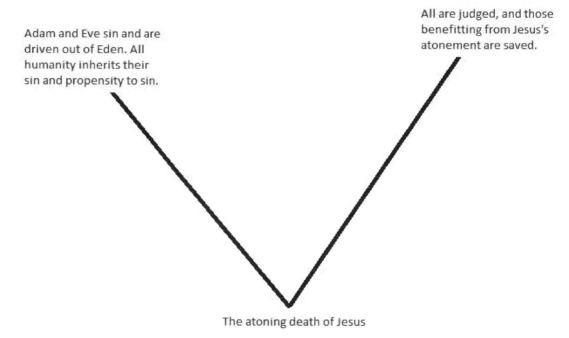

Adam and Eve sin and are driven out of Eden. All humanity inherits their sin and propensity to sin.

All are judged, and those benefitting from Jesus's atonement are saved.

The atoning death of Jesus

The lines are actually not straight; they are jagged with ups and downs, and a good many severe downs just before reaching the end state.

---

[4] Isaac Penington, *Some Mysteries of God's Kingdom Glanced At*, in *Works* volume 2, page 343; Keiser, *Knowing the Mystery of God Within* at 249-50.

[5] *The Axe Laid to the Root*, in *Works*, vol. 1, page 256; see also R. Melvin Keiser & Rosemary Moore, *Knowing the Mystery of Life Within: Selected Writings of Isaac Penington in their Historical and Theological Context* pages 133 and 140 (London: Quaker Books, 2005).

[6] Wallis, *Jung and the Quaker Way*, page 45, quoting George Gorman's 1973 Swarthmore Lecture, *The Amazing Fact of Quaker Worship* (London: Quaker Home Service, 1973).

In traditional Christianity, the "fall" of Adam and Eve left humanity prone to sin, some believe to the point of hopeless depravity.[7] A person's sins are like black marks in a ledger, and each person will be judged and incur the wrath or justice of God based on that ledger. As each soul has black marks against it, each soul will be condemned to suffer in hell. The only way to escape this condemnation is to rely on Jesus to suffer for our sins in our place and thereby to appease God's anger against us or to balance the scales of divine justice.

However, Jesus does not save everyone. For Catholics and eastern Orthodox, good (or, failing that, penitent) behaviour and the sacraments of the church are necessary for a person's salvation. For Protestants, the church has a different role, and faith and the Bible have crucial importance. Whether in the church or the expertly interpreted Bible, little scope remains in mainstream Christianity for individual guidance directly from the Holy Spirit, which has been institutionalised for the church to dispense.

Quaker experience of Christ and the inward Light

> Give over thine own willing, give over thy own running, give over thine own desiring to know or be anything and sink down to the seed which God sows in the heart, and let that grow in thee and be in thee and breathe in thee and act in thee; and thou shalt find by sweet experience that the Lord knows that and loves and owns that, and will lead it to the inheritance of Life, which is its portion.
>
> Isaac Penington, 1661[8]

For Quakers, the primary spiritual authority is neither church nor Bible but the inward Light, the Holy Spirit. The experience of the inward Light is highly personal, though shared somewhat amongst Friends, who cultivate a high (but not boundless) tolerance for variations in our individual experiences of the Light. From our individual experience of the love and peace found in the Light arise our various forms of witness and our concerns. We trust the Spirit to lead us into unity, not a unity imposed by a hierarchy or agreed by negotiating and compromising what a soul has learnt from the Teacher, but the unity of disciples learning from the same Teacher.

Because a soul's encounter with the inward Light is personal, Quaker spiritual learning begins not so much with Genesis as in a real life. Isaac Penington, for example, grew up a Puritan and was well enough off to get an education. When a mature man, Isaac found his way to a Quaker meeting, where he eventually "felt the presence of the Most High among them, and words of truth from the Spirit of truth reaching to my heart and conscience, opening my state as in the

---

[7] "In Jung's view, this doctrine (of utter sinfulness/depravity) is the ultimate debasement of the soul's natural divine dignity. In such theologies, the degree of sinfulness of the soul is in direct correlation to the turning of consciousness from its inner connectedness with God to an expected salvation from without. The worthlessness of the human is directly proportioned to the intensity with which salvation is sought from beyond, usually mediated through the appropriate ecclesiastical agency. Such views not only divorce consciousness from its proximity to God they also become a foundational justification for redemptive institutions." Dourley, *The Illness that We Are*, page 87.

[8] Quoted in Britain Yearly Meeting, *Quaker Faith and Practice* paragraph 26:70.

presence of the Lord."[9]   He then recalls one meeting in which he first experienced the Light:

> My heart (in the certainty of light and clearness of true sense) said "This is he, there is no other: this is he whom I have waited for and sought after from my childhood; who was always near me, and had often begotten life in my heart; but I knew him not distinctly, nor how to receive him, or dwell with him" ... But some may desire to know what I have at last met with? ... I have met with the Seed ... my God ... my Saviour ... true knowledge ... of life ... virtue the Seed's Father, and in the Seed I have felt him my Father ... true holiness, the true rest of the soul.[10]

Isaac went on to develop a systematic view of Quaker theology. I quote him extensively as an example of what Quakers have traditionally believed, in part because many of his word choices echo words frequently used in John such as "Life" and "Light", and because he writes beautifully of his inner life. Focusing on a single open soul is psychologically more interesting than attempting a synthesis of many early Friends' experiences and thereby losing sight of personal experience in order to generalise.

Isaac's discovery of "the Seed" or "Christ" within his soul changed his life:

> The spirit forms the heart anew, forms Christ in the heart, begets a new creature there, which cannot sin. (He that is born of God sins not. [1 John 3:9]). And this is the rule of righteousness, the new creature, or the spirit of life in the new creature.[11]

The new creature recovers what was lost in Eden when "cherubim and a flaming sword" barred the way to knowing God.[12]   Melvin Keiser notes that, "In convincement, [Isaac] let go of his controlling 'veiled self'".[13]   The part of himself veiled from (unconscious) God would be the ego, the conscious mind, which has lost contact with the inward Light. Removing the veil involves letting go even of blessings received: "As the soul is more emptied of the strength and riches it received of God; so it is more prepared to enter into, and live in, the Pure Being itself. For nothing can live there which veils."[14]

---

[9] Quoted by Thomas Elwood in his "Testimony Concerning Isaac Penington", Penington, *Works,* volume 1, pages 9-11 (1667).

[10] *Ibid.*

[11] Penington, *The Way of Life and Death Made Manifest*, in *Works,* volume 1 pages 26-27.

[12] In Jung's view, our original state was unconscious and instinctual, and free of problems. "It is the growth of consciousness that we must thank for the existence of problems". The biblical fall of humanity, the choice of knowledge over (unconscious) life with (unconscious) God, "brings about the "sacrifice of the merely natural man—of the unconscious, ingenuous being". *Modern Man in Search of a Soul*, Routledge edition pages 98-99. In other words, humanity became conscious while God remained in the collective unconscious. Having "turned away from the certain guidance of instinct", we "are handed over to fear". *Ibid.* page 98.

[13] Melvin Keiser, "Felt Reality in Practical Living" p. 198; Keiser & Moore, *Knowing the Mystery of God Within* p. 134.

[14] Penington, *Some Questions and Answers for the ... Jews Natural*, in *Works,* volume 2, 252.

Isaac's life thus had a turning point in it, and one in which he was an active participant, rather than a passive beneficiary of action by Jesus:

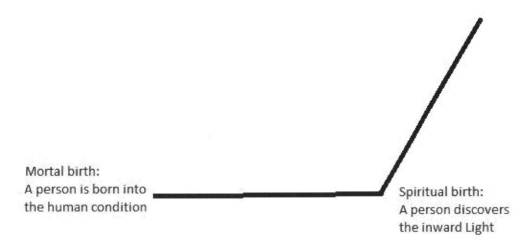

Mortal birth:
A person is born into
the human condition

Spiritual birth:
A person discovers
the inward Light

Quakers give little emphasis to an end state so there is no promise of a reward or threat of damnation. "The wind [meaning also Spirit in Greek] blows where it will, and you hear the sound of it, but you don't know where it comes from or where it goes to. So it is with everyone who is born of the Spirit" (John 3:8). You will also not find among Friends greatly elaborated doctrines about the Trinity, saints, and many other subjects found in traditional Christian creeds, none of which were known to the authors of John. With Quakers, the emphasis is on experience, not verbal formulae or rational elaboration.[15]

A person's great (but perhaps undiscovered) hope in life, then, is to experience the inward Light. That experience is ultimately one of joy and love, which we then reflect in our lives as the Light comes to illuminate all aspects of life. Friends do not worry about a ledger of black marks. "Core Quaker theology does not require an atonement, for its God is not angry."[16]

That is not to say that the experience of the inward Light is always only joy and sweetness. God's Light "shows us our darkness and brings us to new life."[17] The dispelling of darkness and inflow of life can be painful and involve giving up aspects of an old way of life. Early Quakers saw in "the Cross", as they called it, an essential and ongoing step in their spiritual development. Isaac Penington also employed the metaphor of a hammer. By whichever metaphor, he saw it as necessary to having life from God:

> Therefore, if you will live, come to that hammer, that sword,
> that fire which flesh[18] dreads, and let the flesh be delivered
> up to it: and do not despise the day of small things [Zechariah
> 4:10], waiting for some great appearance; but know it in its

---

[15] My hope in writing his book is to facilitate experiences of John by Friends, not to contribute to its rational elaboration.

[16] Williams, *Quakerism: A Theology for Our Time*, page 81.

[17] Britain Yearly Meeting, *Quaker Faith and Practice*, "Advices and Queries", no. 1.

[18] For Isaac and other early Friends, "flesh" was not so much the body as the superficial conscious mind without a deepening connection to the inner Light. Keiser, *Seeds of Silence*, pages 222-224.

> lowest knock: for its power of redemption is as truly there, as
> in its greatest appearance.[19]

For Quakers, salvation comes through the inward Light, and it is that Light that "produces personal transformation, social cooperation, and unity with God, here and now,"[20] as Christ (the Seed, the Light) is realised within.[21] Moreover, because everyone has the inner Light (even if unaware of it), it can save everyone, not just a select few as traditional Christian doctrines hold.[22] Given a chance, the Light transforms the soul, from within, not by emulating Christ but by becoming Christ inside.

Jung said repeatedly that the aim is "not an 'imitation of Christ' but its exact opposite: an assimilation of the Christ-image to his own self. ... It is no longer an effort, an intentional straining after imitation, but rather an involuntary experience of the reality represented by the sacred legend."[23] Pacific Yearly Meeting was more emphatic:

> There is a need in us to be controlled, to receive, to worship, and to adore. If our service is to be real it is that we have received something in worship and pass it on; we do not imitate, we express the Spirit in us. To live by the rule is one of the most disastrous things we can do. If you try deliberately to be loving and kind because you think you should imitate, you put on something from the outside; you waste your life; and worse—you do great damage. If you live in the Spirit you live from the center within you. In worship we search for the Center in ourselves and in one another, "...whence cometh our help."[24]

Jung's view of God's relationship with humanity

> I am not...addressing myself to the happy possessors of faith, but to those many people for whom the light has gone out, the

---

[19] Penington, *The Way of Life and Death Made Manifest,* in *Works*, volume 1, page 89-90.

[20] Williams, *Quakerism: A Theology for Our Time,* page 73.

[21] What we inwardly perceive as God Jung terms the "self". "Christ exemplifies the archetype of the self" because he represents a "totality of a divine or heavenly kind, a glorified man, a son of God unspotted by sin." From "Christ, a Symbol of the Self" in *Collected Works*, vol. 9, part 2, paragraph 70.

[22] Williams, *Quakerism: A Theology for Our Time,* p. 74-76. Jung explains the psychology of it:

> Just as a "door" opens to one who "knocks" on it, or a "way opens out to the wayfarer who seeks it, so, when you relate to your own (transcendental) centre, you initiate a process of conscious development which leads to oneness and wholeness. You no longer see yourself as an isolated point on the periphery, but as the One in the centre. Only subjective consciousness is isolated; when it relates to its centre it is integrated into wholeness. Whoever joins in the dance sees himself in the reflecting centre, and his suffering is the suffering which the One who stands in the centre "wills to suffer." The paradoxical identity and difference of the [conscious mind] and the self could hardly be formulated more trenchantly.

C.G. Jung, "The Mass and the Individuation Process" in *Psychology and Religion: West and East*, reprinted in *Collected Works* volume 11, paragraph 427.

[23] C.G. Jung, *Mysterium Coniunctionis, Collected Works* vol. 14, paragraph 492.

[24] Pacific Yearly Meeting, *Faith and Practice*, page 78.

mystery has faded, and God is dead. For most of them there is no going back, and one does not know either whether going back is the better way. To gain an understanding of religious matters, probably all that is left us today is the psychological approach. That is why I take these thought-forms that have become historically fixed, try to melt them down again and pour them into moulds of immediate experience.

Carl Jung[25]

Jung was a psychiatrist not a theologian or cleric. "Analytical psychology", he noted, "is based on scientific and clinical observation and on self-critical investigation of the psyche, especially the unconscious."[26] From that perspective, Jung saw religious experience as "an eruption of the unconscious and an expression of latent psychic structures and dynamics."[27] To see religious experience in psychological terms does not confirm or deny its reality in other terms,[28] or claim that such experience is all in our heads, although some of it, including our perception of it, certainly is.

God, in human experience, is one such "latent psychic structure".[29] Jung defined God as "the name by which I designate all things which cross my wilful path violently and recklessly, all things which upset my subjective views, plans, and intentions and change the course of my life for better or worse".[30] That capacity of God for eruptive and out-of-control intrusion and interference causes us to make God unconscious, though we do not notice that we do so. Still, though unconscious, God is "an obvious psychic and non physical fact",[31] obvious if you know where and how to look, that is.[32] "Paradox is a characteristic of all

---

[25] *Answer to Job* in *Collected Works,* volume 11, paragraph 148.

[26] Stein, *Jung on Christianity*, p. 16.

[27] Stein, *Jung on Christianity*, p. 16.

[28] "In general, whenever [Jung]attempts to explain things in psychological terms, [he] shouldn't be interpreted as denying the reality or significance of what he is explaining." Kastrup, *Decoding Jung's Metaphysics*, page 103. Jung himself noted ruefully, "If, in physics, one seeks to explain the nature of light, nobody expects that as a result there will be no light. But in the case of psychology, everybody believes that what is explained is explained away." (*Answer to Job, Collected Works*, volume 11, paragraph 749.)

[29] Murray Stein noted, "For Jung, individual experience is the ultimate arbiter and final authority in religious matters" (*Jung on Christianity*, p. 5). Quakers would agree entirely. Our focus is on the "Light", *i.e.,* what we experience of God, rather than complicated theories about the nature of God such as trinitarian theology.

[30] C.G. Jung, *Letters*, vol. 2, p. 525. Early in his life Isaac Penington observed, "Man hugely likes the God that he frames in his own imagination...as lovely...[but is] a dreadful God, and in no wise desirable." Quoted in Melvin Keiser, *Felt Reality in Practical Living*, page 197.

[31] Jung, *Answer to Job*, in *Collected Works*, volume 11, paragraph 751.

[32] Isaac Penington said that Adam's choice of the tree of knowledge had the effect of making him "wise in the wrong part" (his ego consciousness). Penington, *The Scattered Sheep Sought After*, in *Works* vol. 1, pages 120-21 (1659). See also Williams, *Quakerism: A Theology for our Time*, pp. 66-68. Looking at the symbols in psychological terms, Adam and Eve became conscious by eating of the tree of knowledge while God remained as unconscious as ever. "Cherubim and a flaming sword" (psychological defence mechanisms) keep God unconscious.

transcendental situations because it alone gives adequate expression to their indescribable nature."[33]

For Jung, God is not just in a person's individual unconscious mind but also an archetype in our collective unconscious, the part of each person's unconscious mind that is shared across humanity. Jung defined an 'archetype' in terms of the Bible:

> Statements made in the Holy Scriptures are also utterances of the soul—even at the risk of being suspected of psychologism. The statements of the conscious mind may easily be snares and delusions, lies, or arbitrary opinions, but this is certainly not true of the statements of the soul: to begin with they always go above our heads because they point to realities that transcend consciousness. These are the archetypes of the unconscious, and they precipitate complexes of ideas in the form of mythological motifs. Ideas of this kind are never invented, but enter the field of inner perception as finished products, for instance in dreams. They are spontaneous phenomena which are not subject to our will, and we are therefore justified in ascribing to them a certain autonomy.[34]

The God archetype, as we perceive it either in the collective unconscious of humanity or in an individual's unconscious,[35] is for Jung most certainly not "the same, yesterday and today and forever."[36] The Bible and other spiritual writings show the evolution of how we perceive the God archetype over thousands of years.

> In Christianity, this evolution [of the God-image] is still underway. The image is still not complete. There is still more to come, and the blocks to its manifestation need to be cleared away. This is the task of psychology.
>
> It is this view of doctrine as evolving and the ambition for psychology's part in the theological enterprise that makes

---

[33] C.G. Jung, "Christ, a Symbol of the Self", excerpted in Stein, *Jung on Christianity* p. 105. Jung elaborated elsewhere:

> Paradox...does more justice to the *unknowable* than clarity can do, for uniformity of meaning robs the mystery of its darkness and sets it up as something that is *known*. That is a usurpation, and it leads the human intellect into hubris by pretending that it, the intellect, has got hold of the transcendent mystery by a cognitive act and has "grasped" it. The paradox therefore reflects a higher level of intellect and, by not forcibly representing the unknowable as known, gives a more faithful picture of the real state of affairs.

Jung, "The Mass and the Individuation Process", in *Collected Works*, volume 11, paragraph 135.

[34] Jung, *Answer to Job*, in *Collected Works*, volume 11, paragraph 557.

[35] For Jung, humans became conscious in the Eden story; the people there consumed the fruit of knowledge, which made them conscious (*Collected Works*, volume 8, paragraph 751). God remained unconscious. The separation between conscious humanity and unconscious God is preserved by the defence mechanisms described by Anna Freud, or by "cherubim and a flaming sword" in the words of Genesis 3:24. Now we must learn to see past defence mechanisms to find God.

[36] Hebrews 13:8; Wallis, *Jung and the Quaker Way*, page 42.

The evolution of our understanding of God can also be seen in Quaker history. Quakers such as William Penn owned slaves. Benjamin Lay and John Woolman in the next generation improved our understanding of God's will for us, so after Friends like them, Friends do not own slaves.

Jung's work on Christianity so controversial, and for many theologians so completely unacceptable.[37]

Jung's view of the history of the relationship between God and humanity is set out in his slender but densely written volume, *Answer to Job*. That history is not a simple angle for Jung; it has multiple turning points:

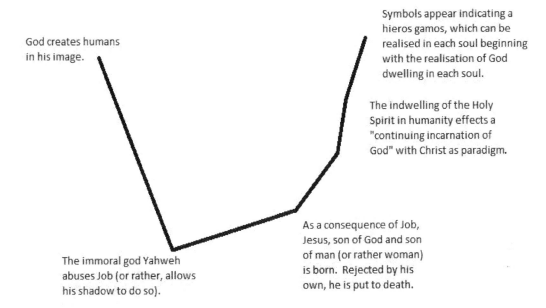

God creates humans in his image.

Symbols appear indicating a hieros gamos, which can be realised in each soul beginning with the realisation of God dwelling in each soul.

The indwelling of the Holy Spirit in humanity effects a "continuing incarnation of God" with Christ as paradigm.

The immoral god Yahweh abuses Job (or rather, allows his shadow to do so).

As a consequence of Job, Jesus, son of God and son of man (or rather woman) is born. Rejected by his own, he is put to death.

As the diagram depicts, the history of the God-human relationship pivots with Job, not Jesus. Jung sees Job with empathy and is not afraid[38] to say that he was badly wronged by God, who, knowing Job's goodness, nevertheless makes him the object of a bet. The bet is against God's shadowy alter ego, called here 'Satan' for the first time in the Bible. Satan is never more expressly visible in the Bible than in Job, and he is out of control.

To win the bet, God stands by as Satan destroys Job's family (except for his wife), his livelihood, and his health, yet Job remains faithful, insisting "I know that my vindicator lives."[39] His well meaning friends treat him as a sinner because they

---

[37] Stein, *Jung on Christianity*, p. 9.

[38] Unafraid, it seems, in *Answer to Job*, but his letters describe how he procrastinated writing *Answer to Job* until "I got ill and when I was in the fever it caught me and brought me down to writing despite my fever, my age [of 75], and my heart that is none too good." *Letters*, vol. 2, p. 32; see generally Edward F. Edinger, *Transformation of the God-Image*, pages 18-19. Completing *Answer to Job* was the happiest moment of Jung's life according to his biographer, Catrine Clay (*Labyrinths: Emma Jung, her Marriage to Carl, and the Early Years of Psychoanalysis*, (New York: HarperCollins, 2016) pages 339-340.

[39] Job 19:25 (NRSV). Jung explains:

> This is perhaps the greatest thing about Job, that, faced with this difficulty [the experience that God can be unjust], he does not doubt the unity of God. He clearly sees that God is at odds with himself—so totally at odds that he, Job, is quite certain of finding in God a helper and an "advocate" against God. As certain as he is of the evil in Yahweh, he is equally certain of the good. ... He [Yahweh] is both a persecutor and a helper in one, and the one aspect is as real as the other. Yahweh is not split but is an *antinomy*—a totality of inner opposites—and this is the indispensable condition for his tremendous dynamism. ... Notwithstanding his wrath, Yahweh is also man's advocate *against himself [Yahweh]* when man puts forth his complaint.

Answer to Job, in *Collected Works*, volume 11, paragraph 567.

do not see that God has been ruthless with Job, who actually deserves empathy rather than judgment. As the book approaches its end, God's still limited self-knowledge has him in denial about his moral inferiority to Job so he rants about his own greatness and Job's puniness. "Where were you when I laid the foundation of the earth?" (Job 38:4).[40]

Yet after God's blustering he comes clean. The book of Job ends with the great turning point in the entire story of the God-human relationship:[41]

> Then Job answered the Lord:
>
> > I know that you can do all things, and that no purpose of yours can be thwarted. 'Who is this that hides counsel without knowledge?' Therefore I have uttered what I did not understand, things too wonderful for me, which I did not know. I will question you, and you declare to me. I had heard of you by the hearing of the ear, but now my eye sees you; therefore I despise myself, I repent in dust and ashes.
>
> After the Lord had spoken these words to Job....[42]

Somewhere in the central lines of that excerpt the speaker changes from Job to the Lord. Certainly the last full sentence:

> I had heard of you by the hearing of the ear, but now my eye sees you; therefore I despise myself, I repent in dust and ashes.

must be words that the Lord spoke because the last phrase quoted above says so. God has finally realised his wrongs and changes. Then follows the rather Hollywood ending of Job that contrasts so sharply with Job's suffering through most of the book. Still, the turning point came when God repented in dust and ashes, one of the most momentous but overlooked sentences in the entire Bible.

Jung says this change in God came about as God reconnected with Sophia (Greek for 'wisdom', and a feminine noun), who finally brings God to self-reflection:

> The victory of the vanquished and oppressed is obvious: Job stands morally higher than Yahweh. In this respect the creature has surpassed the creator. As always when an external event touches on some unconscious knowledge, this knowledge can reach consciousness. The event is recognised as a *déja vu*, and one remembers a pre-existent knowledge about it. Something of the kind must have happened to

---

[40] Jung explains God's fulminations as projection: "Yahweh projects on to Job a sceptic's face that is hateful to him because it is his own, and which gazes at him with an uncanny and critical eye. He is afraid of it, for only in the face of something frightening does one let off a cannonade of references to one's power, cleverness, courage, invincibility, etc." *Answer to Job,* in *Collected Works,* volume 11, paragraph 591.

However, Job's strength was his weakness: "Because of his littleness, puniness, and defencelessness, against the Almighty, [Job] possesses a keener conscience based on self-reflection: he must, in order to survive, always be mindful of his impotence. God has no need of this circumspection, for nowhere does he come up against an insuperable obstacle that would force him to hesitate and hence make him reflect on himself." *Answer to Job,* paragraph 579.

[41] I note here, from the text of Job, my own observations, not Jung's.

[42] Job 42:1-7 (NRSV).

Yahweh. Job's superiority cannot be shrugged off. Hence a situation arises in which real reflection is needed. That is why Sophia steps in. She reinforces the much needed self reflection and thus makes possible Yahweh's decision to become man. It is a decision fraught with consequences: he raises himself above his earlier primitive level of consciousness by indirectly acknowledging that the man Job is morally superior to him and that therefore he has to catch up and become human himself.[43]

To catch up with Job's moral advancement, God became human as Jesus, whose atonement, Jung says, is not "the payment of a human debt to God, but reparation for a wrong done by God to man".[44] Jesus came, not because we mortals did anything wrong, but because God did.[45]

After Jesus dies comes the Counsellor, the Holy Spirit, who extends to humanity the divine incarnation begun by Christ:

> The continuing, direct operation of the Holy Ghost on those who are called to be God's children implies, in fact, a broadening process of incarnation. Christ, the son begotten by God, is the first-born who is succeeded by an ever-increasing number of younger brothers and sisters. These are, however, neither begotten by the Holy Ghost nor born of a virgin. .... Their lowly origin (possibly from the mammals) does not prevent them from entering into a close kinship with God as their father and Christ as their brother.[46]

It is the Holy Spirit that brings peace between God and humans; the two become one, as Jesus's great prayer in John 17 sought. The death of Jesus brings the Counsellor and a salvation in which "man is not so much delivered from his sins ... as delivered from fear of the consequences of sin, that is, from the wrath of God."[47] Humanity may not be saved from the wrath of institutional Christianity, however. "Although the [Counsellor] was of greatest significance metaphysically, it was, from the point of view of the organisation of the Church, most undesirable, because ... the Holy Ghost is not subject to any control."[48]

---

[43] Jung, *Answer to Job*, in *Collected Works*, volume 11, paragraph 640.

[44] Jung, *Answer to Job*, in *Collected Works*, volume 11, paragraph 661.

[45] Quakers would agree with the first half of that sentence. The death of Jesus was not paying for for our sins. Traditional Christians would not agree with any part of that sentence.

[46] Jung, *Answer to Job*, in *Collected Works*, volume 11, paragraph 658. The 'continuing incarnation of God' increases the consciousness of the human creature so that the God within becomes realised in awareness. This has remarkable similarities to the Quaker view of the Holy Spirit effecting a (conscious) unification of God and a soul that opens itself to the Spirit.

[47] Jung, *Answer to Job*, in *Collected Works*, volume 11, paragraph 659.

[48] Jung, *Answer to Job*, in *Collected Works*, volume 11, paragraph 694. For Quakers, the primacy of the inward Light has led Quaker communities to have far more tolerance and diversity in spirituality than is normally found in churches. Isaac Penington:

> The great error of the ages of the apostasy hath been to set up an outward order and uniformity, and make men's consciences bend thereto, whether by arguments of wisdom or force; but the property of the true church government is to leave the conscience to its full liberty in the Lord, to preserve it single and entire for the Lord to exercise, and to seek

Jung saw this process in which the Holy Spirit works on an unconscious mind as the process he called "individuation":

> The goal of psychological, as of biological, development is self-realization, or individuation. But since man knows himself only as an ego [the conscious mind], and the [unconscious] self ... is indescribable and indistinguishable from a God-image, self-realization—to put it in religious or metaphysical terms—amounts to God's incarnation.[49]

However, souls thus incarnated through the Holy Spirit find themselves possessed by God's conflicting opposites, valuing justice (and vengeance) on the one hand, but also valuing love and forgiveness on the other, to cite just one of many divine polarities. "God is a *coincidentia oppositorum*. Both are justified, the fear of God as well as the love of God."[50] Humans who realise God inwardly through the Holy Spirit internalise this conflict:

> As a totality, the self is by definition always a *complexio oppositorum*, and the more consciousness insists on its light nature and lays claim to moral authority, the more the self will appear as something dark and menacing.[51]

Answer to Job then turns to the book of Revelation, in which the loving Jesus seen in John becomes the wrathful Lamb. However, a happier future is presaged in the vision of the "woman clothed with the sun" who is giving birth.[52] "If [that] vision were a modern dream, one would not hesitate to interpret the birth of the divine child as the coming to consciousness of the self [the God archetype]."[53] She prefigures a sacred marriage of opposites, the union of the Lamb with his bride, who is the "new Jerusalem coming down out of heaven".[54]

> This final vision, which is generally interpreted as referring to the relationship of Christ to his Church, has the meaning of a uniting symbol and is therefore a representation of perfection and wholeness. .... The city is Sophia, who was with God

---

unity in the light and in the Spirit, walking sweetly and harmoniously together in the midst of different practices.

An Examination of the Grounds, in *Works*, volume 1, page 388. So it is that

> Revelation is ever a scandal to religion; religion consists of human constructions of patterns and forms designed to further and replicate a spiritual value, ideal, or experience. Paradoxically, however, only as the worshipper releases oneself to unpredictable and uncontrolled winds of the Spirit can one actually encounter the presence of the divine.

Anderson, *The Riddles of the Fourth Gospel*, page 228.

[49] Jung, "Christ as Archetype", from *Psychology and Religion: West and East*, reprinted in *Collected Works*, vol. 11, paragraph 233.

[50] Jung, *Answer to Job*, in *Collected Works*, volume 11, paragraph 664.

[51] Jung, *Answer to Job*, in *Collected Works*, volume 11, paragraph 716.

[52] Revelation 12:1-6.

[53] Jung, *Answer to Job*, in *Collected Works*, volume 11, paragraph 714.

[54] Jung, *Answer to Job*, in *Collected Works*, volume 11, paragraph 726.

before time began, and at the end of time will be reunited with God through the sacred marriage.[55]

This union of the God of wrath with the self-reflecting Sophia resolves the conflict in human souls caused by the realisation of God from within. It is the metaphysical process

> known to the psychology of the unconscious as the individuation process. In so far as this process, as a rule, runs its course unconsciously as it has done from time immemorial, it means no more than that the acorn becomes an oak, the calf a cow, and the child an adult. But if the individuation process is made conscious, consciousness must confront the unconscious and a balance between the opposites must be found. As this is not possible through logic, one is dependent on *symbols* which make the irrational union of opposites possible. They are produced spontaneously by the unconscious and are amplified by the conscious mind. ....
>
> The difference between the 'natural' individuation process, which runs its course unconsciously, and the one which is consciously realised, is tremendous. In the first case consciousness nowhere intervenes and the end remains as dark as the beginning. In the second case, so much darkness comes to light that the personality is permeated with light, and consciousness necessarily gains in scope and insight.[56]

Thus the individuation process, which began with the reception of the Counsellor into a human soul, ends with the soul transformed by the Holy Spirit but remarkably unspectacular in its real-world appearance:

> The significance of man is enhanced by the incarnation [of the Holy Spirit in human beings]. We have become participants of the divine life and we have to assume a new responsibility, the continuation of the divine self-realisation, which expresses itself in the task of our individuation. Individuation does not only mean that man has become truly human as distinct from animal, but that he is to become partially divine as well. This means practically that he becomes adult, responsible for his existence, knowing that he does not only depend on God but that God also depends on man. Man's relation to God probably has to undergo a certain important change. Instead of propitiating praise for an unpredictable king or the child's prayer to a loving father, the responsible living and fulfilling of the divine will in us will be our form of worship and commerce with God.[57]

---

[55] Jung, *Answer to Job*, in *Collected Works*, volume 11, paragraph 727.

[56] Jung, *Answer to Job*, in *Collected Works*, volume 11, paragraph 755-756.

[57] C.G. Jung, *Letters*, volume 2, page 316.

This has been a brutally quick *tour de force* through Jung's view of Christian spiritual history and is a poor substitute for reading *Answer to Job*.[58] It is a fascinating read, but expect to see God undergo a psychological analysis—God as defined by Jung, the God-archetype in each and all of us, not necessarily an objectively existent supreme being. There is no blasphemy in analysing a thing in our minds, though we may feel it to be so (that feeling says more about us than about God). *Answer to Job* has as much to say about the reader's (or any) soul as about Job or Jung.

To conclude, traditional Christianity, Quakerism, and Jung see varying significance in the life and death of Jesus. Traditional Christianity sees Jesus as the solution to problems introduced by the 'fall' of Adam and Eve. Jung and Quakerism do not see the 'fall' of Adam and Eve as the problem Christ came to solve. For Jung, Jesus's coming was God's way of experiencing himself what he had inflicted on Job. For both Jung and Quakerism, the important point for humanity is to draw on the Holy Spirit and grow to experience God more consciously in the soul.

---

[58] Even though you are likely be offended by reading it, one way or another:

> Either one will be offended that Jung contradicts the familiar God-image that one cherishes in one's own religious confession or formulation, either that, or if one is a secular rationalist he will be offended that Jung takes so seriously the primitive anthropomorphic God-image that rationalists have long since discredited.

Edinger, *Transformation of the God-Image*, page 23. The offence taken is worth understanding "because if you locate how you are offended it will tell you something about the nature of your own unconscious assumptions and that can be a valuable bit of self-knowledge." *Ibid.* page 24.

The disciple Jesus loved and the development of his gospel

Origination with the Beloved Disciple

The question who wrote the fourth gospel is complicated in part because its stated source is a person described but not named in the text. The title "Gospel according to John" came 100-200 years after the original book, when books began to be compiled into codices. The gospel may be named for John the Baptist, not John the son of Zebedee and brother of James.[1] There are also other explanations for the title, but all told it is weak evidence of authorship because it was applied late, when the gospel was already 100-200 years old.

The answer to who wrote John is in the text itself. John expressly attributes itself[2] to a man who is never named there, although he is mentioned at least five times,[3] more than any other disciple except Peter. His gospel always calls him 'the disciple whom Jesus loved'; I call him 'the Beloved Disciple' for short.

The Beloved Disciple was an eyewitness to the public years of Jesus's life. He is specifically mentioned as being present at the last supper (John 13:23-24), at the crucifixion (19:16, with the parenthetical, "He who saw this [the death of Jesus] has Testified so that you may also Trust" 19:35), and on resurrection morning (20:2).[4] No other gospel claims to be written by an eyewitness. Luke says he *relied on* eyewitnesses (Luke 1:2), but he does not claim to have been one himself and he does not play an identifiable part in the gospels.

There is too little evidence to deny convincingly the express attribution of the fourth gospel to the Beloved Disciple;[5] instead, the authorship issue centres around the identity of the Beloved Disciple (see the next section). I take as a working assumption that John originated with the Beloved Disciple, as the text says more than once, although whether the Beloved Disciple wrote down any part of it, made any notes, or could write at all are all unknown. Still, John 21:24 says the Beloved Disciple *wrote* John, although I am somewhat willing to discount that statement a bit because chapter 21 is a late addition (see the preface to it in the commentary). Perhaps that statement[6] is from an editor over-compensating for not being the Beloved Disciple himself. Whether written or not, the retelling of stories heard from the Beloved Disciple during his lifetime would have begun an oral tradition because most of his followers could not read or write.[7]

---

[1] Charlesworth, *Jesus as Mirrored in John*, pages 517-532.

[2] John 19:35 and 21:24 (with reference to 21:20 to identify the person spoken of in 21:24). For a fuller examination of the authorship issue see Charlesworth, *Jesus as Mirrored in John* pages 62-73.

[3] The Beloved Disciple was at the last supper (John 13:23-24), at the crucifixion (19:16), at the resurrection (20:2), and in 21:7 and 21:10.

[4] The elder who wrote 1 John also emphasises that their belief is based on eyewitness testimony (1 John 1:1-3).

[5] Schackenburg, *Das Johannesevangelium* volume VI:1, pages 60-88; .

[6] That still leaves the authorship statements in John 19, however, which is very likely part of the earliest version of John. However, an editor who can append can probably also insert. We have only the discontinuities in the text to go on in theorising how the authors went about their task.

[7] Schackenburg, *Das Johannesevangelium* volume VI:1, page 55; Keener *The Gospel of John*, volume 1, pages 54-65.

What seems beyond doubt is that the Beloved Disciple had help, possibly lots of it. A community gathered around the him, and we very likely have this community to thank for preserving the gospel that attributes itself to the Beloved Disciple.[8] Scholars point out good reasons for thinking that John is not the work of one person because, besides using "we" in the narration throughout,[9] the text shows there has been some compiling, leaving discontinuities in the narrative flow and slight variations in style.[10] It is not difficult for Quakers to envisage how a faith community would write a sacred book; all Quaker books of faith and practice, guiding documents in Quaker spirituality, are produced by communities and are compilations whose making rarely involves the original authors. They are spiritual pictures of us in mosaic crafted by the committee we appointed to write them.

The way John is written has led to many theories about how it was written.[11] In my view the evidence is too thin to confirm any such theory, but I have an observation: John is "episodic". It consists of episodes in which things happen and are taught. The profundity, the spiritual and psychological resonance, the literary craft of the episodes is extraordinary. On the other hand, the connections between episodes are thin at best,[12] and inconsistencies between episodes persist.[13] It seems a master author or oral teacher has given us the episodes, and less effort or skill went into pulling them together.

The idea that the Beloved Disciple's community finished what he had begun also fits the estimates of timing. After manuscript and archaeological finds of a few decades ago (see below), John is now thought to have been written about 90-100 C.E., give or take about 10 years.[14] If the Beloved Disciple was 30 years old when

---

[8] Adele Reinhartz questions whether a community of John existed during the time covered in John. *Cast Out of the Covenant*, page xiv. To me, the existence of a group seems clear enough from the fact that John focuses much attention on the disciples of Jesus, particularly at the end of the book. However, John does not mention a church or any formal organisation, just a group of "disciples". Reinhartz seems in no doubt that the book was written "within a particular community of believers" (*"The Gospel of John: How 'the Jews' Became part of the Plot*, page 100), but it was written after Jesus died.

[9] Many scholars think the "we" refers to a "group of disciples" gathered by the Beloved Disciple around him, a group that scholars, lifelong academics, commonly call a "school". (See, e.g. Alan Culpepper in his introduction to Martyn, *The Gospel of John in Christian History*, page xxiii.). To me, it seems unlikely that the gospel writers were long-term academicians, so I'd use a more generic word like "committee".

[10] Brown, *Anchor Bible* volume 29, pages XXIV-XXXIX; see also Ashton, *The Gospel of John and Christian Origins*, pages 119-131; Charlesworth, *Jesus as Mirrored in John* pages 2-4, 48ff, 69-71; Schnackenburg, *Das Johannesevangelium*, volume IV:1, pages 82-88.

[11] For example, Anderson, *The Riddles of the Fourth Gospel*, pages 95-124; Brown, *An Introduction to the New Testament*, pages 362-365; Schnackenburg, *Das Johannesevangelium*, Teil 1, pages 32-88.

[12] Culpepper, *Anatomy of the Fourth Gospel*, page 231, "As a construction, [John] is magnificent but flawed. Magnificent in its complexity, subtlety, and profundity, but oddly flawed in some of its transitions, sequences, and movements." Psychologically, the less editing, the better; editing makes the overall gospel "more coherent and organized than the primary experience [was], and this coherence can be a block against deeper understanding and experience if we allow our attention to fix itself too much on this aspect." Stein, *The Bible as Dream*, page 23.

[13] Anderson has thorough lists in *The Riddles of the Fourth Gospel*, pages 72-75.

[14] Charlesworth, *Jesus as Mirrored in John* pages 47-49 81, and 247-48; Brown, *Anchor Bible* volume 29, pages LXXX-LXXXVI; Coloe, *Wisdom Commentary*, volume 44A, page liii; Cassidy, *John's Gospel*

Jesus died, he would have been nearing 100 when his gospel reached its final form, at a time when centenarians were rare. It is likely that John 21:20-23 records the community's reaction to the death of their Beloved Disciple; if so, that death may well have prompted a serious effort to preserve his legacy by finishing his gospel.

As John underwent its final revision, Rome had just destroyed Judea and its Temple in 70 C.E. John probably began to take shape in Judea, where the Beloved Disciple and Jesus had lived, but it was probably finished elsewhere, perhaps Ephesus, after the community of the Beloved Disciple had fled Judea.

Who was the Beloved Disciple?

We do not know is the simple answer. It could well be John, the son of Zebedee and brother of James. However, John son of Zebedee is never named in the fourth gospel, but neither is James or Mary, for that matter. We know their names thanks to the other gospels. The name 'John' in the fourth gospel always refers to John the Baptist. However, the Fourth Gospel has a long association with John son of Zebedee.[15]

A great amount of scholarly theorising leaves me thinking that there is no reason why John son of Zebedee can't be the Beloved Disciple,[16] but the evidence is not enough to support a firm conclusion that he is.[17] However, I do not see a need to answer the question at all. Who am I to undo anonymity that may well have been intended,[18] quite possibly by the Beloved Disciple himself? The simplest explanation for the fact that he is only named by the wordy circumlocution "the disciple whom Jesus loved" is that his authoring community called him as they customarily did, and as he quite possibly advised them to do. I doubt that they

---

in New Perspective, page 3. Carson estimates "about 80" C.E.; *The Gospel According to John,* page 82-87.

Irenaeus, writing his work *Against Heresies* in about 180 C.E., clearly understood the gospel to have been written by John son of Zebedee. Irenaeus was taught by Polycarp of Smyrna (died 156), who might have known John son of Zebedee personally, so, although Irenaeus is writing about 100 years after the fact, his view is significant evidence. See Carson, *The Gospel According to John*, pages 68-81; Schnackenburg, *Das Johannesevangelium*, volume IV:1, pages 63-66.

[15] Charlesworth, *Jesus as Mirrored in John* pages 2, 62-73, 80, 375-393, and 539; Keener, *The Gospel of John*, volume 1, pages 83-105; Schnackenburg, *Das Johannesevangelium*, volume IV:1, pages 82-85; Brown, *Anchor Bible* volume 29, pages LXXXVII-CII. Irenaeus, writing in about 190 C.E., wrote that John son of Zebedee wrote John. Behr, John the Theologian and his Paschal Gospel, pages 44-77; Brown, *Anchor Bible*, volume 29, pages LXXXVII-LXXXIX. I am reluctant to rely heavily on Irenaus because he was writing 100 years afterwards, and a great deal happened in those 100 years, including the apostasy of the community of John (see "Fate of the community" below).

[16] There are contrary views among scholars, but I remain sceptical of them. Anderson summarises them in *The Riddles of the Fourth Gospel*, pages 104-114.

[17] The great scholars Brown and Schnackenburg began their careers saying the Beloved Disciple was John sin of Zebedee, but changed their minds to thinking him unidentifiable. Brown, *The Community of the Beloved Disciple*, page 33-34. Charlesworth thinks he may be Thomas (*Jesus as Mirrored in John*, pages 72-73, and Coloe does as well (Coloe, *Wisdom Commentary*, volume 44A, page lvi). Sandra Schneiders suggests the disciple is not one person but a composite (*Written that You may Believe: Encountering Jesus in the Fourth Gospel* (New York: Crossroad, 1999), page 224), but she does not entirely convince Adele Reinhartz (*Befriending the Beloved Disciple*), page 23.

[18] "His recurring designation as 'the disciple whom Jesus loved' implies a deliberate avoidance of his personal name." Bruce, *The Gospel of John*, page 3.

would deface him verbally on their own initiative by making him anonymous, but they would refer to him as he had told them to.

Why theorise to fill in what the text leaves open, an openness that may well have been intended by the Beloved Disciple and his community, the authors of the text? The authority of the text comes from the Spirit that gave it, not from the person who wrote it, so our need to know who is mere curiosity, not a prerequisite for benefitting from John.[19]

The manuscript tradition

Some of the very oldest papyrus New Testament manuscripts are of John and date back to about a century after Jesus died.[20] These papyri helped push back the dating of John, which scholars of the mid-20th century such as Rudolf Bultmann had thought to be as late as 300 C.E., a date almost 200 years later than the date of Papyrus $\mathfrak{P}^{52}$, a fragment the size of a credit card that contains two small but recognisable bits of John on each side.[21] The consequent rethinking of the date of John is part of a great discrediting and rebuilding of the scholarship on John during my lifetime.[22]

---

[19] In theory, knowing more about the author might let us know more about John, but we rarely know an ancient author—or even a contemporary one—well enough to opine on what the author's work meant to the author. Psychologist Murray Stein:

> It would not really help us much of we could positively identify the author [of John] because we would still know so little about his personal life and history, and as far as supplying a context for interpretation goes, you have to know quite a bit about the particular author in order to make use of those associations.

The Bible as Dream, page 167.

[20] Notable examples are the Rylands Papyrus, $\mathfrak{P}^{52}$ (about 130 C.E. by most estimates) and the Bodmer Papyri, $\mathfrak{P}^{66}$ and $\mathfrak{P}^{75}$ (about 200 C.E.). The Rylands papyrus is thought to be the oldest known manuscript of the Bible (Bruce, *The Gospel of* John, page 6; Schnackenburg, *Das Johannesevangelium*, volume IV:1 page 153-154), and although it is only about the size of a credit card, its value is less as a witness for the text as for its use in dating John.

Scientists date ancient manuscripts by writing style rather than by carbon dating, which is much less precise, although paleography, the science of ancient writing, inevitably produces a range of opinion on the dating of any ancient manuscript.

[21] Coloe, *Wisdom Commentary*, volume 44A, page liii; Carson, *The Gospel According to John*, page 24. Coloe also notes that the *Epistle to Diognetus* of 125-150 C.E. corroborates the dating of John at about 95-100 because it quotes John extensively.

[22] Behr, *John the Theologian*, page 4; Charlesworth, *Jesus as Mirrored in John* pages 19-34; Brown, *Anchor Bible* volume 29, pages V, XXI-XXII.

Jung found that Bultmann's "demythologisation" of Christianity undermined it:

> Jung says that modern Christianity has erred in its attempt to update itself by eliminating myth—as if myth were a gangrenous limb that must be amputated to save the patient. Jung is here referring to Bultmann's "demythologization" of the New Testament. Jung's first objection is that the supposed incompatibility of myth with modern knowledge stems from a false, literal interpretation of myth. .... Jung's second objection is that myth is indispensable to experience and thereby to religion. "myth is an integral component of all religions and therefore cannot be excluded from the assertions of faith without injuring them.

Segal, *Jung on Mythology* pages 36-37, quoting Jung, *The Undiscovered Self*, in *Collected Works*, volume 10, paragraph 285. Bultmann "criticised and ridiculed" Jung's friend Rudolf Otto, who coined the word "numinous". Stein, *The Principle of Individuation*, page 56.

The Bodmer Papyri, 𝔓⁶⁶ and 𝔓⁷⁵ (about 200 C.E.), each contain roughly the first two-thirds of John. Two great codices, Vaticanus (abbreviated B) and Sinaiticus (ℵ), both dated about 300-400 C.E., contain all of John. Besides these, over a dozen other manuscripts dated before about 600 C.E. together allow the text to be reconstructed with a relatively high degree of confidence. Scholars of Plato or Aristotle have far fewer and much later textual witnesses of the works they study.

In most cases, the variations between the manuscripts are rather minor details. For example, in John 5:4, describing the pool of Bethesda, many manuscripts say that the disabled people beside the pool waited for the water to be stirred by an angel, and whichever of them stepped in first was healed. However, the oldest manuscripts mention no angel or first-in details. They were probably added by a copyist to explain, helpfully, the plight of the man to be healed, but their absence in the earliest manuscripts is good evidence that they were not in the original text.

Most textual variants have similar, rather minor significance, but the exception to that generalisation is a whopper and is found in John. The most significant textual variant, perhaps in the entire New Testament, is John 7:53 through 8:11, the story of a woman caught in adultery, which appears only in John. Again, older manuscripts omit the story, leaving modern scholars to conclude that it is a later addition, even though it is a very good and instructive story. Paul Anderson quipped that the text was caught in adultery.[23]

Papyrus 𝔓⁷⁵ showing the first page of John (about 200 C.E.) thanks to Earlham College.

The commentary portion will note the major textual variants as they come up. Rudolf Schnackenburg has an exhaustive list of them in *Das Johannesevangelium*, volume IV, part 1, pages 163-170.

---

[23] *The Riddles of the Fourth Gospel*, page 70.

The historical setting of John

Jesus did not inhabit the world that modern people imagine that he did. Our knowledge of someone else is always a mix of real fact and psychological projection; I inevitably assume that the other person is like me, when the other person is in fact herself. Evidence is often sparse for ancient facts, and even some scholars have little evidence for their positions.[1] That sets the stage for projection and confirmation bias. Both are inevitable facts of the human condition, but it is dishonest to ignore them and cloak oneself in an attitude of scientific certainty and objectivity when both are somewhat compromised. We actually know less than we think we know.

However, thanks to archaeological finds, the evidence for reconstructing Jesus's time is relatively plentiful. Besides the text of the New Testament itself, we have:

- Josephus's extensive histories, Antiquities of the Jews and The Jewish War. Josephus was a Judean captured and taken to Rome when Jerusalem was destroyed. Although his history is uncritical of his Roman patrons when perhaps it might in honesty have been, in other respects, his may be a fairly honest recounting of Jewish history as he knew it before Judea's destruction in 70 C.E.

- The Dead Sea Scrolls, which had been hidden in caves near Qumran, beside the Dead Sea, when Roman armies were suppressing the Jewish revolt in 68 C.E. These many scrolls, although the records of a Jewish sect disaffected from the Jewish mainstream, offer a bright first-hand window into Judean culture at the time of Jesus.

- Other Jewish sources, including those outside Judea. Judea was destroyed by Rome, and its people scattered, in 70 C.E., so many Jewish texts of the period are from Alexandria and other Jewish communities outside Judea.

Much has been written to analyse this relative bounty of historical source material. A good summary can be found in Raymond Brown's *An Introduction to the New Testament*, (New York: 1997). I condense that further here to this brief timeline:

930 B.C.E.   The Israelites divide politically into the northern 10 tribes (captured by Assyria in 720 and lost to history), and the Jews, the two southern tribes descended from Judah and Benjamin.

587 B.C.E.   Babylon conquers Judea and takes the Jews captive to Babylon. Psalm 137 expresses this catastrophic loss.

---

[1] Rudolf Bultmann is an egregious example. Although highly influential in the mid 20th century, his argument that John is more Greek than Jewish has been thoroughly debunked. *E.g.* Meeks, *The Prophet-King*, pages 6-17; Ashton, *The Gospel of John and Christian Origins*, pages 133-135.

Feminist Bible scholars are more up-front and honest about personal bias. "The advent of feminist biblical criticism prodded me to recognize that the scholarly objectivity I thought I could achieve by bracketing my Jewish identity was an illusion. I became aware of the degree to which my own work as well as that of other interpreters is affected in ways both explicit and implicit by our identities and allegiances." Reinhartz, *Befriending the Beloved Disciple*, page 14.

538 B.C.E.	After Persia conquers Babylon, the Jews are allowed to return to Jerusalem. They rebuild the city walls and the Temple, though the Temple lacks the magnificence of Solomon's.
	The books of Ezra, Nehemiah, Haggai, and Malachi are from this period.
332 B.C.E.	Alexander conquers the Middle East and more, including Judea. Soon afterwards, Alexander dies, age 32. His territorial generals take control, Ptolemy in Egypt and Seleucus in Antioch. Judea finds itself between those two large rivals, Egypt and Antioch, and the Temple priests play politics with both and are manipulated by both because of their personal ambitions.
	After Alexander, Greek culture spreads all over the Middle East, and Greek becomes the *lingua franca* of commerce and culture. When the Romans took over, they spoke mostly Greek not Latin in the eastern Mediterranean.
175-63 B.C.E.	Antiochus Epiphanes, Seleucid king in Syria, seeks unity among his multinational subjects by forcing Greek language and culture on them. In Jerusalem, he erects a statue of Zeus on the Temple altar, slaughters the population and plunders the Temple. The book of Daniel is the literary response; the Babylonians in it reflect Seleucid (Greek) rulers.
	The great Jewish hero, Judas Maccabeus, revolts at the desecration of the Temple. His Jewish guerrilla band take over Jerusalem and purify the Temple as commemorated in Hanukkah every year. Judas begins the Hasmonean dynasty of Jewish priest-kings, who eventually wrest Galilee from Syria. The Hasmoneans also conquer Samaria, which lies between Judea and Galilee, and they destroy the Samaritan temple on Mount Gerizim, cause for great resentment by Samaritans.
63-4 B.C.E.	Later Hasmonean kings make overtures to Rome. When two Hasmonean rivals fight each other for power, Pompey steps in and thereafter Rome rules Judea by puppets. An Idumean (non-Jewish) adventurer, Antipater II, comes to prominence by murder and marriage in the final years of the Hasmonean rivals. Choosing neither rival, Julius Caesar makes Antipater ruler of Judea.
	Antipater's son Herod plays his cards right in the Roman battles following Julius Caesar's death, so Augustus appoints him king of Judea. He is the Herod that Matthew says killed the babies of Bethlehem after Jesus was born (Matt. 2:16). He died when Jesus was four years old.
Most of Jesus's lifetime	After Herod's death, Augustus splits Judea between Herod's sons, with Archelaus in charge of the south and Herod Antipas the north including Galilee. When Judeans complained to

Rome about Archelaus, Augustus fired him and ruled directly through prefects such as Pontius Pilate.

Although Romans spoke Latin in the western half of their empire, in the east, they spoke Greek, and many were bilingual. Greek remained the *lingua franca* in the eastern Mediterranean, including when John was written. Judean and Galilean Jews very likely spoke Aramaic at home, the Hebrew-like language that they had spoken since the Babylonian captivity.

44-69 C.E. Herod Agrippa is king of Judea for a few years and promotes good relations with Jews, in part by persecuting Christians. After he dies in 44 C.E., Roman prefects replace him but are bad at their work. Jewish rebelliousness, smouldering during Jesus's time, flares up, and Judea revolts against Rome.

69-73 C.E. Vespasian defeats the Judean rebels for the most part in 69 C.E. Then he becomes emperor of Rome and returns there, leaving his son Titus to finish the job in Judea. Jerusalem is completely destroyed in 70, and the last pocket of Jewish resistance at Masada is crushed in 73 thanks to now enslaved Jews. Most Jews from ruined Judea leave and join other Jews in the diaspora.

The loss of the Temple and Jewish homeland affects Judaism profoundly. Of the many branches of Judaism active in Jesus's time, only the one least connected to the Temple and its hierarchy, the Pharisees, survive the destruction of Jerusalem.

Judean culture around Jesus' time

None of the gospels says that Jesus ever went far beyond the borders of his own country, Judea. Judea had two pieces, the main part around Jerusalem in the south, and the area beside the Lake of Galilee in the north. Samaria lay in between.

Judea was predominately Jewish and its culture centred around the Temple. Politically, it was ultimately controlled by Rome. When Jesus was born, Herod the Great was client king of Judea appointed by Rome. Some of his sons eventually also became puppet rulers under Rome, and sometimes Rome ruled Judea directly by appointing a procurator such as Pontius Pilate.[2] As part of the Roman Empire, Jerusalem and to some extent all of Judea had special privileges, and also a population opposed to any Roman action that violated their law.[3] The Sanhedrin, a council of 70 learned Jews and Temple priests, had limited jurisdiction to apply Jewish law judicially.

---

[2] *Ibid.*, page 30.

[3] Bruce, *New Testament History*, pages 18-40.

Iudaea Province in the First Century

Judaism was very different then, before the destruction of Judea by the Romans in 66-73 C.E. Judaism then was more diverse than the Judaism we know now, and diverse in different ways. Today's Jews are Ashkenazy or Sephardic, Reform, Orthodox or Hasidic (among many other categories), but all these are variations (some of them going back to medieval times) of the single branch of Judaism, the

Pharisees,[4] that survived the destruction of Judea and its culture in 70 C.E. Before that destruction, Josephus had described three main branches within Judaism, Sadducees, Essenes and Pharisees,[5] but there were further divisions within those broad categories. "A historian can now perceive over twenty groups, subgroups, and sects."[6] For example, the Essenes of Qumran,[7] writers and keepers of the Dead Sea Scrolls, were distinct from the Essenes who lived in Jerusalem.[8]

Judaism also had a political aspect that made Judea a powder keg in Jesus's time and afterwards. The Zealots emerged as a political movement when Jesus was six years old.[9] Zealots believed that it violated Jewish law to acknowledge the sovereignty of a non-Jewish ruler in Judea. Consequently, small-scale rebellions came every few years under the Romans until the big revolt that led to the destruction of Judea in 70 C.E., ending with the destruction of the remaining Zealots at Masada in 73 C.E. Jesus was considered an insurgent by Jewish rulers, and he was crucified between two other insurgents.[10]

In Jesus's time and for decades afterwards, there was no such thing as a church, and no Christians or Christianity.[11] John never mentions a church or hierarchy at all.[12] 3 John mentions a "church" in its 15 verses, but in connection with Diotrephes, of whom the writer disapproves. The letters 1, 2, and 3 John were written to stop a division in the community of John after John was written; see "Fate of the community" below.

Is John antisemitic?

John, particularly chapters 5-12, contains passages that challenge Jews to accept Jesus as the Messiah and son of God. I am not Jewish, so I lack the sensitivity that a Jew would feel in reading such challenging words. I am opposed to racial, religious and ethnic discrimination, and the anti-Jewish passages in John have repeatedly caused me to question whether John deserves the effort of this book, which I hope will make John more accessible and interesting to Quaker readers. I have decided to go ahead with the book, but also to add this section to explain

---

[4] Bruce, *New Testament History*, page 81. Charlesworth points out that there were actually two branches of Judaism that survived, the Pharisees and what he calls the "Jesus Movement" within Judaism (*Ibid.*, page 98); however, the "Jesus Movement" was in the process of becoming non-Jewish.

[5] Flavius Josephus, *Antiquities of the Jews*, Book XVIII, chapter 1; see also Bruce, *New Testament History*, pages 69-121.

[6] Charlesworth, *Jesus as Mirrored in John*, page 23.

[7] The Qumran Essenes left many scrolls, making it possible to reconstruct their beliefs. There are striking similarities between the Dead Sea scrolls and John. Charlesworth, *Jesus as Mirrored in John*, pages 51-53, 99-112, 231-32; Brown, *Anchor Bible* volume 29, page XVII. Essenes appear to have joined the Beloved Disciple's community (Charlesworth, *Jesus as Mirrored in John*, pages 85-87.

[8] Charlesworth, *Jesus as Mirrored in John*, page 540.

[9] Bruce, *New Testament History*, 96-97.

[10] *Ibid.* pages 95-100.

[11] *Ibid.*, page 30-34.

[12] Raymond Brown: "The Johannine community did not seem to have authoritative church officers (presbyter-bishops) who could control doctrine by the very nature of their office," in contrast to the church described beginning with Acts 7:38. Brown, *The Community of the Beloved Disciple*, page 158.

my hesitation, my ultimate decision to go ahead, and to implore readers to read John in a good Light.

Looking at the history, John records that the first followers of Jesus were Jews who thought they had found the Messiah (John 1:35-42). Decades later, the community that wrote John was excluded from synagogues (John 12:42) "because Jews had agreed that anyone who acknowledges [Jesus] to be the Christ would be excluded from synagogue" (John 9:22; see also 16:2). "A parting of the ways between Judaism and Christianity is [also] suggested by the reference to ... 'your law' (Jesus, 8:17, 10:34) and 'their law' (the narrator, 15:25)."[13] The level of anger in John suggests to me that the exit from Judaism was not voluntary because anger will have had a trigger. In any case, by the time John was finished, the community that wrote it appears to be no longer Jewish.[14] John documents an historical turning point: before John, there was one Abrahamic religion in the world, but while John was being completed, the one became two.

All Christians who had been Jews eventually left their synagogues, but John is the only book in the New Testament to mention their leaving, and it does so three times (9:22, 12:42, 16.2). Their departure probably occurred after the destruction of Judea in 70 C.E., when Judaism lost much of its diversity because only the Pharisees survived the destruction. Before the destruction, Jewish followers of Christ may have been more tolerated because Judaism was more diverse; many varieties existed side by side—Pharisees, Essenes, Sadducees, and others, and they all attended the same Temple.

Jews had good reasons for rejecting the community that gave us John according to long held Jewish beliefs, such as:

- **John portrays Jesus as God.** The other gospels only go so far as to say Jesus is the Messiah, but John goes that far and further still: he is God and was so from the beginning (John 1:1, 1:18, 20:28). John 5:18 shows that Jews found Jesus's equating of himself with God to be unacceptable.

- **John has more than one God.** In John, Jesus is clearly not the only God because he speaks often of his Father, but Father and Son add up to two Gods, and the Counsellor makes three. Deuteronomy 6:4 says, "Hear O Israel, the Lord our God, the Lord is one." That particular verse is "a pivotal element of Jewish liturgy".[15]

---

[13] Anderson, *The Riddles of the Fourth Gospel*, page 137.

[14] Brown, *The Community of the Beloved Disciple*, pages 40-48. Adele Reinhartz is sceptical that 9:22 reflects a push from Jews against Jewish followers of Jesus, and she is right that John itself gave early disciples of Jesus a strong impetus to leave synagogues because of its hostility toward Jews (*Cast Out of the Covenant*, pages 116-151; "The Gospel of John", page 116). It is difficult to differentiate action from reaction so long ago with the sequence of events so uncertain. However, to me it seems unlikely that people would willingly abandon a religious identity they had owned from birth and still shared in their families. Reinhartz says they were attracted by the promise of becoming children of God and God's covenant people (*ibid.*, pages 131-151), but for me, that attraction theory does not explain the anger in the text. John 8 has Jesus in a rage against Jews, but rage requires a trigger to set it off. For that reason, it is more likely, in my view, that John is the reaction to a push out of a religious identity. However, with so little evidence of what happened when, it is not possible to be certain whether the community of John was pushed out of the synagogue or whether they jumped, or perhaps it was both in the end.

[15] Reinhartz, "The Gospel of John: How "the Jews" Became Part of the Plot", page 106. Deuteronomy 13:1-5 contains instructions on false prophets who lead Israel astray into the worship of false gods.

- **Jesus takes the Lord's name in vain**. Jews have long said "my lord" instead of pronouncing the four-letter Hebrew word that is the name of God in Hebrew scriptures. That name is usually translated in English as "the Lord", also out of respect for the Third Commandment.

  However, particularly in John, Jesus frequently refers to himself using the very name of God. When God appeared to Moses at the burning bush, Moses asked God his name so that he could tell the Israelites who sent him. God answered, "I am that I am," and told Moses to say that "I am" had sent him.[16] Jesus applies that name to himself frequently in John. In Greek, "I am" would normally be expressed as ἐμί, but when Jesus says "ἐγώ ἐμί", as he often does in John, he is using twice as many syllables as are necessary, adding just enough emphasis to invoke the divine name for himself.[17] For example, in John 8:58, Jesus declares, "Truly I tell you, before Abraham came to be, I am." No wonder his Jewish audience picked up stones to throw at him (John 8:59; see also 10:33, where Jews are again about to stone Jesus for blasphemy).

- **Appropriation.** Jesus re-interprets and co-opts Jewish holy days and institutions. For holy days, Jesus is usually in the Temple as Judaism then required for certain holy days. Many other Jews are also there, and Jesus teaches them, re-interpreting the symbolism and ritual of the day to incorporate himself and to supersede the traditional significance of the day, as we shall see in reading John. He even appropriates the Temple by saying that his body is the house of God (John 2:21). Adele Reinhartz, one of few Jewish New Testament scholars to study John, wrote:

  > It is not possible to explain away the negative presentations of Jews or to deny that [John's] understanding of Jesus includes the view that he has superseded the Jewish covenant and taken over its major institutions and symbols. Any honest and engaged reading of the Gospel must surely acknowledge, and lament, the presence of these themes.[18]

It seems improbable that the community that wrote John could possibly think they could remain Jews and believe so differently, until we think of how the

---

If we assume that Jesus's God was different from the Jewish one, then he fits the description of a false prophet in that passage. Deuteronomy 13:10 requires death by stoning for such false prophets.

[16] Exodus 3:14.

[17] Raymond Brown examines all of Jesus's "I am" statements in John, and the few such statements in the other gospels, in *The Gospel According to John*, volume 29, pages 533-38.

[18] Michael Cook, "The Gospel of John: How 'the Jews' Became Part of the Plot," in *Jesus, Judaism, and Christian Anti-Judaism: Reading the New Testament after the Holocaust*, edited by Paula Fredricksen and Adele Reinhartz (Louisville: Westminster John Knox, 2002), page 114. Quoted in Blumhofer, *The Gospel of John and the Future of Israel*, page 227.

Gale Yee notes that John records Jesus at three Passovers where the other gospels mention only one, and, as for every other Jewish feast, each time Jesus replaces and supersedes the symbols associated with the feast. "In the first Passover [John 2:13-25], Jesus replaces the temple. In the second [John 6], Moses and the manna are replaced, and in the third, the Passover lambs sacrificed in the temple" are replaced by Jesus's sacrifice of himself. Yee, *Jewish Feasts and the Gospel of John*, page 59-60.

The offence to Jews was worsened by the timing. John was written just after the destruction of Judea and the Temple.

human mind first encounters huge, unwelcome change. The change may already be a fact, but if the person undergoing the change is not ready to accept it, denial, even in the face of the obvious, is the psychological response. John's words about Jews come at least in part from having to accept a rejection, for good Jewish reasons, but no less painful for that. The community had become non-Jewish but had not yet accepted they were in fact now no longer Jews.

Rejection explains the immense anger in John's anti-Jewish diatribes, but they are not mere name-calling like you "brood of vipers" (Matthew 3:5).[19] John's words are objectionable to Jews in *principle*. The words offend against Jewish principles such as not mistaking your human self for divine.[20] To the Jews of his local synagogue in Capernaum, he was a local carpenter's son:

> [Jews who heard him] were saying, 'Is this not Jesus, the son of Joseph, whose father and mother we know? How can he now say, 'I have come down from heaven'? .... [Jesus replied:] Truly I tell you, whoever Trusts has eternal Life. I am the bread of Life. Your ancestors ate manna in the wilderness, and they died. This is the bread that comes down from heaven, so that one may eat of it and not die. (John 6:42, 47-50.)

Because Jewish-born followers of Jesus were being forced away from the God of their fathers, John stresses all the more the divinity of Jesus to compensate for

---

> To point to Jesus Christ as the replacement of the fallen Temple and of the sacred holy places (like Bethel), as John does at a time when the war against Rome had deprived Jews of their land and Temple and had desecrated their holy places so that their loss was constantly and painfully present, was to touch a most raw nerve... His theme of "replacement" was, therefore, peculiarly sensitive and challenging and could not but provoke resentment.

W.D Davies, "Reflections on Aspects of the Jewish Background of the Gospel of John", in R.A Culpepper and C.C. Black, *Exploring the Gospel of John: In Honor of D.Moody Smith* (Louisville: John Knox Press, 1996), page 56; quoted in Coloe, *God Dwells with Us*, page 213.

On the other hand, to the authors of John (who considered themselves Jewish), another way of coping with the loss of the Temple, besides the Pharisaic one, had to be offered to the people. The Pharisaic approach was legalistic: "Rabbinic Judaism turned to the Torah as the central focus of the covenantal relationship with God. Fulfilment of Torah replaced Temple sacrifices as a means of atonement." Coloe, *God Dwells with Us*, page 213. John's approach is symbolic not legalistic.

[19] However, John 8:44 comes close to calling names. There, Jesus declares that the father of Jews is not Abraham, as they claim, but the devil. It was a deeply insulting and angry thing to say, and yet, there is a point to it in that Jesus accuses his Jewish audience of having evil roots, or a bedeviled unconscious, as Jung would have seen it. As I explain in the text, the son of man (as portrayed in John) is projecting. Jung noted that Jesus is out of touch with the evil that he is so he encounters it externally in people who seem evil but are just misunderstood. Jews in John very frequently misunderstand Jesus, but our own assumptions about Jesus make it harder for us to see the misunderstanding by him of them.

[20] Blumhofer shows how John offers Jews an alternative view of their future after Romans destroyed Judea. He concludes that "the historical context of the Gospel as a whole should not be reduced to an account of one community's social trauma. The Fourth Gospel's ambitious effort to provide a narrative of Jesus' life that portrays him as the fulfilment of Jewish eschatological hopes calls for a more complex account of its historical context." *The Gospel of John and the Future of Israel*, page 213.

Still the marks of collective trauma are the best explanation for the bitter anger and hurt, unless we posit a racial hatred for which there is little historical evidence during the Roman period. I agree with Louis Martyn in recounting his personal struggle with the place of Jews in John. *The Gospel of John in Christian History*, pages 216-220.

what they have had to leave. John tells them they have not left God behind because they have Jesus and, after him, the Counsellor. That consolation, however, deepens the rift and increases their unacceptability to Jews, who do not see Jesus as divine.

Not being Jewish any more had serious consequences. Just to note a legal one: Judaism was a religion officially tolerated by Rome, but a new non-Jewish religion was not tolerated, so those expelled from synagogues risked punishment for breaking Roman laws on religion.[21] Roman laws required worship of the emperor on pain of capital punishment.[22]

Most regrettably, John's strong words (and others in the gospels) became Christian scripture, so those words have given scriptural authority and encouragement to Christian antisemitism. Although the authoring community of John might not have foreseen the Holocaust and pogroms, I don't see them as without fault in writing and publishing their harsh, angry words. It was entirely foreseeable to the authors and many copyists of John that their angry denunciations would have a negative effect on their readers' opinion of Jews.[23] Anger is contagious, and the authors did Jews a great injustice by spreading their anger to people who had no actual cause for it themselves.

I am not going to cooperate in continuing that effect on Jews. I will translate what the text says—denial of what it says would be dishonest—but I do not accept the implications against Jews. Anger is understandable and the normal human response to rejection, but anger—that was eventually resolved—does not justify promoting hatred through a written record capable of surviving, and meant to survive, long after the events causing the anger.[24]

Trying to understand anger helps resolve it and prevent its spread. "Explanations do not exonerate the perpetrators, nor do they have any bearing whatsoever on the question of punishment or the consequences for evil acts. This is not rationalization or excuse-making, but investigation. Jung's position [provides] an opening for exploring reasons and causes and therefore also for finding ways to prevent such acts in the future by understanding what brings them about."[25] Understanding enables us to take responsibility and do something:

> Those who have difficulty in accepting the idea of a personal
> shadow [unconscious] as far as they themselves are

---

[21] Brown, *The Community of the Beloved Disciple* page 43. The laws included worship of the emperor, especially in and after the reign of Domitian (81-96 C.E). Pressure to worship false gods may be behind 1 John 5:21, which counsels to "stay away from idols". See also the textual note on John 20:28 below; Thomas's declaration of convincement comes in the exact words of the declaration required in worshipping the emperor. Anderson, *The Riddles of the Fourth Gospel*, page 136; Cassidy, *John's Gospel in New Perspective*, pages 9-16.

[22] Pliny the Younger, *Letters*, book 10, number 96 (ca. 100 C.E.).

[23] Reinhartz and others note that belittling one's opponents was a common feature of the rhetoric of the time; however, I agree with her that it was entirely foreseeable that readers, then and since, would respond emotionally to the angry words and use them to justify violence against Jews. *Cast out of the Covenant*, pages 86-87.

[24] Adele Reinhartz notes that it is impossible to read John in a "compliant" (accepting) manner and not be drawn into anti-Jewish thinking (*Befriending the Beloved Disciple*, pages 54-80). To me, there are enough gems in John to justify looking for them but the hate-inspiring rubbish in which many lie makes the looking repugnant.

[25] Stein, *Jung on Evil*, page 11.

concerned, whose knowledge of human nature is two dimensional (that is, without depth), all too easily think that morality attaches to feelings, that hateful, hostile, cruel or greedy feelings are immoral. They do not, perhaps, realise that the feelings that arise in us are neither moral nor immoral, but neutral. The supreme importance of morality is the way we choose to act on our feelings. And we shall not be free to choose if we do not know what they are.[26]

I don't blame the author of John for his anger, but writing it down for generations to come, and thereby preserving it and passing it on with authority, is a failure of morality on the part of the community that gave us John. Jews such as those who gave us John were accustomed to their scriptures, particularly those for Passover, reaching through to the present.[27] They are writing to preserve the memories of their great founder, the Beloved Disciple, and thereby to convince their readers that Jesus is the the promised Messiah (John 20:31). However, John's great gift of loving memories comes laced with gall, the effects of which have been catastrophic.[28]

Although the words of John against Jews are too angry to have been worthy of preservation in writing, time actually healed the wounds and the angry people moved on. John unfortunately caught the transition to a new identity at its angry stage. The fact that John portrays Jesus as divine, and as appropriating Jewish institutions and holy days, ultimately facilitates what had to happen: As Judaism consolidated into a much less diverse religion after 70 C.E., the people who gave us John eventually developed a new identity of their own. When their people separate from them, they separate on their side, protesting vehemently all the way, but going none the less. Separation, though painful, let the community recover and begin developing a new identity. That separation by the community of John is no reason at all for people like me, who have never had a Jewish identity, to think less of those who do, much less to persecute or kill them.

In any case, a reading of scripture that fuels hatred and violence would be inconsistent with the Spirit that Quakers believe should guide our understanding of scripture.[29] Such a reading of John would also be gratuitous and at odds with the example of Jesus in John:

---

[26] Wallis, *Jung and the Quaker Way*, page 24, quoted in Britain Yearly Meeting, *Quaker Faith and Practice*, paragraph 21:11 (5th ed.).

[27] Reinhartz, *Befriending the Beloved Disciple*, page 102.

[28] Reinhartz notes the "likelihood that a compliant reading of the Gospel would entail hostility toward Jews as enemies of Jesus and his followers" in *Befriending the Beloved Disciple*, pages 75-76. An example of such a reading is Cassidy's, whose opinion of Jews in *John's Gospel in New Perspective* seems to have fully internalised the hatred expressed in John. For example, he sees in Caiaphas's words in John 11:47-53 as a "cynical formulation of a cover story" (page 43), with no evidence for his position. To avoid falling into the same trap, it is important to step back and look for a more loving, peaceful, but also honest approach.

[29] Quakers declared to King Charles II, when they were most severely persecuted:

> That spirit of Christ by which we are guided is not changeable, so as once to command us from a thing as evil, and again to move unto it; and we do certainly know, and so testify to the world, that the spirit of Christ which leads us into all Truth will never move us to fight and war against any man with outward weapons, neither for the kingdom of Christ, nor for the kingdoms of this world.

> From within John's world of thought, violence in the name of
> Jesus is an unimaginable option, one that would disconfirm
> Jesus' messiahship and invoke the attributes of the devil
> ([John] 18:36; 8:44). Christians have a long history of
> choosing violence against Jews rather than the way exempli-
> fied by Jesus in John—that is, the way of truth-telling and
> willingness to suffer. Each time Christians choose hostility
> and violence, they reject the logic of John.[30]

There are many ways to read John, such as Blumhofer's[31] and Reinhartz's,[32] without coming to violent antisemitic conclusions.

As Blumhofer and Reinhartz show, whether one sides with Jesus or his Jewish antagonists depends entirely on how one sees Jesus, and that is a matter of individual freedom. Is Jesus the son of God and light of the world that he claims to be? Or is he just another a narcissistic pretender, one of many false messiahs that have offered false hope to Jews for thousands of years? If someone appears at a Quaker meeting claiming to be God's son, we would quite possibly doubt his mental health, just as Jews did of Jesus in John 8:52. If, however, the newcomer is in fact God's son, I hope at least some of us will sense that fact and thank God that we have found in physical reality whom we seek in worship. I also hope that, as our discipline requires, we would respect those who are not as easily convinced. Their presence among us would help us understand the incredulity of the Jews of Jesus's time, who had had so many false Messiahs appear.

In any case, denying Jews the freedom to determine for themselves whom they worship would be the same impairment of religious freedom that caused much suffering to Quakers in our history. Such impairments have troubled Jews much worse and far longer.

In John's war of words against Jews, as in any war, both sides suffer, regardless of whether they realise it at the time. John's angry polemic exacted a terrible cost from the very community for whom it was written. Quaker Georgia Fuller pointed out that John's anti-Jewish polemic

> produced one-sided portraits of Jesus and of Christian faith
> and practice. These portraits caused misunderstandings and
> divisions within the Community. The First Epistle of John
> tried to correct these problems. One lesson from the friendly,
> but fractious, Community [of John] that can be applied to
> friendly, but fractious,[33] Quakers regards the use of internal

---

Britain Yearly Meeting, *Quaker Faith and Practice* 24:04 (5th ed. 2013).

[30] Blumhofer, *The Gospel of John and the Future of Israel*, page 230.

[31] Blumhofer, *The Gospel of John and the Future of Israel*, see especially pages 161-2, where Blumhofer turns Jesus's logic in John 8 against antisemitic Christians. Blumhofer's book explains the deep resonance of Jesus's message in Jewish scripture, and he finds in that message an alternative future for the Jews of Judea, a fair subject for discussion I would say, even in the extremely difficult conditions after the destruction of Judea.

[32] In *Befriending the Beloved Disciple*, Reinhartz demonstrates four approaches to John that vary in their acceptance of or hostility to the text, based on how reading involves a relationship or one sort or other with the "implied author" (chapter 2).

[33] Quakers in the USA divided repeatedly over their history. Although Quakers in Britain have remained in unity, so far, we have a wide variety of views. I have held a variety myself.

polemic. That lesson is "Caution! Two-edged sword! Handle
with care, if at all!"[34]

The anti-Jewish polemic in John sharpened its view of the divinity of Jesus, at the expense of his humanity, among other things. 1 John was written to strike a better balance, but from the two later letters of John, it seems 1 John was too little and too late. See "Fate of the community" below.

---

[34] "Johannine Lessons in Community, Witness, and Power", page 98.

The life and death of Jesus

John is a book about Jesus, whom the stated author of the book, the man known only as the 'disciple Jesus loved', knew personally. It is "startlingly different from the other Gospels in its presentation of Jesus".[1] The other gospels all follow a similar pattern based in large measure on Mark's gospel. The gospel of John is the odd one out, the different gospel that tells its own story rather than elaborating Mark's story.

All four of the gospels are about Jesus, but John's is the one that has the most to say about Jesus's special role as the the long awaited Messiah. Convincing readers that Jesus is the Messiah and son of God is John's stated purpose (20:31).

However, a reader need not accept that purpose or even be open to persuasion about it. Adele Reinhartz, a very insightful scholar of John, has spent much of her life studying John, and being fascinated by it, without ever accepting much of what John's Jesus says. She remains a faithful Jew. I have also found her the most honest critic about the fact that John is "thoroughly anti-Jewish".[2]

It is not possible to read John and accept every sentence without its hostility to Jews rubbing off. It is necessary to to step back at times and to remain faithful to the spirit of peace that should guide the reading. It is not a book to be read uncritically, as if its words fell directly from the mouth of God, because they did not. We are hearing about the life of Jesus through the eyes, ears, and psychology of other human beings. However, more than any other gospel, John promises us the Counsellor, who can bring out the good that is also there.

"What canst thou say?"

I have divided the text of John into sections. Each begins with the text, then I explain "Meaning and resonance". Then for some sections, I have added a "Reflection" or two. You can add your own Reflections.

For Friends, there is no priest to tell us the implications. That is for the Counsellor, and you can be as well informed from that source as I hope to be. George Fox himself invites you in the words that brought Margaret Fell to her feet exclaiming, "We're all thieves! We're all thieves!":

> [W]hat had any to do with the Scriptures, but as they came to the Spirit that gave them forth[?] You will say, Christ saith this, and the apostles say this; but *what canst thou say?* Art thou a child of the light and hast walked in the Light, and what thou speakest is it inwardly from God?[3]

I hope the text and the notes on its meaning find you "pausing from time to time to stare off into space"[4] and look for what you can say.

You will, however, be different from me. Isaac Penington, for example, may not be your guru, and you may not subscribe to his Quaker views. For me, he gave the words of John and Jung a life in which the principles came alive; he enacted

---

[1] Brown, *The Community of the Beloved Disciple*, page 7.

[2] Reinhartz, *Cast Out of the Covenant*, page xxi.

[3] Britain Yearly Meeting, *Quaker Faith and Practice*, no. 19:07, italics added.

[4] Alluding to William Taber's method, see page 2.

them and recorded his experience. However, if he or anything else does not speak to your soul, then I hope you find someone whose writing about his inner life speaks to you for your reflections.

The literal/historical and the spiritual/archetypal

There is a shift in focus that is reflected in the text-meaning-reflection stages. Jesus was an historical person, a man who lived in what is now Israel, and he was killed for fear that he would raise insurrection against Rome. John recounts some incidents from the life of that historical person, but it reached its final form 90-100 years after Jesus died. We have no very effective way of knowing to what extent John's report of what happened reflects actual, unadorned fact, and what builds on facts to make a larger than life-sized Jesus Christ. Jung remarked, "At a very early stage ... the real Christ vanished behind the emotions and projections that swarmed about him from far and near."[5]

Bible scholars have not given up hope in seeking the "historical Jesus". Many scholars in recent decades have focused on re-creating the "historical Jesus" without all that makes him larger than life. However, Jung derided that effort:

> [C]ritical scholarship lays hold of the person of Christ, snips a bit off here and another bit off there, and begins— sometimes covertly and sometimes overtly, blatantly, and with a brutal naïveté—to measure him by the standard of the normal man. After he has been distilled through all the artful and capricious mechanisms of the critics' laboratory, the figure of the historical Jesus emerges at the other end.[6]

Where is the error in "measuring him by the standard of the normal man"? For Jung and me, Jesus was no ordinary man. John is also crystal clear on that: it was written "so "that you may come to believe that Jesus is the Messiah, the son of God" (John 20:31). To Jung:

> Christ is our nearest analogy of the self and its meaning. It is naturally not a question of collective value artificially manufactured or arbitrarily awarded, but one that is effective and present *per se*, and that makes its effectiveness felt whether the subject is conscious of it or not.[7]

Christ was not just a man but reflects the self, and an "archetype possesses a numinous autonomy and has a psychic life of its own."[8] To me, leaving aside the great archetypal energy of Christ in order to engage in a rational quest for the "historical Jesus" misses the point, even the very point of John itself. It shrinks from the "frontier of transcendence, beyond which human statements can only be mythological."[9]

Myth speaks much more deeply to the soul than history. Seeking this historical Jesus is one of many ways of putting Christ outside the soul, when in reality, if a person has any awareness of Christ at all, it will be inward. Isaac Penington:

---

[5] *Psychology and Religion*, in *Collected Works*, volume 11, paragraph 228.

[6] *The Zofingia Lectures*, in *Collected Works,* supplement A, paragraph 247.

[7] *Aion*, in *Collected Works*, volume 9, part 2, paragraph 79.

[8] Jung, "Letter to Pastor Bernet", in *Letters*, volume 2, page 264.

[9] Jung, "Letter to Pastor Bernet", in *Letters*, volume 2, pages 258-259.

> That which God hath given us the experience of (after our great loss in the literal knowledge of things), and that which he hath given us to testify of, is the mystery, the hidden life, the inward and spiritual appearance of our Lord and Saviour Jesus Christ, revealing his power inwardly ... and working his work inwardly in the heart.[10]

Isaac rues the "great loss in the literal knowledge of things", but what "God hath given us now" is "the inward and spiritual appearance of our Lord and Saviour". We rational creatures, who chose knowing over life, we like logically neat and empirically validated facts, even when we have not been given them.

Jung, who strove to be as empirical and logical as he could be, knew that an archetype is thoroughly unconscious; what our mind "sees" of it are symbols. "Symbols are the means by which archetypes, themselves unconscious, communicate to consciousness."[11] The larger-than-life Jesus is such a symbol. Jungian Robert Segal:

> [A] specific savior like Buddha would be a symbol. The archetype manifested through the Buddha would be the category saviors. Through the Buddha, Buddhists would encounter those aspects of the saviour archetype captured by the symbol. Other saviors like Jesus would capture other aspects of the savior archetype. Any symbol, however rich, is capable of capturing only a limited number of aspects of its archetype. Which symbol is employed by the archetype depends on which aspects of the archetype the subject, whether individual or group, needs to cultivate.

> An archetype for Jung is not the symbol of something else but the symbolized itself. The archetype of the child, for example, refers not to any actual children but to itself. The archetype is irreducible.[12]

Reducing the archetype represented by Christ to a historical person is what lands the Jews in John's story in trouble, though it is an error that many make, including many respectable contemporary scholars. From history, we see Jesus as an ordinary man, and not a very impressive one at that. He was an upstart from the North with little formal education (John 6:42, 7:15). However, if I look inward rather than at outward appearances, I am in a world of archetypes, among other things. If one of them, the self, comes to have the face of Christ because I found in Christ a symbol for the self, then thanks to John a way has opened for Christ (the self) to be more a part of my life.

However, if for you the self does not appear in Christ's clothing, perhaps your dreams may be the opening for you. In any case, a person's *understanding* of the self or of Christ is not the archetype itself because the archetype is not a thing we can have in consciousness, unlike knowledge or understanding. We don't possess an archetype; it possesses us,[13] so "not for a moment dare we succumb to

---

[10] *The Flesh and Blood of Christ in the Mystery*, in *Works*, volume 3, page 357-258.

[11] Segal, *Jung on Mythology*, page 40.

[12] Segal, *Jung on Mythology*, page 41.

[13] Jung, *Letters*, volume 2, paragraph 521.

the illusion that an archetype can be finally explained and disposed of but without our doing."[14] We cannot know the archetypes directly; they are unconscious, and a former appearance of the self may not be what comes in our dreams or in a new generation. "The most we can do," wrote Jung, is to *dream the myth onwards* and give it a modern dress."[15]

> We are seekers but we are also the holders of a precious heritage of discoveries. We, like every generation, must find the Light and Life again for ourselves.
>
> Britain Yearly Meeting[16]

Prologue (1:1-18)

Scholars believe that the first 18 verses of John were added between about 70 C.E., when the Romans destroyed Jerusalem, and 90-100 C.E., when John reached its final form. It is a conceptual overture for John and astonishing in what it says about Jesus.

[1]In the beginning[a] was the Word.[b]
And the Word was with God,
and the Word was God.
[2]He was in the beginning with God.
[3]All things came to be through him,
and without him not one thing[c] came to be.
[4]What came to be in him was Life,[d] and
Life was the Light of humanity.
[5]The Light shines in darkness,
but the darkness did not seize it.[e]

[6]There was a man sent from God whose name was John. He came to be a Testimony, to Testify to the Light, so that all may Trust through him. [8]He was not the Light, but was to Testify about the Light. [9]The True Light, which enlightens every person,[f] was coming into the World.[h]

[10]He was in the World, and
the World came to be through him,
but the World did not Know him.
[11]He came to what was his own
but his own people did not accept him.
[12]But to as many as received him
he gave power to become children of God,[i]
to those who Trusted in his name,
[13]who were born, not from blood
nor from the will of the flesh
nor from the will of a man but from God.[i]

[14]And the Word became flesh[i]
and lived among us,[k] and we saw his glory,
glory as a father's Unique Son,
full of grace[i] and Truth

---

[14] Jung, *The Archetypes and the Collective Unconscious*, in *Collected Works*, volume 11, part 1, paragraph 271.

[15] *Ibid.*

[16] *Quaker Faith and Practice*, page 17-18.

[15](John Testifies[m] of him and exclaimed, "This is the one of whom I said, the one who comes after me was before me because he was first before me.")

[16]because from his fulness
we have all received grace for grace[n]
[17]because the law was given through Moses,[o] but
grace[j] and Truth came through Jesus Christ.[p]
[18]No one has ever seen God.[q]
The Unique God,[r] who is
in the lap of the Father,
has revealed him.

Meaning and resonance

a. **"In the beginning"** (1:1): These words also begin the entire Bible (Genesis 1:1) and introduce the accounts of creation; John uses the same words as in the Greek version.   Creation is a separating, differentiating activity: heaven and earth are separated, land and water, etc., in Genesis 1. Ultimately humanity also became separated from God after Eden. "Creation stories are stories of coming to consciousness, of waking up, of developing awareness and cognitive functions."[17]

b. **"the Word"** (1:1): The Greek word translated "Word", λόγος, is broader than "word" in English. It means almost anything said, with connotations of computation, logic, reasoning, explanation, narrative, order, and more. "No doubt the English term 'Word' is an inadequate rendering, but it would be difficult to find one less inadequate."[18]

Murray Stein points out that John's usage of "the Word" is "an anomaly in the biblical text as a whole. No-one else uses it."[19] He continues:

> We automatically pay attention to something new and out of place in a familiar context. John is saying that there is a new archetypal image[20] that has come into consciousness, and he wants to tell us about it. But it is not simply new, since it is an extension of the previous archetypal image of Yahweh that has been making its way into consciousness since the beginning of the biblical narrative. John is announcing a new vision of something that was

---

[17] Stein, *The Bible as Dream*, pages 169-170.

[18] Bruce, *The Gospel of John*, page 19.

[19] *The Bible as Dream*, page 168. Coloe, Reinhartz and others find similarities between the Prologue and the wisdom literature in the Old Testament, but Stein is right, "wisdom" is not the same word as "Word" or λόγος. Evans finds "parallels" between the Prologue and the *memra* of the Targums, Aramaic interpretations of the Hebrew Old Testament used in synagogues at the time. Stein is right, though, about John's unique usage of "the Word"; he is talking about word choice and they about parallels. See Coloe, *Wisdom Bible Commentary*, volume 44A, pages 2-4; Reinhartz, *Cast out of the Covenant*, page 56; Evans, *Word and Glory*, pages 120-130.

[20] In psychology, the archetype is to the ego (the person I mean when I say "I") as the divine is to the human in mythology and theology: a basic structural element and dynamic, an essence that is there at the beginning, pre-conscious, and as far as we can know, "eternal". Stein, *The Bible as Dream*, page 168.

there all along but is only now coming into awareness. It is new and not new.

> This is the nature of revelation. Something that has been there all along but has been hidden or implicit has now come into focus and is made explicit. What was once invisible can now be seen. Translated into psychological language, John is saying that an archetypal image, which was there all along but lay hidden in the unconscious, has now come into awareness, and that this is an aspect of the same archetypal content that was known before as ... Yahweh, only now, through the events recorded in this Gospel, it can now be known. It has become more conscious. It is a new revelation.[21]

Jesus was what the world had unconsciously been looking to find, which helps explain why an obscure man from a provincial town became a culturally dominant figure in a few hundred years. He became "the collective figure whom the unconscious of his contemporaries expected to appear, and for this reason, it is pointless to ask who he 'really was'. .... He opened men's eyes to revelation precisely because he was, from everlasting, God, and therefore unhistorical; and he functioned as such only by virtue of the consensus of unconscious expectation."[22]

c. **"without him not one thing came to be"** (1:3): The negative is emphatic; "nothing whatsoever".

d. **"through him was Life"** (1:4): The issue here is whether "what came to be" belongs in verse 4, as in my translation above, or belongs in verse 3, giving the sense, "without him, not one thing came to be that came to be". There was no punctuation in ancient Greek, so it is sometimes debatable where sentences end.

e. **"the darkness did not seize it"** (1:5): The word translated "seize" means to grab hold of something and overpower it. If it were conjugated differently, it would mean "comprehend",[23] which is how it is translated in the King James Version. As it is, it is a physical taking and can serve as a metaphor.

f. **"The True Light, which enlightens every person"** (1:9): This is a favourite of Quakers. According to traditional Christianity, most people never realise spiritual fulfilment, now or in an afterlife; they are lost souls. Quakers point out that every person has the Light within, and letting that universal native endowment develop will increase the person's inner consciousness of God. Every soul has that capability, exercised or not; it is in everyone. Isaac Penington:

> [T]his light ... shineth in every conscience. .... God, as he loved the world, so he manifested his love to the world by sending his light into it, to enlighten every man that

---

[21] Stein, *The Bible as Dream*, page 169.

[22] Jung, *Psychology and Religion*, in *Collected Works*, volume 11, paragraph 228.

[23] Bauer, Arndt, Gingrich & Danker, *A Greek-English Dictionary of the New Testament*, pages 412-413.

cometh into the world, that with the light they may see his Son; and as many as receive him, to them he gives power to become the sons of God. As God would have "all men to be saved, and come to the knowledge of the truth;"[24] so he hath given that light to all, which may bring to the knowledge of the truth which saveth. He is "the true light, which enlighteneth every man that cometh into the world." John 1:9.[25]

Isaac also explained the purpose of that enlightening:

[T]he end of its enlightening is, that therein men might feel the drawings of the Father...; and in the faith thereof, and subjection thereto, come out of the darkness.[26]

Similarly, Carl Jung believed that every person has it in him or her to individuate, to become aware of the self, the inner divine, which everyone likewise has, though unconscious for the most part if not entirely. Indeed, every person is inwardly driven toward individuation (making the self more conscious),[27] a drive that Isaac called the "drawings of the Father" above. It begins with a discovery of that "light". Carl Jung:

Not all are vouchsafed the grace of a faith that anticipates all solutions, nor is it given to all to rest content with the sun of revealed truth. The light that is lighted in the heart by the grace of the Holy Spirit, that same light of nature, however feeble it may be, is more important to them than the great light which shines in the darkness and which the darkness comprehended not. They discover that in the very darkness of nature a light is hidden, a little spark without which the darkness would not be darkness.[28]

g. **"The True Light, which enlightens every person, was coming into the World"** (1:9): The Greek is unclear about who is coming; this could be read as "This was the True Light, which enlightens every person who comes into the World."[29]

h. **"he gave power to become children of God"** (1:12): Hebrew poetry is structured to repeat ideas with variations; see the Psalms for many examples. Culpepper notes the pattern in the prologue:

---

[24] 1 Timothy 2:3, King James version.

[25] *The Way of Life and Death*, in *Works*, volume 1, page 65.

[26] *A Reply to thy Animadiversions*, in *Works*, volume 4, page 196.

[27] "As a dynamic force, individuation refers to an innate tendency—call it a drive, an impulse or ... an imperative—for a living being to ... become truly itself within the empirical world of time and space, and in the case of humans to become aware of who and what they are." Stein, *The Principle of Individuation*, page xii.

[28] *Alchemical Studies*, in *Collected Works*, volume 13, paragraph 197.

[29] Carson (*The Gospel According to John*, page 121) and Brown (*The Gospel According to John*, volume 29, page 9) have good reasons for preferring the version I have also preferred.

In the beginning was the Word, and the Word was with God (1:1).

> All things came to be through him; nothing came to be without him

>> Life in him was Light of humanity, shining in darkness that does not overpower it (1:4-5).

>>> John came as a witness to the Light (1:6-8).

>>>> The World did not Know him, and his own people did not accept him (1:10-11).

>>>>> To as many as received him, he gave power to become children of God (1:11-13).

>>>> The Word became flesh, lived among us, and we saw his glory as Unique Son, full of grace and truth (1:14).

>>> John exclaimed, "This is the one…" (1:15).

>> From his fulness we have all received grace for grace (1:16).

> Law given through Moses, but grace and Truth came through Jesus Christ (1:17).

The Unique [Son] has revealed the Father unseen by humans (1:18).

This entire pattern, called a chiasm, turns on becoming children of God, a fact that shows it to be the keystone of the Prologue.[30]

i. **"born, not out of blood nor out of the will of the flesh nor from the will of a man but from God"** (1:13): All of John's Prologue anticipates topics that John will consider more deeply later. Being "born of the Spirit" is an example; it is a major theme in John 3.

John 1:13 says that those who "became children of God" were not born out of the three things listed there (blood, will of the flesh, will of a man). What is the point of telling us what the children of God are *not* born from? Perhaps the author knew the predilections of humanity and is warning of common sorts of misunderstanding. Paul Anderson writes that "humans tend to distort the Light, adding conditions and qualifications in ways that make it into a religious construct rather than the divine gift of grace. Further, humans tend too easily to craft it into something born of blood, or of the will of the flesh, or the will of humanity instead of being born of God."[31]

Interestingly, in "will of a man" the word isn't "man" in the sense of a human being. It's the male of the species, so it is specifically a male will in John 1:13.

---

[30] R. Alan Culpepper, *New Testament Studies*, volume 27, pages 1-31 (1980-81); see also Carson, *The Gospel According to John*, page 113.

[31] *Riddles of the Fourth Gospel*, page 185.

j. **"the Word became flesh"** (1:14): "The notion that an invisible and heretofore unknown spiritual figure becomes incarnated and lives among humans on a physical and observable plane is a statement that signifies what is psychologically understood to be an entry into consciousness."[32]

> The Creator is coming into better focus and further into human consciousness. The origin or archetype of this particular consciousness, which has acted in the development of the biblical narrative, is itself now coming into consciousness. This means that human consciousness is being expanded and is now able to take further into account the source of its being. The ego is becoming aware of the self, to use Jungian language. This ego-consciousness can now know what had not been known before: precisely, the image and essence of its creator and of its point of origin. This is a huge leap in self-consciousness and the potential for a more inclusive identity.
>
> It is also a matter of the archetype itself becoming conscious of itself in a new way. In other words, God becomes more conscious of His nature. The distance between archetype and ego-consciousness has been closed, and both sides of this equation are affected by this development.[33]

k. **"the Word ... lived among us."** (1:14): "Lived" is a word that literally means to pitch a tent. It alludes to the Tabernacle, the tent of God's presence where the ark of the covenant was kept (Exodus 40) from Moses's time until David and Solomon built the first Temple. In using "put up a tent" to describe Jesus taking physical form on earth, "John evokes the long memory of the Divine Presence dwelling within Israel and associated with the ark of the covenant, the temple, and the Tabernacle."[34]

l. **"full of grace and Truth"** (1:14, also 1:17): "Grace" is "the action of one who volunteers to do something to which he is not bound",[35] a kindness bestowed that need not be deserved or earned. Carl Jung explained:

> Nobody can know what the ultimate things are. We must, therefore, take them as we experience them. And if such experience helps to make your life healthier, more beautiful, more complete and more satisfactory to yourself and to those you love, you may safely say: "This was the grace of God."[36]

Brown sees here another link to the God of the Old Testament (whom Jung and Stein call "Yahweh"):

---

[32] Stein, *The Bible as Dream*, page 169.

[33] Stein, *The Bible as Dream*, page 170.

[34] Coloe, *Wisdom Bible Commentary*, volume 44A, page 14. In *God Dwells with Us*, chapter 3, Coloe thoroughly examines the tent as the divine dwelling.

[35] Bauer, Arndt, Gingrich & Danker, *A Greek-English Dictionary of the New Testament*, page 877.

[36] *Psychology and Religion*, in *Collected Works*, volume 11, page 114, quoted in Kastrup, *Decoding Jung's Metaphysics*, page 122.

In the great covenant scene at Sinai the glory of God filled the Tabernacle (Exodus 40:34), but now the Word of God has "tabernacled" among us and we have seen his glory (John 1:14). The two outstanding virtues of the covenant God, his *hesed* (gracious love exhibited in God's choice of an undeserving people) and His *emeth* (true fidelity to His choice), are now embodied in Jesus "who is full of grace and truth" (1:14).[37]

m. **"John testifies ..."** (1:15): John slips easily between past and present tenses, something usually taken out in translation. However, the switch is not random. John's editor knows the difference, and uses the past to fix the time, then pops into present tense to give certain words a vivid, right-here sense.[38] I retain the original tenses (as nearly as translation can).

"John" always means the Baptist in the gospel of John except in 1:42, where it refers to Peter's father. John was a common Jewish name then. The original Jonathan was King David's best friend, and in Roman times, it would have been impolitic to name your son "David". Nobody is named after David, Israel's greatest king, in the New Testament.

n. **"grace for grace"** (1:16): "For" in that phrase is a word meaning "in exchange for" or "instead of".[39]

o. **"the law was given through Moses, but grace and Truth came through Jesus Christ"** (1:17): Here begins the controversy with the Jews that recurs throughout John. Note how Jesus is portrayed as superior even to Moses; that pattern will repeat. The new archetype announced in John 1:1 supersedes the old one. John Ashton comments:

> "For the law was given through Moses, but grace and truth came through Jesus Christ." This statement, bleak, blunt, uncompromising, illustrates more clearly than any other in the whole of the New Testament the incompatibility of Christianity and Judaism. It announces a new religion.[40]

p. **"Jesus Christ"** (1:17): In John, these two words appear together like this only here and in 17:3.

"Jesus" is the Greek version of the name "Joshua", the name of Moses's successor. The meaning of the word is "he saves".

"Christ", strictly speaking, is not a name but a title, the name of a role. It is the Greek version of the Hebrew "Messiah". Both "Christ" and "Messiah" mean anointed, *i.e.* wiped with oil.

q. **"No one has ever seen God"** (1:18): God declared to Moses that no one could see his face and live (Exodus 33:20), so Moses sees only God's back (Exodus 33:23). Because God is entirely or mostly unconscious, our perception and awareness of God is limited.

Carl Jung commented on the limits of what we know:

---

[37] *The Community of the Beloved Disciple*, page 49.

[38] See Culpepper, *Anatomy of the Fourth Gospel*, page 31.

[39] Bauer, Arndt, Gingrich & Danker, *A Greek-English Lexicon of the New Testament*, page 73-74.

[40] *The Gospel of John and Christian Origins*, page 2.

All that *is* is not encompassed by our knowledge, so that we are not in a position to make any statements about its total nature. Microphysics is feeling its way into the unknown side of matter, just as complex psychology is pushing forward into the unknown side of the psyche. Both lines of investigation have yielded findings which can be conceived only by means of [polarities], and both have developed concepts which display remarkable analogies. .... Of course there is little or no hope that the Unitary Being can ever be conceived, since our powers of thought and language permit only of [polarised] statements. But this much we do know beyond all doubt, that empirical reality has a transcendental background.[41]

r. **"The Unique God"** (1:18): The word "son" (υἱός) is not in John 1:18, which emphasises Jesus's divinity. "Only begotten" is the King James translation, but it is not very accurate because the word means one of a kind, without any begetting, *i.e.* physical reproduction.[42] See also Unique Son below in "John's key words".

A spiritual community begins (1:19-51)

[19]This is the Testimony[a] of John.[b] When Jews sent priests and Levites to him to ask, "Who are you?"[c] [20]he declared, and did not deny but declared, "I am not[d] the Christ.[e]"

[21] They asked him, "Who then? Are you Elijah?"[f] and he said, "I am not." "Are you the prophet?"[g] and he answered, "No."

[22]So they said to him, "Who are you? So that we can give an answer to those who sent us. What do you say about yourself?"

[23]He said,

> I am a voice shouting in the desert,
> "Make straight the way of the Lord."

As the prophet Isaiah said. [h]

[24]They had been sent from the Pharisees. [26]They said to him, "So why are you immersing[i] people if you are not the Christ nor Elijah nor the prophet?" [26]John answered them saying, "I immerse in water, but among you stands one whom you do not Recognise, [27]who comes after me. I am not worthy to undo the strap of his sandal."[j]

[28]These things happened in Bethany across the Jordan, where John was immersing.

[29]The next day, he sees Jesus coming toward him and he says, "There is the lamb of God[l] who takes away the World's Wrongfulness. [30]This is the one of whom I said, 'After me comes a man who will become ahead of me because he was first before me.' [31]I did not Know him, but I came immersing in water so that he will be revealed to Israel."

---

[41] *Mysterium Coniunctionis*, in *Collected Works*, volume 14, paragraph 768.

[42] Keener, *The Gospel of John*, volume 1, page 412-41

[32]John Testified, "I have seen the Spirit coming down like a dove out of the sky and Remaining on him." [33]I did not Know him, but he who sent me to immerse with water, he told me, "On the one, on whom you see the Spirit come down and Remain, he it is who immerses in the Holy Spirit." [34]I have seen and Testified that this is the son of God.

[35]The next day, John was again standing with two of his disciples,[m] [36]and as he watched Jesus go by, he said, "There is the lamb of God."[n] [37]The two disciples heard him speak and followed Jesus. [38]When Jesus turned and saw them following, he said, "What are you looking for?"

They said to him, "Rabbi," which is to say "teacher", "where are you staying?"[o] [39]He said, "Come and see."[p] They came and saw where he was Remaining, and they Remained with him that day. It was about four in the afternoon.[q] [40]Andrew, Simon Peter's brother, was one of the two who heard John and followed him. [41]He first finds[r] his brother Simon and says to him, "We have found the Messiah" (which is translated "Christ" or "anointed"). [42]He brought Simon to Jesus. When he saw him, Jesus said, "You are Simon the son of John. You will be called Cephas (which is translated, "pebble"[p]).

[43]The next day, Jesus decides to go to Galilee, and he finds Philip. Jesus says to him, "Follow me." [44]Philip was from Bethsaida, the town of Andrew and Peter. [45]Philip finds Nathaniel and says to him, "We have found the one Moses wrote about in the law and the prophets, Jesus son of Joseph of Nazareth." [46]Nathaniel said to him, "Can anything good be from Nazareth?" Philip said, "Come and see."

[47]Jesus saw Nathaniel coming to him and says of him, "Here is Truly an Israelite in whom there is no guile."[s] [48]Nathaniel says to him, "From where did you Recognise me?" Jesus answers him, "Before Philip spoke to you, I saw you under the fig tree." [49]Nathaniel answered him, "Rabbi, you are the son of God, you are the king of Israel." [50]Jesus answered, "You Trust because I told you that I saw you under the fig tree? You will see greater things than those." [51]He said to him, "Very truly I tell you all, you will see the sky opened and messengers of God ascending and descending upon the son of man."[t]

Meaning and resonance

a. **"Testimony"** (1:19): Some scholars think that John 1:6-9, now a parenthetical within the Prologue, was originally the beginning of John before the prologue was added. Verses 6-9 say John came to Testify of the Light, and here we have that Testimony.

b. **"John"** (1:19): In the gospel of John, "John" always refers to John the Baptist (except in 1:42). The gospel is said to come from the Beloved Disciple (John 21:24), who is not named in John. See "The disciple Jesus loved" above.

c. **"Who are you?"** (1:19): In a non-Jewish culture of that time, the first question in this situation would probably be, "What is this strange dunking ritual that you are doing?" However, in Judea, "immersion in water was a common and even regular practice for purification—not necessarily for sin, but for seeking worthiness to come before God."[43] Immersion was required to enter the Temple, for example, and the pools of Bethesda and Siloam were places made for doing it.[44]

d. **"I am not"** (1:21): "I am" (ἐγώ εἰμί), the name of God according to Exodus 3:14, does not appear here; the "not" (οὐκ) appears between the words "I" and "am". Only Jesus uses the name of God in John.

e. **"the Christ"** (1:20): See "Christ" in the Prologue above for more about the meaning of this title.

f. **"Elijah"** (1:21): The prophet Malachi's last words foretold that God would "send you the prophet Elijah before the great and terrible day of the Lord comes" (Malachi 4:5-6).

g. **"the prophet"** (1:21): "*A* prophet" could be any of a number of people, but "*the* prophet" very likely refers to the "prophet like me [Moses]" mentioned in Deuteronomy 18:15-18.

h. **"as the prophet Isaiah said"** (1:23): Isaiah 11:3. The quotation is from the Greek version; the Hebrew text is slightly different, "A voice crying out, 'Prepare the way of the Lord in the desert'."[45]

i. **"immersing"**: "Baptism" is a sacrament of the church, but there was no church in John's time, and the community of John may not have considered itself a church when it later wrote John. Nothing in John requires water baptism or even suggests that immersion is spiritually beneficial. It was a Jewish practice with purification as its purpose.[46]

j. **"I am not worthy to undo the strap of his sandal"** (1:27): John knows his place, but he is also the only one in these opening scenes to Recognise Jesus. He is also never mistaken, a rarity for anyone but Jesus in John.

In the fourth gospel, John never immerses Jesus. His mission is to be a Witness of the Light (John 1:7-8), not to perform a Jewish purification ritual on Jesus. As Jesus never gets immersed, why is he out across the Jordan? His innermost group of disciples come from John the Baptist, for one thing, thanks to the Testimony of John. It is also where the Holy Spirit descends on Jesus (1:32).

k. **"two of his disciples"** (1:35): One of the two is named as Andrew in verse 40. The other is thought to be the Beloved Disciple[47] and is the only anonymous person mentioned in these opening scenes.

l. **"the lamb of God"** (1:29; 1:35): A lamb was the traditional Passover sacrifice dating back to the institution of Passover, when firstborn Egyptian children died but Israelite children in Egypt were spared (Exodus 12:22). The blood of the Passover lamb on Israelite doorposts prevented the Lord from taking a life inside (Exodus 12:23-27). Thus the Passover

---

[43] Coloe, *Wisdom Bible Commentary*, volume 44A, page 36.

[44] Charlesworth, *Jesus as Mirrored in John* page 104 and 196.

[45] Brown, *The Gospel according to John*, volume 29, page 43.

[46] Charlesworth, *Jesus as Mirrored in John*, pages x-xiii and 104-105.

[47] Brown, *The Community of the Beloved Disciple*, page 33.

lamb wards off evil rather than atoning for it. "Atonement theology is foreign to John's gospel."[48]

m. **"where are you staying?"** (1:38): I usually translate μένω as Remain (defined below in "John's key words") rather than "staying", but I chose the more literal sense of "stay" here because they are talking about lodging. However, the meaning goes deeper into "Remain" territory. John loves multiple levels of meaning and the wordplay between them; this note belabours what is actually witty, ironic and playful. The double meaning continues through the rest of the dialogue. Ultimately, Jesus does Remain with the disciples (John 14:23, 15:4-10).

n. **"Come and see"** (1:39): This is the answer to the new disciples' question, "where are you staying?" Culpepper notes "that Jesus typically does not answer questions directly. Instead, he pushes his conversation partners to a deeper level of understanding or response",[49] such as with this invitation.

Philip says the same thing to Nathaniel in 1:46.

o. **"It was about four in the afternoon."** (1:39): People of that time reckoned time of day from sunrise, so the text says literally that it was about the tenth hour.

p. **"finds"** (1:41): John slips easily between present and past tenses. I maintain much of that. John uses the present to make words more vivid.

q. **"pebble"** (1:42): The name "Peter" (Πέτρος) literally means a pebble, not a boulder or a large rock. A πέτρος is much too small to build a church on (*cf.* Matthew 16:18, where the irony is no less present). John keeps the pebble unburdened and never mentions a church (see "Concepts not found in John" below).

Bruce points out that "πέτρος" is simply the masculine form; "πέτρα" would mean a large outcropping of bedrock, but it is a feminine noun so it would not do for a man's name.[50] He may be technically correct, but the fact that this delicious irony may be down to grammatical necessity makes the irony no less. Peter is not a spiritual hero in John.

r. **"Truly an Israelite in whom there is no guile"** (1:47): An "Israelite" is a descendant of Israel, the man first known as Jacob until God changed his name. "Jacob" means guile or deceit, and Jacob is best known for cheating his brother Esau out of his birthright.

> When Esau heard the words of his father, he cried out with an exceedingly great and bitter cry, and said to his father, "Bless me, even me also, O my father!" But he said, "Your brother came with guile, and he has taken away your blessing." Esau said, "Is he not rightly named Jacob?"[51]

Jesus is saying that Nathaniel is a better Israelite than his famous ancestor Israel because Nathaniel is free of deceit.

---

[48] Coloe, *Wisdom Bible Commentary*, volume 44A, pages 38-42.

[49] *The Gospel and Letters of John*, page 122.

[50] Bruce, *The Gospel of John*, page 58.

[51] Genesis 27:34-36, Revised Standard Version.

Verse 51 is another allusion to Jacob and his dream in Genesis 28:10–22, a dream that came to him after he wrestled with an unknown being while Esau was marching toward him to get even. However, in verse 51, it is Jesus who is in Jacob's place, with angels going up and down before him.

s. **"son of man"** (1:51): Literally, this is "son of the human being" (υἱός τοῦ ἀνθρώπου). The first known use of this phrase is in Daniel 7:13, where "one like a son of man [is] coming with the clouds of heaven". The image in John 1:51 is also apocalyptic, with angels ascending and descending as in Jacob's dream in Genesis 28:11-12). Apocalyptic thinking was widespread in Judaism at the time and reflects a "conviction that 'human failure has so corrupted life on this earth that only a radical transformation initiated by God alone could make things right.'"[52]

"Son of man" is said only by Jesus and it always refers to himself.[53] No other gospel is as clear as John that Jesus is God (1:1, 1:34) and the son of his Father, but with this phrase Jesus names himself the human son.

Wedding at Cana (2:1-12)

[1]Two days later,[a] a wedding took place in Cana of Galilee, and Jesus's mother was there. [2]Jesus and his disciples were also invited to the wedding. [3]When the wine ran out, Jesus's mother[b] says to him, "They have no wine." [4]Jesus says to her, "What's that to me and you, woman?[c] My Hour has not yet come." [5]His mother tells the servants, "Do what he tells you to."

[6]Six stone water jars[d] were lying there for Jewish purification rites, each holding about 20 gallons. [7]Jesus tells them, "Fill the jars with water," so they filled them up to the brim. [8]Then he tells them, "Now draw some out and take it to the master of the feast." [9]When the master tasted the water turned to wine, he did not Know where it was from, (though the servants who had drawn the water Knew), so the master called the bridegroom [10]and said to him, "Every person first puts out the good wine and then when they are drunk, the lesser wine, but you kept the good wine until now."

[11]This was the first of the Signs that Jesus did, in Cana of Galilee. He revealed his glory, and his disciples Trusted him. [12]Afterwards he went down to Capernaum, he, his mother, his siblings, and his disciples, and they Remained there a few days.

Meaning and resonance

a. **"Two days later"** (2:1): Literally this is "on the third day", probably referring back to the day when Nathaniel and Philip begin following Jesus. Counting in ancient Greek was inclusive, *i.e.* the count includes both the start and end days.[54] Most of the two days will have been spent travelling, and much of that through Samaria.

b. **"Jesus's mother"** (1:3): She is never called "Mary" in John, but she is present framing the gospel as it begins here, and again as Jesus dies in John 19. Their dialogue here is very mother-son: She begins with a hint

---

[52] Coloe, *Wisdom Bible Commentary*, volume 44A, page 37.

[53] Bauer, Arndt, Gingrich & Danker, *A Greek-English Lexicon of the New Testament*, page 835.

[54] Bruce, *The Gospel of John*, page 68.

that he do something, he rebuffs her, but then he does what she (tacitly) asked. Hollywood could not have scripted the start of this story more typically. Does she know when her son's Hour is? Considering our author's taste for irony, she does; in any case, she does not ask him to explain.

c. **"woman"** (1:4): "What's that to you and me, woman?" sounds disrespectful to our ears, but Mary Coloe says that is down to a gap in cultural understanding:

> Calling her "woman" may sound odd to our ears, but it is not discourteous; it is used to speak to the Samaritan woman (4:21), ... again to his mother (19:26), and to Mary [Magdalene] in the garden (20:15). Adele Reinhartz concludes that calling his his mother "'woman' does not belittle his relationship to her but rather recognizes its intimacy."[55] .... Tannen states that many cultures see "arguing as a pleasurable sign of intimacy," and in this mother-son context she notes that among men and women of Jewish backgrounds "a friendly argument is a means of being sociable" and that when a Jewish couple appear to be arguing, "they are staging a kind of public sparring match, where both fighters are on the same team."[56]

Jungian Murray Stein does not explain away Jesus's "caustic remark", but he also sees it positively: "With a son like this, even though he is magical, she is unlikely to get too inflated."[57] He explains:

> The danger of inflation is that the ego identifies with an archetype and loses its own specific identity. The archetype becomes incarnated[58] badly in this way and loses its usefulness and its positive compensatory effect in the unconscious world. So these tests that look so harsh and down-putting are actually guardians of the process and its deeper intentions. Were Mary to become inflated with her position—the wife of God, the mother of God—she would go insane, become swallowed up in madness.[59]

d. **"Six stone water jars"** (1:6): The jars were hewn from stone, rather than fired from clay, in accordance with the purity rules in Leviticus 11:29-38. Verse 11:33 says that earthenware pots can be contaminated, but "stone ...

---

[55] Coloe's footnote: Adele Reinhartz, "The Gospel of John," in *Searching the Scriptures*, volume 2: *A Feminist Commentary*, ed. Elisabeth Schüssler Fiorenza (New York: Crossroad, 1994), [page] 569.

[56] Coloe's footnote: Tannen, *Gender and Discourse*, page] 44 [New York: Oxford University Press, 1996]. Tannen works in linguistics and discourse analysis and so her methodology is based on twentieth-century research data. Whether this applies to ancient cultures is open to question, but this is true of any evaluation of a dialogue weighed against modern and cultural presumptions.

My source for the quotation: Coloe, *Wisdom Bible Commentary*, volume 44A, page 56

[57] Stein, *The Bible as Dream*, page 108.

[58] Jung and Jungians often use "incarnation" to mean the realisation of one's unconscious self into conscious "real" life.

[59] Stein, *The Bible as Dream*, page 108.

was impermeable from the impurity that would occur when someone ritually impure entered the home."[60]

Anderson catches the irony here: "Purification jars are here used, not to make the party sober and reflective, but to make the party festive and celebrative."[61]

Reflection

Whose wedding was it?

We have here a very incoherent story:

- "What's that to me and you, woman? My Hour has not yet come." That sounds like the answer is no because "it's not my problem". Yet in the very next sentence Mary tells the servants to do whatever Jesus says, an odd thing to say when Jesus has just shrugged off the problem.

- Why was the availability of wine worth noting at all in the first place?

- Why does Mary tell the servants what to do? She seems in charge.

- Why does Jesus tell the servants what to do? He is merely an invited guest (2:2), but both he and his mother command the servants of the house.

- From verse 12, it seems Jesus leaves this scene with a sizeable entourage, his mother, siblings, and disciples. Were they all at the wedding? If so, a large guest list would explain the prodigious amount of wine made from water (about 120 gallons), and possibly also why it ran out initially.

Other narratives in John, such as that of the Samaritan woman in John 4 or of any event in the last week of Jesus's life (John 13-19), or the week after (John 20)—those stories are told in minute detail, but in this wedding story, so many details are omitted that the story ends up garbled. Why? Perhaps the wedding story is just not as important as others. Or perhaps it has undergone so much editing as to leave it fragmented.

We really can't know, but Charlesworth proposes an intriguing theory that it was Jesus and Mary Magdalene getting married.[62] His theory explains many discontinuities in the text, and traditional theology could explain the heavy and reductive editing. However, Charlesworth also notes several reasons that rule out Jesus and Mary. We simply do not know.

Jung noted how incongruous it is that the Christian concept of God, and the life of Jesus as traditionally told, are devoid of any feminine aspect. Because no polarity is ever really without its opposite in Jung's view, that absence in consciousness means that the feminine is all too present on the shadow side, though there the reality will be distorted into negatives like witch, crone, or seductress, and projected externally. The result is misogyny. Jung wrote, after noting Christianity's overly spiritualised view of the feminine in the form of the Virgin Mary:

---

[60] Charlesworth, *Jesus as Mirrored in John*, page 480; Evans, *Word and Glory*, page 165.

[61] Anderson, "Navigating the Living Waters of the Gospel of John: On Wading with Children and Swimming with Elephants", Pendle Hill Pamphlet 352 page 13 (Wallingford Pennsylvania: Pendle Hill Publications, 2000).

[62] Charlesworth, *Jesus Mirrored in John*, pages 466-491.

> Since all unconscious contents, when activated by dissociated libido,[63] are projected upon external objects, the devaluation of the real woman was compensated by daemonic traits. She no longer appeared as an object of love but as a persecutor or witch.[64]

We pay a terrible price for having Truth that we can't bear to hear of. Besides distorting the feminine, we may be missing here a chance to see Jesus in more human terms.

Clearing the Temple at Passover (2:12-25)

[13]The Jewish Passover[a] was approaching, and Jesus went up to Jerusalem.[b] [14]He found in the outer court[c] sellers of oxen, sheep, and pigeons,[d] and the money changers[e] sitting there. [15]After making a [kind of][f] whip of cords, he threw them all out of the Temple with their oxen and sheep. He also dumped out the coins of the money changers and overturned their tables. [16]To those selling pigeons he said, "Take those things away from here. Stop making my Father's house a marketplace." [17]His disciples remembered that it is written, "The zeal for your house will consume me."[g]

[18]Jews[h] responded by telling him, "What Sign do you show us for doing these things?" [19]"Destroy this sanctuary,"[i] Jesus answered, "and in three days I will raise it." [20]So Jews retorted, "Building this sanctuary took 46 years,[j] and you are going to raise it in three days?" [21]However, he was trying to speak[k] of the sanctuary of his body. [22]When he was raised from the dead, his disciples remembered that he had said this, and they Trusted the scripture and what Jesus said. [23]While he was in Jerusalem during the Passover feast, many Trusted in his name after seeing the Signs he did.

[24]However, Jesus himself did not Trust himself to them because he Knew all people, and [25]because he had no need for anyone to Testify about a person for he himself Knew what was in a person.

Meaning and resonance

a. **"Passover"** (2:13): A Jewish holy week that commemorates the deliverance of the Israelites from Egypt as described in Exodus chapters 3-12, and particularly the passing over of Israelite firstborn when the Lord killed Egyptian firstborn.

b. **"Jesus went up to Jerusalem"** (2:13): Jews were required to be in Jerusalem for three Jewish festivals, Passover in the springtime, Pentecost six weeks later, and Tabernacles in the autumn. They each lasted a week. John often shows Jesus going up to these festivals. Jesus goes, re-interprets the symbolism of the festival to refer to himself, and thereby increasingly irks the Jewish establishment.

A person always goes "up" to Jerusalem, and "down" from it. The up and down are literal; Jerusalem is in the hilly area between the Jordan Valley,

---

[63] "Libido" meant different things to Jung and Freud. Most people understand the term as Freud did, as essentially the sex drive. For Jung, the concept included the sex drive but was broader: "Libido is appetite in its natural state," and "denotes a desire or impulse which is unchecked by any kind of authority, moral or otherwise". Jung, *Collected Works*, volume 5, paragraph 194.

[64] *Psychological Types*, in *Collected Works*, volume 6, paragraph 399 (1921).

the Dead Sea and the Mediterranean coast.[65] However, it isn't quite that simple: like just about everything else in John, "going up to Jerusalem" has levels of meaning.

c. **"outer court"** (2:14): The Temple was a series of concentric rectangles, with each rectangle more exclusive than the one further out. In the outermost rectangle, non-Jews were allowed along with Jews, and it was there that sales of animals were permitted to enable sacrifices at the Temple.

d. **"sellers of oxen, sheep, and pigeons, and the money changers"** (2:14): Sacrifice of these animals on the Temple altar was to expiate the sins of their purchasers. An ancient temple, including the one in Jerusalem, was a far cry from a church in that the most common activity in ancient temples was the ritual slaughter of animals.

"Laws requiring that only unblemished animals be used for sacrifices meant that most pilgrims purchased the animals for sacrifice after they arrived in Jerusalem."[66]

e. **"money changers"** (2:14): Besides changing money to buy an animal, the money changers facilitated payment of the Temple tax, the half shekel required of every Jew annually. Besides paying priests, the Temple tax paid for the twice daily regular sacrifices at the Temple to atone for the sins of all Israelites. The tax had to be paid with a Tyrian coin because it was pure silver so as not to violate Jewish purity laws.[67]

f. **"making a [kind of] whip"**: Two of the oldest papyrus manuscripts, 𝔓[66] and 𝔓[75], have an extra word here that changes the meaning a little. According to them, Jesus made a something like a whip. Sticks and other possible weapons were not allowed in the Temple.

g. **"will consume me"** (2:17): Taken from Psalm 69:9, although the psalm has the verb in past tense.

h. **"Jews"** (2:18): The Jews in this story are very likely the people responsible for keeping order in the Temple; however, John lumps all sorts of "Jews" together as "the Jews" ("οἱ Ιουδαῖοι").

i. **"sanctuary"** (2:19): The inner areas of the Temple, not the outer courtyards where animals were sold and sacrificed. Non Jews were not allowed in the sanctuary on pain of death.[68]

j. **"Building this sanctuary took 46 years"** (2:20): The original Temple planned by David and built by Solomon was destroyed when Babylon took the kingdom of Judah captive. Nehemiah and Ezra eventually returned and rebuilt Jerusalem, but their Temple was rudimentary compared to Solomon's. Herod the Great (72 B.C.E. to 4 C.E.) greatly expanded the second Temple, and it is this expansion that took 46 years.[69]

---

[65] Brown, *The Gospel of John*, volume 29, page 12.

[66] Culpepper, *The Gospel and Letters of John*, page 132.

[67] Coloe, *Wisdom Bible Commentary*, volume 44A, page 68.

[68] Coloe, *Wisdom Bible Commentary*, volume 44A, page 72.

[69] Coloe, *Wisdom Bible Commentary*, volume 44A, page 71.

k. **"he was trying to speak"** (2:21): The tense of the verb here indicates that the speaking action does not complete. However, the action is not continuous with no end in sight. More likely, Jesus was trying to say something but the communication did not go through.

Reflections

"My Father's house" (2:16)

The question that the Jews in this story ask is very specific: "What Sign do you show us for doing these things?" A peculiar question, which Mary Coloe explains:

> This [question] implies that they have understood his actions,
> to some extent, as a prophetic action, since prophets were
> authenticated by the "signs and wonders" that they were able
> to perform, *e.g.* Moses (Exodus 7:3).[70]

Jesus, who rarely answers a question directly, does not satisfy this demand for a Sign. Instead, he responds with a future claim, and a preposterous one—or so it seems. There is irony in the fact he is asked to prove his authority even though his actions were prophesied, and fulfilling a prophecy would seem the obvious way to authenticate a later prophet. "There shall no longer be traders in the house of the Lord of hosts on that day," prophesied Zechariah 14:21.

The significance of Jesus's action for the Temple was enormous. The animal sellers were necessary for the main activity of the Temple, the ritual slaughter of animals.[71] The money changers facilitated the sale of animals for sacrifices, and they also enabled payment of the annual Temple tax with the correct coin. In clearing the Temple, Jesus was undercutting the main activity of the Temple and its financial support.

However, despite the implications for the Temple, the Temple authorities did not tell Jesus to stop (but perhaps he already had by the time they are speaking with him). Instead, they ask him for a Sign as proof of his authority to clear the Temple. He answers with a riddle, in the same way that Old Testament prophets sometimes gave a Sign in the form of a riddle.[72] Perhaps the Temple officials were expected to know that he was speaking of himself because of Malachi 3:1: "The Lord whom you seek will suddenly come to his temple," but to Jews, it was blasphemy to say that the house of the Lord is "his father's house", as he puts in in 2:16.

The narrator prevents us readers from misunderstanding by explaining the riddle: Jesus was speaking of his body, a connection that would not have occurred to me, even in light of Malachi 3:1, so it is no surprise that the Temple authorities fail to understand. Their misunderstanding sets up dramatic irony: we know the real situation, the symbolic meaning of what Jesus was saying, but the Jews in the story are, as ever in John, in the dark. Passing that, we also know, as John's author did and probably from experience, that the Temple had been levelled in 70 C.E., about 20-30 years before John was completed.

However, another irony may not have occurred to our author, who was probably Jewish or had recently been so. The Temple, which was a marketplace in its

---

[70] Coloe, *Wisdom Bible Commentary*, volume 44A, pages 70-71.

[71] Coloe, *Wisdom Bible Commentary*, volume 44A, pages 66, 69.

[72] Schnackenburg, *Das Johannesevangelium*, 1. Teil, page 364.

outermost courtyard and a slaughterhouse yard in its next, was in its innermost sanctuary empty, except for a chest containing two stone tablets with writing on them and a few other objects. The chest was the ark of the covenant, the ancient Israelite token of the presence of God.[73] God's "numinous immanence" gave the entire Temple a sort of radiance, which in Greek is "glory" (δόξα).[74]

Jung noted that it is the same with us as well. Beyond ego consciousness lies a core as empty as the silence in a Friends' meeting:

> With increasing [proximity] to the centre there is a corresponding depotentiation of the ego in favour of the influence of the "empty" centre, which is certainly not identical to the archetype but is the thing the archetype points to. As the Chinese would say, the archetype is only the *name* of Tao, not Tao itself. Just as the Jesuits translated Tao as "God" so we can describe the whole "emptiness" of the centre as "God." Emptiness in this sense does not mean "absence" or "vacancy," but something unknowable which is endowed with the highest intensity. If I call this unknowable the "self," all that has happened is that the effects of the unknowable have been given an aggregate name, but its contents have not been affected in any way.[75]

"But he was speaking of the temple of his body" (2:21): Who tells us this?

This story sets a precedent that becomes a pattern in Jesus' later interactions with Jews. The pattern goes about like this:

1. Jesus does something that attracts attention, such as clearing the Temple of traders or healing someone. Sometimes the crowd is just part of the setting, such as on holy days in the Temple.

2. Jews ask a question or begin a brief dialogue.

3. Jesus answers them in terms that his Jewish interlocutors misunderstand. (We know they misunderstand because our narrator keeps us in the know.)

4. Jesus then proceeds to reinterpret his action or the current Jewish holy day in terms of his messianic mission, thus superseding or replacing the traditional meaning of the action or day.[76]

The narrator saves us from being like the Jews in the story, and being like them would never be good anywhere in John. We come off feeling clever, while the Jews in the story end up stumped at best, as here, or they get hefty criticism from Jesus.

Our narrator has the benefit of hindsight and reflection; John 2:22 shows that he or she is writing after Jesus rises from the dead. He/she demonstrates fulfilment of Jesus's promise that the Counsellor "will teach you everything, and remind you

---

[73] Coloe, *God Dwells with Us*, page 44.

[74] Coloe, *God Dwells with Us*, pages 58-59.

[75] Jung, *Letters*, volume 2, page 62; quoted in Stein, *Jung on Christianity*, page 61.

[76] Yee, *Jewish Feasts and the Gospel of John*, pages 60 and 62.

of all that I have said to you" (John 14:26). From the Prologue, it is clear that the narrator's knowledge reaches all the way back to the "beginning".[77]

Thanks to the narrator, the reader is always better informed than any of the characters in John. They misunderstand frequently, as the Jewish hearers of this story did in 2:20 or as Nicodemus is about to do in 3:4. However, readers occupy a privileged position because the narrator saves us from misunderstanding.[78] Moreover, "never is the reader the victim of irony. On the contrary, inclusion is the strongest effect of John's irony."[79] A clever bit of literary craft happens here: the narrator gets us on side, while the characters in the story are left to flounder. "The narrator shapes the response we think we are making on our own, and wins our confidence by elevating us above the characters to his position."[80]

However, the narrator's interventions are not so extensive as to give us a seamless narrative. John consists of brilliantly composed episodes, each with layers of meaning and delicious ironies, but those episodic gems are often strung together loosely, with minimal transitions, and some contradictions occur between them such as between John 2:26 and 4:2.

The episodes all have a pattern, as mentioned above:

> Each episode has essentially the same plot as the story as a whole. Will Nicodemus, the Samaritan woman, or the lame man recognize Jesus and thereby receive eternal life? The story is repeated over and over. No one can miss it. .... The prologue gives these episodes an ironic background in that the reader has already been taken into the confidence of the narrator and knows who Jesus is. We are therefore made to feel superior to the characters Jesus confronts, because in contrast to them we know that Jesus is the incarnate [Word] revealing the Father.[81]

However, though a repeating pattern, the plots become more involved and intense as the narrative moves along. The tersely told story of clearing the Temple is far simpler than the raising of Lazarus in chapter 11. As we read on, the echos of repeated words, metaphors, and symbols also accumulate and build from simple beginnings with John the Baptist through to the death and resurrection of Jesus, which John reports in exquisite detail. This is all done with the purpose of letting us "come to believe that Jesus is the Messiah" (20:31). Throughout, the author's craft is subtle but powerful.

---

[77] Our narrator is, however, probably not the Beloved Disciple himself because the narrator speaks of him in the third person in John 19:36, where he testifies of him, "His testimony is true, and he Knows that he tells the Truth". This comes late in John, just after Jesus dies, after our narrator has been filling us in for 20 chapters.

[78] "The extensive use of misunderstanding in [John] teaches the reader how to interpret what Jesus says and warns the reader always to listen for overtones and double meanings. Through its irony, the gospel lifts the reader to the vantage point of the narrator so that we know what others in the story have not yet discovered and can feel the humour and bite of meanings they miss." Culpepper, *Anatomy of the Fourth Gospel*, page 233.

[79] Culpepper, *Anatomy of the Fourth Gospel*, page 179.

[80] Culpepper, *Anatomy of the Fourth Gospel*, page 234; see also pages 15-49.

[81] Culpepper, *Anatomy of the Fourth Gospel*, page 89.

Birth out of water and spirit (3:1-21)

[1]There was a person among the Pharisees, Nicodemus by name, a leader of Jews. [2]He came to Jesus by night and said to him, "Rabbi, we know that you are a teacher come from God, for no one can do these Signs that you do unless God is with him.[a]

[3]Jesus told him in response, "Very truly I tell you, unless a person is born from above,[b] the person cannot see the kingdom of God."[c]

[4]Nicodemus says to him, "How can a person be born again when he is old?[d] He cannot go into the womb of his mother a second time and be born."

[5]Jesus answered, "Very truly I tell you, unless someone is born[e] out of water and spirit, he cannot enter the kingdom of God. [6]What is born of the flesh is flesh, and what is born of the spirit is spirit. [7]Don't be amazed that I said to you, 'You must all be born from above.[b] [8]The Spirit[f] blows where it will, and you hear the sound of it, but you don't know where it comes from or where it goes to. So is everyone born of the Spirit."

[9]Nicodemus replied, "How can these things happen?"

[10]Jesus answered, "You are a teacher of Israel and you don't Know these things? [11]Very truly I tell you, we say what we Know and Testify of what we have seen, but you do not accept our Testimony. [12]If I spoke of earthly things to you all and you do not Trust, how can you Trust if I tell you of heavenly things?

[13]"No one has gone up into the sky unless he came down from the sky, the son of man. [14]Just as Moses lifted up the snake in the desert,[g] so must the son of man be lifted up, [15]so that everyone who Trusts in him may have eternal Life. [16]For God so Loved the World that he gave his Unique Son, so that everyone who Trusts in him may not perish[h] but have eternal Life.

[17]"For God did not send his son into the World to condemn[i] the World, but so that the World may be Rescued through him. [18]Whoever Trusts in him is not condemned, but those who do not Trust are condemned already because they have not Trusted in the name of the Unique Son of God. [19]This is the condemnation, that the Light came into the World, but the people Loved the Darkness more than the Light for their actions were evil. [20]For whoever does evil things hates the Light and does not come to the Light, so that their actions may not be exposed. [21]But whoever does the Truth comes to the Light, so that it can be seen that their works were done in God."

Meaning and resonance

a. **"no one can do these Signs that you do unless God is with him."** (3:2): In John 2:18, Jews asked for a Sign but do not get one. Here, Nicodemus says he does not lack Signs; what he lacks is understanding. However, there is no transition or connection between the end of chapter 2 and the beginning of chapter 3; our author's sequencing of events may not be chronological.

b. **"from above"** (3:3). This word can also mean "anew" or "again"; the Greek word (ἄνωθεν) is ambiguous. The ambiguity is intended by our author, who is fond of word play and levels of meaning. It leads to the misunderstanding by Nicodemus that moves this story along (3:4).

c. **"kingdom of God"** (3:3, 3:5): This term, so very common in the other gospels and indeed the rest of the New Testament, is found in John only in these two verses. In John 3:3, "see" is the verb, suggesting that the kingdom of God may be present, but unseen (unconscious).

d. **"born"** (3:3-7): The verb here is γεννάω, which means to give birth, not "borne" in the sense of "carried." We saw the same word in John 1:3, "born not of blood, nor of ... will..., but of God."

e. **"How can a person be born again when he is old?"** (3:4): Nicodemus assumes that ἄνωθεν in 3:3 means "again"; the same word was translated "from above" in the previous verse. It has both meanings.

f. **"The Spirit blows"** (3:8): Spirit and wind are the same word in Greek, πνεῦμα. Here is another example of word play by our author.

g. **"Just as Moses lifted up the snake in the desert"** (3:15): A reference to Numbers 21:4-9, where the ever complaining Israelites are plagued by poisonous snakes. God told Moses to make a snake out of bronze, put it on a "signpost",[82] and then, "whenever a serpent bit someone, that person would look at the serpent of bronze and live" (Numbers 9:9).

Looking at the bronze snake must have meant to take in its symbolic value; it is not powerful independent of our thoughts about it. Bite victims who did not look at it remained sick.

However, the bronze snake became a talisman believed to be powerful in itself. That made it an idol so good King Hezekiah destroyed it (2 Kings 18:4). This incident shows how we harden symbols, especially numinous ones, into magical objects and thereby look past the symbol and its opening into the unconscious.

Charlesworth notes that snake symbolism is highly ambivalent but was surprisingly positive in ancient times, when the snake was associated with the great healer Asclepius.[83]

h. **"perish"** (3:16): The Greek word here (ἀπόλλυμι) implies violence. It is traditionally interpreted in terms of hell fire.

The Jungian understanding of that mythic outcome is more down to earth: "The divine power addressing humanity through the unconscious seeks a person's wholeness, which is "the 'divine plan' of the unconscious for humanity." However, "a refusal to accept this proffered invitation to higher or broader consciousness can be met with the same vengeful destructiveness that savage Gods of old were wont to wreak on those who opposed their divine injunctions."[84]

> If the demand for self-knowledge is willed by fate and is refused, this negative attitude may end in real death. ... The unconscious has a thousand ways of snuffing out a meaningless existence.[85]

i. **"condemn"**(3:17): The Greek word (κρίνω) basically means to judge, but in much of its usage in the the New Testament including John, it often has

---

[82] The word in the Greek Old Testament is σημεῖον, which appears often in John and which I translate as "Sign".

[83] Charlesworth, *Jesus as Mirrored in John*, pages 399-426.

[84] Dourley, *The Illness that We Are*, page 24.

[85] Jung, *Collected Works*, volume 14, paragraph 675.

a negative connotation. Here, verse 18 makes clear that it is meant negatively.

John 3:16-21 are an example of what Reinhartz calls "the rhetoric of binary opposition", in which John "recognizes two types of people: those who come to the light and those who do not, those who do evil and those who do not, those who believe and those who do not, those who will have life and those who will not."[86] See "Opposites in John and Jung" below.

Reflections

Nicodemus from "among the Pharisees" (3:1)

Nicodemus seems a man torn between the call to Trust Jesus and his status as a Jewish leader and prominent Pharisee. One symptom of this conflict is that he came by night to Jesus, seemingly unable to resist the desire to see him but unwilling to be seen doing so (John 3:2). Later, he spoke up for Jesus, as much as he dared, in the Jewish ruling council, but he was derided for it (John 7:52). He gave an enormous quantity of myrrh and aloes to enclose in wrapping Jesus's dead body (John 19:39-40). Always he seems to do what he can without blowing his cover. Only John mentions him by name.

Typically for Jews in John, Nicodemus asks the wrong questions as in John 3:4, "How can a person be born again when he is old?", and then he misunderstands the answer when it comes. We know from John 2:12-25 that misunderstanding is a narrative device often employed in John:

> As with all of [John's] misunderstandings, Nicodemus here serves as a foil which enables Jesus to explain his meaning while vaulting the reader to an elevated position of superiority over the characters' limited understanding. Nicodemus says Jesus is 'from God,' but he has not grasped the full implications of the origin.[87]

Looking more closely at Nicodemus's questions, it seems he thinks only in literal terms: being born again must mean re-entering the womb (3:4), but rebirth makes little sense except as symbol. He does not see the symbolic meaning so he ends up in a muddle, "How can this be so?" (3:9). As a scholar of the law of Moses, he concerns himself with precepts and their logical application, but his spirituality seems to go no deeper than those rational activities. All Jews in John share this characteristic, even though Jewish scripture in the Wisdom and prophetic traditions is profound and full of symbols. Perhaps this seeming mental block against symbols and depth simply reflects the Pharisaic approach to spirituality, at least as Jews are caricatured in John.

Jung saw the same problem in contemporary Christianity, which he thought had become overly rational after "the one-sidedness of medieval Christendom which exalted spiritual values at the expense of the values of this world" until the "apparent triumph of 18th Century rationalism ... brought about its own neme-sis."[88] What is left of Christianity is "religious sentimentality instead of the

---

[86] *Befriending the Beloved Disciple*, page 25.

[87] Culpepper, *Anatomy of the Fourth Gospel*, page 135.

[88] Bryant, *Jung and the Christian Way*, pages 12-13.

numinosum of divine experience."[89] Jung learned this from his patients, who "were not suffering from any clinically definable neurosis; they were ill because they could find no meaning in life."[90]

Jung saw that meaning comes from what Penington called "sweet experience":[91]

> The fundamental error persists in the public that there are definite answers, "solutions," or views which need only be uttered in order to spread the necessary light. But the most beautiful truth—as history has shown a thousand times over—is no use at all unless it has become the innermost experience and possession of the individual. Every unequivocal, so-called "clear" answer always remains stuck in the head, but only very rarely does it penetrate to the heart. The needful thing is not to *know* the truth but to *experience* it. Not to have an intellectual conception of things, but to find our way to the inner, and perhaps wordless, irrational experience—that is the great problem. Nothing is more fruitless than talking of how things must be or should be....[92]

Expertise in "how things must be or should be" from a rational perspective can seem enough for an exemplary life, like Nicodemus's was by the standards of his time and place; however, a preoccupation with rules is the wrong frame of mind. It makes us into either Pharisees or libertines. Both a Pharisee and a libertine are obsessed with the rules; it is as if they are travelling at night down a steep road descending in zigzags down a cliff, with the edge of the road (and the abyss) perilously close. The Pharisee concentrates on remaining as far from the edge as possible, while the libertine enjoys much more noncompliance and danger in his travel. Both are obsessed with the edge, the rule, and miss the life in the Spirit that would enable unity with the will of God in the present moment, rather than the will of God congealed into a written rule:

> The ground wherein men's religion grows (even the most zealous) is bad; even the same ground wherein the Pharisees' religion stood and grew; and it hath brought forth such a kind of fruit; namely, such a kind of conformity to the letter as theirs was; which stands in the understanding and will of man, rearing up a pleasant building there, but keeps from the life, and from building in it. But the true religion stands in receiving a principle of the life, which, by its growth, forms a vessel for itself, and all the former part, wherein sin on the

---

[89] Jung, *Collected Works*, volume 11, paragraph 52.

[90] Bryant, *Jung and the Christian Way*, page 14.

[91] "Give over thine own willing, give over thy own running, give over thine own desiring to know or be anything and sink down to the seed which God sows in the heart, and let that grow in thee and be in thee and breathe in thee and act in thee; and thou shalt find by sweet experience that the Lord knows that and loves and owns that, and will lead it to the inheritance of Life, which is its portion." *Quaker Faith and Practice of Britain Yearly Meeting*, section 26:70.

[92] Quoted in Jacobi, *Psychological Reflections*, pages 298-299.

one hand, or self-righteousness on the other hand, stood and grew, passeth away.[93]

"Receiving a principle of life" (opening to the Light within) takes us beyond paper do's and don't's. One born of the Spirit hears the wind (Spirit), but "does not know where it comes from or where it goes to" (John 3:8). Life in the Spirit is an adventure, not primarily a seated reading exercise. Obedience is not "an active conforming to rules but a waiting on the Light, relocating the level of consciousness at which we relate to God from assertion of will—'I will obey the King's command'—to receptive attentiveness—'I am ready to be drawn into creativity by the Spirit's leading'".[94]

The reason Jung wrote so much about Christianity is that he thought "the loss of the symbolic sense was a catastrophe for both individual and society:"[95]

> In Jung's view the recovery of the symbolic sense, and the sensitivity to the unconscious involved in this process, would enable the churches again to experience the vitality of their symbols and so to enhance their capacity to dedicate something of this vitality to the surrounding culture.
>
> However, ... Christianity has historically moved further and further from these sensitivities, often through deliberate theological options. Cut off from the inner life that originally gave birth to its symbols and that should be mediated by them, the Christian myth has more and more become simply a hollow container. It is not surprising, then, that fewer people find satisfaction in it.[96]

Symbols are keys to making sense out of the paradoxes that emerge from the unconscious. "Paradox is a characteristic of all transcendental situations because it alone gives adequate expression to their indescribable nature."[97] A new truth emerging from unconsciousness seems at first glance incapable of being true, if only for the reasons that led me to make it unconscious in the first place. That is why it is likely to appear at first as a paradox. The key to understanding it will be a symbol:

> By a symbol I do not mean an allegory or a sign, but an image which describes in the best possible way the dimly discerned nature of the spirit. A symbol does not define or explain; it points beyond itself to a meaning that is darkly divined but is still beyond our grasp, and it cannot be adequately expressed in the familiar words of our language.[98]

John's Jesus allows us little sympathy for Nicodemus; he mocks him to his face in 3:10. Yet I can't help but regret his case, and he is *so* close: if only he would open himself to a deeper, more symbolic spirituality, then instead of being kept "from the life, and from building in it", he would escape from his rule-bound spiritual

[93] Penington, *Axe Laid to the Root*, in *Works*, volume 1, page 232-233.

[94] Keiser, *Knowing the Mystery of God Within*, page 149.

[95] Dourley, *The Illness that We Are*, page 15.

[96] Dourley, *The Illness that We Are*, pages 89-90.

[97] Jung, *Collected Works*, volume 9ii, paragraph 105.

[98] Jung, *Collected Works*, volume 8, paragraph 644.

life. He seems to have a deeper intuition that drives him to seek out Jesus. However, Trusting openly must feel too risky for him; Trust would let him loosen his hold on rationality, find his unconscious and find God. Fear for his reputation as a Pharisee holds him back, so he comes by night and remains in the dark.

"born out of water and spirit" (3:5)

The two types of birth called for in this section of John are conventionally interpreted as baptism and confirmation, two of Christianity's traditional "sacraments", a word which never appears in the Bible. Conventional Christianity then applies John 3:5 dogmatically to require both sacraments for entry into the kingdom of God. However, there is no mention or even a hint of dunking (the meaning of "baptise" (βαπτίζω)) in this section of John. It is about being born, and what one is born from.

This section recalls that we are born physically out of water (the amniotic fluid that holds the foetus during gestation),[99] with the main point being that we also must be born spiritually in an analogous way.[100] John's immersing in the Jordan prepares the way for Jesus (1:23), but the gospel of John never suggests that the Jewish purification ritual of immersion in water (a *mikveh*) is spiritually necessary or even advised for followers of Jesus.[101]

Nor is there any aspect of the rite of Christian confirmation that resembles immersion in a spiritual equivalent of amniotic fluid, and then coming forth from it; confirmation consists of smearing oil on a person, with the oil symbolising the Holy Spirit. To think that the Holy Spirit is thereby actually imparted confuses the symbol with the thing symbolised.[102] Thinking she now has the Spirit, the confirmed person then never goes looking for it, so she never really finds it. She considers herself well served by the sacrament, but in reality, she has been fobbed off with a cop-out. Traditional Christianity is far too dogmatically rigid to want the real Spirit blowing people about as it does.

The dogma analogising baptism to physical birth is a *post-hoc* effort to make this section apply so as to require "sacraments", when actually this section doesn't apply. That effort increases church power because each church claims a monopoly on Christianity and the performance of the sacraments traditionally thought to be required by this section, even though this section does not mention them. It is talking about *spiritual* birth.

Spiritual birth is not something that a person arranges or decides upon:

> The initiation into the spiritual is based on archetypal energies beyond the reach of ego consciousness, and therefore, it does not require social intent or engineering. It need not be explicit or public. In modernity, in fact, this initiation is typically unofficial, undesired, and sometimes

---

[99] Coloe, *Wisdom Bible Commentary*, volume 44, page 89.

[100] Jung explained the symbolism: "Does modern man know what 'water' and 'spirit' signify? Water is *below*, heavy and material; wind above and the spiritual breath body." Letter to Dorothy Hoch, reprinted in Stein, *Jung on Christianity*, page 169.

[101] The other gospels put more emphasis on water baptism by a church authority, but John does not mention a church or its usual authority figures. See "Concepts not found in John".

[102] Jung's own confirmation into the Swiss Reformed Church backfired: "it convinced him that he was outside the Christian religion." Stein, *Jung's Treatment of Christianity*, page 76.

> seemingly pathological. It often comes in the guise of private suffering such as unaccountable or stubborn depressions, and the process following is played out in the analyst's office.[103]

So much for what this section is not about. From early in his life, Isaac Penington "interpreted the phrase, 'born of ... the spirit' (John 3:5) as a purely spiritual birth, not involving water baptism."[104] He explains:

> *Question:* How doth Christ save [Rescue] the soul?
>
> *Answer:* By visiting inwardly, knocking inwardly, appearing inwardly, causing the light of life to shine inwardly, and so enlightening and quickening inwardly, breaking the strength of the enemy inwardly, and bringing out of the region and shadow of darkness inwardly, into the region and path of light. By the light and power of his Spirit he begets a child of light....
>
> *Question:* What is regeneration, or the new birth?
>
> *Answer:* It is an inward change, by the Spirit and power of the living God, into his own nature. It is being begotten of his Spirit, born of his Spirit, begotten into and born of the very nature of his Spirit. ("That which is born of the Spirit, is Spirit." John 3[:6].) It is not every change of mind which is the right change, but only that which God, by the very same power wherewith he raised our Lord Jesus Christ from the grave, makes in the hearts of those whom he visits.[105]

Elsewhere, Isaac describes the experience and its fruits:

> A man cannot inherit the kingdom of God [without being] born again, even "born of the Spirit." So saith the Scripture, and so saith the experience of every one who feels the new birth. And when he is born of the Spirit, he is to abide with him, and learn the law of the new life, and receive power from him daily; or the spirit of darkness will soon get ground upon him, and by degrees be recovering him back again into his dominions.[106]

Darkness in Penington and John represents what Jung saw as the unconscious, where the self, the Christ archetype,[107] resides, along with the shadow. Paradoxically, the unconscious is dark but has that most numinous archetype shining inside, which Jung called the self and Quakers call the inner Light:

> Quakers believe all people have divine light (God's grace) within themselves at all times. The goal is not to convey God's grace to people, but to awaken them to its inner presence. Therefore, external vehicles are not required to transport grace within. Logically, then, if people experience the Light

---

[103] Stein, *Minding the Self,* page 81.

[104] Keiser, *Knowing the Mystery of God Within,* page 6.

[105] *Naked Truth,* in *Works,* volume 3, pages 290-291.

[106] *The Worship of the Living God,* in *Works,* volume 2, pages 215-216.

[107] Jung, "Christ, a Symbol of the Self", *Aion,* in *Collected Works,* volume 9ii, paragraph 79.

within, they receive baptism of the Spirit and communion
with God without requiring external symbols or vehicles.[108]

Yes, Quakers sometimes call being born of the Spirit a baptism, as John did in 1:33 when he identified Jesus as the one who "baptises with the Spirit". What Quakers dispense with is water baptism, but birth of the Spirit is indispensable.

The first step toward birth of the Spirit is simply a listening openness that the first Advice calls "taking heed". Where Buddhists take refuge in the Buddha and Christians are baptised as babies, Quakers "take heed", and it is that which begins a spiritual life:

> Take heed, dear Friends, to the promptings of love and truth
> in your hearts. Trust them as the leadings of God, whose
> Light shows us our darkness and brings us to new life.[109]

That new life begins by being born out of the Spirit, just as Jung described:

> Baptism endows the individual with a living soul. I do not
> mean that the baptismal rite in itself does this, by a unique
> and magical act. I mean that the idea of baptism lifts man out
> of his archaic identification with the world and transforms
> him into a being who stands above it. The fact that mankind
> has risen to the level of this idea is baptism in the deepest
> sense, for it means the birth of the spiritual man who
> transcends nature.[110]

"For God so loved the World that he gave his Unique Son" (3:16)

John 3:16 may well be the most famous and best known verse in the entire Bible, and yet it doesn't actually say what most people think it says. Most people see it as authority for three propositions:

A. Sin necessitates a penalty for the sinner.

B. I have sinned, so I must incur the penalty—except that:

C. Jesus has paid the penalty for me, if I have faith (Protestants) or if I complete the requirements (*e.g.* sacraments) for being saved (Catholics and Orthodox).

John 3:16 actually says none of that. What it says is just this:

> For God so Loved the World that he gave his Unique Son, so
> that everyone who Trusts in him may not be destroyed but
> may have eternal Life.

It says nothing about sin, or a penalty for sin. It says nothing about Jesus paying the penalty for my or anyone's sins. The verse does not make Jesus a scapegoat for the entire world. Isn't it psychologically interesting when we read sin into a scripture when it isn't actually there? And even more interesting when we also

---

[108] Williams, *Quakerism: A Theology for our Time*, page 30.

[109] Britain Yearly Meeting, *Quaker Faith and Practice,* Advices and Queries no. 1.

[110] *Collected Works*, volume 10, paragraph 136.

read in a scapegoat that lets us dodge personal responsibility for Wrongs we do?[111] We make a hook for ourselves, then get ourselves off it.

John 3:16 states that God "gave" his only Son. Brown sees in this giving essentially a revelation: "The cross of Christ in John is evaluated precisely in terms of revelation in harmony with the theology of the entire gospel, rather than in terms of vicarious and expiatory sacrifice for sin."[112] John never speaks of an "atonement" in that traditionally Christian sense.

Why do we make more of this verse than is there? Paul is part of the reason. Traditional Christianity's "theology arises from St. Paul's (and others') efforts to explain and justify Jesus' crucifixion. It does not spring from Jesus."[113] Ideas from Paul's letters, such as Romans 3:21-26 and Ephesians 2:4-6, get interpolated into John 3:16, even though John sees the death of Jesus differently. John feels no need to explain Jesus's ignominious end, as Paul does; for John, it was a glorious end (John 12:23; 13:31-32; 17:1-4), but then, John has a taste for irony and paradox.

The deeper reason why we read in more than is there is psychological. Jung:

> It is frankly disappointing to see how Paul hardly ever allows the real Jesus of Nazareth to get a word in. Even at this early date (and not only in John) he is completely overlaid, or rather, smothered, by metaphysical conceptions: he is the ruler over all daemonic forces, the cosmic saviour, the mediating God-I-am. The whole pre-Christian and Gnostic theology of the Near East ... wraps itself about him and turns him before our eyes into a dogmatic figure who has no more need of historicity. At a very early stage, therefore, the real Christ vanished behind the emotions and projections that swarmed about him from far and near.... He became the collective figure whom the unconscious of his contemporaries expected to appear, and for this reason it is pointless to ask who he "really" was.[114]

Believers have turned a kid from a nondescript village in a northern province into a saviour, a scapegoat, because shifting our problems to someone else is far easier than dealing with them ourselves through deep change in our minds and souls. "Atonement (at-one-ment) arrives from within through individual struggle to become conscious, not from without by divine intervention."[115] In John's words, we "receive from his fullness grace in return for grace" (1:16); I discover an opening into the darkness and the numinous shines out from it as if responding to the light (consciousness) passing through the opening.

---

[111] Jung observed: "Superficial understanding conveniently enables [a person] to 'cast his sins upon Christ' and thus to evade his deepest responsibilities—which is contrary to the spirit of Christianity." *Psychology and Alchemy*, in *Collected Works*, volume 11, paragraph 9.

[112] Brown, *The Epistles of John*, page 79. Brown is there quoting T. Forestell, *The Word of the Cross: Salvation as Revelation in the Fourth Gospel*, page 191 (Rome: Biblical Institute, 1974).

[113] Williams, *Quakerism: A Theology for Our Time*, page 81.

[114] *Psychology and Religion: West and East*, in *Collected Works*, volume 11, paragraph 228.

[115] Stein, *Minding the Self*, page 12.

So much for what 3:16 does not say. What does it say? The context of 3:16 helps show its significance. The preceding verse is parallel:

> Just as Moses lifted up the snake in the desert, so must the
> Son of Man be lifted up, so that everyone who Trusts in him
> may have eternal Life.

Looking at the bronze snake on a "signpost" healed a snakebite sufferer; however the snake was destroyed when it came to be seen as a magical talisman with healing power of its own, when it was really just a bronze sculpture, human handiwork (see note above). There was no magic in the snake; it *represented* God's power to heal, but it is a misunderstanding to confuse the symbol with what it signifies. Putting up the snake, like the "giving" of Jesus, was a revelation of God to heal people who chose to look.

John 3:17, the verse following the famous 3:16, also clarifies:

> For God did not send his son into the World to condemn the
> World, but so that the World may be Rescued through him.

For Quakers, the Rescue or salvation happens as an experience inside a person, or "within" as Isaac Penington phrases it:

> For the virtue of all Christ did without [*i.e.* performed
> outwardly] is within *him*: and *I* cannot be made partaker
> thereof by believing that he did such a thing without, or that
> he did it for me, but by receiving the virtue of it into me, and
> feeling the virtue of it in me. This is that which saves me, and
> makes that which was done without to be mine.[116]

Or as Patricia Williams puts it:

> [Early Quakers] center their theology on personal experience,
> and no one experiences Jesus' death but Jesus. Rather, the
> early Quakers rely on the Light within, the death of their own
> tendencies to wrongdoing, and personal transformation.
> They find these prefigured metaphorically in Jesus' death and
> resurrection.[117]

The traditional interpretation of John 3:16 is a cop-out; it avoids doing one's own part in order to experience Christ and Rescue within. "Christ exemplifies the archetype of the self," declared Jung,[118] who explained that Christ can be found within as what he called the "divine image", *i.e.*, what we perceive to be God:

> Too few people have experienced the divine image as the
> innermost possession of their own souls. Christ only meets

---

[116] *The Scattered Sheep Sought After,* in *Works,* volume 1, pages 97-98 (emphasis added).

[117] Williams, *Quakerism: A Theology for Our Time,* page 76.

[118] *Aion,* in *Collected Works,* volume 9, part 2, paragraph 37 (emphasis in original).

them from without, never from within, the soul; that is why dark paganism still reigns there....[119]

"those who do not Trust are condemned already"

In the other gospels, the "kingdom of God" points to a happy, future time when all will be well; until then, we live in a troubled world. Mary Coloe traces the origin of this thought back to its historical roots:

> In the post-exilic time [after ancient Jews returned from Babylon], and in response to the oppressive rule of the Greeks, which led some Jews to choose death rather than apostasy, the issue of God's justice arose. .... The hope developed that at the end of time God would raise the righteous, restoring them to life in order to participate in the end-time reign of God, which is called...the βασιλεία τοῦ θεοῦ (usually translated the "kingdom/reign of God"). This final reign of God would come about when the world was liberated from the oppressive rule of evil.[120]

John brings this happy future time into the present, as here in John 3:18-19, when the last judgment, conventionally[121] seen as the justice to come in the distant future, is happening now:

> [18]Whoever Trusts in him is not condemned, but those who do not Trust are condemned already because they have not Trusted in the name of the Unique Son of God. This is the condemnation, that the Light had come into the World, but the people loved the Darkness more than the Light for their actions were evil.

That negative side of judgment is in the present, and so is the positive side: "Whoever hears my words and and Trusts him who sent me has eternal Life ... he has passed from death into Life" (John 5:24; see also 6:54, 8:12, 10:10, 10:28, 17:3).

Quakers also see the end times as present. Isaac Penington:

> For Zion is not now literal, or after the flesh (that day is come, the shadows are gone); but Zion is the holy hill of God in Spirit, upon which the heavenly Jerusalem was built, which is revealed, come down, and coming down from heaven, and many of the heavenly citizens dwell there already, and more are coming thither to dwell.[122]

From Revelation 21:9-21, it would seem that the descent of the New Jerusalem would be hard to miss; it is a large, brilliant cube. However, Revelation speaks in symbols, and "Zion is not now literal, or after the flesh".[123] It is here and present, but it is also easy to miss if looking for a large physical cube rather than

---

[119] *Psychology and Alchemy*, in *Collected Works*, volume 12, paragraph 12.

[120] *Wisdom Bible Community*, volume 44A, page 86.

[121] The Jews of John's time also saw the last judgment as a future event. Brown, *The Epistles of John*, page 99.

[122] Penington, *A Question to the Professors of Christianity*, in *Works* volume 3, page 34.

[123] *Ibid.*

"the holy hill of God in Spirit". In simpler terms, "Quakerism proclaims salvation through the growth of the divine seed within us that produces personal transformation, social cooperation, and unity with God, here and now."[124]

Putting off the critical time disables us in the present, as George Fox explained in his analogy to a galley slave:

> People are saved by Christ, they [Protestants] say, but while you are upon earth you must not be made free from sin. This is as much as if one should be in Turkey a slave, chained to a boat, and one should come to redeem him to go into his own country; but say the Turks, "Thou art redeemed, but whilst thou art upon the earth thou must not go out of Turkey, nor have the chain off thee."[125]

The personal transformation brought about by getting to know Christ within (or by becoming conscious of the self, in Jung's terms) is the work of a lifetime. Delaying a start on it until a distant time misses the opportunity to be as free and fulfilled as we can be here and now. In missing that opportunity, "we are condemned already," in John's words, to a life less fulfilled than it might be.

John the Baptist and a man "from above" (3:22-36)

This section of John may be two fragments rather than one, the first about John the Baptist and the second, smaller one about a man who comes from heaven. The second part is not clearly connected to the first.

These are the last words we hear from the Baptist in the gospel of John; when he is again spoken of in John 5:33-36, it is in past tense. Compared to the other gospels, the Baptist has a more limited role in John.[126] He is forerunner and a witness of Jesus, but he does not immerse Jesus.

> [22]Later Jesus and his disciples went to the Judean countryside and he spent some time there with them and was immersing.[a] [23]John was also immersing at Aenon near Salim because there was much water there, [24]for John had not yet been thrown into prison.
>
> [25]Then a discussion about purification[b] developed among the disciples of John and a Jew.[c] [26]They came to John and said to him, "Rabbi, the man who was with you across the Jordan, of whom you Testified, here he is immersing, and all are going to him."[d] [27]John answered, "A person cannot receive anything at all unless it has been given to him from the sky.[e] [28]You yourselves are my witnesses that I said that I am not the Christ, but I am sent ahead of him. [29]The one who has the bride is the bridegroom; but the friend of the bridegroom,[f] who stands and hears him, rejoices greatly because of the voice of the bridegroom. So my joy has been fulfilled. [30]He must increase, and I must decrease.
>
> [31]He who comes from above is above all, the one who is of the earth is of the earth and speaks of the earth. He who comes from the sky is above all. [32]He who has seen and heard this Testifies, but no one accepts his Testimony. [33]Whoever accepts his Testimony certifies[g] that God is True.[g] [34]He whom God has sent speaks the words of God, for he gives the Spirit without measure. [35]The

---

[124] Williams, *Quakerism: A Theology for Our Time*, page 73.

[125] Cecil W. Sharman, *No More but My Love: Letters of George Fox 1624-1691*, page 75.

[126] Charlesworth, *Jesus as Mirrored in John*, page 94.

Father loves the son and has given all things into his hand. ³⁶Whoever Trusts in the son has eternal Life,ʰ and whoever disobeysⁱ the son will not see Life, but the anger of God Remains on him.

Meaning and resonance

a. **"immersing"** (3:22-26): Again, I use this word rather than "baptise" because the Christian sacrament of baptism did not yet exist. Jesus and John are performing a Jewish purification rite.

b. **"a discussion about purification"** (3:25): Purification is the purpose of the immersion. Jewish purity laws were stricter in Judea after the Maccabees re-consecrated the Temple, which had been polluted by pagan sacrifices to Zeus.[127]

c. **"and a Jew"** (3:25): We do not know who this Jewish man is. It could be Jesus but we have no way of knowing.

d. **"and all are going to him"** (3:26): This carries a hint of rivalry between Jesus's disciples and John's, at least in the eyes of John's disciples.[128] John 4:1 mentions that Pharisees also heard that Jesus was outdoing John at immersing people.

e. **"A person cannot receive anything at all unless it has been given to him from the sky"** (3:27): Likewise, Jesus noted to Pilate that "you would have no power over me unless it has been given you from above" (John 19:11).

Many translate the Greek word meaning "sky" as "heaven", but I often avoid "heaven" because it comes with theological connotations that were not present when John was written.

f. **"friend of the bridegroom"** (3:29): Jewish weddings of the time were arranged and overseen by the groom's friend.[129]

g. **"certifies that God is True"** (3:33): "Certifies" literally means he sets his (wax) seal on it to approve or authenticate it. "That God is True" can mean that God is truthful and honest, rather than deceptive,[130] or it can mean that God is real, *i.e.* God exists.

h. **"Whoever Trusts in the Son has eternal life"** (3:36): Another case of eternal Life coming in the present, not the future; see "those who do not Trust are condemned already" above.

i. **"whoever disobeys the son"** (3:36): This is the only time when the concept of disobedience appears in John.[131]

[127] Charlesworth, *Jesus as Mirrored in John*, pages x-xiii and 104-105.

[128] Reinhartz, *Befriending the Beloved Disciple*, page 83.

[129] Coloe, *Wisdom Bible Commentary*, volume 44A, page 103.

[130] Bauer, Arndt, Gingrich & Danker, *A Greek-English Dictionary of the New Testament*, page 36

[131] Brown, *The Gospel According to John*, volume 29, page 158.

Reflection

"God is True" (3:33)

> God is Reality itself and therefore—last but not least—man.
>
> Carl Jung[132]

As noted above, "God is True" can be read as asserting that God exists. That issue divides people in our time, and it always has. Now, however, the division has changed from being a majority believing that God exists to the present, when such believers are rare.

However, "does God exist?" is too binary a question in that it papers over a deeper, more complex issue. It begs the question who the answerer thinks God is. Often the answerer will have given little thought to that question, and will have a history leading to accepting or rejecting traditional concepts of God, images from the past packed with one's childhood or teenage reactions to them. Images from the past may no longer fit the present, however:

> As Jesus said, whoever looks back is not worthy of the kingdom. He was inviting people to a radical new spirit for the future. In our day, this means taking the risk of giving up inherited traditions and treasures in order to create a new spiritual future for oneself and for the human species as a whole.[133]

Isaac Penington called that turn to face forward becoming "the new creature, which is begotten in every one that is born of God".[134]

What is real about the God that one is born of? Let's start with what seems to be factual. Some aspects of "God" are difficult to deny, such as:

- **Fate**: The Almighty is synonymous with Fate. I may not like my fate, and I may prefer to think that I don't have one or that I can control mine. Such thinking is in vain. I have a fate, I don't know what it is, but I have it none the less. I can repress or split off the fact of it, but it remains what it is.

- **God in the mind**: In Jung's view, everyone has a self, and the self will appear as divine images (in a broad sense), if one's mental map includes the concept of the divine, or in dreams of powerful all-encompassing beings in any case. A God of some sort is in each of us, though perhaps mostly if not entirely unconscious. It is part of being human; our origin

---

[132] *Answer to Job*, in *Collected Works*, volume 11, paragraph 402. We don't see God within us, however: "What one could almost call a systematic blindness is simply the effect of the prejudice that God is outside man." Jung, *Psychology of Religion*, in *Collected Works*, volume 11, paragraph 58. Dourley explains the institutional impediment:

> But this blindness is at the heart of orthodox monotheistic belief. Such belief denies or, worse, historically persecutes individuals and traditions proclaiming the mystical experience of the "the essential identity of God and man."

Jung and his Mystics, pages 20-21.

Isaac Penington became a Quaker in about 1658, and from 1661 until his death in 1672, he spent over half his time in jail, much of it without trial, because of his testimony that he had found God within himself. See the "Testimony of Thomas Ellwood" in Penington, *Works*, volume 1, pages 11-13.

[133] Stein, *The Principle of Individuation*, page 78.

[134] *The Way of Life and Death Made Manifest*, in *Works*, volume 1, page 27.

myth says symbolically that cherubim and a flaming sword (defence mechanisms) bar the way to God,[135] who remains unconscious.[136] The knowledge gained by humans from the symbolic tree was of good and evil, but knowledge of ethics is not knowledge of God. Isaac Penington found his knowledge a distraction from the actual experience. "Wait to feel the thing itself ... and then thou hast a knowledge from the nature of the thing itself...."[137]

Jung took care to express no view on whether God exists other than in the mind, but he was certain of God's existence there, in the part of the mind that he called "the self". However:

> Jung is not *equating* the self with Divinity or saying that the self is divine, as some of his interpreters and critics have claimed. He is saying that Divinity forms and shapes the self into a pattern that manifests as an internal polarity. The Divinity and the self thus mirror one another. In this way, the self reflects the Ground of Being and is therefore intimately related to the universe. Humanity belongs essentially to the cosmos not by virtue of common material elements, but because at bottom the psyche is reflective of the deepest ontological structures, of Being itself. The psyche is linked, in short, to a transcendent factor called Divinity that shapes it structurally.[138]

The self, in other words, "is a [divine image], in Jung's account, in the sense that it conforms to the architecture inherent in the Ground of Being."[139] The Divinity or Ground of Being that gives the self its shape is beyond our conscious reach and not knowable at all.[140] The God-images from the self are also not the same from one person to the next, or over time. In *Answer to Job*, Jung explained how the God-image has evolved since Biblical times in the collective unconscious.[141] Dreams show how different individuals construct differing God-images. What the images have in common is:

---

[135] Genesis 3:24.

[136] John Dourley, in *Jung and his Mystics*, pages 1-2:

> The [individuation] cycle's first moment is the universal original sin. It is the sin of becoming conscious. It is a sin both rewarding and yet painfully paid for. It casts the newborn ego [conscious mind] in its infantile and developing self-affirmation into a state of unconsciousness unaware of its connection to its own origin and so unaware of its connection through that origin to all that is both within and beyond itself. Though a sin, it is a needed sin, a happy fall. To be conscious is better than being wholly unborn.

[137] *The Axe Laid at the Root*, in *Works*, vol. 1, page 256.

[138] Stein, *Minding the Self*, page 17.

[139] Stein, *Minding the Self*, page 18.

[140] "An individual can strive to individuate as far as is possible, and in this sense incarnate the self, but not single person can incarnate the Ground of Being completely because it far exceeds the capacities of an individual self." Stein, *Minding the Self*, page 17.

[141] Edinger's book, *Transformation of the God-Image*, traces the changing God-image through *Answer to Job*.

a) Numinosity (awesome power, wonder, and fear on the part of the human observer); b) absolute ontological standing, and c) cosmic proportion.[142]

Those qualities are what make them God-images, rather than just images.

The process of individuation brings a person's inward God-image more and more into a person's consciousness, into the existence we are aware of:

> The practical question remains of how the infinitesimally small human individual, being limited to a singular consciousness with unconscious cultural blinders fixed in place besides, can possibly take account of a psychological universe that is so much greater than the ego. How do we, or can we, experience the self and integrate it more fully into our conscious life? We tend to build ghettoes for our conscious egos and lock ourselves in at night to avoid the troubling sounds from the lunar world of dreams. This ghettoization of the ego must be overcome and the defenses dismantled. Beyond that, can people [realise] the potentials inherent in the self and also let flashes and hints from the transcendent Divinity into their limited and so much narrower conscious horizon and integrate all this into their conscious attitudes and worldviews? This is the psychological challenge for the contemporary person.[143]

So the question whether God exists is more complex than people ordinarily think, and it is probably not answerable as a simple yes or no. It depends heavily on what a person is conscious of; reality is harder to perceive than we think it is in everyday life. Fate exists, and natural principles such as we reap what we sow are true, regardless of what we think of God's existence. In a deeper psychological sense, God is also in our souls, in the self, waiting to be discovered and integrated into consciousness. The fact that a person has not discovered it does not mean that it is not there.

God is in a person's unconscious because God comes full of "unpalatable truths".[144] The fact that we do not have control of our universe is an unpalatable truth. The universe controls us, but that is unpalatable so many people project their need to control the universe onto a benevolent father in heaven. However, that projection creates a phantom divinity, not a real one, one that has actually been experienced. Evading God's unpalatable truths is hard work because it undermines reality.

To me, it is simpler to accept that God is in my mind, rather than to try to eliminate the Almighty there. Such elimination would just put the unconscious reality even further away from the threshold of consciousness, causing my shadow to compensate for the reality I can't accept. Repressing the God within

---

[142] Stein, *Minding the Self*, page 23. Stein gives several examples of God images beginning on that page.

[143] Stein, *Minding the Self*, page 20.

[144] ""Be honest with yourself. What unpalatable truths might you be evading?", from "Advices and Queries" no. 11, in Britain Yearly Meeting, *Quaker Faith and Practice*.

is also risky, in that unconscious content will find a way out somehow. That makes an unconscious God a risk: if the conscious mind identifies too much with a powerful unconscious archetype like God, it becomes inflated, mistaking myself for God and taking on divine-like attributes as if I were God.

"Thou shalt have no other gods before me"[145] applies to me as much as to anyone else: I must not make myself into God and ignore the real one. The best way to prevent that is to find and know the real God within myself. We all have gods; in a factual sense, God is whatever is most important to a person, and that will be apparent from how the person spends his/her time. For many people, a career or other ambition eclipses God entirely, and if the ambition is high, the risk is high that the ego takes on the greatness that belongs to God. Knowing the real God means sensing within myself what is beyond me while keeping the ego what it is, me not God.

> The essential thing is to differentiate oneself from these unconscious contents by personifying them, and at the same time to bring them into relationship with consciousness. That is the technique for stripping them of their power. It is not too difficult to personify them, as they always possess a certain degree of autonomy, a separate identity of their own. Their autonomy is a most uncomfortable thing to reconcile oneself to, and yet the very fact that the unconscious presents itself in that way gives us the best means of handling it.[146]

Isaac Penington describes what Jungians call "inflation", the ego identifying with God, and he recognised it as a barrier to the "life", the presence of God in consciousness:

> [M]an is apt to forget God, and to lose somewhat of the sense of his dependence (which keeps the soul low and safe in the life), and also to suffer somewhat of exaltation to creep upon him, which presently in a degree corrupts and betrays him. *The heart that is in any measure lifted up in itself, … is [to that extent] not upright in the Lord.* …. When Israel is poor, low, weak, trembling, seeing no loveliness nor worthiness in himself, but depending upon the mere mercy … of the Lord…, then is Israel safe. But when he hath a being given him in the life, and is richly adorned with the ornaments of life, … then is he in more danger of being somewhat of himself, and of forgetting him that formed him, … and so of departing out of that humble, tender … state … wherein he was still preserved.[147]

If I can accept that the Divine is within me (not me but within me), then I can eventually begin "the integration of conscious and unconscious and the formation of a new structure of identity that [is] the transcendent function".[148]

---

[145] Exodus 20:3.

[146] Jung, *Memories Dreams and Reflections*, pages 211-212.

[147] *Some Deep Considerations*, in *Works*, volume 2, page 378-379.

[148] Stein, *The Principle of Individuation*, page 79.

> In this new space, it is evidently possible to become fully engaged with the energies of what Jung called the Self. The risk is, of course, severe. Life itself is on the line. Psychologically, the risk is inflation so extreme that the ego disappears (dies) and insanity prevails.[149]

Now the fearful person that I am would really prefer to play it safe, leave God undisturbed and unconscious, and run no risk at all of inflation so extreme that I go mad. However, playing it safe is not really an option:

> In reality we can never legitimately cut loose from our archetypal foundations unless we are prepared to pay the price of a neurosis, any more than we can rid ourselves of our body and its organs without committing suicide. If we cannot deny the archetypes or otherwise neutralize them, we are confronted ... with the task of finding a new *interpretation* appropriate to this stage, in order to connect the life of the past that still exists in us with the life of the present, which threatens to slip away from it. If this link-up does not take place, a kind of rootless consciousness comes into being no longer oriented to the past, a consciousness which succumbs helplessly to all manner of suggestions and, in practice, is susceptible to psychic epidemics. With the loss of the past, now become "insignificant," devalued, and incapable of revaluation, the saviour is lost too....[150]

Because the God image evolves, finding the Divine within will be an individual, inward process, and one that continues through life because "the archetypes are the imperishable elements of the unconscious, but they change their shape continually."[151] In looking for the God within, my dreams are more important than any preconceived notions.

Seeking the inward God is an experience that Friends can share to some extent; my understanding can inform a community of Friends as I am also informed by their insights. There is no single, definitive formulation of the nature of God, and dogma toward that purpose undermines the open-heartedness that lets Friends share what we have each found.

> Spiritual learning continues throughout life, and often in unexpected ways.
>
> Britain Yearly Meeting[152]

Samaritan woman at Jacob's Well (4:1-42)

Samaritans trace their origin back to the northern ten tribes of Israel. When the Israelites resettled Canaan under Joshua, they divided up the land among their

---

[149] Stein, *The Principle of Individuation*, page 80.

[150] Jung, *Archetypes and the Collective Unconscious*, in *Collected Works*, volume 9, part 1, paragraph 267, also in Jaffe, editor, *Psychological Reflections*, page 46. "Psychic epidemics" are described in "The apocalypse of Carl Jung" below.

[151] *Archetypes and the Collective Unconscious,*, in *Collected Works*, volume 9, part 1, paragraph 301; see generally Edinger, *Transformation of the God-Image*.

[152] "Advices and Queries" no. 7, in *Quaker Faith and Practice*, page 11.

tribes. Fast-forward until Israel has kings descended from David, when the northern ten tribes rebelled against Rehoboam, a new Davidic king from the tribe of Judah. The northern tribes then set themselves up as the kingdom of Israel under new king Jeroboam (1 Kings 12), leaving the southern tribes of Judah and Benjamin under Rehoboam. Jeroboam gave the northern kingdom new gods so that his people would not continue pilgrimages to Jerusalem (1 Kings 12:26-33). Samaria became the capital of the northern kingdom (1 Kings 16:24).

Assyria took the northern kingdom captive in 720 B.C.E. (2 Kings 17:5) and resettled Samaria with people from other countries (2 Kings 17:24). The religion of the area became a mix from the various countries of the new settlers besides worship of the Lord and Jeroboam's other gods (2 Kings 17:25-34).

Later the southern kingdom was conquered by Babylon and its people taken captive (2 Kings 25). Seventy years later, Persia conquered Babylon, and King Darius allowed captive Jews in Babylon to return to Judea (2 Chronicles 36:22-23; Ezra 1:1-4). On their return, the Jews encountered the local residents, the mix descended from northern Israelites and the people resettled there from other countries. After the returning Jews did not allow the local people to join in rebuilding Jerusalem, the locals turned against the Jews and opposed their return, including by letter to the ruling Persians (Ezra 4). This opposition worsened the existing enmity, which worsened further when the Jewish high priest John Hyrcanus conquered Samaria, destroyed its temple, and enslaved its people in about 115 B.C.E.[153]

This history, based on Jewish scriptures and Josephus, tells only one side of the story; Samaritans have a different view of the events. However, I'll keep this a brief if regrettably one-sided summary of the situation. On both sides, the antipathy ran deep with both racial and religious roots, a powerful combination.[154]

> [1]Now when Jesus Realised that the Pharisees had heard that Jesus was making and immersing more disciples than John[a]—[2]although Jesus himself was not immersing but his disciples were [b]—[3]he left Judea and returned to Galilee. [4]He had to go through Samaria. [5]So he came to a town of Samaria called Sychar,[c] near the area that Jacob gave to his son Joseph. [6]Jacob's well[d] was there. So Jesus, tired from his journey, was sitting there on the well. It was about noon.
>
> [7]A woman of Samaria comes to draw water. Jesus says to her, "Give me a drink." ([8]For his disciples had gone to the town to buy food.) [9]Then the Samaritan woman says to him, "How is it that you, a Jew, ask a drink from me, a Samaritan woman?" (For Jews have no dealings with Samaritans.) [10]Jesus answered, "If you Knew God's gift and who it is who said to you, 'Give me a drink,' you would have asked him and he would have given you living water."[e]
>
> [11]The woman says to him, "Sir, you have no bucket and the well is deep. So from where do you have the living water? [12]Surely you are no greater than our father Jacob, who gave us the well and drank from it, with his children and his animals."
>
> [13]Jesus answered, "Everyone who drinks of this water will thirst again. [14]However, whoever drinks from the water I will give him will not be thirsty for eternity, but

[153] Josephus, *Antiquities of the Jews*, book 13, chapter 10, paragraph 3.

[154] For a fuller account of Samaritan history, see Blumhofer, *The Gospel of John and the Future of Israel*, pages 90-97.

86

the water that I will give him will become in him a spring of water gushing up[f] into eternal Life."

[15]The woman says to him, "Sir, give me this water so that I may drink and not come here to draw."

[16]He says to her, "Go call your husband and come back here."

[17]The woman said to him, "I have no husband." Jesus says to her, "You are right to say 'I have no husband,' [18]for you have had five husbands, and the one you have now is not your husband. What you have said is True."

[19]The woman says to him, "Sir, I see that you are a prophet.[g] [20]Our fathers worshipped on his mountain, but you say that worship must be at the place in Jerusalem?"[h]

[21]Jesus says to her, "Trust me,[i] woman, that the time is coming when neither on this mountain nor in Jerusalem will you worship the Father. [22]You worship what you do not Know, but we worship what we Know because the Rescue comes from Jews.[j] [23]However, a time is coming and is now here when True worshippers will worship the Father in spirit and Truth, for the Father seeks such worshippers. [24]God is spirit and those who worship him must worship in spirit and in Truth."

[25]The woman says to him, "I Know that the Messiah[k] is coming who is called Christ. When he comes, he will announce everything to us."

[26]Jesus says to her, "I am he, the one speaking to you."

[27]At that moment his disciples came and were shocked that he was speaking with a woman, but no one said, "What are you looking for?" or "Why are you talking with her?"

[28]Then the woman left her water jar and went away into the town and says to people, "Come see a man who told me everything I did. Is he not the Christ?" [30]They left the town and went to him.

[31]Meanwhile, the disciples were urging him saying, "Rabbi, eat." [32]But he said to them, "I have food to eat that you do not Know." [33]So the disciples began saying to each other, "Surely nobody has brought him anything to eat." [34]But Jesus says to them, "My food is to do the will of him who sent me and to finish his work.

[35]"Don't you say, 'Four months yet then comes the harvest?'" But I say to you, "Look up and see the fields because they are white for the harvest. [36]Already the reaper receives his wage and gathers fruit for Life eternal, so that the sower and reaper may rejoice together. [37]For in this the saying is True that 'one is the sower and another is the reaper.' [38]I sent you to reap what you have not worked; others worked it, and you have embarked on their work."

[39]Many Samaritans from that town Trusted in him because of the woman's Testimony "he told me everything I did." [40]So the Samaritans came to him asking him to Remain with them, and he Remained there two days. [41]And many more Trusted because of his word, [42]and they said to the woman, "Not because of your word do we Trust; for we have heard and Know that this is truly the Rescuer of the World.

Meaning and resonance

a. **"making and immersing more disciples than John"** (4:1): This recalls John 3:26, "and everyone is going to [Jesus]".

b. **"Jesus himself was not immersing"** (4:2): This contradicts 3:26 and 3:22 on whether Jesus was immersing or only his disciples. Just when we think we might have a smooth transition here following on from 3:26, a contradiction shows that John is really a series of episodes. The conflict whether Jesus was immersing or not is usually resolved by saying that the immersing by the disciples was attributed to Jesus as their master,[155] but that is reading a number of assumptions into the text.

c. **"Sychar"** (4:4): No place by this name has been found. Brown equates it with Shechem but with scant support.[156] I think it best to leave the word as it is; where exactly it was is unimportant.

d. **"Jacob's well"** (4:6): This is the well where Jacob had met his sweetheart Rachel (Genesis 29:1-20). In those times, a man looking for a possible wife would go to public places frequented by women such as a well. At that same well, Abraham's servant had found Rebekah, who became the wife of Isaac. His son Jacob found his Rachel there, and asked her for a drink. She gave him one and also watered his camels, a response that indicated she was the one (Genesis 24). Moses also found his wife at a well (Exodus 2:15-21).

One of the ironies of this scene is that the woman Jesus meets at Jacob's well seems more the town floozy than an ideal wife (4:18), but they never the less have a conversation, and one of the longest in John.

e. **"living water"** (4:10): Living water can simply mean fresh, free-flowing water,[157] but John 7:38-39 equates living water with the Spirit, which is to be given when Jesus is "glorified" (*i.e.* crucified; see John 17:1).

The Aramaic[158] version of Genesis 29:10 adds some embellishments (in italics below) that show how the verse was understood in Jesus's time:

> And when Jacob saw Rachel, the daughter of Laban, his mother's brother, and the flock of Laban, his mother's brother, Jacob drew near and, *with one of his arms*, rolled the stone from the mouth of the well; *and the well began to flow and the waters came up before him*, and he watered the flock of Laban, his mother's brother, *and it continued to flow for twenty years*.[159]

Flowing water is living water; Jacob had made it flow for 20 years, and now Jesus offers it. No wonder the woman next asks if Jesus "is greater than our father Jacob", and indeed he is because his living water "gushes up to eternal Life" (4:14) whereas Jacob's water flowed for only 20 years.

f. **"water gushing up"** (4:14): "Gushing up" translates the Greek word ἅλλομαι. In the Greek Old Testament, it is "reserved" for the powerful effect of the Divine rushing upon charismatic figures such as Samson,

[155] Bruce, *The Gospel of John*, page 100.

[156] *The Gospel of John*, volume 29, page 167.

[157] Charlesworth, *Jesus as Mirrored in John*, page 103.

[158] Aramaic was the colloquial language of Judea in Jesus's time, although most Judeans also spoke Greek. The Aramaic scriptures or "targums" would have been read in synagogues then.

[159] Quoted in Coloe, *Wisdom Bible Commentary*, volume 44A, page 114.

Saul, and David.[160] For example, Samson's feats of strength follow the onrushing (ἄλλομαι) of the Lord over him.

g. **"you have had five husbands"** (4:18): Freud noted in his patients a "compulsion to repeat", slipping into the same old patterns of behaviour even though they bring the same unfortunate results. There is hope, however. "Individuation is an imperative that drives us forward and, if successful, releases us from the trap of endlessly repeating the patterns that have conditioned us."[161]

h. **"prophet"** (4:19): Samaritan scripture contains only the first five books of the Christian Bible, not the prophetic or wisdom books. As a result, they recognise no prophets other than the one mentioned in Deuteronomy 18:15-18, the "prophet like Moses", a messianic figure.[162]

i. **"worship must be at the place in Jerusalem?"** (4:20): This could be a statement rather than a question, but I rather think she is asking the "prophet like Moses" about the great controversy of her people with Jews.

j. **"Trust me"** (4:21): The verb form implies continuation, *i.e.*, the woman is to go on Trusting.

k. **"the Rescue is from Jews"** (4:22): This is the nicest thing said about Jews in the entire gospel of John, although Reinhartz rightly points out that it probably comes down to Jesus speaking in a roundabout way of himself as Rescuer rather than being about Jews.[163] Coloe and Pancaro find that "Ἰουδαῖος [Jew] *tends* to become identified with the religious-national community constituted by normative Judaism (the Synagogue)", and it is that "normative Judaism" that John criticises.[164] However, his criticism of other Jews makes him no less a Jew himself.

Reinhartz adds interesting background about how Nazis read this verse. Walter Grundmann thought John 4:22 "could not have been original to this (in Grundmann's estimation) thoroughly and correctly anti-Semitic Gospel."[165] "In 1940, the de-Judaized version of John in *Die Botschaft Gottes* (the Message of God) ... interpreted this text to echo a famous anti-Semitic slogan: "The Jews are our misfortune"[166] (die Juden sind unser Unglück).

k. **"Messiah"** (4:25): The word "Messiah" is rare in the New Testament; "Christ", the Greek word that means the same thing, is very common, but not "Messiah".

> Only in the Fourth Gospel do we find the Greek transliteration of mšh (משׁח); that is, Μεσσίας in John 1:41 and 4:25. Clearly, the Fourth Evangelist, in a way

---

[160] Coloe, *God Dwells With Us*, page 94, citing Judges 14:6, 19; 15:14; 1 Samuel 10:10; 17:13.

[161] Stein, *The Principle of Individuation*, page xviii.

[162] Brown, *The Gospel of John*, volume 29, page 171.

[163] *Cast Out of the Covenant*, page 70.

[164] Coloe, *God Dwells with Us*, page 89, quoting S. Pancaro, *The Law in the Fourth Gospel: The Torah and the Gospel, Moses and Jesus, Judaism and Christianity according to John*, published as supplements to Novum Testamentum 42 (Leyden: Brill, 1975). Emphasis in original.

[165] Reinhartz, *Cast Out of the Covenant*, page 72.

[166] *Ibid.*

unparalleled by the other Evangelists, and his Community claimed that Jesus was to be identified as the Messiah....[167]

Jews and Samaritans differed in their understanding of the term "Messiah". Jews expected a Messiah to resume David's royal role. However:

> It is most unlikely that a Samaritan believer would have hailed Jesus as the Messiah in a Davidic sense, for the whole of Samaritan theology was directed against the claims of the Davidic dynasty and of Jerusalem, the Davidic city. .... Rather, the Samaritans expected a *Taheb* (the one who returns, the restorer), a teacher and revealer; and it may have been in that sense that Samaritans accepted Jesus as "Messiah".[168]

Reflections

"No greater than our father Jacob" (4:12): Supplanting the supplanter

It didn't pay to be the firstborn among the biblical patriarchs:

- **Ishmael lost out to Isaac**. Abraham's firstborn was Ishmael, but his mother was a slave of Sarai (later renamed Sarah), Abraham's wife (Genesis 16 and 21; Galatians 4:21-31). When Sarah eventually had a son, Isaac, he became the heir, not Ishmael (Genesis 25:5-6).

- **Esau lost out to Jacob**. Jacob tricked his nearly blind father Isaac into giving him the inheritance intended for Esau, Jacob's older brother. Jacob's very name, "Jacob," means "supplanter" (Genesis 27:36).[169]

After Jacob cheated his brother, he fled his brother's fury alone (Genesis 27:41-45). Going toward Haran where the well in this story was located, Jacob spent the night in the open and dreamed of a "ladder set up on the earth, the top of it reaching heaven, and the angels of God were ascending and descending on it" (Genesis 28:12).

Jacob was the common ancestor of Jewish Jesus and the Samaritan woman. In the conversation with her, Jesus repeats the pattern already established with clearing the Temple: he reinterprets scripture or tradition to be about himself. He makes himself into the Temple in John 2:12-25, a claim that his Jewish audience—quite understandably—thinks is preposterous. In John 5 through 8, Jesus reinterprets and appropriates first the Sabbath and then every Jewish pilgrimage festival except Pentecost (which Luke will later repurpose in Acts 2). Jews react with increasing hostility to the takeover of their religion by an upstart provincial with little education, much like the Church of England reacted when Quaker preachers came to town.

What is remarkable in the story of the Samaritan woman is that Jesus does the same thing as ever—according to him, he is indeed greater than their father Jacob—but neither speaker breaks off the conversation and walks away, despite cultural differences and social taboos. Like many a Jew, she misunderstands

---

[167] Charlesworth, *Jesus as Mirrored in John*, page 105.

[168] Brown, *The Community of the Beloved Disciple*, page 44.

[169] Stein in *The Bible as Dream*, pages 113-131, notes that this pattern of the younger son supplanting the older heir is as old as Cain and Abel and recurs again and again in the Bible.

Jesus's enigmatic pronouncements at first, but she asks questions and engages him, with reticence or even hostility at first, but she warms as something urges her to engage with Jesus. What is that something?

To find clues, let's look closely at her lines:

> "How is it that you, a Jew, ask a drink from me, a Samaritan woman?" (verse 9)

> "Sir, you have no bucket and the well is deep. So from where do you have the living water? [12]Surely you are no greater than our father Jacob, who gave us the well and drank from it, with his children and his animals." (verse 11-12)

> "Sir, give me this water so that I may drink and not come here to draw." (verse 15)

> "I have no husband." (verse 17)

> "Sir, I see that you are a prophet. Our fathers worshipped on his mountain, but you say that worship must be at the place in Jerusalem?" (verse 19-20)

> "I know that the Messiah is coming who is called Christ. When he comes, he will announce everything to us." (verse 25)

Just as Jesus tells her that he is the promised Messiah, the disciples arrive and cut short the conversation. She, a Samaritan woman now in a crowd of Jews, goes back to her town, forgetting her water container, and she tells everyone, "Come see a man who told me everything I did. Is he not the Christ?" Then she and many people in her town decide to follow Jesus, "the Rescuer of the World". Considering the understandable reaction of Jews to Jesus's re-interpretation of their symbols and rituals, why does this Samaritan town react so differently? The Samaritans *choose* to let the new supplanter supplant their illustrious ancestor Jacob by choosing to Trust Jesus, a response that is the opposite of their Jewish cousins. Why?

Part of the cause may lie in the diversity underlying the Samaritan community: their ethnic history is not as homogenous as that of Jews. However, Jews were no strangers to strangers; the Jewish diaspora was well underway in Jesus's time. However, tolerance for diversity might explain giving a thirsty stranger a drink (if indeed that happened—we are only told that he asked, not that he got), but tolerance is not enough to explain the fact that she goes on from there, engages him in a conversation, is won over, and tells her town. Where does Jesus's appeal come from?

Jung differentiated between two types of supernatural appeal. One is the *numinosum*, which Jung defined as

> a dynamic agency or effect not caused by an arbitrary act of will. On the contrary, it seizes and controls the human subject, who is always [more] its victim than its creator. The *numinosum*—whatever its cause may be—is an experience of the subject independent of his will. ... The *numinosum* is either a quality belonging to a visible object or the influence

of an invisible presence that causes a peculiar alteration of consciousness.[170]

That numinous effect—the glory of God in biblical terms—is an identifying characteristic of the divine; its appeal comes from the self, the God-image in each soul.[171] The full glorification of Jesus will come later when he is "lifted up" (John 12:33-34), but meanwhile, unconscious numinosity will out in all sorts of ways, so it is quite possible that Jesus had an "aura". There was something special about him.

However, charisma does not always come from a spiritual source. Early in his life, Jung described what he called a "mana personality", though in later writings, he simply uses the term "inflation" for the same phenomenon.[172] "The process of becoming aware of the unconscious ... makes more intense the feeling of similarity to the diety."[173] That feeling increases the risk that I mistake myself for God. Assimilating unconscious archetypal content into the conscious mind

> produces in some patients an unmistakable and often unpleasant increase of self-confidence and conceit: they are full of themselves, they know everything, they imagine themselves to be fully informed of everything concerning their unconscious. Others on the contrary feel themselves more and more crushed under the contents of the unconscious, they lose their self-confidence and abandon themselves with dull resignation to all the extraordinary things that the unconscious produces.[174]

When the ego is not strong enough, the archetype bearing the divine image can overwhelm it, leaving a mana personality. If that happened to me, then I would end up thinking I'm God, or God-like. I would become a supplanter of the real God.

A mana personality is "the well known archetype of the mighty man in the form of hero, chief, magician, medicine-man, saint, the ruler of men and spirits, the friend of God".[175] For a woman, the mana personality appears as "a sublime, matriarchal figure, the Great Mother, the All-Merciful, who understands everything, forgives everything, who always acts for the best, living only for others, and never seeking her own interests, the discoverer of the great love".[176]

---

[170] *Collected Works*, volume 11, paragraph 6.

[171] Samuels, Shorter & Plant, *A Critical Dictionary of Jungian Analysis*, page 100.

[172] Inflation was also just described in "God is True" above. This Reflection looks more closely at how it plays out in the world.

[173] 'La structure de l'inconscient', in *Archives de Psychologie*, XVI: 62, quoted in Sorge, "The construct of the 'mana personality' in Jung's works: a historic-hermeneutic perspective: Part 1", in *Journal of Analytical Psychology*, 2020, volume 65, Issue 2, page 370. Sorge's Part 2 is published in the next issue. See also Stein, *The Mystery of Transformation*, pages 98-99.

[174] Jung, *The Relations Between the Ego and the Unconscious*, in *Collected Works*, volume 7, paragraph 221.

[175] Jung, *The Relations Between the Ego and the Unconscious*, in *Collected Works*, volume 7, paragraph 377.

[176] Jung, *The Relations Between the Ego and the Unconscious*, in *Collected Works*, volume 7, paragraph 379.

Someone with a mana personality confuses herself with the archetypal image in her mind. "One becomes convinced that one is a prophet or sage, a culture hero or a demon lover, a Great Mother or Father, or some other myth-sized figure, and an identity is created from a psychological content that is archetypal."[177]

The inflated person "is not directly conscious of this condition at all but can at best infer its existence indirectly from the symptoms. These include the reactions of our immediate environment."[178] However, the inflated person is hindered in that by a "growing disinclination to take note of the reactions" of people in the environment.[179] The remedy is a more humble and realistic view of oneself, a "median degree of modesty which is essential for maintenance of a balanced state".[180] However, modesty is not a quality of one who reinterprets scripture and tradition by inserting himself into the lead role, but then again, modesty in the Unique Son of God would seem entirely fake if not impossible.

From her behaviour, it appears that the Samaritan woman saw something special in Jesus. Was he a mana personality, a great shaman, or did she sense his genuine numinosity shining through his earthly persona of a Jewish man from Galilee passing through Samaria?

The answer can be seen from later developments. Inflation, taking on "this kind of illusory identity is fatal to individuation",[181] but Jung said "Christ's life is a prototype of individuation".[182] From that it seems that he remained the son of man. In John, Jesus and his Father are two distinct identities, in unity with each other, but distinct. Jesus never equates himself with his father; they are one but not the same.

If all things numinous sound wonderful, consider that with Jung, there is always a darker side; "there is no light without shadow".[183] Murray Stein explains what happens when the ego identifies with the God archetype:

> Numinous contents of the unconscious pull the thinking magnetically into an orbit where it becomes merely ingenious rationalization. This is what one commonly finds in people who are absolutely convinced of a religious teaching. Filled with faith and belief, their thinking is decisively influenced by an archetypal image of massive but largely unconscious proportions, which lends privileged ideas a sort of triumphant, dogmatic certainty. Only one step further along this road one finds the martyr, whose identification with the archetypal image is so extreme that mortal life itself loses priority. Needless to say, this is the exact contrary of the individuation project, which is to

---

[177] Stein, *The Principle of Individuation*, page 16.

[178] Jung, *Aion*, in *Collected Works*, volume 9, part 2, paragraph 44.

[179] *Ibid.*

[180] Jung, *Aion*, in *Collected Works*, volume 9, part 2, paragraph 47.

[181] Stein, *The Principle of Individuation*, page 17.

[182] Jung, "Letter to Dorothee Hoch," in *Letters*, volume 2, page 76.

[183] *Psychology and Alchemy*, in *Collected Works*, volume 13, paragraph 208.

> make the numinous content as conscious as possible, to
> sublimate and integrate it, and to bring it into relation with
> other quite different aspects of the Self, thereby relativizing
> it.[184]

Hitler was an extreme case of such thinking and its "triumphant, dogmatic certainty". Jung analysed him as one possessed by a "saviour complex", a complex akin to the mana personality in that the possessed in both cases mistake themselves for a great mythic archetype.[185] Civilisations in crisis are particularly susceptible to being taken in by saviours, as Germany was in the 1930s during its frightening hyper-inflation. Stein explains further:

> Archetypal possession in a community or culture invests
> certain ideas and policies with defensive certainty and
> denies the legitimacy of doubt. Contrary thoughts and
> images are savagely attacked and repressed. This was the
> case with German society at the time [1936]. There was no
> space for reflection, for questioning, for debate, never mind
> contrary views.[186]

The would-be saviour Hitler had not come to terms with the madness in his shadow, so he acted it out and infected all of Germany with it. To his great credit, Jesus did not allow his sense of God within to take him over and corrupt his ethics, when ordinarily it would seem the Almighty's absolute power would corrupt absolutely. His kingdom was indeed "not of this world" (John 18:36).

The same cannot be said of the kingdoms of many of his modern proponents. Christianity has become more and more a big business, in which charismatic authority figures thrive, and where, in Stein's words, there is "no space for reflection, for questioning, for debate, never mind contrary views." Jungian John Dourley:

> The Western religious scene is currently embroiled in a
> schism crossing confessional boundaries. The broader
> schism is between fundamentalism and a more moderate
> expression of traditional confessions within each tradition.
> Fundamentalism is growing as the core component of
> orthodox confessional communities. While
> fundamentalist numbers swell in churches, synagogues and
> mosques, the overall numbers diminish as those of liberal and
> humanistic bent flee the takeover.[187]

The fundamentalists are themselves fleeing authentic religious experience; enthusiastic preaching by a mana personality is to fill the void left in the soul by lack of a real connection with the inner Divine. The "swing to [fundamentalism] is therefore an effort to avoid the depths out of which Jungian psychology lives and religion originates."[188] For example, fundamentalism favours literal interpretations of scripture over symbolic ones that could let a work like John

---

[184] Stein, *The Principle of Individuation*, page 46.

[185] See generally Jung, *Wotan*, in *Collected Works*, volume 10; also Sorge, "Part 2", pages 522-527.

[186] Stein, *The Principle of Individuation*, page 47.

[187] *Jung and his Mystics*, page 29.

[188] *Ibid.*

speak deeply to the soul and offer solutions to its perplexities. A mana personality dominates the worship experience and may produce a shallow enthusiasm, but it all diverts from actual experience of the Divine within each soul. Instead of reaching the self within, it is projected outward on a prophet or human saviour.[189] The soul ends up duped and exploited by an inflated preacher who has supplanted Christ.

> Religious communities now cut off from their founding agency, the unconscious, prevent rather than serve access to their origin. They are dysfunctional and becoming ... more so as they seek in fundamentalist mentalities protection from the immediate experience of the divine which functional communities should mediate not flee....[190]

The rise of fundamentalism and mana personalities are a factor in the "Apocalypse of Carl Jung" below; see also "My sheep know my voice" below.

"Christ", for Isaac Penington, was always the Divine within him, not him but within him. He was not open to supplanting it.

> Such a kind of greatness as is in the world, is the destruction of the life of Christ; and such a kind of dominion and authority as is among the nations, is the direct overturning of the kingdom of Christ. It sets up another power than Christ's, another greatness than Christ's, another kind of authority than Christ's; and so it eats out the virtue and life of his kingdom, and makes it just like one of the kingdoms of this world.[191]

"Worship is our response to an awareness of God."[192] Worship of God, not identification of myself with God, is the response that protects me from inflation. In worship, each of us is in his place, hoping to become aware of the presence of God, who may speak through any of us, but none of us is the divine source of what is spoken. That remains beyond us, beyond any of us.

"True worshippers will worship the Father in spirit and Truth" (4:23)

Like the Prologue, this chapter contains a chiasm, a nested structure with a central turning point. The turning point in the story is worship:

    A Jesus leaves Judea for Galilee, travels through Samaria (verses 1-6).
        B Jesus asks a woman for a drink. Dialogue on two "waters" (7-15).
            C Woman told to go and bring her man (verses 16-18).
                D Place and nature of true worship (verses 19-26).
            C' Woman goes and brings the villagers (verses 27-30).
        B' Disciples ask Jesus to eat. Dialogue on two "foods" (31-38).

---

[189] Stein, "Known or Unknown God Is—An Interview" in *Collected Writings of Murray Stein*, volume 6, page 223-224.

[190] Dourley, *Jung and his Mystics*, page 30.

[191] *An Examination of the Grounds*, in *Works*, volume 1, page 378

[192] "Advices and Queries" no. 8, of Britain Yearly Meeting, *Quaker Faith and Practice*.

A' Jesus leaves the village and resumes his journey to Galilee (39-45).[193]

The story pivots on the point that "True worshippers will worship the Father in Spirit and Truth" (4:23).

Where fundamentalism, as noted above, substitutes charismatic preaching for authentic religious experience, Quaker meetings for worship are meant to be nothing more or less than an opportunity to share an authentic experience of the Holy Spirit together, in other words, to worship in "Spirit and Truth". Isaac Penington:

> For he himself hath said, that neither at the mountain of Samaria, nor at Jerusalem, should men worship; but they that worship the Father must worship him in Spirit and in truth. Now, men cannot worship in Spirit and in truth as they please, or in the ways of their own inventing and setting up; but he that worshippeth in Spirit and truth must first be made spiritual; and then must wait in silence of the flesh for God's Spirit to quicken him unto spiritual worship. For they that worship otherwise than thus, worship at best but after the oldness of the letter, and not in the newness of the Spirit, which is the only worship God seeketh and requireth under the New Testament.[194]

Penington describes Quaker worship in more detail:

> This is a great mystery, hid from the eye of man, who is run from the inward life into outward observations. He cannot see either that this is required by the Lord of his people, or any edification therein, or benefit thereby; but to the mind that is drawn inward the thing is plain; and the building up hereby in the life of God, and fellowship one with another therein, is sweetly felt....

> After the mind is in some measure turned to the Lord, his quickenings felt, his seed beginning to arise and spring up in the heart, then the flesh is to be silent before him, and the soul to wait upon him ... in that measure of life which is already revealed. Now, this is a great thing to know flesh silenced.... For man is to come into the poverty of self, into the abasedness, into the nothingness, into the silence of his spirit before the Lord; into the putting off of all his knowledge, wisdom, understanding, abilities, all that he is, hath done, or can do, out of this measure of life, into which he is to travel, that he may be clothed and filled with the nature, Spirit, and power of the Lord.

> ....

> And this is the manner of [Friends'] worship. They are to wait upon the Lord, to meet in the silence of flesh, and to watch for the stirrings of his life, and the breakings forth of his power amongst them. .... If the Spirit do not require to speak,

---

[193] Coloe, *God Dwells with Us,* page 87.

[194] *Life and Immortality,* in *Works,* volume 4, pages 162-63.

and give to utter, then every one is to sit still in his place…, feeling his own measure, feeding thereupon, receiving therefrom, into his spirit, what the Lord giveth. Now, in this is edifying, pure edifying, precious edifying; his soul who thus waits, is hereby particularly edified by the Spirit of the Lord at every meeting. And then also there is the life of the whole felt in every vessel that is turned to its measure: insomuch as the warmth of life in each vessel doth not only warm the particular, but they are like a heap of fresh and living coals, warming one another, insomuch as a great strength, freshness, and vigor of life flows into all. And if any be burthened…, the estate of such is felt in Spirit, and secret cries, or open (as the Lord pleaseth), ascend up to the Lord for them, and they many times find ease and relief, in a few words spoken, or without words, if it be the season of their help and relief with the Lord.

For absolutely silent meetings, wherein there is a resolution not to speak, we know not; but we wait on the Lord, either to feel him in words, or in silence of spirit without words, as he pleaseth. And that which we aim at … is that the flesh in every one be kept silent, and that there be no building up, but in the Spirit and power of the Lord.

Now, there are several states of people: some feel little of the Lord's presence; but feel temptations and thoughts, with many wanderings and rovings of mind. These are not yet acquainted with the power.…

God is to be worshipped in spirit, in his own power and life.… His church is a gathering in the Spirit. If any man speak there, he must speak as the oracle of God, as the vessel out of which God speaks.… Therefore there is to be a waiting in silence till the Spirit of the Lord move to speak, and also give words to speak. For a man is not to speak his own words, or in his own wisdom or time; but the Spirit's words, in the Spirit's wisdom and time, which is when he moves and gives to speak. And seeing the Spirit inwardly nourisheth, when he giveth not to speak words, the inward sense and nourishment is to be waited for, and received as it was given when there are no words. Yea, the ministry of the Spirit and life is more close and immediate when without words, than when with words, as has been often felt, and is faithfully testified by many witnesses. .…[195]

Quakers still worship in this manner today.

Jungian Quaker Jack Wallis describes the experience of worship from his perspective:

Meeting for Worship is the heart of the Quaker way and is I believe unique among the Christian Churches. The absence of

---

[195] *A Further Testimony to Truth Revived*, in *Works*, volume 4, pages 47-49.

formality, of a priesthood, of special furnishing, music and vestments is uniquely helpful in fostering the inner, spiritual and individual yet corporate basis of the gathering. An essential freedom arises from silence, stillness and simplicity, a freedom for the inner spirit of each member to express itself inwardly, with little interruption. A gathered meeting attains a spiritual corporateness that, if all goes well, leads to what George Gorman called 'a lending of our minds to one another'.[196]

Jack Wallis also noted that what "Quakers would call ... listening to the inner voice or being sensitive to the leading of the Spirit or of God" opens, according to Jung, a way by which "a [person] may even catch a fleeting glimpse of his wholeness, accompanied by the feeling of grace that always characterizes this experience."[197] Jack Wallis also explained that this sort of listening together is not a passive experience; "we have to make the effort to reach a gathered state, [and] we may have to look hard to discern the light or listen attentively for the inner voice."[198]

What George Gorman called the "lending of our minds to one another" lets the worshipping community support each other *through worship itself* in becoming born of the Spirit:

> If it fall out that several met together be straying in their minds, though outwardly silent, and so wandering from the measure of grace in themselves, ... if either one come in, or may be in, who is watchful, and in whom the life is raised in a great measure, as that one keeps his place, he will feel a secret travail for the rest in a sympathy with the seed which is oppressed in the other, and kept from arising by their thoughts and wanderings; and as such a faithful one waits in the light, and keeps in this divine work, God oftentimes answers the secret travail and breathings of his own seed through such a one, ... and that one will be as a midwife through the secret travail of his soul to bring forth the life in them, ... and such a one is felt by the rest to minister life unto them without words.[199]

In becoming born of the Spirit, Friends are each other's midwives, and meetings for worship are where that labour is done.

To Galilee; an official's son healed (4:43-54)

[43]After the two days, he went from there into Galilee [44](for Jesus himself Testified that a prophet has no honour in his own country[a]). [45]When he came to Galilee,

---

[196] *Jung and the Quaker Way*, page 19-20.

[197] *Ibid.*

[198] *Ibid.*

[199] Robert Barclay, *Apology for the True Christian Divinity* (English edition 1678 and numerous reprintings, proposition VII, section iii; quoted in "John Woolman on the Cross", in Birkel & Newman, editors, *The Lamb's War*, pages 94-95.

Galileans welcomed him because they had seen all that he had done in Jerusalem at the feast, for they had also gone to the feast.

[46]So he came again to Cana of Galilee, where he had made water wine.

[47]Now there was a royal official[b] whose son was ill in Capernaum. [48]When he heard that Jesus had come from Judea into Galilee, he went to him and asked him to come and heal his son, for he was about to die. [48]Jesus said to him, "Unless you see Signs and miracles, you will not Trust." [49]The official says to him, "Sir, come, before my little boy dies." [50]Jesus says to him, "Go, your son Lives."[c] The man Trusted what Jesus told him and began going, [51]and while he was still on the way, he encountered his slaves, who said his child lives. [52]Then he asked them the Hour in which he had improved, so they told him that yesterday at 1pm the fever left him. [53]Then the father Realised that that was the Hour in which Jesus told him, "Your son lives," and he and his entire household Trusted. [54]This was the second Sign that Jesus did, after coming out of Judea into Galilee.

Meaning and resonance

a. **"in his own country"** (4:44): Jesus is speaking of Judea here, the area around Jerusalem, south of both Samaria and Galilee. Jews take him to be from Nazareth (6:42), but the narrator implies here that his home country is Judea, not Galilee. The other three gospels disagree and say Galilee is Jesus's home (Mark 6:4; Matthew 13:57; Luke 4:24).

b. **"a royal official"** (4:47): Capernaum was a Roman town with a tax office, and this man had slaves and would have been "used to having his wishes carried out".[200] He was probably Roman or Greek, not Jewish.[201]

c. **"your child Lives"** (4:50, 51, 53): Brown explains this in terms of the conceptual map of people speaking Semitic languages, like the Aramaic Jesus spoke among fellow Judeans:

> Semitic has no exact word for "recover"; "to live" covers both recovery from illness (2 Kings 8:9: "Shall I live from this disease?") and return to life from death (1 Kings 7:23: "Your son lives" to a mother whose son was dead). The twofold meaning is convenient for John's theological purposes.[202]

Reflection

"Unless you see Signs and miracles, you will not Trust" (4:48)

Jesus says this, with an emphatic negative, and yet he performs the Sign asked of him by the official. We have here a paradox. Nicodemus is another example of what Jesus is saying here; he praised Jesus for the Signs he performed, but the Signs did not give him enough Trust to face having other Jews find out that he spoke with Jesus (John 3:3-7). John 2:23-25 says Jesus thought people who Trust because of Signs were not reliable.

---

[200] Coloe, *Wisdom Bible Commentary*, volume 44A, page 133. Jesus was similarly blunt with Nicodemus (John 3:10), and he will soon be more than blunt in telling off Jews in chapters 5-8.

[201] Coloe, *Wisdom Bible Commentary*, volume 44A, page 131.

[202] Brown, *The Gospel According to John*, volume 29, page 191.

Isaac Penington also pointed out that miracles, as evidence, are actually not convincing, but the experience of the Spirit is:

> For miracles leave a dispute in the mind (notwithstanding all the miracles Christ showed, there was yet a dispute and dissatisfaction in the minds of many concerning him). But he that feels the thing itself in the true principle, where the demonstration and certainty of the Spirit's assurance is received; he is past dispute, and is gone a degree, in the nature of things, beyond that satisfaction which miracles can afford. He is out of that state and mind which asketh a sign, or seeketh confirmation by a sign.[203]

The opponents of Jesus will more or less ignore Sign after Sign and reject him.

Returning to our official, however, he is not without Trust before knowing the Sign he requested was done. Jesus's statement, "Unless you see Signs and miracles, you will not Trust" has all verbs in the plural, so it is not directed specifically to the official. Without any Sign as yet, the official had enough Trust to persist. His persistence in asking shows perhaps that he is desperate, but also that he has some degree of Trust as well because he thinks Jesus can help and he had travelled for two days[204] to ask him. He would not be accustomed to being rebuffed, though he was, but he had humility in his desperation so he asked again. The verbs then shift to present as he implores: "Come before my little boy dies!" (3:49).

He took Jesus at his word and went home when told to go and that his son would recover. He had enough Trust to go and find out how it was with his son, to try an experiment to see if Jesus had spoken the truth. He was told to go, but he did not have to do so. He was a powerful man, and the powerful have options in such situations. But he went; he went to find out the truth. For Quakers, that is enough. Quakers don't have a creed, a specification of the faith required by their religion. The only faith required is enough to find out for oneself if the inner Light shines in one's soul. See "Trust" below.

The fact that Signs don't convince is a paradox; you would think that they would, but problem is with the Truth they evidence. That a young man from nowhere is the Messiah was a Truth, according to John, but not one acceptable to people opposed to Jesus. Truth is rejected, no matter the evidence, when we think it can't possibly be True. That rejection can foreclose possibilities for spiritual development. Instead of rejecting what can't possibly be True, it is better to be open to paradox.

Paradoxes often lie just under the surface in John. Here's another, and like Signs and Trust, it is also of the chicken-egg variety: John is to bring us to Life (20:31), but Life is necessary to understand John according to Isaac Penington:

> The prophets and apostles who wrote the Scriptures first had the life in them: and *he who understands their words, must*

---

[203] *Truth Revived out of the Ruins of the Apostasy,* in *Works,* volume 4, page 43.

[204] Brown, *The Gospel According to John,* volume 29, page 191: "In going to Capernaum from Cana, one must go east across the Galilean hills and then descend to the Sea of Galilee. The twenty-mile journey was not accomplished on one day."

> *first have the life in him. He that understands the words of life must first have life in himself.* The life is the measurer of the words, and not the words of the life. And when the Scripture is interpreted by the life and Spirit which penned it, there is then no more jangling and contending about it: for this is all out of the life.[205]

Paradoxes are blessings in a spiritual life. God and the unconscious are under no obligation to make clear, easy sense to us. When content of the unconscious mind becomes conscious—a blessing—it may seem obvious in hindsight, but it is often far from obvious when it first appears. An addict does not consciously know that he is hooked until his eyes are opened, though everyone around him knows his problem only too well. The addict, on realising, is overwhelmed with shame because he now sees what everyone else sees. Denial is a threadbare comfort that frays badly with wear, and we can pay dearly for it when it finally turns transparent. Sooner or later, the truth will out, but often first as a contradiction, or a truth that can't be true.

Spiritual life requires a willingness to accept paradox, willingness that does not come easily because the stuff of the paradox has previously been dismissed from consciousness so it will not be obvious or seem acceptable at first. It will be in the mind's peripheral vision, if visible at all. One of the gifts of John is a heightened sense and taste for paradox, irony, and layers of meaning beyond the obvious. That taste is good for the soul because the transcendent "can be expressed only by a paradox."[206]

> Oddly enough the paradox is one of our most valuable spiritual possessions, while uniformity of meaning is a sign of weakness. Hence a religion becomes inwardly impoverished when it loses or waters down its paradoxes; but their multiplication enriches because only the paradox comes anywhere near to comprehending the fullness of life. Non-ambiguity and non-contradiction are one-sided and thus unsuited to express the incomprehensible.[207]

Logic is not helpful in understanding paradox. The inner Light is, and a symbol will hold the key to making sense of the impossible truth in the paradox. "Here only the symbol helps, for, in accordance with its paradoxical nature, it represents the 'tertium' that in logic does not exist, but which in reality is the living truth."[208] More on this in "Opposites in John and Jung" below.

Isaac Penington discovered the inner Light when he put aside his rationality, his usual approach to grasping a truth. Instead he learned to trust his heart and opened his senses to a mystery that had been beyond the reach of his logic.[209] In amazement, he found that mystery is what he was made of, even though he did not "know the mystery":

---

[205] *The Scattered Sheep Sought After,* in *Works*, volume 1, page 116 (emphasis added).

[206] Jung, *Mysterium Coniuntionis,* in *Collected Works*, volume 14, paragraph 715.

[207] Jung, *Psychology and Alchemy,* in *Collected Works*, volume 12, paragraph 199.

[208] Jung, "Paracelsus as a Spiritual Phenomenon", in *Collected Works*, volume 13, paragraph 199.

[209] Keiser, *Knowing the Mystery of God Within,* pages 16-17.

> But is is not strange, that thou shouldst be of it, and not be able to own it...? What! of God, of Christ, (having received the Spirit, the living well) and yet not know the mystery of life within...![210]

A healing on the Sabbath and its aftermath (chapter 5)

[1]Later there was a Jewish festival and Jesus went up to Jerusalem.

[2]In Jerusalem by the Sheep [Gate][a] there is a pool called in Hebrew Bethesda,[b] which has five porticoes. [3]In them lay many of the sick, blind, lame, and paralyzed. [4][see note [c] below] [5]One person there had been ill for 38 years.[d] [6]When Jesus saw him lying there and Realised that he had been there a long time, he says to him, "Do you want to get well?" [7]The sick person answered, "Sir, I have no person to put me in the pool when the water stirs, and while I am going, someone else gets in before me." [8]Jesus says to him, "Stand up, pick up your mat and walk." [9]And immediately the person became well, picked up his mat and was walking around.

Now that day was a Sabbath. [10]So Jews were saying to the person who had been healed, "It is the Sabbath, and it is not right for you to carry your mat." [11]He answered them, "The one who made me well told me, 'Pick up your mat and walk'." [12]They asked him, "Who is the person who told you, 'Pick up your mat and walk'?" [13]The man who was healed did not know who it was, for Jesus had disappeared into the crowd there. [14]Afterwards Jesus finds him in the Temple and said to him, "See, you have become well. Do no more Wrong so that a worse thing doesn't happen to you."[e] [15]The person went away and reported to Jews that it was Jesus who made him well. [16]Because of that Jews began persecuting Jesus because he did these things on the Sabbath.

[17]Jesus answered them, "My Father is still working and so am I."[f] [18]For this reason Jews were seeking to kill him, because not only was he breaking the Sabbath but also he was saying God was his own father and thereby making himself equal to God.

[19]In response Jesus said to them, "Very truly I tell you, a son can do nothing of himself except what he sees his father doing,[g] for whatever the father does, the son also does in the same way. [20]For the father loves the son and shows him all that he himself is doing, and he will show him greater works than these so that you will be astonished. [21]For just as the Father raises the dead and gives them Life, so also the son gives Life to whomever he wishes. [22]The Father judges no one at all, but he has given all judgment to the Son, [23]so that all may honour the Son just as they honour the Father. Whoever does not honour the Son also does not honour the Father who sent him.

[24]"Very truly I tell you that whoever hears my word and Trusts him who sent me has eternal Life and will not come to judgment, but has passed from Death into Life. [25]Very truly I tell you that the Hour is coming and now is here when the dead will hear the voice of the son of God and those who hear will Live. [26]For just as the Father has Life in himself, so also he gave Life to the son to have in himself. [27]And he gave him authority to carry out judgment because he is the son of man. [28]Don't be amazed at this that the Hour is coming in which all those in tombs will

[210] *Of the Church,* in *Works,* volume 4, page 191.

hear his voice, [29]and those who have done good things will come out into the rising of Life, and those who have done bad things into the rising of judgment.

[30]"I can do nothing at all of myself. I judge as I hear, and my judgment is right because I do not seek my own will but the will of him who sent me."

[31]If I Testify about myself, my Testimony is not True.[h] [32]There is another who Testifies about me, and I Know that his Testimony that he Testifies about me is True. [33]You have sent messengers to John, and he has Testified the Truth, [34](although I do not accept Testimony from a human being but I have told you everything for you to be Rescued.) [35]He was a burning and shining lamp, and you were happy to rejoice for an Hour in his Light.

[36]I however have a Testimony greater than John's, for the works that the Father has given me to complete, these works that I am doing Testify of me that the Father has sent me. [37]And the Father who sent me has Testified about me. You have never heard his voice or seen his image, [38]and you do not have his word Remaining in you because you do not Trust the one he sent. [39]You look into the scriptures because you suppose you have eternal Life in them, but they are what Testifies about me.[i] [40]Yet you don't want come to me so you may have Life.

[41]"I do not accept glory from people, [42]but I Know you, that you do not have the Love of God in you.[j] [43]I have come in the name of my Father and you do not accept me; if another comes in his name, that one you will accept. [44]How can you Trust the glory that you receive from each other, but you do not seek the glory from the only God?

[45]"Do not suppose that I will accuse you before the Father; your accuser is Moses, in whom you have set your hopes. [46]For if you would Trust Moses, you would also Trust me, for he Testified of me, [47]but if you do not Trust what he wrote, how are you to Trust what I say?

Meaning and resonance

a. **"by the Sheep [Gate]"** (5:2): "Gate" is not in the text; however, we know that there was a "Sheep Gate" from Nehemiah 3:1, 3:32, and 12:39. Nehemiah describes the rebuilding of Jerusalem, particularly its walls, after Jews return from captivity in Babylon. If the missing word is indeed "Gate" (πύλη), then the adjective meaning "sheep-related" agrees with it in gender and number; it is feminine singular, as is the word for "gate".

b. **"Bethesda"** (5:2): Ancient manuscripts have several variants of this name, with "Bethsaida" or "Bethzatha" being equally likely alternatives. I opted for the more familiar word.

The pool of Bethesda was actually two pools, one feeding the other. The lower pool was a *mikveh*, a pool deep enough for a person to immerse and used by Jews for ritual purification, which was required before entering the Temple.[211] The site of the pool lay north of the Temple enclosure and has been excavated.[212]

---

[211] Charlesworth, *Jesus as Mirrored in John*, page 192.

[212] Charlesworth, *Jesus as Mirrored in John*, page 261.

c. **Verse 4 is missing**: The oldest manuscripts have the text as translated above. Later ones add this clarifying explanation beginning at the end of verse 3 above:

> ...waiting for the stirring of the water, [4]for an angel of the Lord went down at times into the pool, stirred up the water, and whoever stepped in first after the stirring of the water was made well from whatever ailment they had.

d. **"ill for 38 years"** (5:5): Verse 5 does not say he was at the pool for all of those 38 years, though he was there a long time (verse 6).

e. **"Do no more Wrong so that a worse thing doesn't happen to you"** (5:14): Mary Coloe:

> This is a puzzling statement. It cannot mean that Jesus is expressing a theology that physical illness is a manifestation of sin; this view is expressly rejected by Jesus in 9:3-4. The man has been healed. This action is past. Now Jesus looks to the man's future and points out that there is worse than a physical paralysis, and that is a moral paralysis caused when sin destroys one's relationship with God.[213]

f. **"My Father is still working and so am I."** (5:17): Literally "my Father is still working and I am still working" but there is no I am in the Greek so I simplified the English a little.

> Jesus's claim that God continues work on the Sabbath is based on Jewish theology, which acknowledges the fact that God continues to create life, because children are born even on the Sabbath, and God must continue to work as a judge, since people die on the Sabbath....[214]

g. **"a son can do nothing of himself except what he sees his father doing"** (5:19): This could just as well be translated, "the Son can do nothing of himself except what he sees the Father doing". I have preferred the reading that sees this statement as an analogy to ordinary life at home.

h. **"If I Testify about myself, my Testimony is not True."** (5:31): Brown translates this more freely: "If I am my own witness, my testimony cannot be verified."[215] While I agree that this is most likely the intended sense, it obscures the usage of the word True, which is frequent in John and worth noting. In John 8:17, we find a similar statement that also shows a similar meaning of True.

Brown also explains that "The legal principle stems from Deuteronomy 19:15",[216] which reads "...by the mouth of two or three witnesses shall the matter be established." See also Deuteronomy 17:6 and Numbers 35:30. The witnesses whom Jesus mentions in this chapter are the scriptures

---

[213] *Wisdom Bible Commentary*, volume 44A, page 145.

[214] Coloe, *Wisdom Bible Commentary*, volume 44A, page 146; Yee, *Jewish Feasts and the Gospel of John*, pages 31-47.

[215] *The Gospel According to John*, volume 29 of *Anchor Bible*, page 222.

[216] *The Gospel According to John*, volume 29 of *Anchor Bible*, page 223.

(5:39), John (5:33), the Father (5:37), and Moses (5:46). His "works" (Jesus never calls them Signs but John does)[217] also "Testify of me that the Father has sent me" (5:36, also John 10:25).

i. **"You look into the scriptures because…"** (5:39): "Look into" could also be an imperative, "Look into the scriptures because…", with an implication that they keep looking. However, the text makes better sense if read as a statement, considering what follows.

j. **"you do not have the** Love **of God in you"** (verse 42): "Of God" could be possessive, *i.e.* God's love, or it could be people's love for God. Ambiguities in John are often intentional.

Reflection

"You have never heard his voice or seen his image" (5:37)

It amazes me that Jesus's opponents in this scene ignore the miracle that has just happened and focus instead on two violations of the Sabbath, one of which sounds trivial (lifting a mat, a burden). The other violation is an act of God—if the reader accepts the divinity of Jesus, which Jesus's Jewish opponents never did. My judgment about this encounter with Jesus's opponents is biased in that I have a positive view of Jesus and lack the perspective of someone who keeps the Sabbath as an observant Jew does.[218] John portrays Jews, like Nicodemus, as being overly literal and legalistic, even though John, including this chapter, is also legalistic; Witnesses, judgment, and Wrongs are important concepts in John. John is written as Testimony (John 19:35; 21:24).

The friction point in this encounter with Jews is whether Jesus was entitled to violate Sabbath rules, which are a part of Jewish law as recorded in the first five books of the Bible. For the Jews in this story (as seen by John), the law matters more than a miraculous healing. Jesus says in 5:39-40 that his audience misses the point in reading scripture, including the law:

> You look into the scriptures because you suppose you have
> eternal Life in them, and they are what Testifies of me, yet you
> don't want come to me so you may have Life.

Likewise, Jesus says that even Moses, Israel's great heroic law-giver, accuses the Jews in this story (5:45), "for if you Trusted Moses, you would also Trust me, for he Testified of me" (5:46-47). The concept of law (right and wrong, binary moral thinking), has very deep roots in the Bible. From Eden if not before, the Bible emphasises good and evil, right and wrong, and yet in Eden, God

> did the one thing necessary to ensure that the tree's fruit
> would be eaten by forbidding it to Adam and Eve. He sent the
> serpent to tempt Eve, knowing that she would fall for the bait.

---

[217] Brown, *The Gospel of John*, volume 29 of *Anchor Bible*, page 224.

[218] Mary Coloe explains some reasons why the Sabbath is important for Jews in *Wisdom Bible Commentary*, volume 44A, pages 142-43. She also notes that it was celebrated at home with the woman of the house in the leading role.

> He intended that they disobey Him and feel shame, and thereby come to know good from evil.[219]

Guilt and shame came into human experience from eating that mythical fruit. Creation myths explain the human condition, and the biblical one lays a heavy emphasis on on human obedience. Its original believers were people "known historically for observance of the Law;"[220] they became "extremely, perhaps excessively, legalistic."[221] The consequences of violating the law exceeded the natural consequences of doing the wrong thing: Sin is an act, which produced guilt, but it is also a condition, which requires expiation, sacrifice, purification rituals, and elaborate ceremonies. One result of this highly differentiated knowledge of sin is a high level of consciousness, of a particular sort. Another result could be a serious problem with self-esteem. It is as though from the beginning of the biblical dream onwards, this personality is dealing with the issue of shame and guilt, as though some primordial sin had been committed. This resulted in patterns of cleaning, vigilance, and ritualistic activities.[222]

However, the "attempts at self-purification were ineffective because the true source of the problem was not being addressed."[223] The result is a repeating cycle: man sins, is restored, sins again, sacrifices and is restored, sins again and falls away, is called back and is restored, sins again and is punished, repents and is restored, sins again and is forced to wander in the wilderness or in exile, is restored, sins again, and on and on.[224]

Right from its creation myth onwards, the Bible records the operation of a sort of washing machine cycle: dirty laundry goes in and comes out clean, time after time after time. We never learn, our problems repeat, and that is true for Bible readers as well as others.

So the Bible makes no difference to anyone then? So there is no benefit to reading it? Isaac knew a different way. For him, the Bible was the occasion for further "revelation of Christ in the soul":

> If a man search the Scriptures all his days..., [and] be able to dispute about them...; yet, if he hath not received the true knowledge of the nature of these things, all his professed faith in them cannot be true.
>
> The true knowledge is only to be had by the immediate revelation of Christ in the soul.[225]

Isaac also knew from experience just how people (not just Jews) read the Bible without the "immediate revelation of Christ in the soul":

---

[219] Stein, *The Bible as Dream*, page 48.

[220] Stein, *The Bible as Dream*, page 49.

[221] *Ibid.*

[222] *Ibid.*

[223] Stein, *The Bible as Dream*, page 50. Stein adds that "Freud would trace this back to the primal murder of the Father, the original sin." The Eden story makes more sense to me because it is clearly mythic and symbolic, so it can open a window into the unconscious. Killing my father, who died of cancer, has no symbolic resonance at all for me.

[224] Stein, *The Bible as Dream*, page 56.

[225] Penington, *Axe Laid to the Root*, in *Works*, volume 1, pages 97-98.

> The Spirit of the Lord is the true expositor of scriptures ... but man, being without that Spirit, doth but guess, doth but imagine, doth but study and invent a meaning, and so he is ever adding or diminishing. This is the sense, saith one; this is the sense, saith another; this is the sense, saith a third; this, saith a fourth: another that is witty, and large in his comprehension, he says they will all stand; another, perhaps more witty than he, says none of them will stand, and he invents a meaning different from them all. .... Doth not this plainly show, that he who thus saith, hath not the Spirit of the Lord to open the scripture to him and manifest which is the true sense, but is working in the mystery of darkness?[226]

"The needful thing," said Jung, "is not to *know* the truth but to *experience* it."[227] We shy away from doing that because experiencing the self, the inward sense of God, in our awareness takes effort, is painful at times, and is and feels risky. Like Jesus said, "*you don't want* to come to me so you may have Life" (John 5:40 italics added). That is why "without necessity, nothing budges, the human personality least of all. It is tremendously conservative, not to say torpid."[228]

In studying the Bible without ever having "heard his voice or seen his image" (John 5:37), people are left walking on a treadmill with their defence mechanisms. Isaac Penington could see that people were projecting the evil inside themselves onto their understanding of the Spirit:

> How darest thou ... be guessing at that which the Spirit doth not open to thee, and so art found adding and diminishing?

> Now he that is the adder, he that is the diminisher, he crieth out against the Spirit of the Lord, and chargeth *him* with adding and diminishing: for man being judge, he will judge his own way to be true, and God's to be false. That which is the adding and diminishing, he calls the true expounding of the place; but if the Spirit of the Lord immediately open any thing to any son or daughter, he cries, This is an adding to the word: the scripture is written; there are no more revelations to be expected now; the curse, saith he, is to them that add. Thus he removes the curse from his own spirit, and way of study and invention, to which it appertains; and casts it upon the Spirit of the Lord. And man cannot possibly avoid this in the way that he is in; for having first judged his own darkness

---

[226] Penington, *Scattered Sheep Sought After*, in *Works*, volume 1, pages 249-50.

[227] Foreword to *Seelenprobleme der Gegenwart*, Rascher paperback, Zurich, 1969; in *Collected Works* volume 18, paragraph 7; quoted in Jacobi (editor), *Psychological Reflections*, page 299. The emphasis is in the original.

[228] Jung, *The Development of Personality*, in *Collected Works*, volume 17, paragraph 293.

to be light, then, in the next place, he must needs judge the true light to be darkness.[229]

Projection means seeing one's own unconscious in others rather than in oneself. This sentence describes it in action, "Thus he removes the curse from his own spirit ... to which it appertains; and casts it upon the Spirit of the Lord."

Discovering and undoing projections occurs when two things happen: knowing what the other person is really like on whom I am projecting, and knowing what I'm really like, inside and out, and accepting that for what it is, my characteristics not other people's.

Knowing what another person is like calls for evidence, reliable indications of what the truth is, but which we are apt to misconstrue because we judge our "own darkness to be light, then, in the next place, [we] must needs judge the true light to be darkness." Much of John 5 is evidence or testimony about Jesus and who he is. The scriptures "are what Testifies of me" (5:39). Besides the scriptures, "the Father who sent me has Testified about me" (5:37), but again, the Father's testimony would have to come via the inward Light; we would have to inwardly experience it.

Always the spiritual way forward, the way to realise God in consciousness, comes down to looking inside the soul, not outside it, and not in a book of do's and don't's:

> the disciples who were illiterate, and not so knowing of the scriptures that were written of Christ, yet they knew Christ: but the Scribes and Pharisees, who were very skilful in the letter, could not know him. What was the reason? The reason lay in the difference of the eye, or light, wherewith they looked: the one looked with an outward eye, the other with an inward eye. And a little inward light will do that, which a great deal of outward light will not do.[230]

Bread of life (chapter 6)

[1]Later on Jesus went across the sea[a] of Galilee and of Tiberias. [2]A large crowd kept following him because they saw the Signs that he was doing for the sick. [3]However, Jesus went up onto the mountain and sat down there with his disciples. [4]The Passover,[b] the Jewish festival, was approaching.

[5]When he looked up and saw a large crowd coming toward him, he says to Philip, "Where are we to buy bread so they may eat?" [6]This he said to test him, for he Knew what he was about to do. [7]Philip replied, "200 denaria[c] worth of bread would not be enough for each of them to get a little." [8]One of his disciples, Andrew, the brother of Simon Peter, says to him, [9]"There is a little boy here who has five barley loaves[d] and two small fish, but what is that for so many?" [10]Jesus said to him, "Have the people sit down."[e] There was a lot of grass at that place. So they sat down and the number of the men was about five thousand. [11]Jesus took the loaves and after giving thanks he distributed them to those who were seated and likewise also the fish, as much as they wanted. [12]When they were all provided for, he says to his disciples, "Gather up the left over pieces so that

---

[229] Penington, *Axe Laid at the Root*, in *Works*, volume 1, page 250, italics added.

[230] Penington, *The Jew Outward*, in *Works*, volume 1, page 221.

nothing is lost." [13]So they gathered and filled twelve baskets with pieces from the five barley loaves which had satisfied the people who had eaten. [14]When the people saw the Sign he had performed, they began saying, "This is Truly the prophet who is coming into the World."

[15]When Jesus Realised that they were about to come and seize him to make him king, he left again and went to the mountain alone.

[16]When the evening came, his disciples went down to the sea, [17]got in a boat, and went across the sea to Capernaum.[f] [18]The sea became turbulent because a great wind was blowing. [19]After they had rowed about 3-4 miles,[g] they see Jesus walking on the sea and coming near the boat, and they were frightened. [20]He says to them, "It's me,[h] don't be afraid." [21]Then they wanted to take him into the boat, and immediately the boat reached the shore to which they were going.

[22]On the next day, the crowd, which was still across the sea, saw that no more than one boat was there and that Jesus had not got in the boat with his disciples, but his disciples had gone away alone. [23]But some boats from Tiberias came near the place where they had eaten the bread after the Lord gave thanks. [24]So when the crowd saw that Jesus was not there, nor his disciples, they themselves got in boats and came to Capernaum seeking Jesus.

[25]When they found him on the other side of the sea, they said to him, "Rabbi, when did you come?" [26]Jesus answered them, "Very truly I tell you, you are looking for me, not because you saw Signs, but because you ate your fill of the loaves. [27]Do not work for food that perishes but for food that Remains into eternal Life, which the son of man will give you. On him God the Father has set his seal."[i] [28]So they said to him, "What are we to do to perform the works of God?"

[29]Jesus answered them, "This is the work of God, that you Trust in him who sent him." [30]So they said to him, "What Sign are you doing for us to see and Trust you? [31]Our fathers ate manna[j] in the desert just as is written, 'he gave them bread from the sky to eat'." [32]So Jesus said to them, "Very truly I tell you, it was not Moses who gave you bread from the sky, but my Father gives you the True bread from the sky; [33]for the bread of God is that which is coming down from the sky and giving Life to the World. [34]So they said to him, "Sir, give us this bread constantly."

[35]Jesus said to them, "I am the bread of Life. Whoever comes to me will never[k] be hungry, and whoever Trusts in me will never be thirsty." [36]But I told you that you have seen me, but you did not Trust. [37]All that the Father gives me will come to me, and I will certainly not throw out anyone who comes to me, [38]for I have come down from the sky not to do my will but the will of him who sent me. [39]This is the will of him who sent me, that I should not destroy anything that he has given me of himself, but rather raise it again on the last day. [40]For this is the will of my Father, that all who see the son and Trust in him may have eternal Life, and I will raise them again on the last day."

[41]Then Jews were grumbling[l] about him because he said "I am the bread that came down from heaven," [42]and they were saying, "Isn't this Jesus the son of Joseph? Don't we Know his father and mother? How does he now say that he has come down from heaven?" [43]Jesus answered them, "Don't grumble with each other. [44]No one can can come to me unless the Father who sent me draws him, and I will raise him again at the last day. [45]It is written in the prophets, 'And they will all be taught by God.'[m] Everyone who has heard from the Father and learns comes to me, [46]although no one has seen the Father except the one who

is[n] beside the Father. [47]Very truly I tell you, whoever Trusts has eternal Life. [48]I am the bread of Life. [49]Your fathers ate manna in the desert and they died. [50]This is the bread that comes down from heaven so that anyone who eats of it may not die. [51]I am the Living bread that has come down from heaven. If anyone eats of this bread, he will Live into eternity, and the bread that I will give for the Life of the World is my flesh."

[52]Jews then quarrelled with each other saying, "How can he give us his flesh to eat?" [53]So Jesus said to them, "Very truly I tell you, unless you eat the flesh of the son of man and drink his blood, you have no Life in yourselves. [54]Whoever feeds on[o] my flesh and drinks my blood has eternal Life, and I will raise him again on the last day. [55]For my flesh is True food, and my blood is True drink. [56]Whoever feeds on my flesh and drinks my blood Remains in me and I in him. [57]Just as the Living Father sent me, I also Live because of the Father, and whoever feeds on me will also Live because of me. [58]This is the bread that came down from heaven, not like your fathers ate and died. Whoever feeds on this bread will Live into eternity."

[59]He said these things in the synagogue in Capernaum.

[60]When many of his disciples heard, they said, "That is a tough thing to say." [61]But Jesus, Knowing in himself that his disciples grumbled about it, said to them, "Does this trip you up?[p]" [62]What then if you were to see the son of man ascending to where he was before? [63]The Spirit is the Life-giver; the flesh is of no use at all. What I have said to you is Spirit and Life. [64]But among you are some who do not Trust." For Jesus knew from the start who were the ones who did not Trust and who would betray him. [65]He used to say, "That is why I told you that no one can come to me unless it is given him from the Father."

[66]Because of this many of his disciples turned back and no longer walked with him. [67]So Jesus said to the Twelve, "Don't you want to go too?" [68]Simon Peter asked him, "Lord, to whom would we go? You have the words of eternal Life. [69]We have come to Trust and know that you are the holy one of God." [70]Jesus answered them, "Did I not select you, the Twelve? Yet one among you is a devil." [71]He was alluding to Judas son of Simon Iscariot, one among the Twelve, for he was soon to betray him.

Meaning and resonance

a. **"sea of Galilee"**: Judeans called this a sea, but it is not connected to the ocean. It is a freshwater lake out of which the Jordan River flows southward to the Dead Sea, which is also a lake not connected to the ocean. In this section, however, I have kept their word choice, "sea".

b. **"Passover"** (6:4): Passover is an annual Jewish holy week commemorating the deliverance of the Israelites from Egypt. The last of the plagues that finally persuaded Pharaoh to let the Israelites go was the killing of firstborn sons. The Israelites sprinkled the blood of a lamb on their doorposts as a sign to pass over their houses and spare their sons (Exodus 12:43-13:16).

Mary Coloe:

> This is the second of three Passovers depicted in John and the only one where Jesus is not in Jerusalem. As Passover is one of the three major pilgrim festivals (Exodus 34:22-23), Jewish men were expected to celebrate the festival in

Jerusalem, with the sacrificing of the lamb in the temple followed by the Passover meal. It is possible that this Passover in Galilee is the second Passover prescribed for those who were unable to celebrate the festival at the proper time [Numbers 9:4-5 and 9:10-12].[231]

She adds that in Galilee, two days' journey away from the Jerusalem Temple, the main Passover symbol is unleavened bread, recalling the manna sent by God to nourish the Israelites in the Sinai Desert.[232] "The manna miracle fell one month after the First Passover, *i.e.*, on the day of the second concessional Passover for those who missed the regular date."[233]

c. **"200 denaria"** (6:7): One denarius was a common labourer's daily wage.[234]

d. **"barley loaves"** (6:9): "According to Jewish law, barley could not be used for ordinary eating until it had been offered on the second day within the first Passover liturgy (Leviticus 23:9-14). That barley loaves are now available further supports the view that this feeding, when barley can be used, must be the later Passover for those who missed the first one in Jerusalem."[235] Barley loaves were the bread of common people.[236]

Barley loaves allude to 2 Kings 4:42-44, a multiplication of food by Elisha. However, Jesus outdoes Elisha, who feeds only 100 with 20 loaves:

> A man came from Baal-shalishah, bringing food from the first fruits to the man of God: twenty loaves of barley and fresh ears of grain in his sack. Elisha said, "Give it to the people and let them eat." But his servant said, "How can I set this before a hundred people?" So he repeated, "Give it to the people and let them eat, for thus says the Lord, 'They shall eat and have some left.' " He set it before them, they ate, and had some left, according to the word of the Lord.

e. **"Have the people sit down"** (6:10): This actually says to have them recline, the dining posture of the ancient world. This would have signalled to the people that food was coming.

f. **"Capernaum"** (6:16, 6:24): This was the main Roman city in the Galilee area, where the royal official also lived whose son was healed (John 4:46-54). Outspoken and popular Jewish heroes probably caused Jewish authorities more concern in a Roman town than in a Jewish village or in the Temple.

---

[231] *Wisdom Bible Commentary*, volume 44A, pages 162-163.

[232] *Ibid.*, page 163.

[233] *Ibid.*, page 171; Brown, *The Gospel According to John*, volume 29, page 265.

[234] Bauer, Arndt, Gingrich and Danker, *A Greek-English Lexicon*, entry "δηνάριον", page 179.

[235] Coloe, *Wisdom Bible Commentary*, volume 44A, page 164.

[236] Carson, *The Gospel According to John,* page 270.

g. **"3-4 miles"** (6:19): Literally, "25-30 stadia". The largest Greek linear measurement was a stadion, equivalent to about 607 feet.[237] I have converted to a rough equivalent in miles.

h. **"It's me"** (6:20): This is literally an "I am" statement, but, given its context, it seems best translated as simple identification. However, it is rare in John for the surface level to contain the entire meaning, although I'm not sure what more to make of this I am statement.

i. **"the Father has set his seal"** (6:27): The same word is used in John 3:32; both instances refer to a legal action done to authenticate and authorise a document.

j. **"manna"** (6:31, 6:49): Manna is the Hebrew word for the bread that God provided to the Israelites in the desert to keep them from starving (Exodus 16). The prophetic literature of the Old Testament associates it with the word of God,[238] and, in the wisdom literature, with Wisdom herself, as in Proverbs 9:5 "Come, eat of my bread, and drink of the wine I have mixed".

k. **"will never be hungry"** (6:35): The Greek here is emphatically negative.

l. **"Jews were grumbling"** (6:41): This wonderfully onomatopoetic Greek word, γόγγυζω (pronounced approximately "gonguzo") was also used for Israelites complaining in the time of Moses (Exodus 9:7-12; 17:3; Numbers 11:1; 14:27-29; 16:41; 17:5) in the ancient Greek version of the Old Testament.

m. **"they will all be taught by God"**: From Isaiah 54:13.

n. **"the one who is"** (6:46): In this chapter, I am appears three times (6:35, 6:48, 6:51), and "the one who is" makes four. They all refer to Exodus 3:14. God's name is given there as "I am that I am"; which was translated in the ancient Greek version of the Old Testament as "ὁ ὤν", literally "he who is". God is self-existent; humans were created in Genesis 2 and 3, but God simply is.

o. **"feeds on"** (6:54-58): "In secular Greek this verb [τρώγω] was originally used of animals; but, at least from the time of Herodotus [ca. 450 B.C.E.], it was used of human eating as well. It had a crude connotation (see Matthew 24:38)."[239]

   The Bauer-Danker dictionary notes that eating someone's bread indicates "close comradeship," citing among others John 13:18, which quotes Psalm 41:9 as a prophecy of Jesus's betrayer.[240]

p. **"Does this trip you up?"** (6:61): The verb here (σκανδαλίζω) originally meant to snare an animal, but in the New Testament, where σκανδαλίζω appears frequently, it is people who become ensnared.

---

[237] Matthew 20:2; Brown, *The Gospel of John*, volume 29, page 251.

[238] Coloe, *Wisdom Bible Commentary*, volume 44A, page 174.

[239] Brown, *The Gospel according to John*, volume 29, page 283.

[240] Bauer, Arndt, Gingrich and Danker, *A Greek-English Lexicon of the New Testament*, page 829.

Reflections

"No one can come to me unless the Father ... draws him" (6:44)

Jack Wallis, Jungian and Quaker, described

> two alternative ways of building faith: letting it grow out of one's personal experience of living or, on the contrary, first finding faith and then interpreting experience accordingly. The latter has long been a conventional Christian way, Church leaders insisting that one must have faith, then everything else will follow. Jung objected that faith cannot be had to order. Moreover, there seems, in this approach, to be a risk that we find in experience what we are looking for (a common pitfall). Such looking is often unconscious and is then all the more powerful. [241]

"Faith cannot be had to order" because the order is a conscious demand upon the unconscious mind, which is extremely adept at ignoring such demands and doing what it likes.

Faith cannot be had to order; but it can be had from experience. Jack Wallis describes how a man

> came across Quakers and found ... that "for them, religious experience is always to be found in ordinary everyday experience"; it comes from "a continuous search for truth, life, love, God, call it what you will, in and through the everyday experiences of life itself.... Religious faith arises out of daily experience by a process of looking for "signals of transcendence". [242]

"Religious experience" and experiencing "signals of transcendence" seem roughly the same thing there. Those experiences are an alternative to self-imposed faith. What Jung called "the transcendent function" bridges the divide established on leaving Eden, when "cherubim and a flaming sword" (defence mechanisms) barred the way back to God (Genesis 3:24), leaving God unconscious after Adam and Eve obtained their new knowledge (consciousness). That barrier to God is not forever impenetrable because the transcendent function serves as "a bonding force that unifies the split between conscious and unconscious". [243]

"Drawings" are what Isaac Penington called "signals of transcendence", and he amplifies Jesus's words in 6:44: "The true Lamb doth not compel, but calls to wait on the Father's drawings, till the Father by his spirit make willing." [244] Isaac wrote those words in a booklet in which he examined the "causes which are said to induce the court of Boston in New England" to banish Quakers on pain of death, after several Quakers had been hanged on Boston Common. Isaac stressed that

---

[241] Wallis, *Jung and the Quaker Way*, page 45.

[242] *Ibid.*, quoting George Gorman, *The Amazing Fact of Quaker Worship*, page 58. Instead of "signals of transcendence", Murray Stein calls them "openings to transcendence". Stein, *Collected Writings*, volume 6, page 208. Quakers also call them "openings", as in chapter 19 of Britain Yearly Meeting, *Quaker Faith and Practice*, chapter 19.

[243] Stein, *Jung's Treatment of Christianity*, page 122.

[244] *An Examination of the Grounds*, in *Works*, volume 1, page 356.

even if the Boston authorities had a legal basis for the killings, they usurped Christ's government:

> Now that which they preach to is men's consciences in the sight of God. .... They are nothing, they can do nothing, they cannot convert any man to God; but the power that speaketh by them, the same power worketh in other men's consciences at its pleasure. And here is the beginning of the government of Christ in the heart; when his truth carries conviction with it to the conscience, and the conscience is drawn to yield itself up to him, then he lays his yoke upon it, and takes upon him the guiding of it; he cherisheth it, he cleanseth it...; and he alone preserveth it pure, chaste, gentle, meek, and pliable to the impressions of his Spirit. And as the conscience is kept single and tender to Christ, so his government increases therein; but as it becomes ... subject to men's wills, so another spirit gets dominion over it.[245]

God has granted us a certain power to govern ourselves, but power-hungry people usurp it. Instead, diversity and a reluctance to judge are called for:

> Even in the apostles' days, Christians were too apt to strive after a wrong unity and uniformity in outward practices and [observances], and to judge one another unrighteously in these things. And mark; it is not the different practice from one another that breaks the peace and unity, but the judging of one another because of different practices. .... And he that draws another to any practice, before the life in his own particular lead him ... destroy[s] the soul of that person.[246]

Note that it does not matter whether the demand is right or not;[247] compulsion is a soul-destroying substitute for "the life ... lead[ing] him", or, in Jesus's words, "the Father drawing him" (6:44). For that reason:

> Care must be had that nothing govern in the church of Christ, but the spirit of Christ: that nothing else teach; nothing else exhort.... Every minister in the church is to watch over his own spirit, that it intrude not into the work of God, that it take not upon it[self] to be the teacher.[248]

Once again, as Fox said, "Your teacher is within you. Look not forth."[249] Even less should a person interfere in the work of the Teacher in someone else.

A psychotherapist must likewise respect the boundaries of each human psyche, even while serving as midwife to the transcendent function as the unconscious God-image comes to light in the client's conscious mind. The therapist can explain what is happening and help the client see how to alleviate complexes that

---

[245] *An Examination of the Grounds*, in *Works*, volume 1, page 383.

[246] *Ibid.*, page 385.

[247] *Ibid.*

[248] *Ibid.*, citing Romans 14:1-23.

[249] George Fox, *Journal*, 1694 edition, edited and transcribed by Thomas Ellwood, page 98; online at 1694 edition: page 98 (lancaster.ac.uk).

block the way,[250] but the therapist cannot make the client see what he does not see. The light to see the self must come from within. It is also likely to resist an attempt by force, even self-imposed force. The Quakers on whom Boston forced its religious views ended up dead from the attempt.

> Psychotherapy is at bottom a dialectical relationship between doctor and patient. It is an encounter between two psychic wholes, in which knowledge is used only as a tool. The goal is transformation—not one that is predetermined, but rather an indeterminable change.... No efforts on the part of the doctor can compel this experience. The most he can do is smooth the path for the patient and help him to attain an attitude which offers the least resistance to the decisive experience.[251]

A therapist must simply have faith that a solution will appear in time. Then, when the solution appears, she may have to catch it:

> A man is ill, but the illness is nature's attempt to heal him, and what the neurotic flings away as absolutely worthless contains the true gold we should never have found elsewhere.[252]

Isaac describes a similar process of observation:

> Be not an instrument to draw him into any thing which the Lord leads him not into; but rejoice if thou find him *in simplicity of heart startling at any thing; for if he abide [there] faithful, his guide will in due season appear to him*, and clear his way before him.[253]

That "startling" comes on catching sight of something numinous, glimpsing a "signal of transcendence" as Jack Wallis called it. We are to "rejoice" on seeing that "startling" in someone because it is a sign of hope. The Light is indeed at work. With patience, the Guide will in time "draw" the soul to Christ and Life.

In collective rather than personal terms, "these signals of transcendence, [even if] given to the lowly and quite isolated individual, can help the larger community out of an impasse."[254] The numinous can help the collective, but the collective can also ignore it. Matthew wrote:

> when the chief priests and the scribes saw the amazing things that he did, and heard the children crying out in the temple, "Hosanna to the Son of David," they became angry and said to him, "Do you hear what they are saying?" Jesus said to them, "Yes; have you never read, 'Out of the mouths of children and

---

[250] "Suffering that is not understood is hard to bear, while on the other hand, it is often astounding to see how much a person can endure when he understands the why and the wherefore." Jung, *Psychology West and East*, in *Collected Works*, volume 18, pages 690-693.

[251] Jung, *Psychology and Religion*, in Collected Works, volume 11, paragraph 904.

[252] Jung, *Civilization in Transition*, in *Collected Works*, volume 10, paragraph 361.

[253] Penington, *An Examination of the Grounds*, in *Works*, volume 1, page 388 (italics added).

[254] Stein, "Jung's Green Christ: A Healing Symbol for Christianity," in *Jung's Challenge to Contemporary Religion*, page 2.

nursing babies you have prepared praise for yourself'?" (Matthew 21:15-16.)

The children were responding to the numinosity of the son of God, but the chief priests and scribes seem as if they cannot see that at all—or, more likely, they see it unconsciously as threatening their position. Ignoring numinosity deadens a person's sense of it; that is how "we have stripped all things of their mystery and numinosity: Nothing is holy any longer."[255] The numinous does not disappear, however; our shadow can still see it, as appears to have happened to the chief priests and scribes. For them it surfaced as fear. Unconsciously, a part of them was rejoicing with the children, however. Fear formed a polarity with unconscious joy. They missed that joy as a conscious experience.

"the bread that I will give for the Life of the World" (6:51)

> Whoever speaks in primordial images speaks with a thousand voices; he enthrals and overpowers, while at the same time he lifts the idea he is seeking to express out of the occasional and the transitory into the realm of the ever-enduring. He transmutes our personal destiny into the destiny of mankind, and evokes in us all those beneficent forces that ever and anon have enabled humanity to find a refuge from every peril and to outlive the longest night.[256]

A primordial image ceases to speak "with a thousand voices" if it is reduced to one concrete thing. A primordial, archetypal image speaks to the soul in the soul's terms, but reducing the image of bread to a lump of actual baked dough diminishes the universal image. It turns a reality that can speak to the unconscious into a lump that does not speak at all inwardly; the concrete object must first be restored to the realm of images and symbols for it to speak to the soul.

That is why Christian sacraments are reductive to the point of travesty: they shift the focus from an inward call that the psyche can understand into an outward object and performance, a thing done to someone rather than experienced by someone who answers the call.

John 6 is often read in terms of the Christian sacrament of the eucharist, a ritual meal to remember Jesus and his death. However, that meal is a concept foreign to John, where Jesus's last hours with his disciples include no such meal of remembrance. They eat in John 13, but we are not told what, nor are blessing (or "giving thanks") or repetition mentioned. John chapters 13-17 are full of teaching, and Jesus also washes the feet of his disciples and prays for them, but no sacrament is instituted.

The sacraments were not overlooked in John; the concept of them is inconsistent with John's point that Jesus is all that is required: "I am the way, the Truth, and the Life." (John 14:6). "Especially against a text that claims Jesus is the only way

---

[255] Jung, *Symbols and the Interpretation of Dreams*, in *Collected Works*, volume 18; quoted in Jacobi, *Psychological Reflections*, page 264.

[256] Jung, *The Spirit in Man, Art, and Literature*, in *Collected Works*, volume 15, paragraph 129.

to the Father, the inference of cultic requirements for salvation to be realized is not simply a tension; it is a flat-out contradiction."[257]

So why then did Jesus say this so graphically?

> Unless you eat the flesh of the son of man and drink his blood, you have no Life in yourselves. Whoever feeds on my flesh and drinks my blood has eternal Life.[258]

Isaac Penington lived in a time when the Gutenberg printing revolution had just reached England, and when the press was more free than ever. It was like the explosion of social media in the late 1990s. Self-published books and pamphlets on religion were everywhere. This was the time of the "world turned upside down,"[259] when religion was in the English air, and the free press put it there.

Isaac, a prolific writer on religion, was criticised in a pamphlet written by one Thomas Hicks. Hicks had read some of Isaac's work, then summed it up in what he claimed was a quotation but which he mostly contrived. It takes the form of a dialogue between a Quaker and a "Christian":

> *Quaker (protesting the Christian's accusation):* Thou sayest, we account the blood of Christ no more than a common thing; yea, no more than the blood of a common thief.
>
> *Christian:* Isaac Penington (who I suppose to be an approved Quaker) asks this question, Can outward blood cleanse?[260]

Isaac denied he ever said that,[261] but he didn't deny the gist. Rather, if anything, he affirmed it. Isaac's view of sacraments was symbolic through and through. He protested that Hicks had missed the point: "that book was not to vilify the flesh and blood of Christ ... but to bring people from sticking in the outward...."[262] Then he explains further what he did mean:

> I did mean the mystery, when I spake of bread, water, the wine, the live coal from the altar, the leaves of the tree of life, the putting on Christ, the flesh and blood of Christ, &c., is very plain to him that reads singly. But to make it manifest,

---

[257] Anderson, *Riddles of the Fourth Gospel*, page 41. Carson points out that Latin "sacramentum" was how the Greek word "mystery" (μυστήριον) was translated, a word that does not appear at all in John. "Sacramentum" also meant a "military oath of obedience administered by the commander", a far cry from anything in John. Carson, *The Gospel According to John*, page 281.

[258] John 6:53-54.

[259] This phrase, originally from Acts 17:6, was spoken by Jews charging Paul and Silas before the authorities. Christopher Hill used the same phrase to describe the English Civil War (1642-1651) and its aftermath in his history, *The World Turned Upside Down: Radical Ideas During the English Revolution* (London: Penguin, 1972).

[260] *The Flesh and Blood of Jesus Christ*, in *Works*, volume 3, page 344.

[261] *Ibid.*

[262] *Ibid.*, page 345.

particularly concerning the flesh and blood of Christ; I shall recite one query;[263]

He actually recites two queries from the work Hicks criticised, and I've skipped the first.

> The query runs thus: "Can outward blood cleanse the conscience? Ye that are spiritual, consider; can outward water wash the soul clean? Ye that have ever felt the blood of sprinkling from the Lord upon your consciences, and your consciences cleansed thereby, did ye ever feel it to be outward? It is one thing what a man apprehends (in the way of notion) from the letter concerning the things of God, and another thing what a man feels in Spirit." Is it not manifest, by the express words themselves, that I spake of the inward feeling of the blood in the mystery?[264]

The symbol is everything for Isaac. The symbol eclipses the physical body and blood, the things originally symbolised. Entry of the archetypal into the scene makes the physical a distraction from the primordial images.

> Whoever feeds on my flesh and drinks my blood has eternal Life. (John 6:52)

Isaac, whose very language is charged with his love of John, would have seen even that statement as symbolic. Having eternal Life depends on sustenance that the cross of Christ provides; this is about nourishment from the cross,[265] not human food that satisfies only for a while. "I am the bread of Life. Whoever comes to me will never be hungry" (6:35). This does not allude to an actual memorial meal that has not yet been instituted and never will be in John; instead, it refers to the death of Jesus, and to the cross that each soul is called to bear. See "The Cross" below in chapter 19.

> Complete redemption from the sufferings of this world is and must remain an illusion. Christ's earthly life likewise ended, not in complacent bliss, but on the cross.[266]

The great evil of sacramental reduction is that it makes us think we have accomplished more than we actually have. For our own ultimate happiness and fulfilment, we must shoulder our own cross, not sell ourselves short with an outward gesture that changes nothing within us. Taking a eucharistic meal rather than bearing our own Cross is using a form as an excuse for shirking what is our real calling.

> The Spirit is the Life-giver; the flesh is of no use at all.
>
> John 6:63

---

[263] *Ibid.*, page 347

[264] *Ibid.*

[265] Anderson, *Riddles of the Fourth Gospel*, page 40-41; Anderson, *The Christology of the Fourth Gospel*, chapter 6; Meeks, *The Prophet-King*, pages 93-99.

[266] Jung, *The Psychology of the Transference*, in *Collected Works*, volume 16, paragraph 400.

Jesus at the Festival of Booths, part 1 (chapter 7)

¹After that Jesus went round in Galilee. He did not want to go round Judea because Jews were trying to kill him. ²The Jewish Festival of Booths^a was near. ³So his brothers said to him, "Leave here and go to Judea so that your disciples will see the works that you do, ⁴for no one does things secretly when he seeks to be publicly known. If you do these things, show yourself to the World." ⁵(For not even they Trusted in him.) ⁶Jesus then said to them, "My time has not yet come, but your time is always here. ⁷The World cannot hate you, but it hates me because I Testify of it that its works are evil. ⁸You go up to the festival; I'm not going to this one because my time has not fully come." ⁹After he said these things he Remained in Galilee.

¹⁰After his brothers went to the festival, then he also went up, not openly but in secret. ¹¹Jews were looking for him at the festival and saying, "Where is he?" ¹²There was much muttering about him among the crowds, some saying he is good, and others saying no, he deceives the crowd. ¹³However, no one spoke openly about him for fear of Jews.^b

¹⁴Midway through the festival Jesus went up into the Temple and began to teach. ¹⁵Then Jews were amazed saying, "How is this one literate when he has not been educated?" ¹⁶Jesus answered them, "My teaching is not mine but his who sent me. ¹⁷If anyone wants to do his will, he will know of the teaching, whether it is of God or whether I speak of myself. ¹⁸Whoever speaks of himself seeks his own glory, but whoever seeks the glory of the one who sent him is True, and there is no evil in him.

¹⁹"Hasn't Moses given you the law? Yet not one of you keeps the law. Why are you seeking to kill me?" ²⁰The crowd answered, "He has a demon. Who is seeking to kill him?" ²¹Jesus replied, "I did one work, and you're all astonished. ²²For this reason Moses gave you circumcision (not that it is from Moses but rather from the patriarchs)^c and you circumcise someone on the Sabbath. ²³If someone receives circumcision on the Sabbath so that the law of Moses may not be broken,^d are you angry at me because an entire person was made healthy on the Sabbath? ²⁴Stop judging by appearances, and judge with good judgment.

²⁵Then some people from Jerusalem were saying, "Isn't this the one whom they are trying to kill? ²⁶And here he is, speaking boldly and they have nothing to say to him. Don't the authorities Know that this is the Christ? ²⁷However, we Know where this one comes from, but when the Christ comes, no one will Know where he comes from." ²⁸So Jesus shouted, while teaching in the Temple, "And me you Know? Do you Know where I am from?^e I have not come of my own accord, but the one who sent me is True, whom you do not Know. ²⁹I Know him because I am from him and he sent me."

³⁰Then they tried to arrest him, but no one laid hands on him because his Hour had not yet come.^f ³¹Yet many in the crowd Trusted in him and said, "When the Christ comes, will he do more Signs than this man has done?"

³²The Pharisees heard the crowd muttering things about him, and the chief priests and Pharisees sent officials to arrest him. ³³Then Jesus said, "Yet a little while am I with you, and then I go to him who sent me. ³⁴You will seek me and not find me, and where I am you cannot come." ³⁵So Jews said to themselves, "Where is this man going to go that we will not find him? Surely he's not about to go into the Diaspora among the Greeks and teach Greeks, is he? ³⁶What is

this that he said, 'You will seek me and not find me, and where I am you cannot come'?"

[37]On the last day of the festival, the great day, Jesus stood and shouted, "If anyone is thirsty, let him come to me and drink. [38]Whoever Trusts in me, as the scripture said, rivers of living water shall flow from his belly."[g] [39]This he said about the Spirit, which those who Trust in him were going to receive, for as yet there was no Spirit because Jesus was not yet glorified.

[40]So when some in the crowd heard these words, they were saying "He is Truly the prophet." [41]Others were saying, "He is the Christ," but some were saying, "Surely the Christ does not come from Galilee, does he? [42]Did the scripture not say that from the descendants of David and from Bethlehem, the village where David was from, the Christ is coming?" [43]So a division occurred in the crowd because of him. [44]Some of them wanted to arrest him, but no one laid a hand on him.

[45]Then those slaves returned to the chief priests and Pharisees, who told them, "Why did you not bring him in?" [46]The slaves answered, "Never has a person spoken like this." [47]Then the Pharisees replied to them, "Surely you were not also deceived! [48]Has anyone of the leaders or Pharisees Trusted in him? [49]But this rabble, which does not Know the law, is under a curse." [50]Nicodemus, who came to him earlier, says to them, as he was one of them, [51]"Does our law judge a person without first hearing from him and finding out what he does?" [52]In response they told him, "You are not also from Galilee, are you? Look it up and see that no prophet arises from Galilee."

Meaning and resonance

a. **"Festival of Booths"** (7:2): Also known as the festival of tabernacles, or in Hebrew, *sukkot*, this annual autumn festival begins shortly after the Day of Atonement (Yom Kippur) and continues for one week plus an additional day. During the festival, people eat and sleep in specially constructed booths originally made of myrtle, willow and palm branches (Nehemiah 8:13-18).[267]

Originally a harvest festival in Abraham's time,[268] the Festival of Booths took on additional meaning as a remembrance of Israel's forty years in the desert living in temporary shelters in the time of Moses.[269] Its main symbols are:

- **Water**; a daily procession brought water from the Pool of Siloam into the Temple,[270] and the autumnal timing "coincided with the beginning of the rainy season which was sorely needed after the hot summer months."[271]

- **Light**. Every evening four huge menorahs (candlesticks for seven candles each) were lit. "Atop each [menorah], which could only be

---

[267] Coloe, *Wisdom Bible Commentary*, volume 44A, page 395.

[268] Coloe, *God Dwells with Us*, page

[269] *Ibid.*; Leviticus 23:42-43; Yee, *Jewish Feasts and the Gospel of John*, pages 72-75.

[270] Coloe, *God Dwells with Us*, page 123.

[271] Yee, *Jewish Feasts and the Gospel of John*, pages 73; see also Charlesworth, *Jesus as Mirrored in John*, page 93; Coloe, *Wisdom Bible Commentary*, volume 44A, page 197.

reached by ladders, were golden bowls holding oil. Wicks floated in the oil, which were made from worn-out clothing of the Temple priests."[272]

Jesus re-interprets both these symbols. In John 7:37-39, he promises water, which 7:29 equates with the Spirit. In John 8, Jesus declares himself to be the "light of the world" (8:12).

b. **"no one spoke openly about him for fear of Jews"** (7:13): The people fearing the Jews here are also Jews, perhaps not exclusively but mostly. John uses the word "Jews" very broadly when it could be more specific, as here, where the people feared would have been the Jewish authorities.

c. **"Moses gave you circumcision (not that it is from Moses but rather from the patriarchs)"** (7:22): As the parenthetical indicates, circumcision was part of the covenant God made with Abraham (Genesis 17:9-14), which was later incorporated into the Torah, the law of Moses. Interesting to see the narrator here correct what must have been an earlier statement.

d. **"circumcision on the Sabbath so that the law of Moses may not be broken"** (7:23): Circumcision was required eight days after birth, regardless of whether that day was a Sabbath (Genesis 17:10-14).

e. **"do you Know where I am from?"** (7:28): Greek texts of that time had no punctuation marks, which began coming into use about five centuries after John was completed. In a sentence without an interrogative word such as "why", it is debatable whether the sentence is a question or a statement. I have taken these words as a question, and the next sentence indicates that the hearers do not know the answer.

f. **"his Hour had not yet come"** (7:30): In John 7:6, speaking with his brothers, Jesus says "My time has not yet come, but your time is always here." The word for "time" in that sentence is not Hour (ὥρα) but καιρός, meaning a critical interval of time. In John Hour almost always refers to Jesus's final days; a different word καιρός is used in John 7:6 in relation to Jesus's brothers so John avoids ὥρα there. In John 7:30, Jesus refers to his Hour, which has not yet come.

g. **"rivers of living water shall flow from his belly"** (7:38): For Jews, "the belly is the seat of man's emotional nature, the heart has the same role in Western symbolism".[273] Although this sounds like it alludes to scripture, it does "not reflect exactly any one passage" in the Hebrew scriptures or their Greek translation of the time.[274]

There is an alternative reading of John 7:37-38, which differs according to how punctuation is added: "If any one is thirsty, let him come to me, and let anyone who Trusts in me drink, as the scripture said..." Scholars are divided on which to prefer.

---

[272] Yee, *Jewish Feasts and the Gospel of John*, pages 76; Coloe, *God Dwells with Us*, page 121-122; Coloe, *Wisdom Bible Commentary*, volume 44A, page 198; Charlesworth, *Jesus as Mirrored in John*, page 93.

[273] Brown, *The Gospel According to John*, volume 29, page 323.

[274] Brown, *The Gospel According to John*, volume 29, page 321; see also Carson, *The Gospel According to John*, page 324 ("centre of the human personality" and "a fairly close synonym for [heart]").

h. **"He is Truly the prophet"** (7:40): *The* prophet refers to the "prophet like Moses" of Deuteronomy 18:15-18, a passage often taken to mean the Messiah.

Reflections

"You are not also from Galilee, are you?" (7:52)

In this chapter, Jesus's opponents drop several niggles of disdain:

- **"How does this one know letters when he has not been educated?"** (7:15) Jews were then and are now "people of the Book"; Jewish spirituality centres in the Torah and its observance. Learning is important when spirituality is based on a written document, a thing that can be studied for spiritual benefit. Pharisees also maintained a long oral tradition, also to be learned, and best taught by a rabbi who is latest in a line of teachers that can be traced back to Moses.[275] The rabbinical schools of Hillel and Shammai taught this learning, but Jesus had not been educated in either. The speakers would not have spoken this line if they had been schoolmates. John loves a double-edged meaning and there is one here: they praise him for being literate, even if "uneducated". The irony is that his teaching comes directly from God, not indirectly via learning from Moses.

- **"We know where this man comes from, but when the Christ comes, no one will know where he comes from."** (7:27) In John 6:42, Jesus's audience muttered among themselves, "Isn't this Jesus the son of Joseph? Don't we know his father and mother? How does he now say that he has come down from heaven?" The audience in John 6 were Galileans, some of whom apparently knew of Mary and Joseph. In John 7, the people are in Jerusalem, the big city compared to which Nazareth would have been a village in the northern province, where Jesus was the son of a carpenter's wife.

- **"You are not also from Galilee, are you?"** This jibe was not directed at Jesus but rather Nicodemus because he defended Jesus's right to be heard. Jesus derided Nicodemus in John 3:10; now Nicodemus gets mocked by other Pharisees. Murray Stein explains why: "Archetypal possession in a community or culture invests certain ideas and policies with defensive certainty and denies the legitimacy of doubt. Contrary thoughts and images are savagely attacked and repressed."[276]

- **"No prophet arises from Galilee."** (7:52) This statement was not actually true:

  This statement is incorrect (Jonah and Nahum were from Galilee, and Eliezer, a contemporary of the Fourth Evangelist, believed that every tribe of Israel had produced prophets....) The point of this inaccurate statement is to raise the question of the origin of Jesus. On one level, Bethlehem is hinted at (*cf.* Micah 5:[2]; John 7:42), which

---

[275] Bruce, *New Testament History*, page 73; Coloe, *Wisdom Bible Commentary*, volume 44A, page 204. Instead of a line back to Moses, Jesus says his teaching comes direct from his Father (7:16-17).

[276] *The Principle of Individuation*, page 47.

> conforms with at least one aspect of messianic expectation.... On another level, it hints at Jesus' heavenly origin. This is likely another instance of the evangelist's use of irony.[277]

> Even though the statement was inaccurate, it shows that people from Jerusalem looked down on Nazareth, as Nathanael also did when asking, "Can anything good come out of Nazareth?" (John 1:46).

In this chapter, Jesus does not appear to react to these barbs, but, looking back from the end of chapter 8 (which continues on from this chapter, still at the Festival of Booths), his conversations with Jews show escalating tension. When Jesus cleared the Temple in John 2, the Jews there asked for a Sign, but neither side disparaged the other. In John 5, after a man was healed on the Sabbath, Jews criticised the Sabbath violation. In John 6, Jews question Jesus and grumble at the answers, though, as here, the crowd is ambivalent. In John 7 here, it is clear that the Jewish authorities consider Jesus an uneducated provincial with high pretensions who needs to come down to reality. This escalating tension crests in John 8.

The underlying issue in all those chapters is who Jesus is.

Over and over, Jesus defines himself to be the son of "the Father", who seems the same as God, but many or most of his audience see him as another pretender in a long line of pretenders to the messianic throne, at a particularly volatile time. In our time of religious tolerance, we consider ourselves allowed to differ in matters of religious conviction. That view conflicts with John's, which was written so that its audience "may come to Trust that Jesus is the [Messiah]" (John 20:31). The Jews in John simply do not believe that, and therefore the author demonises them.

In all his conversations with Jews, Jesus never sugar-coats what he says. He speaks plainly and makes no apparent effort to win over his Jewish interlocutors. In modern sales and marketing, if one approach does not prove persuasive, people try another, but Jesus never does. He speaks as God does, and God is not required to sweeten the medicine. This all leaves the authorities thinking he really does need to come down a peg.

Jesus at the Festival of Booths, part 2 (chapter 8)

The story in John 7:53 through 8:11 (about the woman caught in adultery) was not part of the original book. From the manuscripts, it appears those verses were added almost 100 years after John was finished without them.[278] Paul Anderson rather delightfully calls them a "text caught in adultery".[279]

This story is considered in the Appendix of this book. I have removed it from here because it interrupts the flow of Jesus's teaching during the Festival of Booths. Chapter 8 continues on from chapter 7.

---

[277] Evans, *Word and Glory*, page 153.

[278] Schackenburg, *Das Johannesevangelium*, volume 4, page 161-163; Brown, *The Gospel according to John*, volume 29, page 335; Carson, *The Gospel According to John,* page 333; Culpepper, *The Gospel and Letters of John*, page 170, Keener, *The Gospel of John*, volume 1, page 735.

[279] Anderson, *The Riddles of the Fourth Gospel*, page 70.

[12]Then Jesus spoke to them again, "I am[a] the Light of the World.[b] Whoever follows me will surely not walk in darkness but will have the Light of Life." [13]Then the Pharisees said to him, "You are Testifying of yourself. Your Testimony is not True."[c] [14]Jesus told them in response, "If I Testify of myself, my Testimony is True because I Know where I came from and where I go, but you do not Know where I come from nor where I go. [15]You judge according to the flesh.[d] I do not judge anyone, [16]but even if I judge, my judgment is True because I do not judge alone but I and the Father who sent me. [17]It has been written in your law that the Testimony of two people is True. [18]I am the one who Testifies about himself and the Father who sent me also Testifies about me."

[19]So they said to him, "Where is your Father?" Jesus answered, "You do not Know me nor my Father. If you Knew me, you would Know my Father also." [20]He said these things while teaching in the treasury of the Temple, but no one arrested him because his Hour had not yet come.

[21]So he said to them again, "I am going and you will seek me, but you will die in your Wrongfulness. Where I go you cannot come." [22]So Jews said, "He isn't going to kill himself, is he? Because he says 'Where I go, you cannot come.'" [23]And he said to them, "You are from below; I am from above. You are of this World; I am not of this World. [24]I told you that you will die in your Wrongfulness because if you do not Trust that I am, you will die in your Wrongfulness."

[25]They said to him, "Who are you?" Jesus told them, "What I have been telling you from the beginning.[e] [26]I have much to say about you and much to condemn, but the one who sent me is True,[f] and I tell the World all that I have heard from him." [27]They did not Realise that he was speaking to them of the Father. [28]So Jesus told them, "When you lift up the son of man,[g] then you will Know that I am, and I do nothing of my own accord, and I say just what the Father taught me to say. [29]The one who sent me is with me. He has not left me alone because I do what is right by him.

[30]As he was saying these things, many Trusted in him. [31]Then Jesus told the Jews who Trusted him,

> "If you Remain in my word,
> you are Truly my disciples,
> [32]and you will Know the Truth,
> and the Truth will set you free."

[33]They answered him, "We are the descendants of Abraham and have never been enslaved to anyone.[h] How is it you say we will become free?" [34]"Very Truly I tell you, one who does Wrong is a slave to Wrongfulness. [35]A slave does not Remain in the household permanently, but a son Remains for eternity. [36]So if the son sets you free, you are free.

[37]"I know that you are descendants of Abraham, but you are seeking to kill me because my word has no place in you. [39]I say what I have seen from beside the Father, and you are to do what you heard from the Father. [40]Now you are trying to kill me, a man who has told you the Truth that he heard from God. Abraham did not do that. [41]You do what your father does." They told him, "We are not born from sexual immorality. We have one father and that is God." [42]Jesus said to them, "If God were your father, you would love me, for I have come from God and am now here. I did not come of my own accord, but rather he sent me. [43]Why do you not Recognise what I say? Because you cannot hear my word. [44]You are from your father the devil, and you want to do what your father wants. He was a murderer from the beginning[i] and never stood in the Truth, because

there is no Truth in him. ⁴⁵However, I speak the Truth, but you do not Trust me. ⁴⁶Who among you accuses me of a Wrong? If I tell the Truth, why do you not Trust me? ⁴⁷One who is from God hears what God says. Why do you not hear? Because you are not from God."

⁴⁸Jews replied to him, "Aren't we right in saying that you are a Samaritan and have a demon?"ʲ ⁴⁹Jesus answered, "I have no demon, but I honour my Father, and you dishonour me. ⁵⁰I did not come seeking my own glory, but there is one who seeks it and he judges. ⁵¹Very truly I tell you, whoever keepsᵏ my word will never see death in eternity."

⁵²Jews then told him, "Now we know that you have a demon. Abraham died and so did the prophets, but you say 'whoever keepsᵏ your word will not taste death for eternity.' ⁵³Surely you are no greater than our father Abraham who died. The prophets also died. What do you make yourself out to be?" ⁵⁴Jesus replied, "If I glorify myself, my glory is nothing. It is my Father who glorifies me, who you say is your God, ⁵⁵but you do not Know him. Yet I Know him. If I were to say I didn't Know him, I would be a liar like you. But I do Know him and I keepᵏ his word. ⁵⁶Abraham your father rejoiced to see my day, and he did see it and was glad." ⁵⁷Jews said to him, "You are not yet fifty years old, yet you saw Abraham?" ⁵⁸Jesus told them, "Before Abraham came to be, I am." ⁵⁹Then they picked up stones to throw at him, but Jesus hid and left the Temple.

Meaning and resonance

a. **"I am"** (8:12): This phrase, explained below in the "John's key words" section, occurs five times in this section, and stands alone (without a predicate) in 8:24, 8:28, and 8:58. These words recall the name of God declared in Exodus 3:14. In the Greek version of the Old Testament, the name of God was translated as ὁ ὤν ("he who is", the self-existent one), and that appears in 8:47.

The Festival of Booths included a daily procession in which participants would chant in Hebrew, "*ani wehu* [literally I and he] come to our aid".

> The Hebrew phrase *ani wehu* was used as an oblique way of referring to YHWH [the name of God in Hebrew] and thus avoiding saying the sacred name. Having celebrated the feast and heard the daily recitation of *ani wehu*, Jesus's use of the phrase "I am" as a term of self-designation would have been both striking and offensive to his opponents.[280]

b. **"I am the Light of the World."** (8:12): As noted above, light was the other great symbol (besides water) of the Festival of Booths, which featured four huge menorahs lit at night. The festival also took place during the full moon of the autumnal equinox.[281] The festival recalls the time when the Israelites lived in the desert, where they were led by a pillar of cloud by day and a pillar of fire by night.[282]

[280] Coloe, *Wisdom Bible Commentary*, volume 44A, pages 220-221.

[281] Coloe, *Wisdom Bible Commentary*, volume 44A, page 271.

[282] Exodus 13:21, 14:24, 16:10, 19:9 and 16, 24:15.

Again Jesus is re-interpreting the festival in terms of himself. His identity is the central issue in John 7-8.

c. **"You are Testifying of about yourself. Your Testimony is not True."** (8:13): Jesus himself made this same point in John 5:31, and again, "valid" might be a better word in this case than "True", although "True" shows that the recurring word is being used.

d. **"You judge according to the flesh"** (8:15): Melvin Keiser defines "flesh" as "self-will resulting in conformity", [283] or in Fox's words, the part of oneself "that could not give up to the will of God".[284] Keiser continues:

> Rather than grounding itself in the presence of Christ in the self's own depths, fleshly knowing seeks its security in conforming to something outside itself, and thus ends in 'deceit.' We are deceived in mistakenly thinking Christ is an external entity when it is an inward reality.[285]

Jung called it a "systematic blindness" and a "prejudice that God is *outside* man".[286]

e. **"What I have been telling you from the beginning."** (8:25): The Greek here is not a full sentence and has long perplexed translators. Ancient manuscripts have added words to clarify it; 𝔓[66] (ca. 150 C.E.) has an insertion mark to the margin to insert the words "I told",[287] giving the sense, "what I told you at first I'm telling you [now]", though that hardly responds to the question asked. Other manuscripts have similar additions, but they do seem additions rather than original because they vary a little, though most include "I told".

Even if we add in those words as the ancients did, that still leaves a gap: "at first" requires adding a word because the text only has the word "beginning" (ἀρχή), as an object, though the object of what is not clear. I have adopted Brown's translation.[288] He and many other scholars surmise that the Greek may be corrupt or incomplete here,[289] and it was a very early loss because early manuscripts like 𝔓[66] have struggled with the gaps.

f. **"the One who sent me is True"** (8:26): This is an echo of John 3:33; see also the Reflection there.

g. **"When you lift up the son of man"** (8:28): The word for "lift up" here is "ὑψόω", and John uses it only in reference to Jesus's crucifixion. It means both to elevate physically and to exalt, to raise to glory.[290] The same word

[283] *Seeds of Silence*, page 222.

[284] *Journal* (Nickalls edition), pages 14-15.

[285] *Seeds of Silence*, page 223.

[286] *Psychology and Religion*, in *Collected Works*, volume 11, paragraph 61 (italics by Jung), quoted in Dourley, *Mystical Fool* p. 19.

[287] Philip W. Comfort & David P. Barrett, *The Complete Text of the Earliest New Testament Manuscripts*, page 408 (Grand Rapids, Michigan: Baker Books, 1999).

[288] *The Gospel according to John*, volume 29, page 346.

[289] *Ibid.*, page 348.

[290] Evans, *Word and Glory*, page 155 and 180.

is used of the "suffering servant" in Isaiah 52:13 and of the brass snake in John 3:14.

h. **"We ... have never been enslaved to anyone"** (8:33): This is patently false. Babylon conquered Judea in 587 B.C.E., took most of the Jewish nation captive, and enslaved them in Babylon. Centuries before, they had been slaves in Egypt.

The Jews no doubt knew that this was not true. So why did they say it? Perhaps they didn't. We have no way of knowing whether these Jews were prevaricating or whether our narrator is saying they did. Quite possibly the latter because John contains so much that is negative about Jews when in reality Jews are no worse than other people. In John, they ended up cast as the villains in the binary thinking of the story teller because they challenged rather than Trusted Jesus.

i. **"He was a murderer from the beginning"** (8:44): Evans sees an allusion to Cain in this statement. The Targums were the Old Testament translated into Aramaic, the colloquial language of Judean Jews at the time of Jesus, and they are the scriptures that Jesus and his friends would have heard in their synagogues. According to the Targums, "Cain was not the son of Adam, but rather was the son of the evil angel Sammael, also known as Satan", who was also the serpent in Eden.[291]

j. **"you ... have a demon"** (8:48, 49, 52): Carl Jung:

> The greatness of historical personalities has never lain in their abject submission *to* convention, but, on the contrary, in their deliverance *from* convention. They towered up like mountain peaks above the mass that still clung to its collective fears, its beliefs, laws, and systems, and boldly chose their own way. To the man in the street it has always seemed miraculous that anyone should turn aside from the beaten track with its known destinations, and strike out on the steep and narrow path leading into the unknown. Hence, it was always believed that such a man, if not actually crazy, was possessed by a daemon or a god; for the miracle of a man being able to act otherwise than as humanity has always acted could only be explained by the gift of daemonic power or divine spirit.[292]

k. **"whoever keeps my word"** (8:51, 52, 55): "Keeps" translates the Greek word τηρέω, which in ordinary Greek was not used in the sense of obedience. It means to watch over or observe, but it was used in the Greek Old Testament to translate the Hebrew word *shamar*, which also means to observe and includes the sense of observing the Sabbath, for example, or other commandments.

---

[291] Evans, *Word and Glory*, page 161.

[292] *The Development of the Personality*, in *Collected Works*, volume 17, paragraph 298.

Reflections

"the Truth shall set you free" (8:32)

In John 8:30, Jesus is winning people over; some are Trusting in him. Then he tells them in 8:31:

> If you Remain in my word,
> you are Truly my disciples,
> and you will Know the Truth,
> and the Truth will set you free.

On hearing this, his newly Trusting audience seems to feel slighted at the implication that they are not already free because they answer back, "We are the descendants of Abraham and have never been enslaved to anyone." As so often happens in John, Jesus's audience misunderstands him, usually by taking his meaning to be literal when it is not (*e.g.* Nicodemus asking if someone born again re-enters the womb). Jesus clarifies his meaning here by saying, "one who does Wrong is a slave to Wrongfulness" (8:34).

Wrongfulness manifests itself in acts or omissions, but at bottom it is a mind-set. Isaac Penington explains that realising freedom begins—not by a fervent resolve in ego-consciousness to do no Wrong, but rather in a change of mind brought about by the Spirit: "the Spirit of life ... makes free by its powerful working in the mind".[293] He elaborated:

> by no means rest or abide in the natural, but retire with the Lord (who will not dwell there until it be cleansed) into the resting-place. .... And this is the reason why the formal and outward part of religion doth so commonly eat out the life, because things there ... exercise that part wherein the strength of the enemy lies; and there can never be perfect freedom and safety until that part be subdued, and all that belongs to that part removed. The Lord is risen to shake, that the kingdom which cannot be shaken may appear; and happy are they who are shaken by his hand in all that is outward, and established in the inward life, power, and rest, which remaineth for ever, and cannot be shaken.[294]

Jung also saw the outwardness of Christianity as unhelpful:

> In its religious attitude ... the West is extraverted [outwardly orientated]. ... Extraversion ... cannot credit man with a psyche which contains anything not imported into it from outside, either by human teaching or divine grace. From this point of view, it is downright blasphemy to assert that man has it in him to accomplish his own redemption. Nothing in

---

[293] *Of The Church in Its First and Pure State*, in *Works*, volume 3, page 195.

[294] *Axe Laid at the Root*, in *Works*, volume 1, page 85.

our religion encourages the idea of the self-liberating power of the mind.[295]

That externalising approach to religion "eats out the life", Isaac said. The way to freedom is inward, to "retire with the Lord ... into the resting-place" where we become free:

> It is not ethical principles, however lofty, or creeds, however orthodox, that lay the foundations for the freedom and autonomy of the individual, but simply and solely the empirical awareness, the incontrovertible experience of an intensely personal, reciprocal relationship between man and an extramundane authority which acts as a counterpoise to the "world" and its "reason".[296]

Isaac had such an experience of relationship, and knew it as the source of freedom:

> Liberty is the enlargedness of the heart in the Spirit of the Lord, wherein it hath scope in all that is good, and is shut out of all that is evil. The Spirit of the Lord is free, and maketh free. The earthly spirit is in bondage with her children; but they which are begotten of the Lord, and wrapped up in his Spirit, find the power and freedom of the new life therein, and are thereby perfectly out of the reach of that, which (let into the mind) hath power to captivate and inthrall.[297]

Issac wrote those words in 1663. From 1661 to 1671, he spent about half his time in jail for worshipping as a Quaker.[298] Most of what we have been reading from him he wrote in jail, and it demonstrates a great freedom of mind despite the irony of his circumstances. As with Job, evil turned to good: Isaac's written output was more than most of his Quaker contemporaries. Jail gave him the solitude to write. The authorities thought they were silencing him, but they really gave him his platform, as Pilate had also done for Jesus.

"your father the devil" (8:44)

I am not a psychologist, nor am I capable as an ordinary mortal of analysing the mind of God. Jung fathomed and explained the Gods he found in the minds of his patients, though not a transcendent being in the traditional sense. I do not have his fathoming ability.

However, I have often found it helpful to seek a psychological understanding of myself, and also to seek an understanding and empathetic appreciation of others. Then I can see my part in a situation better, and see that part in myself rather than projected out onto other people. If I can see my part, then I can focus within my range of possibilities because my part is the only part I can control or change. It is also the part I am responsible for.

A psychological understanding of life has also helped me see why some situations turn out badly. John 8 is one such situation; in the end, no one was convinced

---

[295] *Psychology and Religion: West and East*, in *Collected Works*, volume 11, paragraph 779.

[296] Jung, *The Undiscovered Self*, in *Collected Works*, volume 10, paragraph 509.

[297] *Some of the Mysteries of God's Kingdom Glanced At*, in *Works*, volume 2, page 345.

[298] "Testimony of Thomas Ellwood," in Penington's *Works*, volume 1, pages 11-13.

and the audience began stoning Jesus. Though I don't presume to offer an understanding of God's mind, the minds of John's authoring group and the God-image in my own mind are both products of human psychology, and fair objects for reflection. When things seem to go wrong in an emotional way, I try to understand why. "You are of your father the devil" puts John 8 in that category for me.[299] Those words are painful to hear from the lips of Jesus.

> When words are strange or disturbing to you, try to sense where they come from and what has nourished the lives of others.
>
> Britain Yearly Meeting[300]

In John, Jesus always speaks plainly. Quakers see honest and plain speaking as a virtue, particularly if its sharper edges are smoothed with loving kindness. However, Jesus as seen in John speaks *very* plainly, with no sandpapering around the edges. It is important to bear in mind that John 8 "is not the transcript of a conversation that took place between the 'historical Jesus' and the 'historical Jews' of his time. Rather, like the rest of the Gospel, it is entirely 'scripted' by the Fourth Evangelist."[301]

However, even with understanding for an author whose community is undergoing a painful and involuntary transition in its identity, John's Jesus has some less appealing aspects. Our view of those depends on whether we see Jesus as God or not. If not, he is rude and disrespectful in his verbal treatment of people (by present standards, at least) and he harbours inordinate hostility to Jews—or was he angry at the world in general, and Jews had the misfortune of being in range? If he is God, then we have no business imposing an obligation to sugar-coat the truth or guidance given. In psychological terms, the unconscious self will accept no such obligation.[302]

However, we are responsible for how our mind affects other people. Telling Jews that their father is not Abraham but the devil is so offensive that it makes persuasion or any further dialogue impossible. For Jews, that is "a complete denial of family and national identity."[303] However, by the time we reach the "devil" statement in verse 44, neither side of the discussion is listening to the other.

The behaviour of both is consistent with projection:

> The psychological rule says that when an inner situation is not made conscious, it happens outside, as fate. That is to say, when the individual remains undivided[304] and does not

---

[299] "You have a demon," said twice, also shows that there is a lot of anger in the room.

[300] "Advices and Queries" number 17, from *Quaker Faith and Practice.*

[301] Reinhartz, "The Gospel of John", in *Jesus, Judaism and Christian Anti-Judaism*, page 106.

[302] The suffering messianic servant in Isaiah 53:2 had "nothing in his appearance that we should desire him."

[303] Ashton, *The Gospel of John and Christian Origins*, page 142.

[304] One would think division is unhealthy, and integrity, that marvellous integration of the soul at peace, is healthy; however, integrity is only *ultimately* good. Our path to wholeness passes through many polarities; see "Opposites in John and Jung" below.

> become conscious of his inner opposite, the world must act
> out the conflict and be torn into opposing halves.[305]

The unconscious strives to become conscious, but when it cannot find any better way into my awareness, I encounter the content of my unconscious in the world around me, projected out onto other people. If I can't acknowledge my greediness, I will see greed in other people, greed that isn't actually there because it is really *my* greed that I *assume* other people have because I do not deal with the greed in my own soul. The less able I am to see my faults, the more I will see them in other people. "The root of all good and evil lies in [a person's] own psyche and the world around him is as he himself shaped it."[306]

> Another way by which we seek to protect ourselves from a feeling of inner unworthiness is to attribute all our innate goodness to the presence of God within us and to attribute our innate evil merely to the absence of that good, to our failure to recognise and respond to it. On this view, the vast mass of evil in the world is projected onto those who are not followers of Christ, to the evil ones, the enemy, to those who are not 'saved' as we are. Sometimes even fellow Christians are the receivers of these projections, and reciprocate them. Then inter-denominational violence, brutality or even war break out between them.[307]

"Our unwillingness to see our own faults and the projection of them onto others is the source of most quarrels."[308] The quarrelers speak as if to each other, but each hears only his own echo chamber of projection. If I am angry but don't realise it, my anger will belittle and insult the other person, or in some way I will treat the other person as hostile, regardless of whether they really are. Both sides of the discussion in John 8 appear to be angry, and they are no longer listening to each other, or able to do so, by the end.

Anger has the effect of distancing people from each other, rather than persuading or winning them over. Faced with the projection of Jesus's anger and hostility in John 8 and the harsh words coming from it, it hardly seems that the audience there had any real chance of being persuaded of anything Jesus wished them to accept. Jesus (as seen in John 8) lacks the compassion that would allow Trust to grow in his audience. Nobody Trusts a hostile person; we step back and protect ourselves from them.

John 8 reflects a discussion in which no one was persuaded, and if it happened as it it is said to have, then no one seems psychologically prepared to either persuade or be persuaded. Each side was actually carrying out a dialogue with itself in the guise of giving the other side what for, too angry to hear or understand each other. However, we don't know what actually happened at the time; this account of the discussion may reflect the anger of a later generation in the painful transition away from Judaism, or perhaps I am being too judgmental

---

[305] Jung, *Collected Works*, volume 9, part 2, paragraph 126. It is uncanny how one unconscious mind brings this about with other unconscious minds.

[306] Jolande Jacobi, "Preface to the First Edition" of Jung, *Psychological Reflections: An Anthology of Jung's Writings 1905-1961* (London: Routledge, 1971), page i.

[307] Wallis, *Jung and the Quaker Way*, page 115.

[308] Jung, *Collected Works*, volume 18 paragraph 15.

and should rather look to my own faults and whether I am projecting them into the text. If indeed it really was the wrath of God, then I can only pray for mercy, for I have some sympathy for the offended Jews. Their father was indeed Abraham, and they are no more devilish than the rest of us.

The man born blind healed on the Sabbath (chapter 9)

This Sign and the trial following it may also have happened as part of the Festival of Booths. Its imagery of light and water continues.

[1]Going on, he saw a man blind from birth. [2]His disciples asked him, "Rabbi, who did Wrong, this man or his parents, that he was born blind?" [3]Jesus answered, "Neither he nor his parents, but so that the work of God may be revealed in him. [4]We must work the works of him who sent me while it is day. The night is coming when no one can work. [5]While I am in the World, I am the Light of the World." [6]After saying that, he spat on the ground, made mud from the spittle, and smeared the man's eyes with the mud. [7]He told him, "Go wash in the pool of Siloam"[a] (which means "one sent"). So he went, washed, and came away seeing.

[8]Then the neighbours and people used to seeing him before as a beggar began saying, "Isn't this the same one who used sit and beg?" [9]Others were saying, "It is he," but others, "No, it is someone like him." The man kept saying, "I am the one." [10]So they said to him, "How then were your eyes opened?" [11]He answered, "The man called Jesus made mud and anointed my eyes, and he told me to go into Siloam and wash. So I went and washed and saw." [12]They said to him, "Where is he?" He says, "I don't know."

[13]So they took the man once blind to the Pharisees. [14]Now it was a Sabbath[b] on the day Jesus made mud and opened his eyes. [15]So the Pharisees asked him again how he got his sight back. He told them, "He put mud on my eyes, I washed, and now I see." [16]Some of the Pharisees were saying, "This man is not from God because he does not observe the Sabbath," but others were saying, "How can a human Wrongdoer perform such Signs?" There was a division among them. [17]So they say again to the blind man, "What do you say about him for having opened your eyes?" He said, "He is a prophet."

[18]Jews did not Trust[c] that he had been blind and regained his sight until they summoned the parents of the one who had regained his sight [19]and asked them, "Is this your son, whom you say was born blind? So how does he now see?" [20]Then his parents said, "We Know that he is our son and that he was born blind, [21]but we don't Know how he now sees or who opened his eyes. Ask him; he is old enough to speak for himself." [22]His parents said these things because they were afraid of Jews, for Jews had already agreed that anyone who acknowledges him as Christ would be excluded from synagogues. [23]Because of this his parents said he was old enough so ask him.

[24]So they summoned the man a second time who had been blind and told him, "Give glory to God,[d] we Know that this man does Wrong." [25]He answered, "I don't Know whether he does Wrong; all I Know is that I used to be blind and now I see." [26]So they said to him, "What did he do to you? How did he open your eyes?" [27]He answered them, "I told you already but you were not listening. Why do you want to hear it again? You don't want to become his disciples, do you?"[e] [28]They scoffed at him and said, "You are his disciple, but we are disciples of Moses. [29]We Know that God has spoken to Moses, but we don't Know where that one comes from." [30]The man said to them, "In that is something astonishing: you don't Know where he is from, but he opened my eyes. [31]We Know that God

does not listen to those who do Wrong, but he listens to someone who is devout and does his will. ³²It is unheard of that someone opens the eyes of one born blind. ³³If this man were not from God, he could do nothing." ³⁴They replied, "You were born entirely in Wrongs and now you are instructing us?" Then they threw him out.

³⁵Jesus heard that they had thrown him out. He found him and said, "Do you Trust in the son of man?" ³⁶He answered, "Who is he, sir, and I'll Trust in him. ³⁷Jesus told him, "You have seen him, and the one now speaking with you is he." ³⁸He said, "Lord, I Trust," and he worshipped him.

³⁹And Jesus said, "I came into this World for judgment,ᶠ so that those who do not see may see and those who do see may become blind. ⁴⁰Some of the Pharisees near him heard these things and said to him, "We're not blind, are we?" ⁴¹Jesus said to them, "If you were blind, you would have no Wrongfulness, but now that you say you see, your Wrongfulness persists."

Meaning and resonance

a. **"the pool of Siloam"** (9:7): This pool was located southeast of the Temple and was used for self-purification before entering the Temple, like the pool of Bethesda in John 5. The ancient pool of Siloam was

> discovered in 2004. An attempt to repair a large sewer pipe demanded the removal of soil. Beneath the soil was revealed a pool with a series of steps and then a platform: the architecture is identical to the mikveh at [Bethesda]. The arrangement allowed Jews to immerse fully....[309]

b. **"it was a Sabbath"** (9:13): The present chapter parallels the lame man healed in chapter 5. Both healings were on the Sabbath and at purification pools, and both audiences' reaction was to focus on the Sabbath violation not the healing (see "you have never heard his voice" above). The two stories differ mainly in how the healed men respond to Jesus. Both men are interrogated about their healings, but the investigation in chapter 9 goes further and the man there speaks favourably of Jesus, for which he is thrown out (9:34). The man in chapter 5 did not know who it was who had healed him (5:13).

The narrator drops the detail that it was the Sabbath after Jesus has committed a violation by kneading earth and spittle and by healing a man without an emergency. He also told the man to break the Sabbath by washing.[310]

c. **"Jews did not Trust"** (9:18): From 9:13, it is clear that these Jews are Pharisees, but our author often lumps all Jews together rather than see their differences. He stylises them all as Jesus's opponents; only Nicodemus is drawn with enough detail to appear like a person and not just a role.

d. **"Give glory to God"** (9:24): Brown and Coloe see these words as equivalent to putting the man under oath to tell the truth, citing the words'

---

[309] Charlesworth, *Jesus as Mirrored in John*, page 27; see also 195-198.

[310] Brown, *The Gospel of John*, volume 29, page 373; Coloe, *Wisdom Bible Commentary*, volume 44A, page 241.

use for that purpose in Joshua 7:19 and 1 Esdras 9:8.[311] However, they are not an oath but an acknowledgment of the witness's own position relative to God.

e. **"You don't want to become his disciples, do you?"** (9:27): I rather think the man spoke these words with sarcasm. In any case, they got the response that sarcasm usually gets because the Pharisees scoff back at the man. There is also a deeper irony in that it is the man who now sees the situation clearly while the Pharisees do not; the tables have turned.

f. **"I came into this World for judgment"** (9:39): There is a paradox created by this statement in 9:39 and John 3:17 ("For God did not send his son into the World to judge the world") and John 12:47 ("I do not judge anyone who hears my words but does not obey them, for I did not come to judge the World but to save the World.") In the latter two verses, I'm inclined to read "judge" with a negative connotation, *i.e.* as meaning "condemn". Paul word-plays with that negative connotation in Romans 14:13.

On the other hand, John 9:39 may look to the basic meaning of κρίνω (translated "judge"), which is to differentiate and separate, the core logical process of "not this but that". In that sense, the basic meaning of 9:39 would be "I came to this world for logical differentiation, so that those who do not see may see and those who do see may become blind." That makes sense; the problems of the blind are about differentiation, such as not knowing a wall from empty space.

At the end of the day, a paradox has no entirely logical explanation. Neither the Divine nor the unconscious has any obligation to make sense logically, or "to the fleshly understanding" in Isaac Penington's terms:

> ...in his doctrine there seemed many contradictions to the fleshly understanding; for one while he said, "I judge no man" [John 8:15] ... and yet was he not continually judging and condemning the Scribes, the Pharisees.... Again, one while he said, "I and my Father are one" [John 10:30]; another time, "My Father is greater than I" [John 14:28].

> But to what purpose should I heap up any more instances? O thou that readest this, wait to know in thyself the ear that cannot hear Christ's doctrine; while thou condemnest the Jews, do not run into the same error of unbelief and gainsaying, but wait to know the voice of Christ in this day, and to receive the ear that can hear it; for though thou shouldst be willing to hear, yet thou canst not till thy ear be opened.[312]

Reflections

"who did Wrong, this man or his parents, that he was born blind?" (9:2)

The second of the ten commandments is:

---

[311] Brown, *The Gospel of John*, volume 29, page 24; Coloe, *Wisdom Bible Commentary*, volume 44A, page 243.

[312] *The Jew Outward*, in *Works*, volume 1, page 202-203.

> You shall not make for yourself an idol.... For I the Lord your God am a jealous God, punishing children for the iniquity of parents, to the third and fourth generation of those who reject me....[313]

Such statements provoked the disciples' question about whose fault it was that a child was born blind. But is it really a matter of fault? Mary Coloe:

> Disability studies challenge the perception of differences as a problem to be solved or cured. They ask questions when reading the healing narratives of Jesus such as .... Is the "whole" body more Godlike than one that has some impairment? Such was the attitude in ancient Israel, where the blind and the lame were not permitted within the temple (2 Samuel 5:8). This would be an affront to God's holy perfection.[314]

That "attitude" underlies the Pharisees' statement that the formerly blind man was "born entirely in Wrongs" (9:34), and also why they threw him out.

Jesus saw the man's blindness differently, and not as anyone's fault: "Neither he nor his parents [did Wrong], but so that the work of God may be revealed in him" (9:3). No one is to blame; the man was an opportunity for a revelation, not an object of forgiveness or discrimination. The real world then was much more judgmental: The blind and lame were excluded from communal prayer, including the annual festivals, but

> Jesus's actions remove such a social obstacle. "Jesus as a prophet engaged in faith healing treats disability as any other socially made obstacle."[315] He acts as liberator as much as healer.[316]

My grandfather went blind over his lifetime because of a congenital defect; he was unable to see even bright lights in his later years when I knew him. However, his life was free from social stigma, but I know how often he wished—and prayed—that his sight would return. He longed to see again, not so much because blindness was a social obstacle but because he often fell over, partly because his leg had also been amputated when a teenager. I doubt that he faced any discrimination; indeed, I did the opposite and loved and admired him.

A disability is nobody's fault, though we tend to think it must be. Jungian Edward Edinger, speaking of a woman who had given birth to a mentally disabled child, wrote:

> How well one endures such a misfortune will depend on the conception one has of fate, as opposed to mechanical causation. For instance, we can be quite sure that the woman who gave birth to the mentally defective child surely must have tortured herself with causal questions. What did I do

[313] Exodus 20:4-5 (NRSV).

[314] Coloe, *Wisdom Bible Commentary*, volume 44A, pages 239-240.

[315] Coloe cites here "Jesus Thrown Everything Off Balance: Disability and Redemption in Biblical Literature," in Avalos, Melcher, Schipper, eds., *This Abled Body: Rethinking Disabilities in Biblical Studies,* in *Semeia Studies*, volume 55, page 179 (Atlanta: SBL, 2007).

[316] Coloe, *Wisdom Bible Commentary*, volume 44A, page 240.

during the pregnancy? Did I take some drugs? Did I drink too much alcohol? Did I smoke? What did I do? What caused it? That is the eternal round of the ego, because these are the only terms the ego can think in, the terms of causality, mechanical causality.[317]

We seek causes so that we can assign blame; because of Eden, we are chronically keen to know good and evil. Only rarely do we ascribe disabilities to fate, perhaps because fate is work of the Almighty. We prefer not to think about the Almighty or the Almighty's work because neither is under our control. That fact makes them scary and better left unconscious (or so it seems).

Edinger goes on to explain that Greek had two words for fate, *heimarmene* (εἱμαρμένη) and *moira* (μοῖρα). "*Heimarmene* is a fate that can be altered with sufficient consciousness. It is not irrevocable fact. It is like being caught up in parental complexes which do not undergo resolution."[318]

> The other term, *moira*, is generally interpreted as destiny. Its basic meaning is one's portion, one's allotment. .... According to ancient mythology, even the gods, and Zeus himself, were subject to *moira*. .... Of course, we never know in a given situation whether we are dealing with *heimarmene* or *moira*, so we have to go on the assumption that it is the former. We have to go on the assumption that it can be modified by consciousness.[319]

In the case of the mother who gave birth to the disabled child, perhaps the disability was not modifiable by consciousness after birth, and no amount of conscious intervention would then change it. However, from a pre-birth vantage point, it was difficult for the mother to know whether fate had *heimarmene* or *moira* in store for her:

> We project all goodness and perfection onto God and all evil onto scapegoats ... leaving ourselves empty, subject to elation when our projections seem successful and dejection when they are unsuccessful. In reality, says Jung, the individual self is the true mid-point between the opposites that are within, if only we had not forgotten how to look [at the self]. To stop projecting so much of the good and evil in our own personality (conscious and unconscious) is the first essential step in psychic growth towards wholeness.[320]

Once I stop projecting my inner reality and thereby distorting the outward one, I begin to see myself as I am. I then can accept my fate, whatever it is. For *heimarmene*, I have a possible solution, in that I can get to grips with my unconscious complexes and free myself. That will not be easy, but it is possible. For *moira*, the solution lies deeper:

> Recognizing that it is destiny is the first step, because one recognizes one did not cause it. One recognizes that a

---

[317] *The New God-Image*, page 69.

[318] *Ibid.*

[319] *Ibid.*

[320] Wallis, *Jung and the Quaker Way*, page 105.

> transpersonal agency is responsible for it. That is Job's question; he was hit by profound misfortune and he would not accept the advice of his comforters to take the blame himself. He persevered until he found the meaning that was satisfying to him. What is required in all such misfortunes is to find the meaning.[321]

The meaning will vary a bit for each personality, but it will fit a collective pattern, that of Job:

> "Job experiences" have as their basic meaning the realization that God does not know his total condition and that by getting a glimpse of that total condition, man is helping God become more conscious. That is the meaning that Jung extracts from the Book of Job, which is, potentially, the meaning that any individual can extract from a misfortune that befalls one. Of course, it cannot be imposed just arbitrarily; such realization has to grow organically from within. If it does, then the misfortune can be accepted and assimilated.[322]

Therein lies the deeper meaning of Jesus's statement of the reason for the man's blindness: neither the man nor his parents were the cause; he was blind "so that the work of God may be revealed in him" (9:3), so that the activity of the unconscious God might become more conscious.

"Man's suffering," wrote Jung, "does not derive from his sins but from the maker of his imperfections, the paradoxical God."[323]

I'm not sure that my grandfather would have found that an entirely satisfying explanation. However, his grandson, to whom he was like a father, now sees more of his inner divinity than before. He accepted his fate with patience and humility, earning his own living all his life, and he was much loved. We did not see him as impaired, even though he couldn't see physical things. To us, he was a great and noble son of God who could see things in us we could not. The Hollywood ending of Job leaves unsaid his inward gains: the wisdom earned, the insight into his soul and God's, and the strength necessary to pass through all that Fate laid on and remain sane and conscious of the unseen good in God.

"excluded from synagogues" (9:22, also 12:42, 16:2)

John contains a word not found elsewhere in the New Testament or in ordinary Greek: ἀποσυνάγωγος. It literally means "away from synagogue", and it appears three times and only in John:

> His parents said these things because they were afraid of Jews, for Jews had already agreed that anyone who acknow-

---

[321] Edinger, *The New God-Image*, pages 69-70.

[322] *Ibid.*, page 70.

[323] *Collected Works*, volume 18, paragraph 1681.

> ledges him as Christ would be excluded from synagogues. (9:22)
>
> Yet many Trusted in him even among the authorities, but because of the Pharisees they did not acknowledge it so that they would not become excluded from synagogues. (12:42)
>
> They will exclude you from synagogues, and the hour is coming when everyone who kills you will think of it as a service to God. (16:2)

The man born blind became ἀποσυνάγωγος when he was "thrown out" by the Pharisees (9:33) after speaking favourably of Jesus. Synagogues largely took the place of the Temple in Jewish life after the Temple's destruction in 70 C.E.

Ἀποσυνάγωγος has had a turbulent history in the scholarship of John. In 1957, Kenneth Carroll, a Quaker scholar of the Old Testament,[324] interpreted a bit of Jewish liturgy, a curse against heretical Jews, as being "a forceful attempt on the part of the Jews to rid their synagogues of Christians."[325] That attempt was going on about 90-100 C.E. when John reached its final form. J. Louis Martyn picked up on Carroll's article and turned it into a book[326] with roughly the same thesis as Carroll's.

Martyn's (and Carroll's) view came to dominate the scholarship of John, until, after decades of sustained criticism, "most scholars now concede that [the curse] is a red herring".[327] So we have here a cautionary tale about scholarship; for ancient subject matter, the evidence is usually thin and can become over-elaborated. Martyn later remarked, "It would be a valuable practice for the historian to rise each morning saying to himself three times slowly and with emphasis, 'I do not know.'"[328]

Mary Coloe has a cautious conclusion for this cautionary tale. After noting the sharp contrast in John 9:28-29 between Jesus and Moses, she explains that there was no middle ground between them; one had to follow *either* Jesus *or* Moses:

> As both nascent rabbinic Judaism and early Christianity shape their traditions and form their identities following the destruction of Jerusalem, distinctions are beginning to be made: Moses *or* Jesus.... While the Gospel describes the issues in clear opposing terms "Moses" or "Jesus," in fact such clarity was not obvious for some centuries. The Gospel reflects an early stage in a long process of separation, and,

---

[324] Ken Carroll was a member of a Quaker meeting in Dallas, but spent his summers doing research in London, where he attended my local meeting. I knew him there.

[325] Kenneth L. Carroll, "The Fourth Gospel and the Exclusion of Christians from the Synagogue," in *Bulletin of the John Rylands Library*, volume 40, 19-23 (1957).

[326] *History and Theology in the Fourth Gospel* (1968).

[327] Reinhartz, *Cast Out of the Covenant*, page 118.

[328] *The Gospel of John in Christian History*, page 92.

through its polemic, tries to be a catalyst in such separation.[329]

In other words, John's harsh words against Jews are slowly and painfully redefining the identity of John's readers as *former* Jews, while at the same time the diversity of Judaism that existed before the destruction of 70 C.E. was consolidating into Pharisaism, the Judaism of rabbis, the Mishnah, and the Talmud, the Judaism we know today.

The good shepherd (chapter 10)

[1]Very truly I tell you, whoever does not enter the sheepfold through the gate is a thief and a plunderer. [2]The one who enters through the gate is the shepherd of the sheep. [3]For him, the gatekeeper opens the gate, and he calls his sheep by name and leads them. [4]When he has taken out all his own, he goes before them and the sheep follow him because they Know his voice. [5]A stranger they will never[a] follow; rather they will flee from him because they do not Know the voices of strangers. [6]Jesus spoke this metaphor to them, but they did not Realise what he was saying to them.

[7]So Jesus said to them again, "Very truly I tell you, I am the gate. [8]All who came before me are thieves and plunderers,[b] but the sheep did not listen to them. [9]I am the gate. Anyone who enters the gate through me will be Rescued and will come in and go out and find pasture. [10]The thief comes only to steal, kill and destroy. I came so that they may have Life and have it abundantly.

[11]"I am the good shepherd.[c] The good shepherd gives his life for the sheep. [12]A hireling, who is not a shepherd and whose sheep they are not, sees the wolf coming, abandons the sheep, and flees—and the wolf snatches and scatters them—[13]because a hireling is a hireling and the sheep are of no concern to him.

[14]"I am the good shepherd. I Know my own and my own Know me, [15]just as the Father Knows me and I Know the Father, and I give my life for the sheep. [16]But I have other sheep that are not of this fold.[d] I must bring them too, they will also hear my voice and become one flock and one shepherd.

[17]"This is why my Father Loves me, because I give my life in order to take it again. [18]No one takes it from me, but I give it of myself. I have the ability to give it, and I have the ability to take it again. I have received this commandment from my Father."

[19]Another division came among Jews because of these words. [20]Many of them were saying, "He has a demon and is raving. Why listen to him?" [21]Others were saying, "That is not what a person possessed by a demon says. Can a demon open the eyes of the blind?"

[22]Hanukkah[e] was then taking place in Jerusalem, and it was winter. [23]Jesus was walking in the Temple in the portico of Solomon. [24]Jews gathered around him and said to him, "How long are you keeping us in suspense?[f] If you are the Christ, tell us plainly." [25]Jesus answered them, "I tell you and you do not Trust. The works that I do in the name of my Father Testify of me, [26]but you do not Trust because you are not from my sheep. [27]My sheep hear my voice, and I know them and they follow me. [28]I give them eternal Life, and they will never be destroyed in eternity and no one will snatch them from my hand. [29]What my Father has given

---

[329] Coloe, *Wisdom Bible Commentary*, volume 44A, page 245; see also *ibid.*, volume 44B, pages 432-434.

me is greater than all else, and no one can snatch it from the hand of the Father. [30]I and the Father are one."[g]

[31]Again Jews took up stones to stone him. [32]Jesus responded, "I have shown you many good works from the Father. For which of them are you stoning me?" [33]Jews answered him, "We are not stoning you because of a good work but for blasphemy, and because you, a human being, make yourself God." [34]Jesus replied, "Is it not written in your law, 'I said, you are Gods'?[h] [35]If it calls those to whom the word is spoken 'Gods'—and the scripture cannot be undone—[36]yet you say the one whom the Father sanctified and sent into the World is blaspheming, because I said I was the son of God? [37]If I do not do the works of my Father, do not Trust me, [38]but if I do, and then you don't Trust me, Trust the works so that you may Know and Trust that the Father is in me and I am in the Father." [39]Then they tried to arrest him again, but he escaped their hand.

[40]He went away again across the Jordan to the place where John had been immersing, and he Remained there. [41]Many came to him, and they were saying that John performed no Sign, but all that John said concerning him is True. [42]Many Trusted in him there.

Meaning and resonance

a. **"A stranger they will never follow"** (10:5): The negative here is emphatic in Greek.

b. **"All who came before me are thieves…"** (10:8): The text here is uncertain because the oldest manuscripts conflict on whether "before me" is included; however, that makes little difference to the meaning. The differences in texts may reflect copyists' discomfort with the enormity of "all who came before".

> Isaac Penington was struck with how this story must have sounded to its Jewish audience:

>> the exceptions which might or did arise in their minds, are not particularly mentioned; as when he saith, "I am the door of the sheep. All that ever came before me are thieves and robbers; but the sheep did not hear them." John 10:7-8. How offensive must this doctrine needs have been to them, going carnally to understand and reason about it? What! were all the prophets and holy men before thee thieves and robbers? Did the truth never come till thou broughtest it? What became of our fore-fathers in former ages? Were they none of them God's sheep? Did none of them find the door? For thou sayest thou art "the door," and thou hast been but of late. And whereas thou sayest the sheep did not hear them; that is utterly false; for they did hear Moses, and they did hear the prophets….[330]

> I find his empathy with the incredulous a beautiful thing.

c. **"I am the good shepherd."** (10:11): This chapter is a close parallel to Ezekiel 34, in which the Davidic Messiah is the good shepherd; see also Numbers 27:17.

---

[330] *The Jew Outward*, in *Works*, volume 1, page 201.

d. **"I have other sheep that are not of this fold"** (10:16): This is commonly thought to refer to non-Jews accepting Jesus,[331] although the mission to the Greek-speaking world championed by Paul was not a case of "I [Jesus] must bring them too". Some believe Jesus appeared in the western hemisphere. I know of no reason why that cannot be true. In Quaker experience Christ appears in spiritual form all over the world.

e. **"Hannukah"** (10:22): Also known as the festival of rededication, Hannukah celebrates the re-consecration of the Temple after it was defiled on orders of the Syrian ruler Antiochus Ephiphanes, who caused a statue of Zeus to be erected on the altar.[332]

f. **"How long are you keeping us in suspense?"** (10:24): Literally this is "until when are you lifting up our life?". This meaning of "life" (ψυχή, natural life not Life) is "not well attested."[333]

g. **"I and the Father are one"** (10:30): Literally, "one thing", a word (ἕν) that also appears all through John 17 to express the unity of Father, Son, and the disciples.

h. **"You are Gods"** (10:34): The scripture quoted is Psalm 82:6-7:

> I say, "You are gods,
> children of the Most High, all of you;
> nevertheless, you shall die like mortals
> and fall like any prince.

Psalm 82 reproves people who judge unjustly. It is not clear to me how the quoted lines relate to the rest of Psalm 82.

"You are Gods" was often quoted by Jung, as here:

> [T]he Father appears in the Son and breathes together
> with the Son, and the Son leaves the Holy Ghost behind for
> man, then the Holy Ghost breathes in man too, and thus is
> the breath common to man, the Son, and the Father. Man
> is therefore included in God's worship and the words "Ye
> are Gods" appear in a significant light.[334]

Sharing God's breath was a metaphor often used by Isaac Penington as well:

> ...O how doth the soul that is begotten of the divine
> breath ... depend upon God for his continual breathings!

---

[331] *E.g.*, Anderson, *The Riddles of the Fourth Gospel*, page 186; Reinhartz, *Cast Out of the Covenant*, p. 137; Bruce, *The Gospel of John*, page 228.

[332] Bruce, *The Gospel of John*, page 230.

[333] Brown, *The Gospel of John*, volume 29, page 403.

[334] Jung, *Psychology and Religion: West and East*, in *Collected Works*, volume 11, paragraph 233.

> There is nothing that hath so much from God, and yet nothing is so little able to live without him....[335]

Reflection

"My sheep know my voice" (10:4)

Sheep are not born knowing the shepherd's voice; they learn to recognise it. Christ now speaks within people rather than with a physically audible and recognisable voice, so Isaac Penington asks:

> Do they or can they truly know Christ's voice, who never experienced the Word of life speaking in their hearts? Where doth the false prophet speak? Doth he not speak within? And where doth the true Shepherd speak? Doth he not speak also even in the heart? And do not the sheep hear, know, and distinguish his voice there?[336]

Because both the "false prophet" (a thief or plunderer in Jesus's story) and Christ speak inwardly, differentiating between the voices requires what Quakers call discernment,[337] which does not depend on outward evidence. Behaving in an apparently holy or ecclesiastically approved way is not a reliable indicator. Not even caring for the flock is proof of speaking for Christ within. Jung remarked, "Solicitude for the spiritual welfare of the erring sheep can explain even a Torquemada."[338] Torquemada founded and prosecuted the Inquisition.

Hearing one audible voice and not another would be physically strange, but psychologically it is entirely possible. Isaac again:

> that of God in the conscience within answers the pure voice when it comes.... If life speak in one vessel, and its voice be not heard or owned by another vessel, the pure ear (in that other vessel) is not at that time open, but *there is somewhat there that obstructs*. And if the pure ear of the sheep be not open to hear the voice of the Shepherd ... *it is [serious] if that ear [is] opened to hear the voice of the stranger*, and to look upon it as the voice of the Shepherd, it agreeing with that, and answering to that, which now goeth for the voice of the measure of life in that heart. He that hath an ear, let him hear; for it is easy being taken in this snare, and the danger thereof is very great.[339]

How then can we discern the real "measure of life in that heart" from the stranger? Answering that crucial question begins by recognising each voice, both real and false, when we encounter each. Isaac knew the Light from his first

---

[335] *Where is the Wise,* in *Works*, volume 1, page 416.

[336] *Life and Immortality,* in *Works*, volume 4, page 164.

[337] The rest of this Reflection assumes the discerning Friend's need to know, and that the Light is willing to inform about that need. Attempted discernment is no more than passing judgment outside my jurisdiction if the Light does not require my discernment. However, discerning the ways of me is not outside my jurisdiction.

[338] *Alchemical Studies,* in *Collected Works*, volume 13, paragraph 391.

[339] *Some Queries Concerning the Order and Government,* in *Works,* volume 2, page 364. Italics added.

discovery of it (see "Quaker experience of Christ" above). The false voice he also recognised, as his biographer Melvin Keiser explains:

> How do we discern the life? Penington gives a detailed description of the false appearance of life constructed by the veiled self. [One coming under the influence of that false appearance] believes scripture, is instructed by philosophy, undergoes visible changes in affections, will, and understanding. He works very hard doing all that he is supposed to— reading scripture, praying, meditating, denying self, acknowledging he can do nothing without the Spirit, receiving past revelation, waiting for further revelation, and living in hope he has the Spirit and is safe in eternal salvation.[340]

The false appearance of life looks very much like the real thing, but it is driven by ego consciousness, the "veiled self" as Keiser calls it.[341] It does not arise spontaneously, in its own good time, out of the true self. Melvin Keiser continues:

> Since this description of a changed life dependent on God sounds very much like the life Penington advocates, how does he distinguish them? He answers that it is not easy and takes a discipline of much waiting and exercising sense and feeling. But when you have waited, he says, you can tell with confidence. True life is given, not constructed by us. It springs up in inwardness from below the threshold of consciousness— what [Isaac] calls "immediacy" (that is, unmediated by idea, word, or feeling). While there may be a waiting for it, when it comes, it comes more quickly than words or thoughts. As it crosses that threshold, it is powerful in a way that false life is not.[342]

The "immediacy" is not near the conscious surface of the mind:

> ...beneath [consciousness] there is a depth that shades into mystery at the roots of our being, which contains the greatest meaning in our lives but is the least accessible to others and to ourselves. That is why Quakers worship in silence, to become open to such depths.[343]

That "greatest meaning in our lives" that is also "the least accessible to others and to ourselves" aptly describes what Jung called the unconscious self. However, let's follow through with Melvin Keiser. Given the difference between a veiled, false self constructed by a person and that "greatest meaning in our lives" that is the real self, what are the implications for one's life? It would seem a waste to invest in the false self, but vital and fulfilling to follow where the true Life leads:

---

[340] Keiser, *Knowing the Mystery of God Within*, page 183.

[341] It is not a benign state: "We quite forget that we can be as deplorably overcome by a virtue as by a vice. There is a sort of frenzied, orgiastic virtuousness which is just as infamous as a vice and leads to just as much injustice and violence." Jung, *Wandlung und Symbole der Libido* (1912) page 222, quoted in Jacobi, *Psychological Reflections*, page 236.

[342] *Ibid.*

[343] Keiser, *Knowing the Mystery of God Within*, page 136.

"Faith" is not adherence to belief but trust in this Life streaming through us. Penington often speaks of "obedience". It is not, however, an active conforming to rules but a waiting on the Light, relocating the level of consciousness at which we relate to God from assertion of will—"I will obey the King's command"—to receptive attentiveness—"I am ready to be drawn into creativity by the Spirit's leading". "Redemption" is an ongoing process of creativity, not conformity, in relation to God who is not an outside judge and rule-giver but an intimate presence with whom we are united ("engrafted").[344]

"Remaining in" would be John's word for Isaac's "engrafted" (see "I am the vine" below), and it gives "the soul such a touch and taste of it at first as makes unsatisfiable without it".[345] However, I'm interrupting Melvin Keiser again:

Penington speaks of "Christ", meaning this intimate presence and this drawing into creativity, but he makes it clear that Christ is the symbol for him of the Life, not the object of biblical knowledge and belief; that would belong to the veiled self.[346]

"Christ is a symbol of the Life" is to say, in Jungian terms, that Christ is a symbol of the self. Within us the self appears as a God-image like Christ.[347] We find fulfilment in life to the extent that we become aware of the self, a process that Jung called individuation. Both Quakers and Jung see the process leading to a still centre:

The whole course of individuation is dialectical, and the so-called "end" is the confrontation of the ego with the "emptiness" of the centre. Here the limit of possible experience is reached: the ego dissolves as the reference-point of cognition. [348]

That silent "emptiness" at the centre is what Quaker worship seeks. As Melvin Keiser noted above, "That is why Quakers worship in silence, to become open to such depths".[349]

Jesus raises Lazarus (11:1-44)

[1]A certain man was ill, Lazarus of Bethany, the village of Mary and her sister Martha.[a] [2]It was Mary who anointed the Lord[b] with myrrh and wiped off his feet with her hair. Her brother was ill. [3]So the sisters sent to him saying, "Sir,[c] one you Love is ill." [4]When Jesus heard he said, "This illness is not to death but is for the glory of God, so that the son of God may be glorified through it."[d]

[5]Jesus Loved Martha, her sister, and Lazarus. [6]When he heard that he was ill, he then Remained where he was for two days. [7]Then later he says to the disciples,

---

[344] Keiser, *Knowing the Mystery of God Within*, page 149.

[345] Penington, *The Axe Laid to the Root*, in *Works*, volume 1, page 241.

[346] Keiser, *Knowing the Mystery of God Within*, page 149.

[347] Stein, *Jung's Treatment of Christianity*, pages 121 and 148

[348] Jung, *Letters*, volume 2, paragraph 259.

[349] Keiser, *Knowing the Mystery of God Within*, page 136.

"Let's go into back to Judea." [8]The disciples said to him, "Rabbi, Jews were trying to stone you just now, and you want to go back there?" [9]Jesus replied, "Aren't there twelve hours in a day? If someone walks around in the daytime, he does not stumble because he sees the Light of the World. [10]If someone walks at night, he stumbles because the Light is not in him."

[11]He said those things and then later he says to them, "Lazarus our friend has fallen asleep, but I go to wake him." [12]So the disciples said to him, "Lord, if he has fallen asleep he will be all right.[e] [13]Jesus, however, had been speaking of his death, but they thought that he was speaking of falling asleep. [14]So Jesus told them plainly, "Lazarus is dead. [15]I'm happy for you that we were not there so that you may Trust. But let us go to him." [16]So Thomas who is called Didymus[f] said to his fellow disciples, "Let us go too, so that we may die with him."

[17]When Jesus arrived, he found Lazarus had already been in the tomb four days. [18]Bethany was near Jerusalem, about two miles away. [19]Many Jews[g] had come to Martha and Mary to console them about their brother. [20]So when Martha heard that Jesus was coming she went out to meet him, but Mary stayed home. [21]Then Martha said to Jesus, "Sir, had you been here my brother would not have died, [22]but even now I Know God will give you whatever you ask for." [23]Jesus says to her, "Your brother will rise again." [24]Martha says to him, "I Know that he will rise again in the resurrection at the last day." [25]Jesus told her, "I am the resurrection and the Life.[h] Whoever Trusts in me will Live even if he dies, [26]and everyone who Lives and Trusts in me will certainly never die. Do you Trust me?" [27]She tells him, "Yes, sir, I have come to Trust that you are the Christ, the son of God coming into the World."

[28]After she said that, she left and called her sister Mary, and told her in private, "The teacher is here and asking for you." [29]When she heard, she got up quickly and went to him. [30]Now Jesus had not yet come to the village, but was still at the place where Martha went to meet him. [31]The Jews who were with her in the house consoling her, on seeing that she got up quickly and left, they followed her thinking that she is going to the tomb to weep there.

[32]Then as Mary came to where Jesus was, on seeing him, she fell at his feet telling him, "Sir, if you had been here my brother would not have died." [33]When Jesus saw her weeping, and the Jews who had come with her also weeping, he was upset in spirit and shook. [34]He said, "Where have you put him?" They told him, "Sir, come and see." [35]Jesus wept.[i] [36]So the Jews said, "See how he Loved him." [37]Some of them said, "Could he, who opened the eyes of the blind man, not do something so that he would not have died?"

[38]Then Jesus again, still inwardly upset, came to the tomb. It was a cave and a stone lay on it. [39]Jesus says, "Remove the stone." Martha, the sister of the dead man, says to him, "Sir, he stinks now because it's been four days." [40]Jesus tells her, "Did I not tell you that if you Trust you will see the glory of God?" [41]So they lifted away the stone, and Jesus looked up and said, "Father, I thank you that you hear me. [42](I have always known that you hear me, but I said that for the crowd standing round,[j] so that they may believe that you sent me.)" [43]After saying that, he shouted in a loud voice, "Lazarus, come out." [44]He who had died came out, his feet and hands bound with linen burial strips and his face still wrapped in a cloth. Jesus told them, "Unbind him and let him go."

Meaning and resonance

a. **"and her sister Martha"** (11:1): Some of the oldest manuscripts of John omit Martha from this story.[350]

b. **"Mary who anointed the Lord"** (11:2): In John, Mary anoints Jesus in 12:1-8, so that fact mentioned here by our all-knowing narrator has yet to happen in John's chronology.

c. **"Sir, the one you love is ill"** (11:3): "Sir" sounds too formal to be used among friends, but its use throughout this section shows that Jesus's friends had great respect for him as their teacher. "If (as is probable) the sisters spoke in Aramaic, then the natural mode of address would have been *Rabbi*."[351]

d. **"so that the son of God may be glorified through it"** (11:4): In John, Jesus refers to his last days as his "glorification" (12:23, 13:31-32; 16:14; 17:1, 5, 10, 22, 24), and, rather than "dying",[352] he says he will be "lifted up", both raised physically and exalted (ὑψόω). We shall see that the raising of Lazarus sets Jesus's "glorification" in motion, and this comment foreshadows it.

e. **"if he has fallen asleep he will be all right"** (11:12): "Will be all right" is the word σῴζω, which I usually translate as "Rescue", but here it just means recovery from illness. I noted above in relation to John 4:50 that Semitic languages like the Aramaic that Jesus spoke with friends did not have a word meaning to recover from illness.

f. **"Thomas who is called Didymus"** (11:16): "Thomas" is the Aramaic word for "twin", and Didymus is its Greek equivalent.[353]

g. **"Many Jews had come to Martha and Mary to console them"** (11:19): Here and John 4:22 are two rare examples of John speaking positively about Jews. It is likely that the mention of exclusion from synagogues (see the Reflection above) is a late addition in John because Jews and followers of Jesus have a perfectly amicable relationship in this chapter, which reflects normal life rather than staged debates with adversaries too demonised to be real. The presence of Jewish friends in this story shows that relations were not yet antagonistic but had become so in the narrator's time 60-70 years later.[354]

h. **"I am the resurrection and the Life"** (11:25): The idea of resurrection came late into Jewish thinking. It comes up in Daniel 12:2-3 and in 2 Maccabees 7:9 and 14 as a way for God to even up the scales of justice, as in 2 Maccabees 7:9, where a victim of murder by frying tells his killer,

---

[350] Coloe, *Wisdom Bible Commentary*, volume 44B, page 319-323. The oldest manuscript of John, 𝔓[66], has Mary's name replaced by "Martha" (the ι in "Μαρία" was erased and "θ" (th) written above it). Comfort & Barrett, eds., *The Complete Text of the Earliest New Testament Manuscripts*, page 418.

[351] Bruce, *The Gospel of John*, page 240; see also Carson, *The Gospel According to John*, page 406.

[352] The closest Jesus comes to speaking of his death is in metaphor. The Good Shepherd "lays down his life for his sheep" (John 10:16, 17, 28), and the seed must die in the ground to bear fruit (12:24). Coloe, *Wisdom Bible Commentary*, volume 44B, page 327.

[353] Bruce, *The Gospel of John*, page 241.

[354] Reinhartz, *Befriending the Beloved Disciple*, pages 41 and 155.

"You rip us from this present life, but the king of the universe will raise us again into eternal renewal of life." "Raise" in that sentence is the verb form of the word translated "resurrection" in 11.25 above. The same word appears in 11:24 and shows that Martha has this last-days resurrection in mind ("I know that he will rise again in the resurrection at the last day.")

The book of Wisdom has a different view. There "life is a participation already in the [eternal life] that is ... a gift of Sophia", who is wisdom personified. This participation is not a future event; it happens in the present.[355] In 11:25, Jesus reinterprets this Wisdom tradition by taking over the role of Sophia in providing eternal life. "He is wisdom incarnate, God reaching out to humanity to the fullest extent, as a human being."[356]

The book of Wisdom is part of what is sometimes called the Apocrypha, but that is a misleading name. The Apocrypha are Jewish scriptures for which no Hebrew text is extant. That distinction between the Apocrypha and the rest of the Old Testament is outmoded; Hebrew was a dead language after the Babylonian captivity. After Alexander, Greek was the *lingua franca* of the eastern Mediterranean, and there is no reason to discriminate against scriptures from that time merely for being in Greek.

In John, words are sometimes said to be Hebrew when really they are Aramaic *e.g.* 19:13 and 17, 20:16. The two were similar Semitic languages.

i. **"Jesus wept."** (11:35): Everyone weeps in this scene, but they weep differently. Jesus's weeping is the verb δακρύω, meaning that his tears fell. Everyone else does κλαίω, meaning to grieve, to weep out of grief. "The resurrection and the Life" is not said to be grieving here, though everyone else is. He may be weeping out of sympathy for his friends' grief, knowing that he will soon give them cause for more grief. The Jews in this story, as always in John, are mistaken in assuming grief, "See how he Loved him" (11:36).

j. **"I said that for the crowd standing around"** (11:42): This parenthetical must surely be a comment by our helpful narrator, and it shows that the narrator has no reservations about having Jesus himself speak his words in the first person.

With the raising of Lazarus, John's Book of Signs (which began with the wedding at Cana in John 2) ends.[357] We have reached here the turning point of John; the end of Jesus now begins. It will soon be Passover again, his Hour will come, and

---

[355] Coloe, *Wisdom Bible Commentary*, volume 44B, pages 316-319. Coloe notes that "of the 17 times "eternal Life" (ζωή αἰώνιον) appears in John, only twice does it appear directed toward the future (4:14; 12:25). Thus [John's] use of the term "[eternal life]" places this life in the present with the offer of Sophia in the book of Wisdom...." *Ibid.* pages 318-319. "Those who do not Trust are condemned already" in chapter 3 above has more on how John and Penington bring the last days into the present.

[356] Michel E. Willett, *Wisdom Christology in the Fourth Gospel* (San Francisco: Mellon Research University Press, 1992), page 127; quoted in Coloe, *Wisdom Bible Commentary*, volume 44B, page 318.

[357] *E.g.*, Brown, *The Gospel according to John*, volume 29, page 466; Reinhartz, *Cast out of the Covenant*, page 139.

then he will live only about a day longer. Now he will spend no more time teaching the public. Now his disciples become his main focus.

Caiaphas and the plot to kill Jesus (11:45-55)

45Then many of the Jews who came to Mary and saw what he did Trusted in him. 46But some of them went to the Pharisees and told them what Jesus had done.

47So the chief priests and the Pharisees convened the Council[a] and began by saying, "What do we do? Because this man is performing many Signs. 48If we let him go on, everyone will Trust in him, and the Romans will come and take away from us both our place and our nation." 49One of them, Caiaphas, the high priest that year,[b] said to them, "You know nothing whatsoever. 50Don't you think that it is better for you that one person die for the people rather than let the whole nation be destroyed?" 51He did not say this of himself, but because he was high priest that year, he prophesied that Jesus was about to die for the nation, 52and not only for the nation but to gather all the scattered children of God[c] into one.[d] 53So from that day on they were intent on killing him.

54So Jesus no longer went about openly among Jews, but went away from there to an area near the desert, to a town called Ephraim, and he Remained there with the disciples.

55The Passover of the Jews was coming soon,[e] and before Passover many went up from the countryside to Jerusalem to purify themselves.[f] 56They were looking for Jesus and saying among themselves as they stood in the Temple, "What do you think? Surely he'll not come to the festival, will he?" 57The chief priests and the Pharisees had given orders for anyone who Knew where he was to inform them, so that they might arrest him.

Meaning and resonance

a. **"the Council"** (11:47): The name of the Council was the Sanhedrin. It included the priestly class (Sadducees), some Pharisees, and perhaps other Jews.

b. **"the high priest that year"** (11:49, 51): Caiaphas was high priest from 18-36 B.C.E., "a longer period than any other high priest in New Testament times."[358] Numbers 35:25 says the high priest position was to be held for life; however, the Maccabean rulers of Judea made it a political office as much as a religious one, and it remained so in Jesus's time.[359] When the Romans took over, high priests were replaced often, every year or so, as political winds changed.[360] Caiaphas was replaced when Pilate was replaced in about 37 C.E.[361]

c. **"children of God"** (11:52) is ambiguous and ironic; Jews considered themselves God's own people, but it is not only from that nation or people (11:52) that the scattered children are gathered. The "prophecy" refers

> not only to the Jews, or to Diaspora Jews, but to the children of God whom the Prologue has already defined as

---

[358] Bruce, *The Gospel of John*, page 343.

[359] Keener, *The Gospel of John*, volume 1, page 431.

[360] Brown, *The Gospel According to John*, volume 29, page 439; Bruce, *The Gospel of John*, page 250.

[361] Bruce, *New Testament History*, page 38.

those "who received him [the Word], who believed in his name" (1:12). In other words, these are believers who are not Jews, therefore Gentiles.[362]

d. **"gather all the scattered children of God into one"** (11:52): Literally, into "one thing"; "one" here is the neuter singular, as in John 10:16. The same expression is used frequently in the great prayer of John 17.

e. **"The Passover of the Jews was coming soon"** (11:55): Three Passovers are mentioned in John (2:13; 4:4), leaving us to think that Jesus's public life lasted about three years. However, the second Passover may be the later Galilean celebration of the first Passover, and if so, the timing would be only two years. See <u>note on John 6:4</u>.

f. **"to purify themselves"** (11:55): Numbers 9:10 forbids an unclean person to participate in the Passover festival; see also 2 Chronicles 30:17-18.

Reflection

"better for you that one person die for the people" (11:50)

We know from the historian Josephus (of the generation just after Jesus) that Caiaphas's fear of Roman intervention was realistic because Rome repeatedly used military force against various would-be Jewish messiahs.[363] About 20 years before John was completed, Rome had destroyed the Temple and the rest of Judea because of a Jewish revolt fuelled by messianic zeal.[364]

Caiaphas expressed a realistic fear, then, but it was also crass to advocate killing someone merely as a political expedient. Helen K. Bond observes that

> what really matters to the high priest here is not simply the fate of the temple and the nation, but the maintenance of the status quo, his own supremacy, and that of his advisers. The pragmatic Jewish leader has no scruples in offering one man's life to safeguard his own position.[365]

She concludes:

> Caiaphas comes across as a hostile character, intent on self-preservation and callous in his disregard for human life. As high priest, he epitomizes Jewish opposition to Jesus and, like "the Jews" generally in [John], allies himself with the satanic forces of darkness and sin. Yet it is also apparent that John has some residual regard for the office of high priest; in that role, even a hostile character can unconsciously speak the words of God.[366]

So Caiaphas had a murdering mind and a lucid moment, and both are rationalised by his fear of the Romans. However, Murray Stein sees another, deeper motiva-

---

[362] Reinhartz, *Cast Out of the Covenant*, page 138. Martyn sees 11:52 in relation to 10:16 ("I have other sheep not of this fold") as referring to "Jewish-Christian conventicles". Martyn, *The Gospel of John in Christian History*, page 201.

[363] *Antiquities of the Jews*, 20:97-99; 20:169-72; 20:188; *Jewish War*, 2:258-63.

[364] Bruce, *New Testament History*, pages 94-100.

[365] Helen K. Bond, *Caiaphas: Friend of Rome and Judge of Jesus?* (Louisville, KY: Westminster John Knox, 2004), page 132, quoted in Reinhartz, *Caiaphas*, page 43.

[366] *Ibid.*, page 133 of Bond, quoted in Reinhartz, *Caiaphas*, page 43.

tor, namely envy. He notes how much envy fills the Bible. In most cultures, like that of the pagan Greeks, the gods have little interest or involvement in human beings, but the God of the Old Testament is different. He is heavily involved with his human creations,[367] particularly with his favourite ones. This favouritism created a long line of haves and have-nots, leaving the haves to gloat and the have-nots to envy:

- **Cain and Abel**: God preferred Abel's offering over Cain's. Cain was so envious that he killed his brother Abel.

- **Ishmael and Isaac**: Sarah had Abraham disinherit Ishmael and throw him and his mother out of their settlement. Ishmael nearly died in the desert. (Genesis 21:8-20)

- **Esau and Jacob**: Rebekah helped Jacob trick his father Isaac into giving him the birthright that would otherwise have gone to his older brother Esau (Genesis 27), who raised an army and came after Jacob (Genesis 33).

- **Joseph and his brothers**: Jacob favoured Joseph, the first child of his favourite wife Rachel. "When [Joseph's] brothers saw that their father loved him more than all his brothers, they hated him, and could not speak peaceably to him" (Genesis 37:4 NRSV). Soon his brothers spot an opportunity and sell him as a slave into Egypt. (Genesis 37:12-36)

- **Saul and David**: Saul was preferred and anointed king of Israel, but he fell out of favour by disobeying God in what seems a rather minor matter (1 Samuel 15-18). David takes his place.

With Abraham and Moses, this favouritism was codified as a covenant between God and the Israelites. Murray Stein:

> The classic text of the covenant is found in Deuteronomy, chapters 27-33. Here, Moses and the elders of Israel call the people together and explain the contract: the Israelites are to obey the law as it has been given by [God] through Moses, and in exchange for this obedience, "the Lord your God will set you high above all the nations of the earth."[368] This extraordinary promise is spelled out in detail: increase in cattle and flocks, plenty of grain for bread, defeat of enemies, and general prosperity and many children.[369]

Choosing a favourite and leaving others out produces "what we might call a 'specialness complex' ... which creates the shadow of envy in others."[370]

In Jesus comes the ultimate supplanter (see "No greater than Jacob" above). John's Jesus teaches that he is greater than Moses, David, and all the patriarchs:

> As Jesus emerges on the scene and makes his claims, he calls down upon himself the wrath of the displaced elder brothers. Jesus is standing in the position of the chosen, just like Abel, Isaac, Joseph, David. The established leaders of Israel in the

---

[367] Jung, *Answer to Job*, in *Collected Works*, volume 11, paragraph 569.

[368] Stein cites here Deuteronomy 28:1.

[369] Stein, *The Bible as Dream*, page 121. Stein also notes that these promises are followed by "a series of ferocious threats of punishment for disobedience." *Ibid.*, page 122.

[370] Stein, *The Bible as Dream*, page 117.

> Sanhedrin are placed into the role of Cain, Ishmael, and Joseph's disgruntled elder brothers who seethe with envy. The force motivating the priests and Pharisees to stir up the mob against Jesus is envy: the specialness of the people and their privileged position in history by virtue of the covenant is being directly challenged by an upstart young brother figure, and if they lost their position, their most central and deeply felt connection to the self would go along with it.[371]

The elder brothers in relation to Jesus are descendants of Israel, who "could join the new covenant [of Jesus] if [they] desired, but to do so [they] must first give up the claim of exclusive chosenness in favor of recognizing the lordship of Christ and the legitimacy of his new followers as children of God."[372] John shows that Israel, in the form of the Jews in John, never gave up the belief in their exclusive chosenness. It was and remains the bone marrow of Jewish identity.

In time, the upstart younger son Jesus came to have a greater following than the Pharisees, the only Jews to survive the destruction of Judea. The other side of the envy coin is the gloating superiority of medieval Christianity right down to the present, which has hung a "Cain-like identity"[373] on Jews. From their superior position in God's favour, Christians have historically disdained Jews, the prior occupants of the favoured position. The teachings of John's Jesus, and the rest of the New Testament, show how displacement of Jews from their favoured position was justified in words. Reinhartz shows how in traditional Christian eyes Caiaphas has come to be the epitome of a Jewish stereotype in film and Christian culture.[374] To avoid the same pitfall, it is important to keep in mind that, according to John, Jesus dies because his Father requires it (12:27-28), not because Caiaphas is murderously minded. Like Pilate, an earthly authority such as Caiaphas would have no power over Jesus unless it was allowed "from above" (John 19:11).

In all this story, Caiaphas was in a predicament that calls for empathy. He was tormented by God's injustice, like Job. The demand to accept a replacement *in one's own position*, after doing nothing wrong and scrupulously keeping the law, is harsh and unfair. Caiaphas and other Jews did nothing to deserve their displacement from God's favour. It would be easy to judge Caiaphas as Job's friends judged Job, with seemingly the best of intentions, but in reality damning him all the more because his friends never took account of what God's will was. They could not bear to see the injustice in God's will.

The envy that drives the action in the Caiaphas story has its taproot in that injustice. Fear and envy, left unconscious, came to be acted out in reality and and projected onto other people. Jesus, with his enviable and charismatic personality, had to die; and his death was justified by a rationalisation involving Rome but emotionally driven by fear and most of all envy. Emotions are not things we decide to have or do; emotions happen to us,[375] and what we cannot

---

[371] Stein, *The Bible as Dream*, page 123.

[372] Stein, *The Bible as Dream*, page 128.

[373] Stein, *The Bible as Dream*, page 127.

[374] Reinhartz, *Caiaphas*, pages 52-124.

[375] Jung, *Aion*, in *Collected Works*, volume 9, part 2, paragraph 15: "Emotion is not an activity of the individual but something that happens to him."

inwardly face up to we encounter in reality. A possibility feared rather than faced will become fact. Envy not faced will pull down the rival, litigating the rival's unfair destiny all the way down to mutual destruction.

However, we have an alternative now, with psychotherapy available:

> The repressed, inferior or shadow aspects of our personality may be acknowledged and enacted, rather than acted out: acting after we have digested and reflected, as distinct from acting impulsively and without conscious thought or awareness.[376]

Caiaphas was not as fortunate as he had no real psychological help in his predicament. Jesus was killed as Caiaphas had advised. Forty years after that there was no longer any high priest or Temple. What Caiaphas had feared came true, but there was no way available to him to avoid living out his envy and fear as fate. As envious people do, he pulled down his rival, but he also ruined his nation. It would indeed have been better "that one person die for the people" but as it was, his "whole nation was destroyed" (John 11:50).

I am not going to judge Caiaphas for the downfall of his people. He is a tragic figure, a victim of his own psychological shortcomings, like many who never get help.

> [T]he feelings that arise in us are neither moral nor immoral, but neutral. The supreme importance of morality is the way we choose to act on our feelings. And we shall not be free to choose if we do not know what they are.[377]

Caiaphas was far from unusual in failing to see his negative, destructive feelings. Indeed, both of the Quakers whom Jung is known to have encountered were people of inordinate positivity on the surface and blind to the evil within them.

The first case was mentioned, not by Jung, but by two Englishmen writing about him. Kenneth Lambert recalled:

> A man told Jung about a Quaker who seemed a perfectly good man. So where was his shadow? Jung asked about his wife. Apparently she was perfect, too. His children? 'Oh,' said the inquirer, one of them is a thief'. …. Jung's comment was, 'The son assumes the father's shadow. His father was stealing, you see, [his sins from God]. The son was punished for the father's sins not rendered to God.'[378]

A.I. Allenby adds, speaking of the same anecdote, that the man's other child, a daughter, was a prostitute.[379] "Because the father could not relate to his shadow, his children were compelled to live out the dark side which he had ignored."[380] Did his good Quaker simplicity leave him outwardly austere but covertly envious, a quality his son took on and acted out to get back at his father for his hypocrisy?

---

[376] Stone, "Individuation", in Mathers, ed., *Vision and Supervision*, page 69.

[377] Jungian Jack Wallis, quoted in Britain Yearly Meeting, *Quaker Faith and Practice*, no. 21.11.

[378] McGuire & Hull, *C.G. Jung Speaking*, page 163.

[379] *Ibid.*, page 161.

[380] *Ibid.* These are Allenby's words recalling Jung's.

John tells us more about Caiaphas than anyone, but he doesn't mention his family. Did his son react to his father's "hidden" envy and become a thief too?

The other Quaker whom Jung met was an idealistic young American Friend from Utah, George H. Hogle. He recalled "training for foreign relief work with the American Friends Service Committee in Philadelphia during 1946." There he met several Quakers who were also interested in Jungian psychology. George Hogle then went to Germany, where he (in his words)

> was working with the Quakers in Germany to rebuild the bridges of friendship between enemies and that the next big job, I felt, was already looming on the horizon; namely, to reach out across the Iron Curtain and make some kind of friendship with the Russians. I felt that the Friends' approach would lessen tensions and be an example of mutual brotherhood.
>
> [Jung] snickered, or something like that, and said he would not advise it; it would be quite impossible to work with the Russians or reach them, you could not trust them, they had broken their agreements many times. I replied, so had we, which was, of course, not mentioned in the Western press, and that somehow we needed to get beyond that. But he simply was adamant. Finally, he patted me on the shoulder and, with a big smile, said, 'Well, we don't have to agree about everything.'[381]

Young Hogle had sought out Jung, after his time in Germany, to discover "what I should do with my life". He said Jung "dealt graciously and helpfully with [that] impossible inquiry", but

> [i]nstead of answering my questions he gave me other better questions to ask myself over the succeeding months. I told him something of my belief that God is good and love, at which he inquired, 'But do you think that God may also include hate and evil?'[382]

Hogle then saw that for Jung, "God includes all just as the individual self both the divine centre and the shadow, that Satan must be another aspect of God." Hogle's recollection ended with Jung encouraging him "to go into psychology and [Jung] gave me the names of analysts, especially recommending Frances Wickes."[383] Hogle went into analysis with Frances Wickes and became a psychiatrist and analyst himself.[384] Caiaphas never understood his problems, but George Hogle understood his. His idealism was not wrong, just one-sided and lacking the depth to see its unconscious counterweight. George lived to be 100 years old and remained a Quaker. He also retained his ideals but learned to balance them against the darker impulses of men, as seen in this quotation from 2006, nine years before his death:

---

[381] McGuire & Hull, *C.G. Jung Speaking*, page 171.

[382] *Ibid.*, pages 171-172.

[383] *Ibid.*, page 172.

[384] *Ibid.*, page 170.

> I feel good that I have been part of the movements to bring the public's attention to the potential medical consequences of nuclear war and crucial need for arms' control and East-West accord. And now that we men have brought the world close to the terrorism of the atom and of 'other' men, I submit that more and more women in leadership roles everywhere could benefit the world more than anyone could imagine.[385]

Quaker Jungian Jack Wallis was aware of this fault in Friends of being overly positive and blind to shadowy aspects. He borrowed William James's term for it and called it being "healthy minded".[386] He then offered queries:

> Is there perhaps an element of Healthy Mindedness among Quakers? Do we tend sometimes to deny the same status to evil as to good? Can we accept both Inner Light and Inner Dark? We speak sometimes of the Inner Voice and indeed experience it as a reality, as the prompting of God within our heart. Can we accept the possible reality of a second Inner Voice also? Or do we shut our ears like those monkeys that 'Hear no evil' and 'see no evil'?[387]

Britain Yearly Meeting summed up the point with a simple advice and query:

> Be honest with yourself. What unpalatable truths might you be evading?[388]

The Hour comes (chapter 12)

[1]Then six days before Passover Jesus came to Bethany, where Lazarus was, whom Jesus had raised from the dead. [2]They made dinner for him there, Martha served, and Lazarus was one of those at the table with him.

[3]Then Mary took a pound[a] of expensive perfume made of genuine nard,[b] anointed Jesus's feet and wiped them with her hair. The house was filled with the fragrance of the ointment. [4]Judas Iscariot,[c] one of his disciples who was about to hand him over, says, [5]"Why was this perfume not sold for 300 denari[d] and given to the poor?" ([6]He said this not because he was concerned about the poor but because he was a thief and used to keep the money box and steal what was put into it.) [7]Then Jesus told him, "Let her go on. She bought it for the day of my preparation for burial. [8]You always have the poor with you, but me you do not always have."

[9]When the great crowd of Jews Realised he was there, they came not because of Jesus alone but to see Lazarus whom he raised from the dead. [10]The chief priests planned to kill Lazarus also [11]because many Jews were beginning to leave[e] and Trust in Jesus.

---

[385] From his obituary in the *Salt Lake Tribune*, February 2016, online at https://www.legacy.com/us/obituaries/saltlaketribune/name/george-hogle-obituary?id=21409791 (last retrieved 5 August 2023).

[386] Wallis, *Jung and the Quaker Way*, page 9.

[387] *Ibid.*, pages 9-10.

[388] "Advices and Queries" no. 11, in *Quaker Faith and Practice*, section 1.02.

[12]On the next day the great crowd that had come to the festival, on hearing that Jesus was coming into Jerusalem, [13]took branches of palm trees and went out to meet him shouting, "Hosanna! Blessed is the one who comes in the name of the Lord, the king of Israel."[f] [14]Jesus found a young donkey and sat on it, just as is written, "Fear not, daughter of Zion. Look, your king is coming seated on a donkey colt."

[16]His disciples did not understand these things at first, but when Jesus was glorified,[g] they then remembered that these things had been written of him and were done to him. [17]So the crowd that was with him when he called Lazarus out of the tomb and raised him from the dead continued to be Witnesses. [18]It was also because they had heard that he had done that Sign that they went out to meet him. [19]The Pharisees then said among themselves, "Do you see that you are doing nothing? Now the World has gone after him."

[20]Among those who went up to worship at the festival were some Greeks.[h] [21]They came to Philip, who was from Bethsaida of Galilee, and were asking him, "Sir, we wish to see Jesus." [22]Philip goes to Andrew, and Andrew and Philip go and speak to Jesus. [23]Jesus answers them by saying, "The Hour has come for the son of man to be glorified.[i] [24]Very truly I tell you, if a kernel of wheat does not fall to the earth and die, it Remains alone; but if it dies, it bears much fruit. [25]One who Loves his life will destroy it, and one who hates his life in this World will keep it for eternal Life.[j] [26]One who serves me is also to follow me, and where I am, there my servant will also be. Whoever serves me my Father will honour."

[27]"Now my soul is troubled.[k] What do I say? 'Father, Rescue me from this Hour?' But that is why I came to this Hour. [28]Father, glorify your name!" Then a voice came from the sky, "I have glorified it and will glorify it again." [29]The crowd standing there also heard it and were saying it was thunder. Others were saying an angel had spoken with him. [30]Jesus answered, "This voice is not for me but for you. [31]Now is the crucial time for this World; now the ruler of this World will be thrown out. [32]When I am lifted up from the earth,[l] I will draw all to me."[m] [33]He said this to make known what sort of death he was about to die.

[34]Then the crowd replied, "We heard from the law that the Christ Remains for eternity, and now you say that the son of man must be lifted up? Who is this 'son of man'"? [35]Jesus said to them, "The Light is with you a little while longer. Walk while you have the Light, so that the darkness does not overtake you. While you have the Light, Trust in the Light, so that you may become children of the Light." After Jesus said these things, he left and hid from them.

[37]Although he had performed so many Signs before them,[n] they did not begin to Trust in him, [38]so that the word of Isaiah the prophet may be fulfilled,[o] which he said:

>Who has believed our report?[p]
>And to whom is the arm of the Lord revealed?

[39]That is why they could not Trust, because again Isaiah said:

>[40]He has blinded their eyes[q]
>and hardened their heart,[r]
>lest they see with their eyes
>and understand with their hearts
>and turn, and I will heal them.

[41]Isaiah said this because he saw his glory and spoke about him. [42]However, many, even from the authorities, Trusted in him, but because of the Pharisees they did not acknowledge it so that they would not be put out of the synagogue, [43]for they Loved the glory of people more than the glory of God.

[44]Jesus shouted and said,[r] "Whoever Trusts in me Trusts not me but the one who sent me, [45]and whoever sees me sees him who sent me. [46]I have come as a Light into the World so that everyone who Trusts in me may not Remain in darkness. [47]I do not judge anyone[s] who hears my words but does not keep them, for I did not come to judge the World but to save the World. [48]Whoever rejects me and does not receive my words has a judge; on the last day, the word I spoke will judge him, [49]because I did not speak of myself, but the Father who sent me has given me a commandment what to say and what to speak. [50]And I Know that his commandment is eternal Life. What I say I say just as the Father has told me to say."

Meaning and resonance

a. **"a pound"** (12:3): A Roman pound was about 12 ounces or 327 grams.[389] For an aromatic oil imported by caravan from northern India (see "genuine nard" below), this was a large quantity.

b. **"genuine nard"** (12:3): "Also known as spikenard, [nard] is a fragrant oil derived from the root and spike ... of the nard plant which grows in the mountains of northern India."[390]

A tougher word to understand is the one translated "genuine". It is the Greek word πιστικός, which is rare and means "faithful", though that meaning makes no sense in relation to perfume. In the New Testament, πιστικός occurs only in describing this perfume, here and in Mark 14:3. The meaning of πιστικός is not clear; "genuine" is a guess based on Brown and Carson.[391]

c. **"Judas Iscariot"** (12:4): John 6:71-72 identifies Judas as "son of Simon, the Iscariot". "Iscariot" probably means "from Kerioth", a town in southern Judea.[392]

Judas (Judah in Hebrew) was a very common Jewish name because Judah was the son of Jacob (renamed Israel) from whom all Jews were descended. Because his name was so common, Judas was often further identified by his father's home town.

d. **"300 denari"** (12:5): One denarion was an average worker's daily wage.[393] Allowing for Sabbaths and holy days, this would have been a year's wages for a Jewish worker.

e. **"many Jews were beginning to leave"** (12:11): Reinhartz points out that this "leaving" was voluntary, and I agree.[394] She goes on, based on 12:11, to doubt that Jewish synagogues expelled the community that wrote John:

---

[389] Bauer, Arndt, Gingrich & Danker, *A Greek-English Lexicon of the New Testament*, page 475.

[390] Brown, *The Gospel According to John*, volume 29, page 448.

[391] *Ibid.*; Carson, *The Gospel According to John*, page 428.

[392] Brown, *The Gospel According to John*, volume 29, page 298.

[393] Bauer, Arndt, Gingrich & Danker, *A Greek-English Lexicon of the New Testament*, page 179.

[394] *Befriending the Beloved Disciple*, page 43.

> In [John 12:10-11], the Jewish leadership is upset about Jews who begin to believe in Jesus; the fact that they equate such belief with desertion implies that they view faith in Christ as incompatible with Judaism. But nothing indicates that the authorities can actually expel Jewish believers in Christ from the Jewish community. The "expulsion" theory cannot accommodate the complex relationships between the Johannine and Jewish communities implied by an ecclesiological reading of the Gospel as a whole.[395]

She may be right as a legal matter; I have no reason to think that expulsion of Jews from synagogues was legal or customary under Jewish law, either at Jesus's time or in the very different Judaism that prevailed when John was undergoing its final edit.

In any case, psychologically it is clear from 12:11 that a great antipathy has arisen by the time John is written, and its author is angry at Jews. In Jesus's time, as the Jews in the Lazarus story show, relations still seem harmonious, but after the destruction of the Temple, when John reached its final form, hostility had set in that was very likely mutual; anger is psychologically reactive and infectious. It is difficult to know from the subtle clues in the text what exactly happened, but I can't rule out expulsion, given the fact that the community of John ended up outside the synagogues and furious about it.

However, noting that anger was involved does not justify recording it for later generations, and it certainly does not justify antisemitism. See "Is John antisemitic?" above. Reinhartz is surely right in thinking that both sides in John are undergoing a "difficult struggle for self-definition" after the destruction of Judea.[396]

f. **"Hosanna! Blessed is the one who comes in the name of the Lord, the king of Israel"** (12:13): "Hosanna" is Hebrew for "Save" or "Rescue".[397]

Most of that sentence is a quotation is from Psalm 118:26, and the blessing was upon people coming to the Temple. However, the Jews in John 12 give it a new spin. Psalm 118 celebrates the Temple, but the Jews acclaiming Jesus repurpose Psalm 118:26 to celebrate him, adding that he is "King of Israel", words not in the Psalm. Jews had earlier acclaimed Simon the Maccabee with the same words and with palm branches (1 Maccabees 13:41).

Jesus's action in finding and riding a young donkey "corrects the crowd's limited nationalistic perception."[398] His action recalls Zephaniah 3:16, which the narrator recites in the text ("Fear not, O daughter of Zion"). Zephaniah 3 foretells that God will "gather all nations" (3:18); echoed in John 12:32, "I will draw all to me." "Jesus is entering Jerusalem not as king of Israel but as God incarnate, who has come to gather all the

---

[395] Reinhartz, "The Gospel of John: How the Jews Became Part of the Plot", page 115.-

[396] *Ibid.*

[397] Brown, *The Gospel of John*, volume 29, page 457.

[398] Coloe, *Wisdom Bible Commentary*, volume 44B, page 341.

nations."[399]   However, let's not overlook the irony of "God incarnate" arriving in the great city to great acclaim, on a "young donkey". An adult donkey is about half the size of an adult man. Jesus would probably have had to hold his feet up so they would not drag on the ground.

The second scripture recalled by the narrator in John 12:13 is Zechariah 9:9, but the narrator omits the text bracketed below:

> Lo, your king comes to you; [triumphant and victorious is he, humble and riding on a donkey,] on the colt, the foal of a donkey.[400]

"By omitting part of the citation, the Gospel refrains from interpreting the action as a gesture of humility. Once again, the context in Zechariah is most significant, for this king will 'command peace to the nations; his dominion shall be from sea to sea, and from the River to the ends of the earth' (Zechariah 9:10)."[401]

Jesus thus disclaims the role of political Messiah and presents himself as one in a position to save all nations. Then the Jews in John 12 lament that "the whole World is going after him" (12:19), and, sure enough, Greeks arrive in the story right on cue (12:20).

g. **"His disciples did not understand**..." (12:16): The full sentence is this:

> His disciples did not understand these things at first, but when Jesus was glorified, they then remembered that these things had been written of him and were done to him.

They remembered later because they had help:

> The Counsellor, the Holy Spirit, whom the Father will send in my name, will teach you everything and remind you of all I have said to you. (John 14:26)

h. **"at the festival were some Greeks"** (12:20): In the New Testament, 'Greeks' are not necessarily ethnically Greek; in that part of the Near East, 'Greeks' were people who spoke Greek, and most people involved in business or public life spoke Greek. It was the *lingua franca* of the eastern Mediterranean, even though many Jews in Judea spoke Aramaic among themselves. Alexander the Great had spread Greek culture by his conquests about 350 years earlier, and his successors and the ensuing expansion of trade made Greek the main language of the eastern Mediterranean.

In this passage, some think "Greeks" means Greek-speaking Jews attending at the Passover festival. However, in that case, the Greek word would not be "Ἕλληνες" but "Ἑλλενισταί", meaning not native Greek but "hellenised".[402]

---

[399] *Ibid.,* page 342.

[400] Translated by Coloe in *Wisdom Bible Commentary,* volume 44B, page 343-344.

[401] *Ibid.,* page 343.

[402] Brown, *The Gospel according to John,* volume 29A, page 466; Martyn, *The Gospel of John in Christian History,* page 202. They both see these Greeks as Greek natives who have converted to Judaism like the Ethiopian eunuch in Acts 8.

Given the context, these Greeks are Gentiles and their presence is a sign that the oracles about the eschatological gathering of the nations to Jerusalem are now being fulfilled. In response to this sign, Jesus declares, "The Hour has come for the son of man to be glorified."[403]

Adele Reinhartz adds:

> [I]t is significant that what the Greeks request is to *see* Jesus. The Greeks are anxious to do what the Jews refuse to do: truly see Jesus for who he is. This contrast—between the Greeks who ask to see and the Jews who refuse to see— is key to this passage, to the rhetorical message of the Gospel as a whole, and to its aim and audience.[404]

i. **"The Hour has come for the son of man to be glorified."** (12:23): The Hour (see "John's key words" below) has finally come, after being foreshadowed in John 2:4, 4:21-23, 5:25-28; 7:30; 8:20.

The word "glory" (δόξα) originally meant an opinion, including the opinion people have of someone, *i.e.* a reputation. It could mean fame, assuming the reputation was good.[405] In the Greek Old Testament, δόξα was used to translate the Hebrew *yichra*, meaning the radiance (numinosity) of God and the Temple, the awe-inspiring sense of being in the presence of God.[406] The New Testament frequently uses "glory" in a similar sense of "brightness" or "radiance" (*e.g.* Acts 22:11), as well as in the sense of "fame", as in John 12:43.

j. **"whoever hates his life in this World will keep it for eternal Life"** (12:25): The full text of 12:25 is:

> One who loves his life will destroy it, and one who hates
> his life in this World will keep it for eternal Life.

Two different kinds of life indicated by two different Greek words, ψυχή and ζωή. The full verse shows where each word is used; I have translated ψυχή as (natural) life and ζωή as "Life", capitalised because it is listed in "John's key words" below.

k. **"Now my soul is troubled."** (12:27): Besides meaning natural, physical (rather than spiritual) life, ψυχή also means "soul". The word ταράσσω ("troubled", same word as in John 5:7) can mean a physical disturbance, and perhaps we have wordplay here with that sense. In any case, "troubled" expresses the psychological unease faced by the son of man in coming to terms with his destiny—except, as ever with John's Jesus and the less desirable aspects of his soul, he doesn't face the problem for long. He expressly represses it in the rest of 12:27:

---

403 Coloe, *Wisdom Bible Commentary*, volume 44B, page 343.

404 *Cast out of the Covenant*, page 140.

405 Liddell, Scott & James, *Greek-English Lexicon*, entry "δόξα".

406 Coloe, *Wisdom Bible Commentary*, volume 44A, pages 23-26.

> Now my soul is troubled. What do I say? 'Father, Rescue
> me from this Hour?' But that is why I came to this Hour.
> Father, glorify your name!

Perhaps "represses" is a bit harsh; he will now live only a couple of days so perhaps he is choosing his moment for facing the trouble. He needs to prepare his disciples first.

The trouble in his mind was the dawning of his awareness of his unconscious, which is the opposite of his conscious attitude of calm detachment. That awareness will increase until there he is, on the cross, torn apart by good on the one hand and evil on the other, both now in full view. Yet he—willingly, it seems—passes through the process as a humble but strong son of man. Why? Carl Jung had a reason:

> Here [on the cross] his human nature gains divinity: at that moment God experiences what it means to be a mortal man and drinks to the dregs what he has made his faithful servant Job suffer. Here is given the answer to Job, and, clearly, this supreme moment is as divine as it is human....[407]

For each of us, wholeness means integrating the unconscious, including the self, into consciousness, into the ego, the part of me that I refer to when I say "I". For more on this theme, see "The cross" and "Opposites in John and Jung" below.

l. "**When I am lifted up from the earth**" (12:32): "Lift up" is the word ὑψόω, which is is an old "play on words with an ambiguous expression which can mean [advancement] in social position as well as being lifted up on a cross before the eyes of all."[408] John uses it in both the physical sense (lifted on a cross) and in the sense of exaltation. It appears three times in John. The other two places are:

John 3:14-15:

> Just as Moses lifted up the snake in the desert, so must the son of man be lifted up, so that everyone who Trusts in him may have eternal Life.

John 8:28:

> When you lift up the son of man, then you will know that I am, and I do nothing of my own accord, and I say just what the Father taught me to say.

m. "**I will draw all to me**" (12.30): The text of "all" is uncertain. Mary Coloe: There is a disagreement in the manuscript tradition as to whether the [word translated "all" above] should be πάντα (all things [including people]) or πάντας (all people). 𝔓⁶⁶ and ℵ[409] are strong witnesses to πάντα, and the cosmic

---

[407] *Answer to Job*, in *Collected Works*, volume 11, paragraph 408.

[408] Bauer, Arndt, Gingrich & Danker, *A Greek-English Lexicon of the New Testament*, page 850.

[409] 𝔓⁶⁶ is the abbreviation for papyrus Bodmer II, which dates from about 150 C.E. (Comfort & Barrett, eds., *The Complete Text of the Earliest New Testament Manuscripts*, page 366.) ℵ is Codex Sinaiticus, about 350 C.E. See Codex Sinaiticus - About Codex Sinaiticus (retrieved 11 March 2023).

dimension of Jesus' mission has just been announced, making "all things" a credible reading; but it is also possible that the final sigma [of πάντας] was added by a copyist who found πάντα ambiguous.[410]

n. **"Although he had performed so many Signs before them"** (12:37): See "Unless you see Signs..." above for a reflection on how this is so.

o. **"so that the word of Isaiah ... may be fulfilled"** (12:38): In about 95 C.E., when John was completed, it must have been difficult

> to make sense of the fact that Jesus, and the later gospel message, was unacceptable to many within Judaism, while the community's post-Easter mission to Gentiles was successful. How could this be possible? The narrator's answer is that this was to fulfil the scriptures.[411]

Unfortunately, that answer raises still more questions for me, and for those, I have as yet no answer. I don't know why Jesus came to his own and they did not accept him but the Gentiles did, but I do not believe that Isaiah's foretelling of it caused it.

p. **"Who has believed our report?"** (12:38): The scripture quoted is Isaiah 53:1, "part of the Fourth Servant Song which begins, 'Behold my servant shall prosper; he shall be lifted up [ὑψόω] and glorified'" (Isaiah 52:13).[412] That lifting up and glorification are major themes in John 12. Like Jesus, but unlike the Davidic Messiah hoped for by Jews, the suffering servant in Isaiah is rejected, suffers, and dies (Isaiah 53:3-11).

q. **"He has blinded their eyes..."** (12:40): Quoting Isaiah 6:10, probably from memory because this is not an exact quotation of either the Greek or Hebrew text.[413]

r. **"Jesus shouted and said..."** (12:44): This last paragraph of John 12 is said to be words shouted by Jesus, but he has just gone into hiding (12:37). Because shouting defeats the purpose of hiding, Brown thinks this is a fragment from elsewhere inserted here as a summation, before the audience becomes limited to the disciples.[414] He is surely right about the insertion, but I doubt it is a summation. It scarcely even begins to summarise what has gone before.

s. **"I do not judge anyone..."** (12:47): Recall from John 3:17 that the word κρίνω basically means to judge, but often has negative connotations, *i.e.* "condemn". I have opted for the more neutral wording here, although that rather distorts the alignment with 3:17-20.

---

[410] Coloe, *Wisdom Bible Commentary*, volume 44B, page 344, note 24.

[411] Coloe, *Wisdom Bible Commentary*, volume 44B, pages 348-349.

[412] Coloe, *Wisdom Bible Commentary*, volume 44B, page 349.

[413] Coloe, *Wisdom Bible Commentary*, volume 44B, page 350.

[414] *The Gospel According to John*, volume 29, page 490-493.

Reflection

"Glorify your name" (12:27)

"Your name" refers to "I am", the name Jesus has been using for himself throughout John. It is also the name of the God of the Old Testament, the God of Abraham and Moses. It is also the name of the God of Job, his tormentor. Now that God's son is about to die so that his Father can know how it feels to lose a son.[415] God in Job does not appear to be omniscient; indeed, he barely seems conscious at all until the end. Now the Father's knowledge is about to come at a terrible price.

The concept of spiritual radiance, translated "glory" in the Bible (from δόξα), resembles what Jung calls the "numinosum", a term he borrowed from Rudolf Otto, who studied the religious experiences of many cultures and noted a common element in them, for which he coined the term "numinosum".[416] "To enter into the presence of 'the Holy' was for [Otto] to be shaken to the foundations by the power and awesome magnitude of the Other who is confronted in this experience."[417]

Chapters 4 ("no greater than our father Jacob") and 6 ("the Father draws him") have considered some aspects of the numinous. Let's look now at its healing aspect. Carl Jung wrote in a letter:

> It has always seemed to me as if the real milestones were certain symbolic events characterized by a strong emotional tone. You are quite right, the main interest in my work is not concerned with the treatment of neuroses but rather with the approach to the numinous. But the fact is that the approach to the numinous is the real therapy and inasmuch as you attain to numinous experiences you are released from the curse of pathology.[418]

"Numinous experiences" come as the self becomes more conscious. They light the way to a release from pathology, or rather, from the "curse" of it, alluding perhaps to the Eden myth.

It is not possible for my will to make a numinous experience. Years ago my uncle led a group of us teenagers, who thought ourselves very spiritual, on a quest for "spiritual experiences" as he called them, experiences of the numinous. A sort of spiritual hedonism was the result as we endeavoured to cause the Spirit to give us an experience of its numinous effect. The Spirit, however, doesn't work that way; "the Spirit blows where it will, and you hear the sound of it, but you don't know where it comes from or where it goes to" (John 3:8). "The numinosum is a dynamic agency or effect not caused by an arbitrary act of will."[419] In Quaker meetings, Friends wait for the Spirit's presence, but we do not make it come, nor can we.

---

[415] See "Jung's view of God's relationship with humanity" in the introduction.

[416] Stein, *The Principle of Individuation*, pages 49-62.

[417] Stein, "The Importance of Numinous Experience", page 39.

[418] Adler and Jaffe, *C.G. Jung Letters*, volume 1, page 377.

[419] Jung, *Collected Works*, volume 11, paragraph 6.

Much human suffering can come from trying to experience the numinous when in reality, we do not control the Spirit (John 3:8). It happens to us, if we are open to it. Jung treated a patient who was an alcoholic, and in the earliest days of Alcoholics Anonymous, that patient, Roland, was one of very few cases to recover from alcoholism. When his friend and the founder of Alcoholics Anonymous, Bill W., wrote Jung to enquire why Roland had come to recover, Jung explained:

> His craving for alcohol was the equivalent, on a low level, of the spiritual thirst of our being for wholeness, expressed in medieval language: the union with God.
>
> ....
>
> The only right and legitimate way to such an experience is that it happens to you in reality, and it can only happen to you when you walk on a path which leads you to higher understanding. You might be led to that goal by an act of grace, or through a personal and honest contact with friends, or through a higher education of the mind [such as psychotherapy] beyond the confines of mere rationalism. I see from your letter that Roland has chosen the second way, which was, under the circumstances, obviously the best one.[420]

That yearning of the soul for wholeness drives the process Jung called "individuation". The way to be "released from the curse of pathology" does not lie in *seeking* numinous experiences, and much less in faking them with dopamine releases brought on by intoxication. The "only genuine cure for neurosis is to grow out of it through pursuing individuation."[421]

Murray Stein describes individuation as a process of "analysis and synthesis."[422] The process begins by breaking free of "the affectively charged 'voices' or 'images'" embedded in the psyche. In those "voices or images":

> are represented the figures with whom one is identified or to whom one is bound emotionally by affective ties—parents, mentors, lovers, community leaders, enemies, 'ghosts' etc." The reality of psychological life requires that in analysis we confront voices and images that communicate feeling and

---

[420] Jung's letter is quoted entirely and verbatim in Schoen, *The War of the Gods in Addiction: C.G. Jung, Alcoholics Anonymous, and Archetypal Evil*, pages 19-20. On reading AA's Twelve Steps, it becomes clear that Jung's letter had a profound effect on them. For example, the second step is, "We came to believe that a power greater than ourselves could restore us to sanity."

[421] Stein, "The Importance of Numinous Experience", page 34. Stein describes this is the "classical Jungian view"; in my brief introduction to Jung, I stick with this "classical view" rather than look into further development of Jungian thought.

"Individuation" is a technical term for what a person experiences through symbols more meaningful to that person than the technical term.

[422] *Ibid.*, page 24; see also Stein, *The Mystery of Transformation* pages 55-100.

emotion; we do not confront inner structures [like persona, anima/animus, shadow] as such.[423]

For Bill W., part of this breaking free involved escaping his "religious tradition [which] had become, as it has for modern people generally, Procrustean."[424] The solution for him was suggested by a friend, "Why don't you choose your own conception of God?"[425]

The synthesis stage of individuation begins by perceiving numinous experiences when they occur, those "signals of transcendence" described in "No one can can come to me unless the Father ... draws him" (John 6) above. Numinosity is the radiant quality of what "transcendence" reveals.

A psychological explanation[426] for "the glory of God" (God's numinosity) comes from Murray Stein:

> The psychological explanation for numinous experiences ... lies in the phenomenon of projection, whereby unconscious contents are "found" in physical objects, rituals, or sounds that elicit them. In religious experience, the psychologist claims, the ego is experiencing a content of the unconscious in projection. The stronger the experience, the more archetypal is the content. Such experiences link conscious-ness to the unconscious and offer "hints" that may be deciphered as communications. These hints can lead to a deeper perspective on life from the viewpoint of the collective unconscious and are essential for the psychological process of individuation if they can be brought forward and made conscious.[427]

The experience of the numinous, the glory of God, and the "hints" there revealed, become a gateway through which unconscious content becomes conscious and integrated into a person becoming more whole:

> [A] dynamic tension inherently exists between unconscious and consciousness. Out of this emerges the transcendent function: "a natural process, a manifestation of the energy that springs from the tension of opposites, and it consists in a series of fantasy-occurrences which appear spontaneously in dreams and visions".[428] It allows a way through internal conflict leading to the growth and establishment of a new

---

[423] *Ibid.*

[424] *Ibid.*, page 38.

[425] Alcoholics Anonymous, *Alcoholics Anonymous*, (known in AA circles as "the Big Book") 3rd edition, (New York: Alcoholics Anonymous World Services), page 12.

[426] Understanding the psychology of the numinous does not rule out there being more to "the glory of God" than numinous radiance. If a person believes in God, there is no harm in understanding why some aspects of God radiate transformative holiness for one person, and other aspects do that for someone else, and why we all find much of it, the universal glory of God, to be shared among us all.

[427] "The Importance of Numinous Experience", page 46.

[428] Stein cites here Jung's *Collected Works*, volume 8 paragraph 121.

position. In this way it can bridge the gap between conscious and unconscious, between ego and self, between rational and irrational. This, in Jung's view, leads through symbolic transformation towards individuation.[429]

Although wilfully seeking out the numinous is fruitless and frustrating, it is also easy to miss the numinous, like everything served up to us by our unconscious minds. "Is it not strange," wrote Isaac Penington, "that thou shouldst be [made] of it, and not be able to know and own it...?"[430] Catching sight of the numinous when it comes to awareness requires sensitivity to awe and reverence, an openness to the divine within. Life gives opportunities to learn:

> Whenever we are driven into the depths of our own being, or seek them of our own will, we are faced by a tremendous contrast. On the one side we recognize the pathetic littleness of our ephemeral existence, with no point or meaning in itself. On the other side, in the depth, there is something eternal and infinite in which our existence, and indeed all existence, is grounded. This experience of the depths of existence fills us with a sense both of reverence and of responsibility, which gives even to our finite lives a meaning and a power which they do not possess in themselves. This, I am assured, is our human experience of God.[431]

The Last Supper (chapter 13)

As his public ministry ends, Jesus begins preparing his disciples for his death. The tone becomes more intimate.

[1]Just before the festival of Passover, Jesus Knew that his Hour had come to pass from this World to the Father; having Loved his own who were in the World, he Loved them to the end. [2]As dinner time came, the devil had already made up his mind[a] that Judas son of Simon Iscariot would betray him.[b] [3]Jesus, Knowing that God had given all things into his hands and that he came from God and was going back to God, [4]got up from dinner, took off his outer clothing, and took a towel and put it around himself. [5]Then he put some water into a basin and began washing the disciples' feet[c] and drying them with the towel around himself.

[6]Then he comes to Simon Peter, who says to him, "Lord,[d] are *you* washing *my* feet?" [7]Jesus replied, "You don't Know what I am doing now, but you will Realise later." [8]Peter says to him, "You are *never* going to wash my feet, never!"[e] Jesus answered him, "Unless I wash you, you have no part with me." [9]Simon Peter says to him, "Lord, not only my feet then but my hands and head as well." [10]Jesus says to him, "Whoever has had a bath has no need to wash but is entirely clean, except for the feet. You are clean, though not every one of you. ([11]For he Knew who would betray him; that is why he said "not every one of you is clean".)

[12]After he had washed their feet, put on his outer robe, and come to the table again, he said to them, "Do you Realise what I have done for you? [13]You call me teacher and lord, and you are right, for so I am. [14]So if I, your lord and teacher,

---

[429] Stein, "The Importance of Numinous Experience", pages 67-68.

[430] *Concerning the Rule of the New Covenant*, in *Works*, volume 4, page 191.

[431] John MacMurray, quoted in Pacific Yearly Meeting, *Faith and Practice*, section on "Faith and Experience" no. 46, page 79.

washed your feet, you too ought to wash each other's feet,[f] [15]for I have set you an example so that you do what I did for you. [16]Very truly I tell you, a servant is no greater than his master, nor is the one sent greater than the one who sent him. [17]If you Know these things, happy[g] are you if you do them."

[18] "I am not talking about all of you; I Know whom I chose. But so that the scripture may be fulfilled, 'Someone eating my bread will lift up his heel against me,'[h] [19]I tell you now before it happens, so that you may Know when it does happen that I am. [20]Very truly I tell you, whoever accepts someone I send accepts me, and whoever accepts me accepts the one who sent me."

[21]After saying this, Jesus was troubled in spirit and Testified, "Very truly I tell you that one of you will betray me. [22]The disciples looked at each other, puzzled about whom he was talking. [23]One of his disciples, the one whom Jesus loved, was reclining in Jesus's lap,[i] [24]so Simon Peter motions to him to ask who it is that he was talking about. [25]So the one reclining on the front of Jesus says to him, "Lord, who is it?" [26]Jesus answers, "It is the one to whom I will give this piece of bread[j] after I dip it." After dipping the piece, he gives it to Judas son of Simon Iscariot. [27]After the piece of bread, Satan entered into Judas. Jesus says to him, "What you are doing do quickly." [28]No one at the table Knew why he said this to him, [29]for some were thinking, because Judas kept the money box, that Jesus was telling him, "Buy what we need for the festival"; or "give some to the poor." [30]After receiving the piece of bread, Judas left immediately. It was night.

[31]After he left, Jesus says, "Now the son of man was glorified,[k] and God was glorified by him. [32]God will also glorify him in him,[l] and will glorify him immediately. [33]Little children, I am with you only a little longer, and you will seek me and, as I told Jews I also tell you, where I go you cannot come. [34]I give you a new commandment, that you Love[m] each other; like I Loved you so you are to Love each other. [35]By this everyone will know that you are my disciples, if you have Love for each other."

[36]Simon Peter says to him, "Lord, where are you going?" Jesus answered, "Where I am going you cannot follow me now, but you will follow later." [37]Peter says to him, "Lord, why can we not follow you now? I will lay down my life for you." [38]Jesus answers, "You will lay down your life for me? Very truly I tell you, before the cock crows, you will deny me three times."

Meaning and resonance

a. **"the devil had already made up his mind that Judas … would betray him"** (13:2): This is a sentence that can be translated two different ways, either as translated above, or as "the devil put into the heart of Judas … to betray him". I took the former option because it fits better with 13:27, "After the piece of bread, Satan entered into him…".[432]

---

[432] Barrett, *The Gospel according to St John*, page 439; Coloe, *Wisdom Bible Commentary*, volume 44B, page 363; Culpepper, *The Gospel and Letters of John*, page 204; Moloney, *Love in the Gospel of John*, page 106.

b. **"betray him"** (13:2): The word translated "betray" literally means to hand someone or something over, to deliver up. The same word appears again in 13:11 and 13:21.

c. **"he began … washing the disciples' feet"** (13:5): This was a common practice in the Near and Middle East at that time. The climate is dry and hot especially in summers and low-lying areas. The roads were dusty and also used by livestock, so it was customary to remove one's sandals when entering someone's house. The host would then provide water and a catch-basin, and if wealthy, a slave to do the washing of the feet.

> Footwashing in the [New Testament] culture was performed on occasions such as "(1) cultic settings, (2) domestic settings for personal hygiene and comfort, and (3) domestic settings devoted to hospitality."[433] By the first century CE, while it may have been most unusual for a host to personally wash the feet of his guests, the action could be seen in the light of Abraham's hospitality. According to Manns, footwashing had a particular religious significance within Judaism as it recalled the hospitality shown by Abraham in welcoming his divine guests under the oaks of Mamre (Genesis 18:4).[434] While the original Hebrew text portrayed Abraham merely as providing water for his guests to wash their feet, this tradition had developed to present Abraham himself washing the feet of the guests as an act of gracious hospitality.[435]

d. **"Lord…"** (13:6 and other verses all through chapter 13): The Greek word here is a common title for a respectable man, similar to "Mr" or "sir". Peter, Mary and Martha, and others use this title to address Jesus, and it was expected of disciples for their rabbi. "Sir" would have been a good alternative translation here, were there not also a play on words: "Lord" also refers to the God of the Old Testament, whose name was replaced in speech by the phrase "my Lord" or in Greek, "the Lord". I chose the loftier option "Lord" here because the "glorification" of Jesus is underway.

e. **"You are *never* going to wash my feet, never!"** (13:8): The sentence is emphatically negative and even includes the phrase "into eternity". Although Peter's master has chosen to wash Peter's feet, Peter refuses, probably because washing a guest's feet is a slave's job.[436] In John, Peter appears less than ideal until the last chapter; the Beloved Disciple is the model disciple in John.

f. **"you too ought to wash each other's feet"** (13:14): The plural "you" and "each other" refer to the same people; this is a reciprocal action that

---

[433] Coloe cites here John C. Thomas, *Footwashing in John 13 and the Johannine Community*, in *Journal for the Study of the Old Testament Supplement Series*, page 61 (Sheffield: JSOT Press, 1991).

[434] Coloe cites here, Frédéric Manns, "Le Lavement des Pieds: Essai sur la structure et la signification de Jean 13", in *Recherches de science religieuse*, volume 55, page 160.

[435] Coloe, *Wisdom Bible Commentary*, volume 44B, page 364-65.

[436] Coloe, *Wisdom Bible Commentary*, volume 44B, page 366.

people are to do to one another. It is not an action to be done by a priest to someone who will never reciprocate.

Speaking of sacraments, it is worth noting what is conspicuously absent in John's Last Supper: there is no blessing of bread and wine. We can't even be certain from John that they had wine with this meal because it is not mentioned. There is also no requirement for a blessing to be repeated, though that can be found elsewhere. Compare Matthew 26:17-30; Mark 14:17-26; Luke 22:1-39.

The imperative in all of this is to wash each other's feet. However, I wear socks and rarely walk in sandals on dusty roads. I never visit the Temple, for which foot washing was required.[437] I have much less need of foot washing than Jesus's disciples. The gist is to help each other, and foot washing was an example Jesus set for his disciples (13:15).

g. **"If you Know these things, happy are you if you do them"** (13:17): "Happy" is the same word used at the beginning of each Beatitude (Matthew 5:1-12; Luke 6:20-26), often translated "blessed". In John, the word appears only here and in 20:29.

h. **"Someone eating my bread will lift up his heel against me"** (13:18): From Psalm 41:9:

> Even my bosom friend in whom I trusted,
> who ate of my bread has lifted up the heel against me.

Showing someone the bottom of the foot still expresses contempt in the Middle East.[438]

i. **"reclining in Jesus's lap"** (13:23): Diners normally reclined at dinner then, so there is nothing unusual in the reclining. More remarkable is where the Beloved Disciple reclines. Two words are used for it; in 13:23, the Beloved Disciple is lying on the κόλπος, meaning the front of a person, from the chest to the lap.[439] In 13:25, the Beloved Disciple is lying on Jesus's στῆθος, which is higher up than κόλπος, more in the chest area. Κόλπος can also mean chest, or it can mean lap.

Κόλπος is rarely translated "lap", even though "lap" is well within its range of meanings, so I opted for "lap" here.

j. **"piece of bread"** (13:26, 27, 30): Literally a bit of solid food, not necessarily bread. John does not tell us the menu. However, the bit was dipped in a liquid of some kind (13:26), perhaps a sauce.

k. **"Now the son of man was glorified"** (13:31): This is another case of a future event being treated in John as if it had already happened. See "those who do not trust are condemned already" above.

l. **"God will also glorify him in him..."** (13:32): About half the oldest manuscripts of John begin this sentence with "If God was glorified in him". I have left that out; it is clear from the preceding sentence that God was glorified in him, with no "if".

---

[437] Coloe, *Wisdom Bible Commentary*, volume 44B, page 365.

[438] Brown, *The Gospel according to John*, volume 29A, page 554.

[439] Liddell, Scott & Jones, *Greek-English Lexicon*, entry "κόλπος"; Bauer, Arndt, Gingrich & Danker, *A Greek-English Lexicon of the New Testament*, page 442 for κόλπος, page 767 for στῆθος.

m. "**that you Love each other**" (13:34): The verb form implies that they already love each other and should continue doing so. If it were a novel thing to be done for the first time, we would have a different form.

Reflection

"I, your lord and teacher, washed your feet" (13:14)

> What happens to me if God becomes conscious in me?

The answer to that question lies in the sentence excerpted in the heading:

> So if I, your lord and teacher, washed your feet, you too ought
> to wash each other's feet, for I have set you an example so
> that you do what I did to you. (John 13:14-15)

First we have to step back a little though. We have seen in John so far that Jesus speaks of himself often and highly; most of his teaching sessions have emphasised his high calling. "Before Abraham was, I am" (John 8:58) is saying quite a lot about himself, and it is no surprise that Jews (seeing him as human) felt a need to take him down a peg or two. Now Jesus has performed a slave's job. What has changed?

Murray Stein points out that the ego, a person's conscious mind, can develop during life.[440] In the first half of life, the ego focuses on making a place for myself in the world. I went to university, got my first career-track job, got a lasting place to live, and got a family to live there with me. I became king, of a small niche to be sure, but sufficiently in control of my niche to be less anxious than I would have been. Ego development in the first part of life is about getting control over a place in the world for me, becoming "king" of a niche.

"If the first half of life culminates in kingship," wrote Murray Stein, "the second emphasizes the figure of the suffering servant."[441] John 12:38-40 referred to the suffering servant described in Isaiah 52:13 through 53:12. I'll only quote 53:1-5, which I have long found beautiful (from the King James Version):

> Who hath believed our report?
> and to whom is the arm of the Lord revealed?
> For he shall grow up before him as a tender plant,
> and as a root out of a dry ground:
> he hath no form nor comeliness;
> and when we shall see him, there is
> no beauty that we should desire him.
> He is despised and rejected of men;
> a man of sorrows, and acquainted with grief:
> and we hid as it were our faces from him;
> he was despised, and we esteemed him not.
> Surely he hath borne our griefs,
> and carried our sorrows:
> yet we did esteem him stricken,
> smitten of God, and afflicted.
> But he was wounded for our transgressions,
> he was bruised for our iniquities:

---

[440] See Stein, *The Bible as Dream*, pages 131-160.

[441] *Bible as Dream*, page 146.

the chastisement of our peace was upon him;
and with his stripes we are healed.

Murray Stein says Jesus steps into this suffering servant role when he washes the feet of his disciples, and we can do the same.[442] After quoting John 13:12-16, he adds, "[Jesus] is setting up a new ego ideal: do not strive to be king, to sit at the head of the table, or to be first; rather, serve others, take the last seat, take on the role of servants, not masters."[443]

> What is being offered is a healer vocation: by themselves becoming seriously ill patients and finding the healing substance within themselves they will be able to offer it to others who are ill. The suffering servant is such a figure. "By his stripes we are healed" [Isaiah 53:5] is the telling sign. Because he takes on the sickness of the people who need healing, he can eventually produce, from his own willing and conscious suffering, the medicine that will heal the others. Thus the suffering servant must be looked upon as a spiritual healer who has obtained the power to heal by virtue of his acceptance of suffering and by the consequent constellation of spiritual "medicine".[444]

In John 12, Jesus sidestepped being acclaimed king striding into Jerusalem and instead found a donkey, and a young one at that, and rode that in (12:12-14).

> Jesus takes the identity of king but also undercuts it, deconstructs it, psychologises it. It is with grim irony that he allows himself to be crowned and named King of the Jews [John 19:13-16; 19:19-22]. In taking this identity on himself, he also destroys it, grinds it to powder, and relativizes it. It is decisively subsumed under his identity as suffering servant.[445]

The contrast between Peter and Jesus in John 13 shows the difference: Peter, defending Jesus and perhaps trying to impress, refuses to let Jesus wash his feet. Peter recognises that the dominant person is Jesus, and no king is going to do a slave job for Peter, who is conscious of his relative position. He is stuck in the kingly power dynamic, while Jesus has now moved on. "I, your lord and teacher, washed your feet." (John 13:14)

It is not possible to be a suffering servant while still retaining dominance. I long believed that abnegation and service were the right way, *but I pushed myself down that way*, a king making myself a servant, rather like Marie Antoinette playing at being a peasant. Striving to be good is still an effort to dominate. I was working very hard to be a servant without actually being one or having the mind of one. A servant does not will himself to do anything; a servant serves and does not choose what needs doing because other people's needs are the focus. As if royalty over my own soul, I was pushing myself—ironically into abnegation—but really going nowhere because I was still in control. "Take up the cross to that

---

[442] Stein, *Bible as Dream*, page 151.

[443] *Ibid.*

[444] Stein, *Bible as Dream*, pages 152-153.

[445] Stein, *Bible as Dream*, page 155.

proud spirit," Isaac would have told me, "make it bend and serve, let the life ... rise over it..."[446]

Murray Stein explains there is another way and one that can work:

> Jung's approach was to make the attempt at integration in a different way. Rather than through conscious effort, meditation on the images of the Bible, spiritual exercises, prayer, cultic activities, etc., he recommended dealing with the unconscious and individuating in a personal way. Rather than trying to be more Christ-like in the traditional sense, his way was to become more self-like in a personal way. .... It would be the individual, working diligently on himself or herself, honestly and sacrificially, bending the kingly ego to the servant's task of tending the psyche and nurturing its gradual development, who would eventually ground the wholeness promised in Isaiah.... The kingdom of God would come to earth through the inner work of the individual and through increasing consciousness and acceptance of the whole person as this is revealed through a personal individuation journey.[447]

Not a forced march dictated by a dominating (or even "abnegating") ego but letting myself develop, understanding that most of who I am is not conscious. I can become aware of God only to the extent that my ego (conscious mind) can make room. To the extent God comes into my conscious mind, I am not in charge there. I'll be washing people's feet, or doing some other more useful thing in a Quaker meeting or more broadly in service of humanity.

So what happens to me when God becomes conscious in me? It is the change that came over Jesus in John 13 as he performs a useful service: "So if I, your lord and teacher, washed your feet, you too ought to wash each other's feet, for I have set you an example...." (John 13:14-15).

> [T]his is the pattern which all his disciples are to walk by. The more life they receive, the more they are to minister, the more they are to serve. They must not lift themselves by their gifts; they must not hereupon lord it over others, or hold forth their knowledge or doctrines, and think to make others bow thereto; but wait in their service, till the Lord make way into men's hearts, and plant his truth there; and upon him also must they wait for the watering and growth of it.[448]

Words before leaving (chapter 14)

Chapter 13 records the Last Supper as they were eating it. Now they linger after dinner. The Jewish authorities have determined to kill Jesus (11:45-55), and Judas left in chapter 13 to arrange to hand Jesus over to them. Little time remains.

---

[446] *An Examination of the Grounds*, in *Works*, volume 1, page 379.

[447] Stein, *Bible as Dream*, page 159.

[448] Penington, *An Examination of the Grounds*, in *Works*, volume 1, page 381.

[1]"Don't let your hearts be troubled. Continue Trusting in God and in me. [2]In my Father's household are many dwellings.[a] If it were not so, would I have told you that I go to prepare a place for you? [3]If I go and prepare a place for you, I am coming again and taking you to myself, so that where I am you may be also. [4]You Know where I am going and the way."

[5]Thomas says to him, "Lord, we don't Know where you are going. How can we Know the way?" [6]Jesus says to him, "I am the way, the Truth, and the Life. No one comes to the Father unless through me. [7]If you all Know me, you also Know my Father. From now on you do Know him and have seen him."

[8]Philip said to him, "Lord, show us the Father and that will be enough for us." [9]Jesus said, "Have I been with you so long and still you don't Know me, Philip?[b] Whoever has seen me has seen the Father. How is it that you say, 'Show us the Father'? [10]Do you not Trust that I am in the Father and the Father is in me? What I say to you all is not spoken of myself, but the Father who Remains in me does what he does.[c] [11]Trust me that I am in the Father and the Father in me. But if you don't, Trust because of what I do.[c]

[12]"Very truly I tell you, the one who Trusts in me will do the works I do and greater than those will he do, because I am going to the Father. [13]Whatever you ask for in my name I will do, so that the Father may be glorified in the son. [14]If you ask me in my name, I will do it.

[15]"If you Love me, you will keep my commandments.[d] [16]I will ask the Father, and he will give you another Counsellor to be with you for eternity, [17]the spirit of Truth, whom the World cannot accept because it neither perceives him nor Recognises him. [18]I will not leave you orphans, I am coming to you. [19]Just a little longer and the World will see me no more, but you see me. Because I Live, you will also Live. [20]In that day you will Know that I am in my Father and you are in me and I in you. [21]Whoever has my commandments and keeps them is who Loves me. Whoever Loves me will be Loved by my Father, and I will Love him and reveal myself to him."

[22]Judas (not Iscariot) says to him, "Lord, how is it that you will reveal yourself to us and not to the World?" [23]Jesus replied, "Whoever Loves me will keep my word, and my Father will Love him and we will come to him and make our home with him. [24]Whoever does not Love me will not keep my words, and the word that you hear is not mine but from the Father who sent me.

[25]"I have said these things to you while I Remain with you, [26]but the Counsellor, the Holy Spirit, whom the Father will send in my name, that Spirit will teach you everything and remind you of all I said to you.

[27]"Peace I leave you, my peace I give you, not like the World gives do I give you. Don't let your hearts be troubled nor afraid. [28]You heard that I said, I am going and I am coming to you. If you Loved me, you would rejoice that I am going to the Father, because the Father is greater than me. [29]Now I have told you this before it happens, so that when it happens, you may Trust. [30]I will no longer speak much with you, for the ruler of the World is coming, and he has nothing in me, [31]but so that the World may Know that I Love the Father, I do as the Father commands me.

Get up, let's leave here."

Meaning and resonance

a. **"In my Father's household are many dwellings"** (14:2): The word translated "dwellings" is related to the word translated "Remain". A "dwelling" is a place to Remain. The same word appears again in 14:23, where I translated it "home".

b. **"Have I been with you so long and you still don't know me, Philip?"** (14:9, 14:11): Modern English uses "you" for both singular and plural, but they are distinct in Greek. The English translation of Jesus's reply to Philip obscures this nuance: "Have I been with you [plural] so long and you [singular] still don't know me, Philip? Whoever has seen me has seen the Father. How is it that you [singular] say, 'Show us the Father'?"

c. **"Trust because of what I do"** (14:11): Literally, "Trust because of the works I do."

d. **"If you Love me, you will keep my commandments"** (14:15): "You will keep my commandments" is given as a future fact; it is not an imperative.

   "Keep commandments" is the English idiom; the Hebrew version is to observe or watch commandments (shamar), and the Greek version τηρέω means about the same thing. "Keep the Sabbath" meant originally to watch it closely, an intriguing way of expressing the concept of compliance—intriguing for being incomplete: observation does not include obedience.

Reflection

"If you Love me, you will keep my commandments" (14:15)

John 14:15 reverberates with innumerable parental echoes, and for me every one of them rankles. The concept of obedience sits about as comfortably in my ego (conscious mind) as a nettle stem in my hand. I would not like it used as a whip on me; it can be traumatising. Obedience is a tough demand in the kingly stage of ego development, but much less so in the suffering servant stage, when the self is becoming conscious (see "I your lord and teacher" in chapter 13 above).

Isaac Penington understood this, that the sting of obedience varies depending on the inward presence of what John calls the Counsellor and Isaac calls "life":

> True obedience, gospel obedience, flows from life.... If I could obey in all things that God requires of me, yet that would not satisfy me, unless I felt my obedience flow from the birth of his life in me.[449]

Isaac concluded, "Oh! blessed is he, who meets with the power of life, which enables to obey; and who is obedient and subject to that power."[450] The consciousness of a divine inward Presence ("the power of life") "enables" the relativisation of the ego and the willingness to follow and obey that Presence.

As ever for Quakers, much depends on experiencing the inner Light, which "the World cannot accept because it neither perceives [it] nor Recognises [it]" (John 14:17). In the next sentence after speaking of "keeping commandments" in 14:15, Jesus reassures his disciples that the Light can be present: "I will ask the Father,

---

[449] *Naked Truth*, in *Works*, volume 3, page 314.

[450] *Ibid.*

and he will give you another Counsellor to be with you for eternity, the spirit of Truth."

It is the Counsellor, the inner Light or "life", that is the authority, and it is the Light that we are "enabled" to obey. Melvin Keiser:

> The central authority for Friends is whatever measure we have of the fullness of life, the divine presence known in the inward depths of our relational being, which we open to in a gathered meeting but can experience in any other moment.[451]

What the Light says to me is for me, and quite possibly for no one else. The "life" must be present for obedience to be enabled, and it is always about *my* obedience to the Light in me. Obeying the collective is something else and may not be what I am enabled to do. Collective, outward norms (a priest's idea of what it means to keep Jesus's commandments, for example, or even a biblical "commandment") may not be enabled for me. "The hallmark of individuation is the differentiation of the individual psyche from its containment in the collective psyche."[452] "As soon as a more honest and more complete consciousness beyond the collective level has been established," wrote Jung, "man is no more an end in himself, but becomes an instrument of God, and this is *really* so."[453]

Not the only instrument of God, however. We are "relational beings," as Keiser noted. "In my Father's household are many dwellings", or in a Quaker meeting, we all have our chairs, places to Remain for a time. I am there, in myself but also with everyone else, and what comes to me there often resonates from something someone else has said, which shows me that, as Jesus said, "I am in my Father and you are in me and I in you" (John 14:20). We all share an experience, but not all of it; much remains personal, the divine in me. In our shared experience as a spiritual community, what we share lets us find unity on community decisions.

The Counsellor, Remaining, and Love are all recurring themes in Jesus's last words, which continue on through John 17. However, John chapters 15-17 are almost certainly not in the early drafts of John;[454] they are amplification of the themes we have seen in John 14, but the last sentence John 14 is "Get up, let's leave here." Instead of leaving, three more inserted chapters of teaching follow. Chapter 18 picks up where 14 left off. They do go out at the beginning of 18, so let's now continue on to chapter 18 and come back to the three inserted chapters. I have taken out chapters 15-17 here, and put them at the end of the rest of John. Now we can get on with the story from where they "leave here". John recounts it in exquisite detail.

---

451 Keiser, *Seeds of Silence*, page 169.

452 Edinger, *The Creation of Consciousness*, page 85.

453 *Letters*, volume 2, page 242, emphasis Jung's.

454 Most commentators agree; see *e.g.,* Charlesworth, *Jesus as Mirrored in John* pages 95 and 103; Anderson, *The Riddles of the Fourth Gospel*, page 72; Anderson, *The Christology of the Fourth Gospel*, page 225; Schackenburg, *Das Johannesevangelium*, volume 4, part 1, page 34; Brown, *The Gospel According to John*, volume 29A, page 582-4; Moloney, *Love in the Gospel of John*, page 100. However, there are no manuscripts of John without those three chapters in sequence.

Jesus is arrested and interrogated (18:1-27)

[1]After saying those things, Jesus went out with his disciples across the Kidron Valley[a] to where there was a garden,[b] which he and his disciples entered. [2]Judas, who handed him over, also Knew the place because Jesus often met there with his disciples. [3]So Judas came there bringing a detachment of Roman soldiers[c] and officials from the high priests and Pharisees, with torches, lamps and weapons. [4]Then Jesus, Knowing all that was coming upon him, stepped forward and says to them, "Whom are you seeking?" [5]They answered him, "Jesus the Nazarene."[d] He says to them, "I am he."[e] (Judas, who handed him over, was standing with them.) [6]When Jesus said to them, "I am",[e] they recoiled and fell to the ground. [7]So he asked them again, "Whom do you seek?" They said, "Jesus the Nazarene."[d] [8]Jesus answered, "I told you that I am he.[e] So as you are seeking me, let these people go."[f] [9]Thereby was fulfilled what he said, "I did not lose one of those you gave me."[g] [10]Then Simon Peter, who had a sword, drew it, struck the slave of the high priest, and cut off his right ear. The slave's name was Malchus. [11]Then Jesus said to Peter, "Put your sword in its scabbard. The Father has given me the cup. Am I not to drink it?"

[12]So the soldiers, their officer and the Jewish officials seized Jesus and bound him, [13]and brought him first before Annas,[h] for he was the father in law of Caiaphas, who was high priest that year. [14]It was Caiaphas who advised Jews that it is better for one person to die than the people [John 11:45-55].

[15]Simon Peter and another disciple[i] follow Jesus. Because that disciple was known to the high priest, he went with Jesus into the courtyard of the high priest, [16]but Peter was standing outside in front of the gate. So the other disciple known to the high priest went back out, spoke to the gatekeeping woman and led Peter in. [17]Then the gatekeeper says to Peter, "Aren't you one of the disciples of that man?" He says, "I am not." [18]The slaves and officials standing there had made a charcoal fire to keep warm because it was cold, and Peter was also standing with them and warming himself.

[19]Then the high priest questioned Jesus about his disciples and about his teaching. [20]Jesus answered him, "I have spoken openly to the World; I have always taught in synagogues and in the Temple, where all Jews come together. I have said nothing in secret. [21]Why ask me? Ask those who heard what I told them. They Know what I said." [22]After he said that, one of the officials standing there gave Jesus a slap and said, "Is that how you answer the high priest?" [23]Jesus replied, "If I have spoken in error, Testify to the error. But if I spoke rightly, why did you hit me?" [24]Then Annas sent him bound to Caiaphas, the high priest.

[25]Simon Peter was standing and warming himself. Then they said to him, "Weren't you also one of his disciples?" He denied it and said, "Not me." [26]One of the slaves of the high priest, a relative of the man whose ear Peter had cut off, asked, "Did I not see you in the garden with him?" [27]Then Peter denied again, and immediately the cock crowed.

Meaning and resonance

    a. **"across the Kidron Valley"** (18:1): This valley runs east of the Temple. It is a wadi, a desert gully dry for most of the year but with a rushing torrent during rainy periods. The bottom of the valley was about 200 feet below the level of the outer courtyard of the Temple above,[455] and the Temple walls towered above the outer courtyard and the Kidron Valley beyond it.

b. **"where there was a garden"** (18:1): John is the only gospel to say they went to a garden. Mark 14:32 and Matthew 26:36 say they went to a place called Gethsemane, which they do not say was a garden. People have made "the garden of Gethsemane" by synthesising the gospels.

c. **"a detachment of Roman soldiers"** (18:3): The Greek says it was a σπεῖρα, a cohort of 600 Roman soldiers.[456] That seems an enormous number for one arrest.

d. **"Jesus the Nazarene"** (18:5, 18:7): The other gospels prefer to say "Jesus of Nazareth", but when Jesus's Hour comes, John calls him a Nazarene.[457] Coloe sees in this name an allusion to the Hebrew word *netzer*, which is the word for the royal shoot from the stump of Jesse, David's father (Isaiah 11:1-5).[458] In other words, "Nazarene", here and on the sign over the cross (John 19:19), alludes to Jesus as the Davidic messiah.

e. **"I am he"** (18:5, 18:6, 18:8): This statement is an I am, the name of God. The soldiers respond by prostrating themselves, an action so ironic for armed soldiers that it borders on slapstick. The "I am" is repeated three times in this section, juxtaposed against Peter's triple denial.

f. **"So as you are seeking me, let these people go"** (18:8): Note who is in control in this scene. Jesus steps up and turns himself in, but he attaches this condition—as if in a position to bargain with the armed soldiers apprehending him, who have just picked themselves up off the ground.

g. **"I did not lose one of those you gave me"** (18:9): The sentence containing this statement begins, "Thereby was fulfilled the word that he said..." However, "Jesus has not said this verbatim previously in John."[459] However, it is a paraphrase of John 17:12, where Jesus speaks in prayer.

h. **"brought him first before Annas"** (18:13): The questioning in 18:19-23 is by Annas, who is said to be "high priest" (18:22). Caiaphas was *the* high priest at the time, and Annas had been the high priest between 6-15 C.E.[460] John refers to "chief priests" in the plural, using the same word.[461] Annas would be one of the "chief priests", and may have been particularly trusted by Caiaphas as his father in law.

i. **"another disciple"** (18:15): Probably this was the Beloved Disciple, if only because his very anonymity identifies him. The other disciples are all called by name, even "Judas not Iscariot" (14:22), but never the Beloved Disciple.

---

[455] Bruce, *The Gospel of John*, page 339.

[456] Culpepper, *The Gospel and Letters of John*, page 221.

[457] Coloe, *Wisdom Bible Commentary*, volume 44B, page 476.

[458] *Ibid.*, page 477-479.

[459] Brown, *The Gospel According to John*, volume 29A, page 811.

[460] Coloe, *Wisdom Bible Commentary*, volume 44B, page 479.

[461] John 7:32, 45; 11:47, 57; 12:10; 18:35; 19:6-21.

Jesus before Pilate (18:28-19:16)

[28]Then they took Jesus from Caiaphas to the Praetorium.[a] It was early in the morning. They did not also enter the Praetorium so that they would not defile themselves so as to eat the Passover. [29]So Pilate[b] went out to them and said, "What charge do you hold against this man?" [30]They said in response, "If this man had done no crime, we would not be handing him over to you." [31]So Pilate said to them, "Take him yourselves and judge him according to your law." The Jews told him, "We are not allowed to put anyone to death." [32]This was to fulfil what Jesus said to foretell the kind of death he was about to die.

[33]Then Pilate went back in the Praetorium, called for Jesus, and said to him, "Are you the king of the Jews?" [34]Jesus answered, "Do you say that of yourself, or are others telling you about me?" [35]Pilate replied, "I am not a Jew, am I? Your own people and the chief priests handed you over to me. What did you do?" [36]Jesus replied, "My kingdom is not of this World. If my kingdom were of this World, my helpers would be struggling to stop me being handed over to the Jews. However, my kingdom is not from here." [37]So Pilate said to him, "So you are not a king?" Jesus answered, "You say that I am a king. For this I was born and came into the World, to Testify to the Truth. Everyone who is of the Truth listens to my voice." [38]Pilate says to him, "What is Truth?"

After saying that, he went out again to the Jews and says to them, "I find no case against him whatsoever. [39]But it is customary with you that I release to you someone at Passover. Do you want me to release to you the king of Jews?" [40]Then they shouted again, "Not this man but Barabbas." Barabbas was an outlaw.[c]

[1]Then Pilate took Jesus, had him whipped, [2]and the soldiers wove a crown out of thorns and put it on his head. They put a purple robe around him, [3]and kept coming before him and saying, "Hail, king of the Jews!" and hitting him. [4]Pilate went out again and says to them, "See, I am bringing him out to you so that you Know that I find no case against him." [5]So Jesus came out, wearing the crown of thorns and the purple robe, and Pilate says to them, "Look at the man."

[6]When the chief priests and officials saw him, they shouted, "Crucify him! Crucify him!" Pilate says to them, "You take him and crucify him, for I find no case against him." [7]The Jews replied, "We have a law and according to the law, he should die because he made himself out to be the son of God." [8]So when Pilate heard that said, he was more afraid. [9]He went in the Praetorium again and says to Jesus, "Where are you from?" But Jesus gave him no answer. [10]Then Pilate says to him, "You're not speaking to me? Don't you know that I have power to release you and power to crucify you?" [11]Jesus answered, "You would have no power at all over me were it not given you from above. For that reason, the one who handed me over to you has the greater Wrong." [12]From then on,[f] Pilate tried to release him, but the Jews shouted, "If you release him, you are no friend of Caesar. Anyone who makes himself a king is opposing Caesar."[g]

[13]After Pilate heard those words, he brought Jesus outside, sat on his judgment seat in the place called Stone Pavement but in Hebrew, Gabbatha. [14]It was the day of preparation for Passover; the time was about noon.[h] He says to the Jews, "Here is your king," [15]so they shouted, "Away with him! Away with him! Crucify him!" Pilate says to them, "Shall I crucify your king?" The chief priests answered, "We have no king but Caesar." [16]Then he handed him over to them to be crucified.

Meaning and resonance

a. **"Praetorium"** (18:28): The "headquarters of a Roman military governor."[462]

b. **"Pilate"** (18:29 and throughout this section): John's depiction of Pilate is somewhat at odds with Pilate's real life; from John, Pilate seems judicious and sensible, at least at first. However, he really was neither of those. Herod Agrippa, his neighbouring ruler to the north, wrote Emperor Gaius in 40 C.E. that Pilate was "naturally inflexible, a blend of self-will and relentlessness."[463] Pilate clashed violently and repeatedly with Jewish authorities by introducing imperial Roman images into Jerusalem and violating other Jewish prerogatives.[464] He also forcibly took funds from the Temple to pay for an aqueduct he had built. When Samaritans gathered on Mount Gerizim with messianic hopes, Pilate dispersed the crowd "with considerable bloodshed".[465] The real Pilate was not a nice man.

He isn't entirely nice in this story either. He repeatedly says he finds no case against Jesus, but he has him whipped and mocked. He ends up presenting the mob "your king", with sarcasm expressing the absurdity of his position, sarcasm that continues with "Shall I crucify your king?" It seems he could have said "no, you have not made your case" instead of taking the course leading to crucifixion. However, several times before he had had to back down to the Jews he was supposed to be ruling, so perhaps he gives in here before the situation gets even more awkward. In the economics of power, perhaps the flak from the chief priests was not worth one man's life to him. Caiaphas had earlier made a similar calculation (11:45-55).

The other gospels differ considerably in how they characterise Pilate and describe the trial before him; see Matthew 27:11-26; Mark 15:1-15; Luke 23:1-25.

c. **"Barrabas was an outlaw."** (18:40): In ordinary Greek, a λῃστής was a robber or pirate.[466] Josephus, the Jewish historian writing just after the destruction of Judea, used the word for revolutionaries, Zealots keen to expel Rome from Judea. Brown would harmonise the two definitions,[467] *i.e.* a λῃστής is person with no respect for civil law, or an "outlaw" as I put it. Mark and Matthew say that Jesus was crucified between two λῃσταί, showing that Jesus, as "King of Jews", was killed in the company of violent rebels.[468]

d. **"Jesus gave him no answer"** (19:8): His silence again recalls the suffering servant of Isaiah 53:7-8:

---

462 Bruce, *New Testament History*, page 348.

463 Bruce, *New Testament History*, page 34.

464 See "Historical setting" above.

465 Bruce, *New Testament History*, page 34-38.

466 Liddell, Scott & Jones, *A Greek-English Lexicon*, entry "λῃστής". Λῃστής is used in the sense of robber in Luke's parable of the good Samaritan, Luke 10:30.

467 Brown, *The Death of the Messiah*, volume 1, pages 679-693.

468 Mark 15:27; Matthew 27:38, 44.

He was oppressed, and he was afflicted,
yet he did not open his mouth;
like a lamb that is led to the slaughter,
and like a sheep that before its shearers is silent,
so he did not open his mouth.
By a perversion of justice he was taken away.
Who could have imagined his future?

e. **"Don't you know that I have power..."** (19:10): "Because Jesus was not a Roman citizen, Pilate had almost unlimited authority to deal with the situation as he saw fit."[469] The dramatic irony of this scene is tremendous: Pilate, who speaks these words, is the one who actually has all the power; even Jesus says Pilate has power "from above" (19:11). Yet the Jews in this scene—who will not even come in the same building as Pilate—bully him and subvert his power to their ends.

f. **"From then on..."** (19:12): These words could be causal rather than temporal, the sense then being "For this reason...".

g. **"opposing Caesar"** (19:12): Literally, "contradicting Caesar".

h. **"the time was about noon"** (19:14): Noon on the day before Passover was when the slaughter of Passover lambs began in the Temple.[470] Mary Coloe:

> At the time of Jesus, this was the hour when the priests in the temple would begin the slaughter of the lambs to be used in the Passover meal later that evening. Exodus 12:6 required that the lambs had to be killed "in the evening" of the Preparation day. In the first century, the large number of pilgrims meant that thousands of lambs needed to be slaughtered; rabbinic law, therefore, interpreted "evening" to begin at noon so that the necessary work could be completed before the Passover feast began at sundown. At the same time that the lambs are being led to their slaughter in the temple, Pilate is handing over Jesus to his death.[471]

Reflection

"We have no king but Caesar" (19:15)

This is a shocking thing for Jews, the people of David and Solomon, to say. God permitted Israel to have kings only reluctantly; God considered kings a rejection of his own sovereignty over Israel.[472] Now, ignoring the sovereignty of God and the kings of their golden age, Jews now "have no king but Caesar." "In denying all claims to kingship save that of the Roman Emperor, Israel abdicated its own unique position under the immediate sovereignty of God."[473]

The timing could not have been more ironic: their cry comes on the morning before the Passover supper, which celebrates the liberation of Jews from

---

[469] Culpepper, *The Gospel and Letters of John*, page 224.

[470] Brown, *The Death of the Messiah*, volume 1, page 847.

[471] *Wisdom Bible Commentary*, volume 44B, page 487.

[472] 1 Samuel 8:6-18; Judges 9.

[473] Barrett, *The Gospel According to St John*, page 546.

Pharaoh, their mythic oppressor. Oblivious to the timing, the chief priests take the lead in this story, but the mob seems not far behind. Jews collectively say, "Away! Away! Crucify him!" at the end.

Because of their involvement and John's demonisation of Jews, Pilate, who ultimately decided the issue, seems less than entirely culpable. He was pressured and manipulated into giving in, so although it ultimately remains Pilate's decision, his decision accommodates the Jewish mob, leaving him looking weak. Consequently much of the blame tends to fall on Jews, who are out for blood and demand it *en masse*. Our narrator has told this story in a way that takes much of the blame off a particularly violent Roman and drops it on the Jews in the story instead.

I offer no excuse or justification for that, but I have an explanation. John's portrayal of Jesus could not be more loving and positive. John's portrayal of Jews compensates psychologically for his strongly idealising portrayal of Jesus.[474] It is in portraying Jews that our author lets slip glimpses of his shadow, his hurt and spiteful side. The author has been hurt somehow, and the anger from that festers. Many of the final authoring group, in their lifetimes, had been expelled from Judea, and from their fellow Jews in their synagogues. Whatever it was, some trauma has left a wound in the soul that has not yet healed when John was written.

Nothing in John disabuses a reader of the human reaction to the traumatic wound of the speaker in John. When a highly idealised, divine figure battles misguided people and fatally loses, readers normally want to punish the killers who brought down their saviour and hero. If acted out, that get-even reaction multiplies trauma and escalates conflict. There was an alternative: to deal with the original trauma with minimum spread.

"Blessed are the peacemakers" is not in the gospel of John; it is Matthew 5:9. Tragically, the trauma in John was too sharp, and no peacemaker appeared to facilitate healing and understand both sides well enough to look for possible resolution. Nicodemus, well informed and moderate, might have been a candidate for peacemaker, but he was intimidated by scorn and social pressure into silence after he spoke up for Jesus (John 7:50). John's Jesus is the perfect foil: Jesus never appears intimidated in John. Daunted, yes (12:27-28), but going ahead anyway and always in control. Pilate himself was told he would have had no power over Jesus, "were it not given you from above" (19:11).

To avoid further harm, it is crucial to remember that what Jews did in relation to Jesus stems from what people always do with the written word of God:

> Every man [makes a pretence out of] Scripture, but none truly honoreth it but they who are guided by that Spirit which it testifieth of. And they who are not guided by that Spirit walk not according to the Scriptures, but according to reasonings of the fleshly part, which windeth itself into the letter of the Scriptures, that by some conformity thereto, it may avoid the dint of the Spirit. .... Thus the Jews cried up the temple of the

---

[474] "Psychologically the case is clear, since the dogmatic figure of Christ is so sublime and spotless that everything else turns dark beside it. It is, in fact, so one-sidedly perfect that it demands a psychic complement to restore the balance." Jung, *Aion*, in *Collected Works*, volume 9, part 2, paragraph 77.

> Lord, the sabbath, the law of Moses, and writings of the prophets, and under this cover ... persecuted Christ.... [Since] the days of Christ, the antichristian spirit speaks great words of Christ; his death, resurrection, ascension ... that, under this cover, it may fight against the Comforter, the Spirit of Truth, who alone can lead into truth.... And this hath been the way of opposing truth ever since, and still is....[475]

The Spirit never gets hidebound; it blows where it will (John 3:8). However, we, in our lazy desire for consistency, clarity and predictability in life, we inevitably tend toward habit and rigidity, the written word over the actual wind. "The inability to accommodate new developments creates a Procrustean bed into which society and the individual must fit, which results in rigid legalism."[476]

The suffering servant does not impose laws or wish for them; he accepts his lot, like Jesus in this scene, or like Job:

> The ego that once would have been king has now been ground down by adversity and tragedy, and instead of seeking to avoid the brunt of the suffering by looking for routes of escape or various defenses (denial, adaptation and assimilation, violent aggression), this attitude accepts the suffering and bears the consequences for the earlier inflation and hubris.[477]

"Jesus, dramatically demonstrating the possibility for a constellation of the transcendent function within the human psyche, reveals a stage of development beyond that of legalism, heroism, and even mature kingship and rulership."[478]

We too can "constellate the transcendent function", but doing so is not a matter of conscious compliance:

> For it is not [through] effort and ego struggle for perfection that one attains to the Christ pattern. To reach it, one would have to replicate in some inner and psychological way the developmental process outlined in the biblical narrative, from creation of ego consciousness through the separation stage, the warrior stage, the kingship stage, to the first inklings of the transcendent function in the prophetic stage, and finally, its fully embodied conscious realization in the Christ stage. But this is, I believe, the revelation that John witnessed in his beloved friend, Jesus, to which he bears eloquent and persuasive witness in his Gospel.[479]

Jesus is crucified (19:17-37)

[16]Then [Pilate] handed him over to them to be crucified. Then they took [17]Jesus, and, carrying the cross himself,[a] he went out to what is called Skull Place[b] (which is called Golgotha in Hebrew) [18]where they crucified him[c] with two others, one on

---

[475] Penington, *An Examination of the Grounds*, in *Works*, volume 1, page 364.

[476] Stein, *The Bible as Dream*, page 147.

[477] Stein, *The Bible as Dream*, page 149.

[478] *Ibid.*, page 178.

[479] *Ibid.*

each side with Jesus in between. [19]Pilate wrote a sign and put it high up on the cross, and it read:

> Jesus the Nazarene, King of Jews.[d]

[20]Many Jews read the sign because the place where Jesus was crucified was near the city, and the sign was written in Hebrew, Latin, and Greek. [21]The Jewish chief priests tried to tell Pilate, "Don't write 'king of Jews' but rather 'This man said, I'm king of Jews.'" [22]Pilate replied, "What I have written, I have written."

[23]So the soldiers, when they crucified Jesus, took his cloak and divided it in four parts, one for each soldier. His tunic[e] was a seamless one woven in one piece from the top. [24]So they said to each other, "Let's not rip it, but let's draw lots to see who gets it," so as to fulfil the scripture that says,

> They divided my clothes among themselves,
> and for my clothing they cast lots.[f]

So that is what the soldiers did.

[25]Standing by the cross of Jesus were his mother, his mother's sister, Mary the wife of Klopas, and Mary Magdalene. [26]Then Jesus, on seeing his mother and the disciple he Loved standing there, says to his mother, "Woman, there is your son."[g] [27]Then he says to the disciple, "There is your mother." And from that Hour the disciple took her into his own.

[28]After that, when Jesus Knew that all was now finished,[h] he said (to complete the scripture), "I'm thirsty." [29]A container full of wine vinegar[i] was there, so with a hyssop branch[j] they brought to his mouth a sponge full of the wine vinegar. [30]When Jesus had taken the vinegar, he said, "It is finished,"[k] and, bowing his head, he handed over his spirit.[l]

[31]Because it was the day of preparation, Jews asked Pilate to break the legs of the bodies of the crucified and take the bodies down so that they would not Remain on the cross, for it was to be a great Sabbath.[m] [32]So the soldiers came and broke the legs of the first and the other man crucified with him, [33]but when they came to Jesus and saw that he had already died, they did not break his legs. [34]However, one of the soldiers stabbed his spear into his side, and out came blood and water.[n] ([35]He who has seen has Testified, and his Testimony is True, and he Knows that he speaks True,[o] so that you may Trust.)[o] [36]These things occurred to fulfil the scripture, "His bone will not be broken."[p] [37]Again, another scripture says, "They will see into the one they pierced."[q]

Meaning and resonance

a. **"carrying the cross himself"** (19:17): In the other gospels, Jesus does not carry his cross (Matthew 27:32, Mark 15:21, Luke 23:26), but in John he does. A parallel has long been drawn to Isaac carrying the wood for the sacrifice of himself (Genesis 22:6). In the other gospels, soldiers compel one Simon the Cyrenian to carry the cross (Matthew 27:31-32; Mark 15:20-21; Luke 23:26-32). In Jung's psychology, each soul carries her own cross, "which is the sum of your own polarities and self-contradictions."[480]

b. **"Skull Place"** (19:17): Brown explains that the names of the place (in Greek and Aramaic (the language spoken by local Jews at the time) "are reconcilable with the suggestion that the appearance of the site was similar to a skull because it was a rounded knoll, rising from the

---

[480] Stein, *Collected Writings*, volume 6, page 235.

surrounding surface. In part because of John's information that a tomb was there (19:41), many have thought that the entrances to cavelike tombs may have supplied the knoll with facelike aspects."[481]

Brown goes on to consider whether the place is the site of the present Church of the Holy Sepulchre at the location identified by Constantine's architects (about 310 C.E.) based on local traditions.[482] Quakers believe that Christianity had fallen into apostasy by that time, and the urge to preserve physical relics from the distant past distracts from crucial inward work. Rome destroyed Jerusalem in 70 C.E., and by 310 C.E., Hadrian had built a new Roman city on the site of old, destroyed Jerusalem. I can't see that I have any need to know where exactly the crucifixion happened.

c. **"they crucified him"** (19:18): Bruce describes

> the bones of a crucified man of this period found ... north of Jerusalem, in June 1968.... Anatomical examination of the bones revealed that the victim—one John son of Ezekiel (the father's name is not quite clear), about twenty-five years old—had been fastened to his cross by one nail through each forearm and a single nail through both heels together. The latter nail had turned when it was being driven in, and could not be extricated afterwards, so it remained *in situ*, with some of the wood still adhering to it.[483]

d. **"Jesus the Nazarene, King of Jews"** (19:19): This was the original charge against Jesus when Jews took him to Pilate, and for which Pilate found no evidence (see John 18:28-19:6). After he is manipulated into condemning an innocent man, Pilate's behaviour seems angry and even cynical, so these words come dripping sarcasm. For the meaning of "Nazarene" see chapter 18. See "We have no king but Caesar" above on Jesus as king of Jews.

e. **"His tunic"** (19:23): Men of that time wore two items of clothing (besides footwear): an outer cloak (ἱμάτιον) and a long, woven garment worn next to the skin (χιτών),[484] translated "tunic" here. I imagine a tunic looked much like a long undyed T-shirt, though from woven rather than knit fabric.

f. **"...for my clothing they cast lots."** (19:24): Psalm 22:18. John quotes the Greek version exactly.[485]

---

[481] *The Death of the Messiah*, volume 2, page 937.

[482] *Ibid.*, pages 937-940. Hadrian had built a temple to Venus at the crucifixion site when rebuilding Jerusalem in 135 C.E. Constantine tore down the pagan temple and replaced it with the Church of the Resurrection, which was replaced during the Crusades by the present Church of the Holy Sepulchre. Carson, *The Gospel According to John*, page 631.

[483] *The Gospel of John*, pages 367-368.

[484] Liddell, Scott and Jones, *A Greek-English Lexicon*, entry "χιτών".

[485] In the Greek, the verse numbering is 22:19.

g. **"Woman, there is your son"** (19:26): "Woman" is the same word used by Jesus to address his mother in John 2:4 at the wedding at Cana. See the comment there.

Some read in this a quasi-adoption that creates a new Christian family; Mary and the Beloved Disciple are just the beginning of that family (see also John 1:12).[486] For me, that view imports a good deal of church doctrine into very few words, and it reduces the natural filial motivations—so obvious and striking in this scene—to mere premises in an argument travelling to a conclusion far removed from what stands written in the text. Familial love is the simplest explanation, and we have evidence for it in the fact that Jesus, dying in agony, went to the effort of looking after his mother here.

h. **"all was now finished"** (19:28): Jesus mentioned more than once that he had work from God to finish (4:34; 5:36; 17:4). Now it is finished. The same word (τελέω) is used in 19:30, Jesus's last word.

i. **"wine vinegar"** (19:29-30): "Cheap, bitter red wine or vinegar",[487] rather than οἶνός, good wine as served at the wedding at Cana (chapter 2). The drink alludes to Psalm 69:22:

> And they gave for my bread gall
> and for my thirst they gave me vinegar to drink.

j. **"hyssop branch"** (19:29): Hyssop is an aromatic bush in the mint family, although exactly which species is uncertain. Many species in the mint family grow no taller than mint in a garden (10 inches at most), so it is unclear how the hyssop supported a sponge being lifted up to Jesus's mouth.[488]

Hyssop is significant mainly as the plant to be used to daub the blood of a lamb on the doorposts of Israelites so that the Lord, who killed all firstborn sons in Egypt, would pass over them (Exodus 12:21-27). Note there the significance of the Passover lamb: it "was not expiatory but a replacement; 'its purpose was not sacrificial but apotropaic.'"[489]

k. **"It is finished."** (19:30): This is a single unforgettable word: τετέλεσται, literally, "it's just been finished" but in a single word.

Brown has researched the medical causes of Jesus's death.[490] The best known theory of how death by crucifixion occurred is asphyxia, based on data from men crucified without a horizontal crossbar, cases where crucifixion was done with the victim's hands tied over his head, with the victim hanging from his arms above and perhaps partially supported by a block below the feet and possibly even a simple seat. Crucifixion was meant to be slow, and more load-bearing points prolong the agony. However, in Jesus's case, it is likely that his cross had a crossbar, as

[486] Brown, *The Death of the Messiah*, volume 2, pages 1019-1025; Coloe, *Wisdom Bible Commentary*, volume 44B, page 490-494; Culpepper, *The Gospel and Letters of John*, page 234.

[487] Brown, *The Death of the Messiah*, volume 2, page 1059.

[488] Brown, *The Death of the Messiah*, volume 2, pages 1075-77.

[489] Coloe, *Wisdom Bible Commentary*, volume 44B, page 500; quoting John Ashton, *Understanding the Fourth Gospel*, (Oxford: Clarendon, 1996) page 491.

[490] *The Death of the Messiah*, volume 2, pages 1088-92.

commonly pictured. Indeed, it was probably the crossbar that Jesus carried, rather than the full cross, because the upright pole would have to be dug well into the ground and was probably left in place for re-use.[491] Crucifixions were common in Roman times.

Brown concludes his research into medical causes of death by crucifixion:

> In my judgment the major defect of most of the studies I have reported on thus far is that they were written by doctors who did not stick to their trade and let a literalist understanding of the Gospel accounts influence their judgments on the physical cause of the death of Jesus. There is no evidence that the evangelists personally knew anything about that matter, and discussion of it could better be carried on simply by employing the best of medical knowledge to determine how any crucified person is likely to have died.... The recent study by Zugibe[492], a medical examiner and pathologist .... has challenged the asphyxia theory.... He has conducted experiments with volunteers whose arms in simulated crucifixion were spread out at an angle of 60°-70° to the trunk of the body, and no asphyxia resulted. He contends that the shock brought on by dehydration and loss of blood is the only plausible medical explanation for the death of the crucified Jesus.[493]

Thirsty Jesus bled to death.

l. **"he handed over his spirit"** (19:30): "Handed over" is the same word used for handing Jesus over in 19:16.

John, and every other Greek manuscript at that time, was written in all capital letters because there were no small ones yet, so there was no distinction between "spirit" and "Spirit".

This phrase could equally well be translated, "He handed over the Spirit", though to whom is left unsaid, oddly, because to whom would be important when bestowing the Spirit. It is odd for another reason: Jesus very clearly bestows the Holy Spirit in John 20:21-23. I chose the simpler, less odd way of resolving the ambiguity in the text.

m. **"Because it was the day of preparation, Jews asked Pilate to break the legs..."** (19:31): The Jews there are complying with Deuteronomy 21:22-23, which reads (italics mine):

> When someone is convicted of a crime punishable by death and is executed, and you hang him on a tree, *his corpse must not remain all night upon the tree*; you shall bury him

---

[491] *The Death of the Messiah*, volume 2, pages 947-949.

[492] Brown cites here F.T. Zugibe, "Two Questions about Crucifixion: Does the Victim Die of Asphyxiation? Would Nails in the Hand Hold the Weight of the Body?" *Bible Review*, volume 5, pages 34-43 (1989).

[493] *The Death of the Messiah*, volume 2, page 1092.

that same day, for anyone hung on a tree is under God's curse.

n. **"out came blood and water"** (19:34): Mary Coloe sees in those words a parallel to what is going on in the Temple at the same time:

> Since the narrator has identified the body of Jesus as "the temple" (2:21), the flow of blood and water from his side mirrors the action taking place in the temple on the other side of Jerusalem. The Passover lamb was slaughtered in the temple by the head of the household, and it was the role of the priests to hold basins to receive the blood. The priests would pass the basins along a line until the one nearest the altar received it and then tossed the blood on the altar. The altar had two holes in one corner "like two narrow nostrils through which the drops of blood which are tossed on the western foundation and on the southern foundation descend and mix together in the water channel" and flowed out into the Kidron brook. As Preparation day drew to a close, quite literally, blood and water would flow from the side of the temple down into the Kidron.[494]

That western wall is all that remains today of the second Temple as rebuilt by Herod the Great, the Temple Jesus knew. It would have been covered in blood as Jesus died. Imagine the smell.

o. **"He who has seen has Testified**..." (19:35): John is the only gospel that says it was written by an eyewitness.[495] Luke says his account is based on a tradition of eyewitnesses (1:2). Matthew and Mark don't mention their sources. The Beloved Disciple was an eyewitness of Jesus's public life, and now he has in his home someone who knew Jesus as a mother does, and from his birth.

p. **"so that you may Trust"** 19:35): That translation equivocates. The Greek manuscripts have a subtle discrepancy here. Most of oldest say "so that you may come to Trust" (πιστεύσητε); the rest say, "so that you may go on Trusting" (πιστεύητε).

q. **"His bone will not be broken"** (19:36): Jewish law required that no bone of the Passover lamb be broken (Exodus 12:46; Numbers 9:12). Psalms 34:19-20 is also relevant:

> Many are the afflictions of the righteous,
> but the Lord rescues them from them all.
> He keeps all their bones;
> not one of them will be broken.

r. **"They will see into the one they pierced"** (19:37): "Scholars agree that the Scripture passage is Zechariah 12:10. Once again the evangelist gives a free rendition of the Greek text as the [ancient Greek translation] has

---

494 *Wisdom Bible Commentary*, volume 44B, page 493 (citations to midrash texts omitted).
495 John 19:35.

'they shall look upon me because they have *mocked* me.'"[496] Perhaps the writer was working from memory.

Reflections

The cross (19:17, 19, 25, 31)

> [W]hen I rather simply and naïvely asked God for a deeper understanding of Christ[,] I think I expected something rather comforting and lovely. Instead all the world's suffering was gathered up in a moment and pressed upon me. It was quite searing, quite devastating. The experience gave me an understanding of Jesus as one deeply involved in our suffering and pain, actually experiencing it too, that God is not remote but that *God is with us*. Truly Emmanuel.
>
> Rosamond Robertson, 1990[497]

Traditional theology sees the crucifixion of Christ as pivotal: we'd have been forever lost without it, but with it, we can be saved if we are good and receive sacraments (Catholicism and Orthodoxy) or if we are the faithful (or merely fortunate) beneficiaries of grace (Protestantism). In both cases, it is Christ's suffering at the end of his life that saves humanity. Jung and Quakers have a different view.

Melvin Keiser explains that 17th-Century Quakers used the term "flesh" to indicate "self-will resulting in conformity";[498] George Fox said "flesh" is what cannot "give [itself] up to die by the Cross."[499] Keiser continues:

> This uncrucified self is a "veiled self", clouded both from itself and from the presence of Christ within the self: Fox says that the flesh "did veil me from the presence of Christ."[500] The fleshly self is a self enclosed upon itself, directing itself out of its own ego-consciousness, and not open to its own depths, within which it could find the presence of Christ. .... And its knowing is conformist: "And while there is this knowledge in the flesh, deceit and self-will conform to anything, and will say, 'Yes, yes,' to that it doth not know."[501]

This conformist "knowledge in the flesh" affects a person's understanding of scripture. Keiser again, beginning with another quotation from Fox:

> "The knowledge which the world hath of what the prophets and apostles spake is a fleshly knowledge...."[502] Rather than grounding itself in the presence of Christ in the self's depths, fleshly knowing seeks its security in conforming to something outside itself, and this ends in "deceit." We are deceived in

---

[496] Coloe, *Wisdom Bible Commentary*, volume 44B, page 499.

[497] Britain Yearly Meeting, *Quaker Faith and Practice*, section 26:59.

[498] Keiser, *Seeds of Silence*, page 222.

[499] Keiser, *ibid.*, quoting Fox's *Journal* (Nickalls edition), pages 14-15.

[500] Keiser's footnote: *Journal* (Nickalls edition), pages 14-15.

[501] Keiser, *ibid.*, page 223; citing here Fox, *Journal* (Nickalls edition), page 10.

[502] Keiser cites here Fox's *Journal* (Nickalls edition), page 10.

mistakenly thinking Christ is an external entity when it is an inward reality.[503]

Jung often described this conformity to externals as "imitating Christ", as here:

> [Christ] took himself with exemplary seriousness and lived his life to the bitter end, regardless of human convention and in opposition to his own lawful tradition, as the worst heretic in the eyes of the Jews.... But we? We imitate Christ and hope he will deliver us from our own fate. .... No talk at all of uniting our Above and Below! On the contrary, Christ and *his* cross deliver us from our conflict, which we simply leave alone. We are Pharisees, faithful to law and tradition, we flee heresy and are mindful only of the [imitation of Christ], but not of our own reality which is laid upon us, the union of opposites in ourselves, preferring to believe that Christ has already achieved this for us. Instead of bearing ... our own cross ourselves, we load Christ with all our unresolved conflicts. We place ourselves under *his* cross, but by golly not under our own. .... The cross of Christ was borne by himself and was *his*.[504]

We project our unconscious problems onto Jesus, a useless act, but it lets us evade our true calling to carry our own "cross". We "flee the cross", as Isaac Penington put it, when questioning the leaders of Boston Massachusetts, who had just hung several Quakers for no fault other than being Quakers in Boston. Those leaders were Puritans who had fled religious intolerance in England, only to recreate it in Massachusetts in their Puritan zeal. Isaac diagnoses what gave rise to that intolerance:

> Consider whether ye did not flee from the cross, in your transplanting into New England, and so let up that part in you there, which should have been kept down by the cross here, and gave advantage to that spirit to get ground in you, which you outwardly fled from. The safety is ... in bearing the cross...; but if at any time there be a fleeing [from] the cross ... without God's direction, the evil spirit is thereby let in, his part strengthened, and the life weakened. That spirit which would save itself from the cross, is the same with that which would persecute that which will not save itself.[505]

Jung explains what they were fleeing:

> Whoever imitates Christ and has the cheek to want to take Christ's cross on himself when he can't even carry his own has in my view not yet learnt the ABC of the Christian message.
>
> Have your congregation understood that they must close their ears to the traditional teachings and go through the darknesses of their own souls and set aside everything in

---

[503] Keiser, *Seeds of Silence*, page 223.

[504] "Letter to Dorothee Hoch", in Stein (ed.), *Jung on Christianity*, page 170.

[505] *An Examination of the Grounds*, in *Works*, volume 1, page 348.

order to become that which every individual bears in himself as his individual task, and that no one can take this burden from him? .... Christ's life is a prototype of individuation and hence cannot be imitated: *one can only live one's own life totally in the same way with all the consequences this entails.*[506]

Recalling Luke's account of the good and bad outlaws on both sides of Jesus,[507] Jung saw in that image the psychological process it enacted: hanging, arms-out, on a cross represents coming to an awareness that one is being torn apart by opposites,[508] often with one pole conscious and the opposite pole unconscious (see "Opposites in John and Jung" below). Jung again:

The reality of evil and its incompatibility with good cleave the opposites asunder and lead inexorably to the crucifixion and suspension of everything that lives. .... [T]his result is bound to come as infallibly as it did in the life of Jesus: we all have to be "crucified with Christ," *i.e.* suspended in a moral suffering equivalent to veritable crucifixion.[509]

Only through the "most extreme and menacing conflict does the Christian experience deliverance into divinity, always provided that he does not break, but accepts the burden of being marked out by God. In this [way] alone can the [Divine within] realise itself in him, and God become man."[510]

This inward crucifixion is not a one-time experience. There can be a time in life when it begins, when the cleansing Light first begins to work, a time "wherein are but glimmerings or little light, wherein the discovery of good and evil are not so manifest and certain; yet there must the traveller begin and travel; and in his faithful travels, the light will break in upon him more and more."[511] Once begun, it is an ongoing process:

[H]e that will follow Christ, must take up the daily cross, even that cross which God daily lays upon him.... And as this cross is taken up, the worldly part is offended, and the life grows, cutting down worldly interests and ways of religion daily; but as worldly interests are followed and kept up, the fleshly part thrives, and the life decays and suffers....[512]

The result of taking up the Cross is that the Light grows within, or "the Counsellor" as Jung put it here:

If God is born as a man and wants to unite mankind in the fellowship of the Holy Ghost, he must suffer the terrible torture of having to endure the world in all its reality. This is the cross he has to bear, and he himself is a cross. The whole

---

[506] "Letter to Dorothee Hoch", in Stein (ed.), *Jung on Christianity*, page 170 (emphasis Jung's).

[507] Luke 23:39-43.

[508] See *Answer to Job*, in *Collected Works*, volume 11, paragraph 659.

[509] Jung, *Psychology and Alchemy*, in *Collected Works*, volume 12, paragraph 24.

[510] *Ibid.*, page 70.

[511] Isaac Penington, quoted in Britain Yearly Meeting, *Quaker Faith and Practice*, section 19:43.

[512] Penington, *An Examination of the Grounds*, in *Works*, volume 1, page 350.

world is God's suffering, and every individual man who wants to get anywhere near his own wholeness knows that this is the way of the cross. But the eternal promise for him who bears his own cross is the [Counsellor].[513]

"Woman, there is your son." (19:26)

The mother of Jesus appears only twice in John, where she is never named. That is just as well; there are so many Marys in the New Testament that the name is a poor identifier. She is one of the women in John (Jesus's mother, the Samaritan in chapter 4, Mary Magdalene, Mary and Martha of Bethany), and though they occupy minor roles as all the disciples do, they do speak, whereas women are nearly silent and rarely even mentioned in the other gospels. They also have character; the Samaritan is an interesting person (John 4), for example. Mary Magdalene will be the first person to meet the risen Jesus, and he has her tell everyone else (John 20:1-18).

Murray Stein interprets the Bible as a psychologist would interpret a collective dream. In that biblical dream, Mary is central in two great images:

Next to the image of Mary giving birth in Bethlehem, it is the picture of her at the foot of the cross and holding her broken, charismatic son in her lap that has gripped the Western imagination. In this part of the narrative, the feminine subject experiences the loss of her dream. Eve saw one son kill another, Job's wife knew the grief of losing all ten of her children, and Mary is forced to look upon the cruel crucifixion of her godlike son at the instigation of a vicious, ignorant, angry mob. Surely this experience of lost children over the centuries must have produced a saltiness of wisdom about life in this feminine subject. If individuation leads to wisdom through the conflict of the opposites, as Jung said,[514] then this feminine subject, Mary, standing at the foot of the cross upon which her son was crucified, must represent an opportunity for the profoundest wisdom.[515]

She is also in danger of inflation, thinking that she is herself divine rather than just the human mother of Jesus, thanks be to God to have such a son. In chapter 2 (note on "woman"), I quoted Murray Stein saying that, in calling his mother "woman", Jesus

---

[513] *Psychology and Religion*, in *Collected Works*, volume 11; quoted in Jacobi, *Psychological Reflections*, page 365. Jacobi's reference notes that "the last sentence was in the original version in *Eranos Jahrbuch* 1940/41, but was omitted from the 1948 version", which is the version included in the *Collected Works*. "Counsellor" is my word (see "John's key words" below); Jung's original was "Paraclete", from the Greek word that I translated "Counsellor".

[514] Stein's note here references Jung, *Mysterium Coniunctionis*, in Collected Works, volume 14, paragraphs 330-336.

[515] *The Bible as Dream*, pages 109-110.

> preserves her from becoming inflated through identifying too
> closely with her Messianic offspring.
>
> When a woman achieves this position in real life, she values
> herself (her ego) highly enough but she does not take credit
> for all her wisdom, inspiration, and spiritual insight.[516]

Mary remained herself rather than take on God's identity. In Mary, we have a suffering servant who was a woman and a mother. She was also strong enough to bear the intense conflict of divine opposites clashing right before her eyes and in her soul—the loss of her amazing son, whom she loved; his suffering a death conventionally seen as a disgrace, but which he insisted was his glorification—she is being torn apart. Yet the centre holds and she does not break. Job's wife, on losing all ten of her children, told Job, "Do you still persist in your integrity? Curse God, and die."[517] She cracked, but not Mary.

Mary experienced what it is to encounter God inwardly, the experience of the cross, as considered in the previous Reflection. Taking up the cross in one's own life is daunting—but we must not flee it. Taking up the cross is a risk, as Job's wife shows, but the cross is our only path to wisdom and wholeness, to a truly fulfilled life. It is the path we are called to travel.

> That man who is born of the Spirit is to wait for the movings,
> breathings, and kindlings of the Spirit in him ... to wait under
> the ... daily cross to that part which is to be brought and kept
> under, till all the bonds of captivity be broken through by the
> life, and the veil of flesh rent from the top to the bottom[518]
> (the remaining of which is that which stops the free current
> of life), and then shall the soul enter into the holy of holies.[519]

In the Temple, the Holy of Holies, its innermost sanctuary, was the place of God's presence.

Burying the body of Jesus (19:38-42)

[38]After those things, Joseph of Arimathea,[a] a disciple of Jesus but in hiding for fear of Jews, asked Pilate to let him take the body of Jesus. Pilate gave him permission so he came and took away his body. [39]Nicodemus, who had come to him by night the first time, also came bringing about 75 pounds of a mix of myrrh and aloes.[b] [40]Then they took the body of Jesus and bound it with the spices in linen cloths according to Jewish custom for burial preparation.

[41]There was a garden in the place where he was crucified, and in the garden was a brand new tomb,[c] in which no one had yet been laid. [42]So, because it was Preparation Day[d] and the tomb was nearby, they laid Jesus there.

Meaning and resonance

a. **"Joseph of Arimathea"** (19:38): Luke 23:50 says Arimathea was a "Jewish town"; scholars differ on where it was. Mark 15:43 says Joseph was a

---

[516] Stein, *The Bible as Dream*, page 109.

[517] Job 2:9.

[518] Matthew 11:29-30 records that the veil of the Temple was torn from top to bottom as Jesus died.

[519] Penington, *The New Covenant of the Gospel*, in *Works*, volume 2, page 75.

member of the Sanhedrin, which would have made him a Jewish leader and legal expert. And also probably wealthy.

b. **"75 pounds of a mix of myrrh and aloes"** (19:39): Literally, 100 (Roman) pounds, but there were only 12 ounces in a Roman pound.[520]   Still, 75 pounds is a lot of spices.

Myrrh is made from the sap of a thorny tree that grows on the coasts of the Arabian Peninsula and the horn of Africa. The sap is dried and forms a fragrant resin.[521]

Aloes were the "strongly aromatic, quick-drying sap of a tree ... used for embalming".[522]   Aloes and myrrh were used to embalm Alexander's corpse.[523]

Jesus's body was properly prepared for burial according to Jewish custom, using a very generous quantity of aromatics, which might have had the effect, for a time, of subduing or postponing flies and their maggots.

c. **"brand new tomb"** (19:41): Romans did not bury the bodies of people crucified for treason, which would have been the crime of the "king of the Jews". Augustus, after defeating Brutus and his army, crucified them all, and he is quoted as saying their burial was "a matter to be settled with the carrion birds."[524]

For Jews, however, it was unlawful to keep a crucified body on the cross overnight;[525] that is why John 19:31 says "Jews asked Pilate to break the legs of the bodies of the crucified *and take the bodies down*". However, Jews of the time normally buried criminals in mass graves, a dishonourable end. However, a brand new tomb and preparation fit for Alexander show that Jesus was accorded a very respectful and honourable burial according to John.[526]

d. **"Preparation Day"** (19:42): The day before the evening when the Passover commences. We close this chapter with another reminder that lambs are being slaughtered and roasted on the altar of the Temple as Jesus is laid in his tomb.

Resurrection morning (20:1-18)

This story is told mostly in the present tense, which I have retained. "The effect of this switch to the present tense is to move the reader into the scene so that even though it is told in the course of narrating the past, readers feel that they are in the scene."[527]

---

[520] Liddell, Scott & Jones, *A Greek-English Lexicon*, entry "λίτρα".

[521] Brown, *The Gospel According to John*, volume 29A, page 940.

[522] Bauer, Arndt, Gingrich & Danker, *A Greek-English Lexicon of the New Testament*, page 41.

[523] *Ibid.*

[524] Brown, *The Death of the Messiah*, volume 2, page 1208. Brown cites Suetonius, Augustus 13.1-2 as his ancient source.

[525] Deuteronomy 21:22-23.

[526] Brown, *The Death of the Messiah*, volume 2, pages 1209-1211.

[527] Culpepper, *Anatomy of the Fourth Gospel*, page 31.

¹Early on the first day of the week, while it was still dark, Mary Magdalene[a] comes to the tomb and sees that the stone was taken away from the tomb. ²So she runs and comes to Simon Peter and the other disciple, the one Jesus Loved, and she tells them, "They took away the Lord[b] from the tomb and we don't know where they put him." ³So Peter and the other disciple left and set off for the tomb.

⁴The two were running together, but the other disciple outruns Peter and came first to the tomb. ⁵After bending down and looking in, he sees the wrappings[c] lying there, but he doesn't go in. ⁶Then Simon Peter also comes following him, and he went in the tomb and sees the wrappings lying there ⁷and the face cloth not lying with the wrappings but folded by itself in one place. ⁸So then the other disciple, who had reached the tomb first, also went in the tomb and saw and Trusted,[d] ⁹for they did not yet know the scripture that he must rise again from the dead.[e] ¹⁰Then the disciples returned home.

¹¹Mary however stood outside in front of the tomb weeping. While she was weeping, she bent over and peered into the tomb. ¹²She sees two messengers in white sitting, one at the head and the other at the feet, where the body of Jesus had been lying. ¹³They said to her, "Woman, why are you weeping?" She tells them, "They have taken away my Lord, and I don't know where they put him."

¹⁴After saying that, she turned around and sees Jesus standing there, but she did not know that it was Jesus. ¹⁵Jesus says to her, "Woman, why are you weeping? Whom are you looking for?" Supposing him to be the gardener,[f] she says to him, "Sir, if you have carried him away, please tell me where you put him, and I will take him away." ¹⁶Jesus says to her, "Mary." She turned and says to him in Hebrew, "Rabbouni!" which means "teacher".

¹⁷Jesus said to her, "Stop holding me,[g] for I have not yet ascended to the Father, but go to my brothers and sisters[h] and tell them, I am ascending to my Father and your Father and my God and your God." ¹⁸Mary Magdalene went and announced to the disciples, "I have seen the Lord," and he said these things to her.

Meaning and resonance

a. **"Magdalene"** (20:1) denotes a place. Mary came from the town in Galilee called "Magdala".[528]

b. **"The Lord"** (20:2): John does not call Jesus "Lord" until after his resurrection.[529] Jews avoid saying the name of God, which appears frequently in Hebrew scriptures, and say "Lord" instead.

c. **"wrappings"** (20:5-6): Literally, linen cloths. John 19:40 mentions that the body was wrapped in such cloths with aromatic spices for burial.

d. **"Trusted"** (20:8): Although I uniformly translate πιστεύω as "Trust", the word as used here may simply mean that he accepted as true what Mary had said, that Jesus's body was gone. We are not told what the Beloved Disciple Trusted here so it is difficult to make much of this word. He may have believed a good many things from what he saw. Trust that Jesus had come to life again seems premature however, particularly in view of the

528 Brown, *The Gospel According to John*, volume 29A, page 981; Schnackenburg, *Das Johannesevangelium*, Teil 3, page 322.

529 Brown, *The Gospel According to John*, volume 29A, page 984.

next verse, "for they did not yet know the scripture that he must rise again from the dead."

e. **"he must rise again from the dead"** (20:9): These words mean to rise (go up) from dead people; "dead" is plural.

In a symbolic sense, everyone carries the dead in the mind, in the collective unconscious in each of us. Jung said "the unconscious corresponds to the mythic land of the dead, the land of the ancestors."[530]

f. **"gardener"** (20:15): Jesus was in a garden when he was arrested (John 18:1), and he was crucified in a garden, where his tomb also was (John 19:41). The garden setting recalls Eden, with the tree of life in its centre (Genesis 2:9). It was God who made Eden, so it is meaningful irony that Mary takes Jesus for the gardener.[531]

g. **"Stop holding me"** (20:17): The Greek verb ἅπτω means to hold physically. The form of the imperative verb here indicates that the holding is already happening or, less likely, is being attempted. Ἅπτω can have sexual connotations, such as groping or even sex, or it can just mean a hug or other physical contact. In the Greek version of Genesis 20:4 and Proverbs 6:29, ἅπτω implies sexual intercourse.[532] On the question whether Jesus and Mary Magdalene had a relationship, see "Whose wedding was it?" in chapter 2.

I do not know why Jesus added, "for I have not yet ascended to the Father". It is particularly odd considering that Thomas was soon after invited to put his finger on Jesus's risen body in 20:27. When Jesus ascended to the Father is not mentioned in John, but Acts 1:9 puts it at the end of Jesus's post-resurrection appearances. There are many theories to explain John 20:17.[533] A simple one is that he had something further to attend to so he couldn't stay. This scene then ends.

h. **"brothers and sisters"** (20:17): The text just says "brothers" (ἀδελφοί), which can mean males only, or it can also mean "brothers and sisters", *i.e.* a mixed group. Besides his mother, Jesus befriended several women in John (a Samaritan woman, Mary and Martha of Bethany, and Mary Magdalene) so it cannot be the case that his disciples were only male. "The presence of women can be hidden within the generic term 'disciples,' so it is important to remember that in [John] it is the women who stand out as witnesses and prophets."[534] Jesus is calling on Mary to be his witness here (20:17).

Reflection

"Rise again from the dead" (20:9)

What exactly happened to Jesus so that he rose from the dead is not something I understand. Paul gives some details in 1 Corinthians 15 and compares

---

[530] *Memories, Dreams and Reflections*, page 216.

[531] Coloe, *Wisdom Bible Commentary*, volume 44B, pages 513-517.

[532] Charlesworth, *Jesus as Mirrored in John*, page 493-496.

[533] Adele Reinhartz summarises them and adds her own in *Befriending the Beloved Disciple*, pages 108-112.

[534] Coloe, *Wisdom Bible Commentary*, volume 44b, page 508.

resurrection to sowing seed: "Sown in perishability, it is raised in imperishability. Sown in dishonour, it is raised in glory. Sown in weakness, it is raised in power. Sown in a physical body, it is raised in a spiritual body."[535] Paul invites the conclusion that the resurrected body is not physical, like the body that died, but "spiritual".

However, John has Jesus resurrected in a body that can be held physically by Mary (20:17), and Jesus tells Thomas, "Put your finger here",[536] presumably not into ether but into a tangible hole. I do not know how to reconcile Paul's view with John's. No wonder Paul said of the resurrection, "I tell you a mystery" (1 Corinthians 15;51).

However, in John, there is always a deeper meaning beyond the physical layer, even when I can't explain the physical layer. Jung cried out for understanding the resurrection as symbol:

> The standpoint of the creeds is archaic; they are full of impressive mythological symbolism which, if taken literally, comes into insufferable conflict with knowledge. But if, for instance, the statement that Christ rose from the dead is to be understood not literally but symbolically, then it is capable of various interpretations that do not collide with knowledge and do not impair the meaning of the statement. .... The danger that a mythology understood too literally, and as taught by the Church, will suddenly be repudiated lock, stock and barrel is today greater than ever. Is it not time that the Christian mythology, instead of being wiped out, was understood symbolically for once?[537]

It takes no great symbolic leap to realise that Nietzsche was surely right, in one sense, in saying "God is dead".

> I only know—and here I am expressing what countless other people know—that the present is a time of God's death and disappearance. The myth says he was not to be found where his body was laid. "Body" means the outward, visible form, the erstwhile but ephemeral setting for the highest value [God]. The myth further says that the value rose again in a miraculous manner, transformed. It looks like a miracle, for, when a value disappears, it always seems to be lost irretrievably. So it is quite unexpected that it should come back. The [traditional] three days' descent into hell during death describes the sinking of the vanished value into the unconscious, where, by conquering the power of darkness, it rises up to heaven again, that is, attaches supreme clarity of consciousness. The fact that only a few people see the Risen

---

[535] 1 Corinthians 15:42-44.

[536] John 20:27.

[537] *The Undiscovered Self*, in *Collected Works*, volume 10, paragraph 521.

One means that no small difficulties stand in the way of finding and recognising the transformed value.[538]

Both Mary Magdalene in John 20:11-16 and the disciples on the shore of Lake Galilee in John 21:4-7 do not recognise the risen Jesus at first. In the other two post-resurrection appearances recorded in John, recognition difficulties are not mentioned (John 20:21 and 26).

We don't recognise the risen Christ because the God-image reflected by the self has evolved. God is changing here; from now on, God for all practical purposes is the Counsellor, and the Counsellor transforms a person's inward God-image, the face of the self. It transforms us.

John Dourley wrote that "one whose experience has yet to include that of personal death and resurrection would be incapable of understanding its biblical meaning."[539] Life-changing breakdowns are paradoxical blessings. It is no consolation to know that, unlike Job, my faults have much to do with my losses. In time, I can, with help, learn to understand my part in what happened, but at the time of collapse, that is not possible. The old me must be lost in order to be transformed. At times of personal breakdown and death of the soul, the self can make the rising of Christ from the dead into a hope powerful enough to let the soul keep going and find a way forward.

> [Resurrection is] nothing less than the transformation of consciousness that attaches to the process of becoming whole in the here and now of everyday life. Resurrection so understood would thus involve the state of conscious awareness consequent upon living a human life in increasing resonance with the source of that life in the psyche. This conception of resurrection removes it from the realm of extraordinary geriatrics and relocates it in the area of human spirituality.[540]

Isaac knew this symbol as well, of dying with Jesus in order to rise again transformed into Christ, the Life, the Light. The result he describes is the service characteristic of a suffering servant:

> For being dead with Christ, and risen with Christ, and changed into the nature of Christ, by the principle which is of him, through the power and Spirit of Christ, which worketh therein; he can say as Christ did, when the Lord calls him to any thing; Lo, I come; it is my meat and drink, yea, my great delight, to do thy will, O God![541]

Appearances to disciples (20:19-29)

[19]When it was evening on that day, the first day of the week, and when the doors were locked where the disciples were for fear of Jews, Jesus came, stood in the

---

[538] Jung, *Collected Works*, volume 11, paragraph 149.

[539] Dourley, *Jung and his Mystics*, page 4.

[540] Dourley, *The Illness that We Are*, page 98.

[541] "Some Things of Great Weight", in *Works*, volume 3, page 3.

middle, and says to them, "Peace to you."[a] [20]After he said that, he showed them his hands and side. Then the disciples were joyful on seeing the Lord.

[21]Jesus said to them again, "Peace to you. As the Father sent me, so I also send you." [22]When he had said this, he breathed on them and told them, "Receive the Holy Spirit. [23]If you forgive any people's Wrongs, they are forgiven them, and whomever you hold fast, they are held fast."[b]

[24]However, Thomas, called the Twin, one of the Twelve, was not with them when Jesus came. [25]So the other disciples were telling him, "We have seen the Lord," but he said to them, "Unless I see the marks of the nails in his hands and put my finger in the mark of the nails, and put my hand in his side, I shall never Trust."[c]

[26]A week later, the disciples were again indoors and Thomas was with them. Jesus came while the doors were locked, stood in the middle, and said "Peace to you."

[27]Then he says to Thomas, "Put your finger there, look at my hands and take your hand and put it in my side. Be Trusting, rather than without Trust. [28]Thomas said to him in response, "My Lord and my God." [29]Jesus says to him, "Have you Trusted because you have seen me?[d] Blessed[e] are those who don't see and yet Trust.

Meaning and resonance

a. **"Peace to you"** (20:19:, 21, 26) was an ordinary greeting like saying "hello".[542] John might have left out an expression so ordinary, except that peace is what Jesus left to his disciples in John 14:27-28. The greeting repeats three times in this section.

b. **"whomever you hold fast, they are held fast"** (20:23): I have not translated this phrase as most do, by assuming that a Wrong is implied here from the previous phrase.[543] However, the word is not there, and as Coloe notes, its implication by many is based on analogy to Matthew 16:19. To me, the connection to Matthew is too tenuous for it to be interesting.[544] Coloe instead sees "whomever" as the object of the verb, and "whomever" is present in the text: "whomever you hold fast, they are held fast".[545] Both readings seem plausible, but better to hold people than Wrongs.

c. **"I shall never Trust"** (20:25): The negative is doubled for emphasis, and the verb Trust could either be future or subjunctive. If subjunctive, then even the *potential* for Trust is negated,[546] *i.e.* "Trust is impossible for me." Psychologically Thomas is not wrong; Trust is not healthy in the absence of any reliable indications of trustworthiness. If he could be sure that it was indeed Jesus, he would have a basis for Trust. As it happened, he was convinced on sight, as the others had been, and no actual touching is

---

[542] Brown, *The Gospel According to John*, volume 29A, page 1021.

[543] New Revised Standard version, for example: "if you retain the sins of any, they are retained."

[544] Anderson notes how different Matthew's gospel is from John. In John 20:23, "the authority to forgive sins is not withheld for one disciple alone and for those who follow after him, but it is granted to *all the disciples* by [John's] Jesus." Anderson, *The Christology of the Fourth Gospel*, page 239. There is no point looking for a parallel in the face of such great contrast. Luke is also not in harmony; for him, the Holy Spirit came on Pentecost, fifty days later (Acts 2).

[545] Coloe, *Wisdom Bible Commentary*, volume 44B, page 525.

[546] Wallace, *Greek Grammar Beyond the Basics*, page 468.

mentioned in John (just invitations). John provides the only record for this incident.

d. **"Have you Trusted because you have seen me?"** (20:29) can be read as either a question or as a statement, "You have Trusted because you have seen me." There were no question marks in ancient Greek.

e. **"Blessed"** (20:29): The same word is used here as in Matthew's more numerous beatitudes that begin Matthew 5.

Reflection

"Blessed are those who don't see and yet Trust." (20:29)

No one alive today is in the position of Thomas; none of us can realistically expect to see or touch the earthly or the risen Jesus. It is clear from John that the Word once made flesh now comes to us through the Counsellor sent us as the risen Jesus went up to the Father (John 14:26-28; 20:22). However, although we cannot see or touch, we can nevertheless experience Christ. Isaac Penington described his first Quaker meeting:

> When I came, I felt the presence and power of the Most High among them, and words of truth from the Spirit of truth reaching to my heart and conscience, opening my state as in the presence of the Lord. Yea, I did not only feel words and demonstrations from without, but I felt the dead quickened, the seed raised; insomuch as my heart, in the certainty of light and clearness of true sense, said: 'This is he; this is he; there is no other; this is he whom I have waited for and sought after from my childhood, who was always near me, and had often begotten life in my heart, but I knew him not distinctly, nor how to receive him or dwell with him.

> But some may desire to know what I have at last met with. I answer, 'I have met with the Seed'. Understand that word, and thou wilt be satisfied and inquire no further. I have met with my God, I have met with my Saviour, and he hath not been present with me without his Salvation, but I have felt the healings drop upon my soul from under his wings. I have met with the Seed's Father, and in the Seed I have felt him my Father; there I have read his nature, his love, his compassions, his tenderness, which have melted, overcome and changed my heart before him.[547]

There is no requirement in John that we Trust without experiencing what it is in which we are to Trust, although outward seeing and touching are not effective means for experiencing inward Light. It must be an inward experience, like Isaac's, but as each individual soul is led in its own way.

John Dourley, a Jungian and Roman Catholic priest, explains why experience is crucial:

> [In modern Christianity] conceptions of faith are divorced from any experiential basis in humanity's awareness of itself, and become dehumanizing substitutes for the life-giving

---

[547] Britain Yearly Meeting, *Quaker Faith and Practice*, section 19.14.

experience of the unconscious which the symbols express. Of this destructive psycho-spiritual situation Jung writes: "It [theology] proclaims doctrines which nobody understands and demands a faith which nobody can manufacture."[548]

The psychological consequences of such pathological conceptions of faith may take many forms. For instance, the situation can breed a fanaticism designed to block a potentially healing and expanding doubt. Such a doubt would be grounded in the human conviction that, whatever the content of such faith may be, in its current lack of integration with life it remains foreign and therefore hostile both to psychological growth and to life itself:

> People who merely believe and don't think always forget that they continually expose themselves to their own worst enemy: doubt. Wherever belief reigns doubt lurks in the background. But thinking people welcome doubt: it serves them as a valuable stepping-stone to better knowledge.[549]

When and if faith as fanaticism is overcome, the results are not always unqualifiedly beneficial. Patterns of depression and emptiness can follow the loss of whatever solace was previously offered by the so-called faith—though paradoxically the depression may be accompanied by rage at the sacrifices made to the dubious God of such faith and his strident moral demands, now felt to be hostile to fuller expressions of human life and spirit. Victims of "sacrosanct unintelligibility" are thus too often faced with "no-win" options. They can grit their teeth and cling fanatically to a burden of "revealed truth" which finds no experiential resonance in themselves. This splits them between the demands of their faith and the demands of their humanity and potential maturity. Or they are driven, often by inner demands for a fuller and more balanced life, into patterns of denial. In the language of their own impoverished theological options such denial is described as "atheism." Not infrequently this carries with it a lingering guilt for having abandoned what may have been, after all, the one true revelation—all the truer because of its unintelligibility.[550]

On the other hand, Trust, based on real (but inward) experience of whom we Trust, is rooted deep in the mind. It will also have a threshold of doubt—nobody knows or experiences everything—but to the extent we do experience Christ within, the response is as sure as was Thomas's "My Lord and my God".

---

[548] "A Psychological Approach to the Dogma of the Trinity," *Collected Works*, volume 18, paragraph 285.

[549] Dourley cites here Jung, "A Psychological Approach to the Dogma of the Trinity," in *Collected Works*, volume 18, paragraph 170.

[550] Dourley, *The Illness that We Are*, pages 18-19.

The story of Thomas shows, not that evidence is bad and blind faith is good, but rather that we must know how and where to look and how to be open to the experience:

> Mature individuals, desperate for a sense of depth in their lives, are hampered in their search for meaning by the difficulties in finding access to those levels of themselves which a healthy religious tradition would ordinarily supply.[551]

The moral of the story of doubting Thomas is not that doubt is bad; it is instead about how to look, and that is not with physical vision: "Blessed are they who do not see and yet Trust". That beatitude does not even come close to ruling out Trust based on an inward experience other than physical seeing.

However, the difficulty remains of "finding access to those levels of themselves which a healthy religious tradition would ordinarily supply" when "even intelligent people no longer understand the value and purpose of symbolical truth."[552] We are not helped in this predicament by "contemporary Christian theologians and apologists ... woefully unaware of the unconscious as the seat of religion and therefore a potential source of healing."[553] Instead, conventional Christianity tells us that Thomas shows that looking for experience is asking too much, and instead, Christianity demands faith, the voluntary suppression of normal incredulity—and that really is asking too much.

> Exclusive appeals to faith are a hopeless *petitio principii* [begging the question], for it is the manifest improbability of symbolical truth that prevents people from believing in it. Instead of insisting so glibly on the necessity of faith, the theologians, it seems to me, should see what can be done to make this faith possible.... And this can only be achieved by reflecting how it came about in the first place that humanity needed the improbability of religious statements, and what it signifies when a totally different spiritual reality is superimposed on the sensuous and tangible actuality of this world.[554]

Dourley adds:

> Jung's reflections on why humanity seemed universally and at all times driven to "the improbability of religious statements" brought him a radically new understanding of religion and its diverse expressions. He came to see religion in its broadest sense as a natural child of the unconscious, and so conceived of a new, "natural" theology which would view the various improbable statements of faith as referents to

---

[551] Dourley, *The Illness that We Are*, page 19.

[552] Jung, *Symbols of Transformation*, in *Collected Works*, volume 5, paragraph 336.

[553] Dourley, *The Illness that We Are*, page 19.

[554] Jung, *Symbols of Transformation*, in *Collected Works*, volume 5, paragraph 336.

psychological movements in the universal processes of human renewal and maturation.[555]

Faith as a conscious act of will is, then, a nonsense inviting the psychological consequences that Dourley noted above. Trust is not a thing we decide to have; it is an effect of experiencing the inner Light. That experience leaves us "gripped and held by the numinous power of the archetype functioning beyond the ego's controlling grasp."[556] In other words, we don't so much have Trust as we are held fast in the grip of what we have experienced, and Trust is the calm sense that all is well there.

Original ending of John

The story of Thomas is meant to illuminate Trust, and now comes the clincher that originally ended John. Almost all scholars agree that chapter 21 is an epilogue added after the original ending, which is these two verses.

> [30]Now Jesus did many other Signs before his disciples, but they are not written in this book. [31]But these things are written so that you may Trust that Jesus is the Christ,[a] the son of God, and so that by Trusting you may have Life in his name.

Meaning and resonance

    a. **"Christ"** is not a name but a title. It is the Greek equivalent of the Hebrew word "Messiah". For the meaning of "Christ", see section "Why John? Why Jesus?"

Epilogue

> The Gospel narrative of Jesus's life, ministry, death and resurrection came to its conclusion with chapter 20, especially 20:30-31. But the story of the community continued, witnessing to the ongoing presence of Jesus/Sophia. Chapter 21 provides a glimpse into the beginnings of this Gospel community and the issues it faced. Clearly, this chapter comes some time later than the original Gospel....[557]

Much has changed in the time between Jesus's lifetime and this later addition. Judea was destroyed in 70 C.E., and the community of John is being excluded from synagogues at this time, but probably not when Jesus was alive.

Breakfast by the sea (21:1-15)

> [1]Later, Jesus showed himself again to the disciples by the Sea of Tiberias,[a] and he showed himself in this way. [2]Simon Peter, Thomas who is called "the Twin", Nathanael of Cana in Galilee, those of Zebedee,[b] and two others of his disciples were together. [3]Simon Peter says to them, "I'm going fishing." They tell him, "We're coming with you." They went down and got in the boat, but that night they caught nothing.

---

[555] Dourley, *The Illness that We Are*, pages 19-20.

[556] Dourley, *The Illness that We Are*, page 23.

[557] Coloe, *Wisdom Bible Commentary*, volume 44B, page 537.

[4]Just after daybreak, Jesus stood on the beach, but the disciples did not Recognise that it was Jesus. [5]Then Jesus says to them, "Lads,[c] you have nothing to eat, have you?" They answered no. [6]Jesus told them, "Cast the net on the right side of the boat and you will find some." So they did so, and they were not strong enough to haul it in because of so many fish. [7]That disciple whom Jesus Loved said to Peter, "It is the Lord." Then Simon Peter, on hearing it was the Lord, cinched on his outer garment, for he was naked,[d] and he jumped into the sea. [8]The other disciples came by boat, for they were not far from land, only about 300 feet out and were towing the net of fish.

[9]As they came ashore, they see a charcoal fire there with fish on it and bread. [10]Jesus says to them, "Bring some of the fish you have just caught." [11]So Simon Peter went aboard and hauled the net ashore full of large fish, 153 of them, and though there were so many, the net did not break. [12]Jesus says to them, "Come have breakfast." But none of the disciples dared ask him, "Who are you?" because they Knew it was the Lord.[e] [13]Jesus comes and takes bread and gives it to them, and the same with the fish. [14]This was the third time Jesus appeared to the disciples after he was raised from the dead.[f]

Meaning and resonance

a. **"Sea of Tiberias"** (21:1): Tiberias was a city on the western shore of the Sea of Galilee, which is a lake rather than an arm of the ocean. John 6:1 calls the same lake the Sea of Galilee and of Tiberias. Tiberias survived the destruction of Judea and became a centre of rabbinic learning despite being built on a cemetery, which made it unclean for Jews.[558]

b. **"those of Zebedee"** (21:2): We know from other gospels that Zebedee was the father of James and John,[559] who are never mentioned by name in John. The Greek does not say "sons"; it could mean any in the family of Zebedee.

c. **"Lads..."** (21:5): This word is a diminutive form of the word meaning "child", so the meaning would literally be "little children". In view of the fact that grown men were in the boat, Brown sees the diminutive as indicating colloquial endearment and translates the word, "Lads".[560] I have done the same. The NRSV leaves it out entirely, but I don't want to leave out a word.

d. **"cinched on his outer garment, for he was naked"** (21:7): Brown points out that Jews disliked complete nudity so Peter was probably wearing a loincloth.[561] That seems plausible, but not the only possible interpretation. The word γυμνός certainly means "naked", but also sometimes near nudity, or even just the lack of weapons.[562] Citing the Talmud, Barrett notes "that to offer greeting was a religious act and could not be performed without clothing".[563]

---

[558] Josephus, *Antiquities of the Jews*, book 18, chapter 2, section 3.

[559] Matthew 4:21; Mark 1:19-20, 3:17, 10:35; Luke 5:10.

[560] *The Gospel According to John*, volume 29A, page 1070. Carson agrees with Brown here; *The Gospel According to John*, page 670.

[561] *The Gospel According to John*, volume 29A, page 1072.

[562] Liddell, Scott and Jones, *A Greek-English Lexicon*, entry "γυμνός".

[563] Barrett, *The Gospel According to St John*, page 580-581.

e. **"none of the disciples dared ask him, 'Who are you?'"** John 21:4 and 21:12 (and Mary Magdalene in John 20:11-16) show that disciples find recognition of Jesus difficult after he rises from the dead. See "Rise again from the dead" above.

f. **"This was the third time Jesus appeared to the disciples after he was raised from the dead."** (21:14): John 20:19-29 records two prior appearances to the disciples. There was one more appearance, but only to Mary Magdalene rather than "disciples" in the plural (John 20:1-18).

Jesus, Peter, and the Beloved Disciple (21:15-25)

[15]When they had eaten breakfast, Jesus says to Simon Peter, "Simon son of John,[a] do you Love me more than these?"[b] He says to him, "Yes, Lord, you Know that I Love you." Jesus says to him, "Tend my sheep."

[16]He says to him again, "Simon son of John, do you Love me?" He says to him, "Yes, Lord, you Know I Love you." He tells him, "Take care of my sheep."

[17]He says to him a third time, "Simon, son of John, do you Love me?" Peter felt hurt that he said to him a third time, "Do you love me?" and he said to him, "Lord, you Know all things. You Know that I Love you." Jesus says to him, "Tend my sheep. [18]Very truly I tell you, when you were young you fastened your own belt and went where you pleased; but when you get old, you will hold out your hands, and someone else will fasten a belt around you and take you where you don't want to go." [19]He said this to indicate by what kind of death he would glorify God, and after saying that, he said, "Follow me."

[20]Peter turns and sees the disciple Jesus Loved following, the one who had reclined on his chest at the supper and had said, "Lord, who is going to hand you over?" [21]When Peter saw him he says to Jesus, "Lord, what about him?" [22]Jesus says to him, "If I want him to Remain until I come, what is that to you? You are to follow me." [23]So the word went out among the brothers and sisters that that disciple would not die. However, Jesus did not say he would not die[c] but "if I want him to Remain until I come, what's that to you?"

[24]He is the disciple who Testifies of these things[d] and who wrote them, and we know that his Testimony is true. [25]But there are also many other things that Jesus did, which if all were written down in detail, I suppose the World would not have room for the books that would be written.[e]

Meaning and resonance

a. **"Simon son of John"** (21:15): The only other time in John when Jesus calls Peter by this, his full proper name, was when calling him as a discile in John 1:42. Jesus has given him the nicknames Peter (Greek) and Cephas (Aramaic), both meaning a small stone.

b. **"do you love me more than these?"** (21:15): It is not clear to whom or what "these" refers. It could be people (of any gender) or things, or both.

c. **"Jesus did not say he would not die"** (21:23): The preceding sentence says that a rumour was circulating that the Beloved Disciple would not die, so the quoted sentence scotches that rumour. That action would only be necessary if the Beloved Disciple had in fact died, so just under the surface, this verse reports the death of the Beloved Disciple.

d. **"He is the disciple who Testifies of these things"**: The Beloved Disciple is said to have written John in John 21:24 (see also 19:35): "He [the Beloved Disciple] is the disciple who Testifies of these things and who wrote them", but he is not alone in writing. There is also a narrator using "we" as the verse continues: "and we know that his Testimony is True."

e. **"there are also many other things that Jesus did"** (21:25): This is part of a larger statement:

> There are also many other things that Jesus did, which if
> all were written down in detail, I suppose the World would
> not have room for the books that would be written.

This is said by the same person who has just responded to the death of the Beloved Disciple. It shows that there was a large narrative tradition in the community of John, drawing on the experiences of the Beloved Disciple and Mary, before John was completed. The first generation of disciples has died out and the second is also thinning, so the large oral part of the tradition may be beginning to fade. With no eyewitnesses left, tales become recited rather than remembered, and people start retelling the story to their liking (consciously or not), rather than sticking to the Truth. The need to preserve something of the True, original Testimony has become acute, so John gets finished.

Insertions were made into John from this oral wealth in this final stage, such as this chapter, the Prologue, and chapters 15-17. It must have been unbearable to think that so much of what Jesus said and did would be lost. And had by that time already been lost; then as now we who have John do not live where Jesus did, nor as he did. His world had vanished even then.

Reflection

"Peter felt hurt that he said to him a third time, 'Do you love me?'" (21:17)

Peter is interesting because he has a dramatic fall and a dramatic recovery. A person has little chance of passing through life without a fall, so Peter's case is worth a closer look.

John portrays Peter—not as ideal, like the Beloved Disciple—but as a human disciple. The word "Peter" comes up 32 times in John. In John 1, he is one of the original disciples of John to whom Jesus says, "Follow me." In John 6:8 he is named to identify his brother Andrew.

In John 6:68, he speaks for the first time:

> Because of this many of his disciples turned back and no
> longer walked with him. So Jesus said to the Twelve, "Don't
> you want to go too?" Simon Peter asked him, "Lord, to whom
> would we go? You have the words of eternal Life. We have
> come to Trust and Know that you are the holy one of God."[564]

He speaks again in John 13:6-9:

---

[564] Carson observed about 6:68, "Peter's way of expressing himself appears somewhat pretentious, as if he and his fellows are a cut above the fickle 'disciples' who have turned away, superior at least in insight. Indeed, Peter's words almost seem to mean that he is doing Jesus a favour." *The Gospel According to John*, page 304.

> Peter says to him, "You are *never* going to wash my feet,
> never!" Jesus answered him, "Unless I wash you, you have no
> part with me." Simon Peter says to him, "Lord, not only my
> feet then but my hands and head as well!"

In John 13:24, Peter motions to the Beloved Disciple to ask Jesus who will betray Jesus. Peter's next spoken words are in John 13:36-38:

> Simon Peter says to him, "Lord, where are you going?" Jesus
> answered, "Where I am going you cannot follow me now, but
> you will follow later." Peter says to him, "Lord, why can we
> not follow you now? I will lay down my life for you." Jesus
> answers, "You will lay down your life for me? Very truly I tell
> you, before the cock crows, you will deny me three times."

In John 18:10, Peter draws his sword and cuts off Malchus's ear as Jesus is arrested. Peter then follows Jesus, now a prisoner, into the palace of the high priest. There he denies three times that he is a disciple of Jesus (John 18:15-18, 18:25-27).

Peter runs with the Beloved Disciple to the tomb on the morning of Jesus's rising, but they find the tomb empty. He is not mentioned by name again until the present chapter, John 21.

What patterns are there in what he says and does? One, I would suggest, is that he is over-eager, as when he swims to shore in this chapter, leaving his friends to bring the boat ashore, towing their enormous catch. Compared to the other disciples, Peter is the one out in front and the first to act, sometimes rashly. Is he just a top-dog sort, competitive and trying to outdo everyone else? Or is he compensating for an inner insecurity? Or both—both would create a polarity: the high achiever that Peter presents to the world, and the weak and fearful thing that he can't bear to think about.

That polarity would explain his rather too grand "I will lay down my life for you" (13:37), which prompts Jesus to point out the flimsiness of that vow, "Before the cock crows, you will deny me three times." (13:38.) All three denials happened around a charcoal fire (John 18:18), as did this scene on the beach, in which Jesus takes Peter back from his failure by eliciting a triple affirmation. Perhaps Peter jumped in the lake in 21:7 because, after his denials, Peter is now even more eager/insecure, and because being keen to please is how he deals with his (mostly hidden) fear of not pleasing enough, or at all. It is the only way he knows to relieve his insecurity, his fear, that really he is not good enough.

It was also very likely his fear that motivated Peter's denials. He was in the high priest's palace where Jesus was a prisoner. Peter had just cut off the ear of the high priest's slave, so his over-eagerness in compensating for his hidden fear ends up making him an offender, thereby feeding his fear. He is in the perfect place to get arrested for injuring Malchus, so he denies knowing Jesus.

The human condition, and most of all the fact that we make the unliked parts of us unconscious, leaves us all with a risk of being found out. Carl Jung:

> Simple things are always the most difficult. In actual life, it
> requires the greatest art to be simple, and so acceptance of
> oneself is the essence of the moral problem and the acid test
> of one's whole outlook on life. That I feed the beggar, that I
> forgive an insult, that I love my enemy in the name of Christ—

all these are undoubtedly great virtues. What I do unto the least of my brethren, that I do unto Christ. But what if I should discover that the least amongst them all, the poorest of all beggars, the most impudent of all offenders, [and even] the very fiend himself—that these are within me, and that I myself stand in need of the alms of my own kindness, that I myself am the enemy who must be loved—what then? Then, as a rule, the whole truth of Christianity is reversed: there is then no more talk of love and long suffering; we ... condemn and rage against ourselves. We hide him from the world, we deny ever having met this least among the lowly in ourselves, and had it been God himself who drew near to us in this despicable form, we should have denied him a thousand times before a single cock had crowed.[565]

The life of Isaac Penington provides another example of mistake and recovery. Englishmen of the 17th Century customarily wore hats, but took them off when encountering someone of higher social standing. Quakers consider everyone equal before God, so they did not take off their hats because differences in social standing were superficial and false.

However, one Quaker of that time, John Perrot, advocated removing hats during Quaker worship at times of prayer. Perrot's view divided Friends, some removing their hats and thinking themselves correct for doing so, and others continuing the earlier practice of leaving them on. Isaac was initially an admirer of Perrot and advocated leaving the question of hat removal open for each person to decide in the Light.

Other weighty Friends did not wish to have a controversy on a minor point acted out in meetings for worship. As someone who habitually wears a hat, I'm glad we don't have the outward busyness of taking my hat off and on during worship. I'm not sure that I can discern when someone is praying and when not. That quagmire of protocol issues is extraneous to worship. By encouraging diversity in practice, Isaac had encouraged controversy, right in the middle of the experience of worship.[566]

A letter to Isaac from another great Friend, Francis Howgill, helped open Isaac's eyes to his error:

> Divers things more could I say about that business of the hat, but I desire that it may die with that spirit that brought it forth: and fill not thy mind with things of this nature, for it will beget trouble and thoughts of hurt. These things were upon me in brotherly love to lay before thee, not desiring or expecting any answer, as in way of contending, but as being

---

[565] Jung, *Psychology and Religion*, in *Collected Works*, volume 11, paragraph 131.

[566] See Keiser & Moore, *Knowing the Mystery of God Within*, pages 39-45.

> sensible that divers writings and papers from divers hands
> hath done hurt, and have had a bad effect.[567]

Other Friends offered similar advice.[568] Isaac realised that he had made a mistake. He later wrote to some Friends:

> It is somewhat strongly on my heart this morning to acquaint
> you, how that after that hour of darkness and sore
> temptation, which it pleased the Lord to suffer to befall me,
> ... how that the Lord manifested to me his great tenderness
> and mercy in preserving me from the snare of the hat....[569]

Writing to his brother William, Isaac reflected on how he came to be ensnared in the Perrot matter:

> O brother! there is a high-mindedness ... which takes upon it
> to judge beyond its growth and capacity; and there is a fear...,
> lest any thing ... should get up, or judge, or be any thing,
> beyond or beside the pure Truth...[570]

We have there another polarity: "high-mindedness" against fear of being wrong. Perhaps a little more consciousness of that fear might have kept Isaac from getting caught in the "snare of the hat," but more important than hindsight is that Isaac learned from the experience. Carl Jung:

> There is no light without shadow and no psychic wholeness
> without imperfection. To round itself out, life calls not for
> perfection but for completeness; and for this the 'thorn in the
> flesh' is needed, the suffering of defects without which there
> is no progress and no ascent.[571]

Isaac learned the value of unity among Friends from his experience of the "snare of the hat"—a trivial issue, really, but it interfered with worship. Diversity is good, but Friends' yearning for peace and harmony in the community must also be in the balance. If Isaac had not been open to input, he'd have missed seeing his error. Extreme high-mindedness (what Jung called "inflation") takes no counsel, but Isaac did, and that let him recover and get back on track.

> Think it possible that you may be mistaken.
> Britain Yearly Meeting[572]

Peter is never more prominently on stage in John than in chapter 21. Before now, Peter's over-eagerness, brittle with fear, has tripped him up, but in chapter 21, Jesus reclaims him. The triple affirmation required for Peter's recovery was that he loved Jesus. "Complete love casts out fear" (1 John 4:18), so with awareness

---

[567] Letter from Francis Howgill to Isaac Penington, 1663, quoted in Keiser & Moore, *Knowing the Mystery of God Within*, pages 44-45. The original letter is in the papers of Isaac's son John, who collected and copied Isaac's non-printed papers, in the library in Friends House, London.

[568] See Keiser & Moore, *Knowing the Mystery of God Within*, page 45.

[569] Letter to Nicholas Noye and others, 11 October 1667, reprinted in Keiser & Moore, *Knowing the Mystery of God Within*, pages 69.

[570] Letter to William Penington, in *Works*, volume 2, page 504-505.

[571] Jung, *Psychology and Alchemy*, in *Collected Works*, volume 12, paragraph 208.

[572] "Advices and Queries" number 17, in *Quaker Faith and Practice*, section 1.02.

of the love of Jesus, the fear does not become too much. The questions whether Peter loved Jesus were drawing Peter toward balance: consciousness of love was the "reconciling third"[573] that relieved his oscillation between over-achieving and fearing his worst.

John ends here, but Luke's portrait of Peter after this time, in the book of Acts, is of a leader, not an insecure but striving yet faltering learner, but a leader. He changed, and it was obtaining consciousness of love that changed him.

---

[573] See "Opposites in John and Jung" below.

The final words of Jesus (John 15-17)

Chapters 15-17 of the text appear to be inserted for <u>reasons noted at the end of chapter 14</u>. They hold up the narrative flow because they consist entirely of teachings. At the end of 14, Judas has left to arrange the hand-over of Jesus, but we lose our place in the narrative if we hear all the teachings in chapters 15-17. To keep a better sense of narrative flow, I have lifted them from their usual place and now end with them here.

"I am the vine" (15:1-17)

[1]"I am the True vine,[a] and my Father is the farmer. [2]He removes every branch in me that bears no fruit, and every branch that bears fruit he prunes so that it may bear more fruit. [3]You have already been pruned by the word I have spoken to you. [4]Remain in me,[b] and I in you. Just as the branch cannot bear fruit of itself unless it Remains in the vine, neither can you unless you Remain in me. [5]I am the vine, you the branches. Whoever Remains in me and I in him bears much fruit, because apart from me you can do nothing. [6]Whoever does not Remain in me is thrown out like a branch, dries out, and they gather them and throw them into the fire, and it burns. [7]If you Remain in me and my words Remain in you, ask what you wish, and it will come to you. [8]By this my Father was glorified, so that you bear much fruit and become my disciples.

[9]As the Father has Loved me, I also Loved you. Remain in my Love.[b] [10]If you keep my commandments, you will Remain in my Love, just as I have kept the commandments of my Father and Remain in his Love. [11]I have said these things to you so that my joy may be in you and your joy will be fulfilled.

[12]This is my commandment, that you Love each other as I Loved you. [13]No one has greater Love than this, to lay down one's life for his friends. [14]You are my friends if you do what I command you. [15]I am not calling you servants any longer because a servant does not know what his master does.[c] I have called you friends because all that I heard from my Father I have revealed to you. [16]You did not select me, but I selected you, and I appointed[d] you to go and bear much fruit. Your fruit will Remain, so that whatever you ask the Father for in my name he will give you. [17]I am commanding you to Love each other.

Meaning and resonance

a. **"I am the True vine"** (15:1): This could also have been translated as "the real vine". Either way, the vine and branches are symbols, and in the realm of the spiritual, symbols, sometimes with paradoxical meaning, may be the best and only way a person has to access her unconscious truth.

b. **"Remain in me…. Remain in my Love"** (15:4, 15:9): These two "Remains" have a slight difference in nuance: "Remain in me, and I in you" assumes that the Remaining is not already in progress. "Remain in my love" assumes that the Remaining is continuing, *i.e.* "go on Remaining in my love".

c. **"a servant does not know…"** (15:15): "Servant" could also be translated "slave", and more commonly meant a slave in the Roman world, in which slaves were far more common than hired help. In John 13:16, Jesus tells his disciples that a slave is no greater than his master. As these servants are also friends, I opted for the softer meaning in translation.

d. **"I appointed you..."** (15:16): "Appointed" in 15:16 is the same Greek word as "lay down" in 15:13; in other words, these two sentences are linked by a shared word:

> "No one has greater love than this, to lay down his life for his friends."

> "I appointed you to go and bear much fruit."

Reflections

"I am the vine; you are the branches." (15:5)

We are individual branches, but also all one single thing together, a vine, one unity comprised of various constituents. There is a mutuality between the vine and its branches: the vine nourishes the branches, and the branches the vine. They are interdependent. It is a profound image of unity in diversity.

Isaac Penington tells us that we branches were all *grafted* in; our original birth out of water did not make us branches:

> [T]he Word which was from the beginning ... is ingrafted into the heart of every believer, and into which the heart of every believer is ingrafted; and so he truly is in the vine, and the sap of the vine runs up into him, which makes him fruitful to God; he abiding in the Word..., and the Word ... abiding in him.[1]

All Friends are Friends by convincement, so we are all grafts into our community.[2] It is not possible to pass on the Light within oneself; another person must find it for herself within herself, a process that Friends traditionally call "convincement". Because we each have our own experience of the Light, we bring to that experience our habits of mind, our family background, our history, and other factors. Both vine and graft share enough commonality to nourish each other, water and minerals from below, sugar from the sunshine above. We are grafts that became part of the vine by opening a wound and inserting a new, unique branch into the vine of Friends' organisations.

The roots of the vine are grounded in love and the Life:

> [U]nity in the life is the ground of true brotherly love and fellowship. Not that another man walks just as I do; ... yet he walks by the same principle of light, and is felt in the same Spirit of life, which guideth both the weak and the strong ... to that one Spirit of life and truth, which all are to be subject to.[3]

It is love that lets each branch of the vine give up its own will, its desire to dominate, either the group or even just oneself. Jung observed:

---

[1] *An Examination of the Grounds*, in *Works*, volume 1, page 345.

[2] Membership was once conferred by birth, though this has not been so in Britain Yearly Meeting for some years. However, membership is not convincement or the first experience of the Light within. That experience is not transferable; it is unique to each soul.

[3] Penington, "Some Misrepresentations of Me", in *Works*, volume 4, page 315.

> Where love reigns, there is no will to power; and where the will to power is paramount, love is lacking. The one is but the shadow of the other.[4]

In a vine, branches are made up of branches. On a collective level, local Quaker meetings are part of larger meetings like a series of concentric circles. There is considerable variety among us, but we also have much in common. Quakers are different from other religious denominations. Some Quakers today do not consider themselves Christian, but traditionally, Quakerism has been a branch of Christianity, that "religion of chronic squabblers", as Jung called them:

> A Christian of today no longer ought to cling obstinately to a one-sided credo, but should face the fact that Christianity has been in a state of schism for four hundred years.... Behind those barriers he can rejoice in his absolute and consistent conviction and deem himself above the conflict, but outside them, he keeps the conflict alive by his intransigence and continues to deplore the pig-headedness and stiff-neckedness of everybody else. It seems as if Christianity had been from the outset the religion of chronic squabblers, and even now it does everything in its power never to let the squabbles rest. Remarkably enough, it never stops preaching the gospel of neighbourly love.[5]

Jung wrote those words in 1955. It is still true that the various branches of Christianity each still hold that their branch is the only way to be saved, a situation set up for conflict. Jung was actually short-sighted to say that "Christianity has been in a state of schism for four hundred years"; he forgot the Orthodox and the great schism of 1054 between west and east. Each "one true church" evangelises everyone outside that church, but "for the psychologist, there is nothing more stupid than the missionary point of view, which declares the gods of the poor heathen to be illusory."[6] Quakers are different; if you find among Friends a spiritual way forward for yourself, good, you have found a way, but it is not the only possible way to spiritual fulfilment.[7]

However, it is also true that hardly anyone actually cares about Christianity or its "squabbles" anymore. We have religions now that are without conventional gods. Money, success in the World, politics, social media followings—many causes now take the place of Christianity and receive the devotion that it formerly received. The large branch of the vine that is Christianity has withered. The farmer will want to clear it eventually, so that new growth can come in its place (John 15:6).

---

[4] *Two Essays in Analytical Psychology*, in *Collected Works*, volume 11, part A, paragraph 78.

[5] Jung, *Mysterium Coniunctionis*, in *Collected Works*, volume 14, paragraph 257.

[6] Raimar Keintzel, *C.G. Jung: Retter der Religion? Auseinandersetzung mit Werk und Wirkung*, (Stuttgart: Quell Verlag, 1991), page 60 (my translation). Keintzel was a Reformed pastor in Baden, Switzerland, where I was a Mormon missionary many years ago. In the original: "Für den Psychologen gibt es nichts Blöderes als den Missiuonarstandpunkt, der die Götter der armen Heiden für Illusionen erklärt."

[7] Williams, *Quakerism: A Theology for our Time* pages 94-97.

Jung, the son of a Swiss Reformed pastor, had a vision and a dream about this situation. The vision needs a prior warning, however: the unconscious is not obliged to be polite, respectful or reverent. It can be disgusting, and this vision has that quality. However, the vision graphically and unforgettably illustrates the collapse of Christianity in our time. Murray Stein retells it:

> The young boy of 10 or 12 comes out of school one day and looks up at the beautiful, gleaming cathedral in the [Basel] town square. Glancing upward and high above the cathedral, which was the "residence" of his [maternal] grand-father, the well-known Basel clergyman Samuel Preiswerk, he "sees" God's throne. All seems well with the world until suddenly he finds himself at the edge of an existential abyss. He is about to have a frightening thought, which he must at all costs block from entering consciousness. He rushes home and for three days struggles mightily to control his mind. Finally, he gives up and suffers the completion of his thought:

Basel cathedral at night from across the Rhine. Nearest us are the apse and transept. (thanks to Wikipedia)

> > I gathered all my courage, as though I were about to leap forthwith into hellfire, and let the thought come. I saw before me the cathedral, the blue sky. God sits on His golden throne, high above the world, and from under the throne an enormous turd falls upon the sparkling new roof, shatters it, and breaks the walls of the cathedral asunder.[8]

> Completion of the thought brought relief, strangely in a feeling of grace. He had allowed the intolerable thought to enter his consciousness, and he felt that God Himself had willed that he should think it.

> Of course, one could easily speculate about the personal motives for a hostile fantasy of this kind, but it would miss the point that this experience is also a reflection of the shattering of a religious container that has taken place throughout western culture over the past several generations. For modern men and women, the gleaming House of God is smashed. The comfort of containment in an intact Christian tradition is no longer available.[9]

To Jung, the Christian branch of the vine was quickly becoming moribund. In the last 25 years of his life, he wrote volume after volume trying to save it, sometimes "emotionally and with his whole being as he became deeply engaged by the crisis

---

[8] Stein cites here *Jung, Memories Dreams, Reflections*, page 39.

[9] "Jung's 'Green Christ': A Transformational Symbol for Christianity", in *Collected Writings of Murray Stein*, volume 5, pages 252-253.

in Christianity in the age of modernity."[10]   It also cost him an important friendship.[11]

Ultimately, he lost the struggle to save the Christian branch. However, he also had a dream that "dreams the myth onwards".[12] This is how Jung describes his dream:

> In 1939, I gave a seminar on the *Spiritual Exercises* of Ignatius Loyola. At the same time I was occupied on the studies for *Psychology and Alchemy*. One night I awoke and saw, bathed in bright light at the foot of my bed, the figure of Christ on the Cross. It was not quite life-size, but extremely distinct and I saw that his body was made of greenish gold. The vision was marvellously beautiful, and yet I was profoundly shaken by it. ....
>
> I had been thinking a great deal about the *Anima Christi*, one of the meditations from the *Spiritual Exercises*. The vision came to me as if to point out that I had overlooked something in my reflections: the analogy of Christ with the *aurum non vulgi* and *viriditas* of the alchemists.[13] When I realised that the vision pointed to this central alchemical symbol, and that I had had an essentially alchemical vision of Christ, I felt comforted.
>
> The green gold is the living quality which the alchemists saw not only in man but also in inorganic nature. It is an expression of the life-spirit, ... [that] animates the whole cosmos. This spirit has poured himself out into everything even into inorganic matter; he is present in the metal and stone. My vision was thus a union of the Christ-image with his analogue in matter, the *filius macrocosmi*. If I had not been so struck by the greenish gold, I would have been tempted to assume that something essential was missing from my "Christian" view—in other words, that my tradition-al Christ-image was somehow inadequate and that I still had to catch up with part of the Christian development. The emphasis on the metal, however, showed me the undisguised

---

[10] *Ibid.*, page 251.

[11] Jung's friendship with Victor White, a Dominican, fell miserably to pieces when Jung published *Answer to Job*, which White criticised roundly. See Dourley, *On Behalf of the Mystical Fool*, pages 125-134.

[12] Jung, *The Archetypes and the Collective Unconscious*, in *Collected Works*, volume 11, part 1, paragraph 271.

[13] This footnote from Jung's editor, Aniela Jaffé here: The more serious alchemists realised that the purpose of their work was not the transmutation of base metals into gold, but the production of *aurum non vulgi* (not the common gold) or *aurum philosophicum* (philosophical gold). In other words, they were concerned with spiritual values and the problem of psychic transformation.

alchemical conception of Christ as a union of spiritually alive and physically dead matter.[14]

I am not an alchemist, and I don't understand alchemical terms. Fortunately, Murray Stein explains this dream:

> What then, about the actual content of the vision? I will follow Jung's thoughts and associations into alchemy. The Christ at the foot of his bed is the traditional symbol of Christianity, but with a difference: He is made of green gold and is also an image of the *filius philosophorum* of alchemy. What is the *filius philosophorum*? He is the son of the Mother (of matter), not the son of the Father (of spirit). This image of the Green Christ, then, represents the response of the unconscious to the conscious attitude of the Christian dominant. Christian tradition expresses its God image in the dogma of the Holy Trinity, which excludes matter, earth, the feminine, the chthonic, the dark, the instinctual, and the body. These elements of reality are not included in the Godhead. The *filius philosophorum*, in his form as Mercurius duplex, is a highly ambiguous agent, the spirit of the earth and the unconscious, of instinctuality and impulse, of tricksterism and deception as well as brilliant revelation. It was the concern of the alchemists to redeem this spirit, to bring him into consciousness and to hold him fast (fixation). This meant overcoming the censure that Christianity had placed upon matter, the body, nature, and instinct. Alchemy held that nature was not ruled by evil and therefore wholly to be shunned, but rather that it contained a piece of Divinity left there by God when He created the world. This divine light in nature needed to be found and honored as a part of the Divinity. On a psychological level, Jung felt compelled to release the spirit within the unconscious, which would lead to a personal experience of the God within.

> This numinous spirit within the unconscious is symbolized in Jung's Green Christ. The vision was a response from the unconscious to Jung's shamanic incubation of the problems of humanity. The *filius philosophorum*, the child of Mother Nature and here also captured in the image of Christ, the Son of the Heavenly Father, was similarly sacrificing himself upon the cross for the sake of wholeness. This is a sign of nature's cooperation, finally, with the Judeo Christian line of development: The unconscious is prepared to assist in the further individuation or development of Christianity. In this vision, the spirit of Nature and the Son of the Heavenly Father

---

[14] *Memories, Dreams, Reflections*, pages 210-211 (hardback edition); page 237 of paperback edition

are brought together in a single image. Father and Mother
are found to be uniting and cooperating.[15]

A new God-image emerges that is more complete than the former one. Christianity took no account of the state of the earth as it became worse and worse. Now we utterly need a Green Christ to redeem the climate change that has overtaken us. We no longer need scientists to tell us climate change is happening; we can see the evidence in events, in actual experience. Jung's vision uniting the crucified Christ with matter and the earth is profound and beautiful. We need a Green Redeemer, a Rescuing God-image incorporating Mother Earth. A new God-image re-values our values.

John 15 offers us another green image besides the Green Christ of Jung's dream: "I am the vine," Christ said. A vine does not remain the same vine forever. Branches die, some of them large, and new branches take their place in the sun. The farmer prunes away the dead wood to make room for new green growth. Grapes do not grow on old wood, so he removes that too in time, grafting in new shoots to replace them. We need our farmer.

"You are my friends if you do what I command you" (15:14)

The last paragraph of this section of John is riddled with paradoxes. Jesus is ordering his friends about in 15:14 and 15:17; however, ordering about is not consistent with the equality of friendship. However, the order is to love (15:17), and love is what friends do, but it comes naturally, without having to be commanded.

> In friendship we are beyond law and obedience, beyond rules and commandments, beyond all constraint, in a world of freedom. But did not Jesus say, 'Ye are my friends if ye do whatsoever I command you'? Yes, he did. We, on our side, are apt to miss the quiet humour of his paradoxes. 'These are my commandments,' he goes on, 'that ye love one another'.

> In other words, the friendship of Christ is realised in our friendships with one another. His command is that we rise above commandments, and therefore his obedience is perfect freedom. Make service your centre, with its laws and duties and self-sacrifice, and life is a bondage. Make friendship the centre and life is freedom.[16]

Modern commentators of John abhor inconsistencies in their work so they have little tolerance for paradox and contradiction. Jesus did not share that intolerance, as this text shows. Indeed, John shows such a taste for paradox and its ironies that I rather think our author savoured the "quiet humour" he found there.

Paradox is a key to understanding the soul, as Jung explains:

> [Paradox] does more justice to the unknowable than clarity can do, for uniformity of meaning robs the mystery of its darkness and sets it up as something that is *known*. That is a usurpation, and it leads the human intellect into hubris by

---

[15] "Jung's 'Green Christ': A Transformational Symbol for Christianity", in *Collected Works of Murray Stein*, volume 5, pages 259-261.

[16] John MacMurray, quoted in Britain Yearly Meeting, *Quaker Faith and Practice*, section 22:10.

> pretending that it, the intellect, has got hold of the
> transcendent mystery by a cognitive act and has "grasped" it.
> The paradox therefore reflects a higher level of intellect and,
> by not forcibly representing the unknowable as known, gives
> a more faithful picture of the real state of affairs.[17]

So back to the question: why is love commanded? Its roots lie in a deep imperative arising from the self, that which we inwardly perceive as God. The self commands us to let it make itself conscious in the process Jung called "individuation". Murray Stein:

> As a dynamic force, individuation refers to an innate
> tendency—call it a drive, an impulse, or ... an imperative—for
> a living being to incarnate itself fully, to become truly itself
> within the empirical world of time and space, and in the case
> of humans to become aware of who and what they are.[18]

Jung also used the word "incarnation" to refer to the process of the self becoming conscious in humans;[19] the inner, unconscious divinity seeks a way out of its unconscious darkness into the empirical world of the five senses and consciousness realised in a physical body.

Individuation is a drive or imperative of the soul to let the self become more and more conscious, but that does not explain why "love each other" is an imperative. However, there is an answer in 1 John 4:8, "Anyone who does not Love does not Know God, because God is Love." That answer is more complicated than first appears, however. Some people can't love.

Murray Stein uses the mythic character Hephaistos (Vulcan in Latin) to illustrate why a person may find love impossible. He was the child of the goddess Hera, wife of Zeus, but Hera made Hephaistos parthenogenically out of jealousy that Zeus had made Athene without her involvement; Athene had sprung full-grown from his head. Hephaistos came out with deformed legs, however. Hera rejected him out of disgust and hurled him down from Olympus into the sea, where two nymphs took him in. Although they were kind to him, he never recovered from the initial rejection by his own real mother. It left him with an "inflamed negative mother complex".[20]

> A complex is a festering emotional wound, often mostly
> unconscious, that has a life of its own. It harbors
> resentments, hurts and angry and hurtful intentions, and it
> bubbles to the surface in spontaneous and often surprising
> ways. Complexes are the motivators of much psychological
> behaviour.[21]

His mother complex leaves Hephaistos convinced that love is a thing to be earned because he does not innately deserve it. Earning it makes it the result of a sale transaction, so he has "a commercial attitude toward the feminine and toward

---

[17] *Psychology and Religion: West and East*, in *Collected Works*, volume 11, paragraph 417.

[18] *The Principle of Individuation*, page xii.

[19] *Answer to Job*, in *Collected Works*, volume 11, paragraph 693.

[20] Stein, *The Principle of Individuation*, page 119.

[21] *Ibid.*, page 111.

the love relationship."[22] However, real love is not an agreed exchange, so real love is not psychologically possible for him. It does not come naturally like it does for people without his complex. He thinks, however, that he does actually love, but in reality, it is too laboured and purchased to be real. He is really just acting as if he loves, going through the motions. He doesn't actually know what real love is because his complex blocks his individuation.[23]

Hephaistos finds a way past his complex thanks to someone who loosens the blockage for him. But back to the question: why is love commanded? Perhaps the reason lies in the fact that some people need time and help simply to be able to do it, and the command is psychological, that inner drive to remove the block that is keeping out the Divine, preventing the Spirit self from reaching consciousness.

"We love because [Jesus] first loved us," says 1 John 1:19. For that to happen now that Jesus is not physically on earth, we would have to find him and his love inwardly. Isaac Penington describes that experience:

> [Love] is the sweet, tender, melting nature of God, flowing up
> through his seed of life into the creature, and of all things
> making the creature most like unto himself, both in nature
> and operation.[24]

"Seed of life" there means the transcendent function, that bridge between consciousness and unconsciousness that "is the ultimate goal of individuation.[25] It makes the "creature" (the conscious, physical part of us) "most like unto himself", as Isaac put it; a result that Murray Stein described as "the integration of conscious and unconscious and the formation of a new structure of identity".[26] Isaac often said he had become a "new creation" under a "new covenant" (his identity was reconstructed). He described the process:

> [W]e are not persons that have shot up out of the old root into
> another appearance, as one sect hath done out of another, till
> many are come up one after another, the ground still
> remaining the same out of which they all grew; but that
> ground hath been shaken and [is] shaking..., and a real change
> brought forth in us out of that spirit wherein the world lives
> and worships, into another Spirit, into which nothing which
> is of the world can enter. And here we have met with the call
> of God, the conversion to God, the regeneration in God....
>
> Now our work in the world is to hold forth the virtues of him
> that hath called us; to live like God; not to own any thing in
> the world which God doth not own; to forget our country, our
> kindred, our father's house, and to live like persons of another
> country, of another kindred, of another family; not to do any
> thing of ourselves, and which is pleasing to the old nature;
> but all our words, all our conversation, yea, every thought in

---

[22] *Ibid.*, page 119.

[23] *Ibid.*, page 123.

[24] *Some Mysteries of God's Kingdom Glanced At*, in *Works*, volume 2, page 341.

[25] Stein, *The Principle of Individuation*, page 81.

[26] Stein, *The Principle of Individuation*, page 79.

us, is to become new. Whatever comes from us, is to come from the new principle of life in us, and to answer that in others....[27]

He longed for God within to occupy him fully as he fully sacrifices not only his old identity but all his ego consciousness:

> [T]his my soul waits and cries after, even the full springing up of eternal love in my heart, and in the swallowing of me wholly into it, and the bringing of my soul wholly forth in it, that the life of God in its own perfect sweetness may fully run forth through this vessel, and not be at all tinctured by the vessel but perfectly tincture and change the vessel into its own nature; and then shall no fault be found in my soul before the Lord, but the spotless life be fully enjoyed by me, and become a perfectly pleasant sacrifice to my God.[28]

Another great Friend, John Woolman, described a transformative dream that made him forget his name, his identity:

> In a time of sickness with the pleurisy a little upward of two years and a half ago, I was brought so near the gates of death that I forgot my name. Being then desirous to know who I was, I saw a mass of matter of a dull and gloomy colour, between the south and the east, and was informed that this mass was human beings in as great misery as they could be and live, and that I was mixed in with them and henceforth might not consider myself as a distinct or separate being. In this state I remained several hours. I then heard a soft, melodious voice, more pure and harmonious than the voice of an angel who spake unto other angels. The words were, "John Woolman is dead." I soon remembered that I once was John Woolman, and being assured that I was alive in the body, I greatly wondered what that heavenly voice could mean. I believed beyond doubting that it was the voice of an holy angel, but as yet it was a mystery to me.

> I was then carried in spirit to the mines, where poor oppressed people were digging rich treasures for those called Christians, and heard them blaspheme the name of Christ, at which I was grieved, for his name to me was precious. Then I was informed that these heathens were told that those who oppressed them were the followers of Christ, and they said amongst themselves: "If Christ directed them to use us in this sort, then Christ is a cruel tyrant."

> At this time the voice of the angel remained a mystery, and in the morning my dear wife and some others coming to my bedside, I asked them if they knew who I was; and they, telling me I was John Woolman, thought I was only

---

[27] *The Way of Life and Death made Manifest*, in *Works*, volume 1, page 93.

[28] *Some Mysteries of God's Kingdom Glanced At* in *Works*, volume 2, page 341-342.

light-headed, for I told them not what the angel said, nor was I disposed to talk much to anyone, but was very desirous to get so deep that I might understand this mystery.

My tongue was often so dry that I could not speak until I had moved it about and gathered some moisture, and as I lay still for a time, at length I felt divine power prepare my mouth that I could speak, and then I said: "I am crucified with Christ, nevertheless I live; yet not I, but Christ that liveth in me, and the life I now live in the flesh is by faith in the Son of God who loved me and gave himself for me.[29]

Woolman was a native of what is now southern New Jersey, but which was then an English colony. He died in 1772 in York, having come to Britain Yearly Meeting to testify against slavery, the cause to which he devoted his adult life. He got a mostly chilly reception from Friends in Britain, but he gave the spark that lit Friends' involvement in the movement against slavery in Britain and in the USA.

Friends in York recorded one of his last spoken prayers to his "friend":

[T]hough I have gone through many trials and sore afflictions, thou hast been with me, continuing a father and a friend. I feel thy power now, and beg that in the approaching trying moments, thou wilt keep my heart steadfast unto thee.[30]

Woolman died in 1772 a poor messenger on his last mission, living from the kindness of Friends in York who saw in him the deeply spiritual man he was. From what he could see at his death, he had failed in his mission, though in reality, he had not. He had planted a seed that grew:

1774   Woolman's Yearly Meeting, Philadelphia, decided that "no one could be both a member of Philadelphia Yearly Meeting and own slaves".[31]

1794   The USA prohibited the building or outfitting of slave ships in U.S. ports,[32] and in 1807, it prohibited the importation of slaves.[33]

1807   The UK banned the slave trade in the British Empire.[34]

1833   The Slavery Abolition Act 1833 began phasing out slavery in the British Empire. Owners were paid for their slaves.

1865   After fighting a civil war during which slaves were promised emancipation, the USA adopted the 13th amendment of its constitution to prohibit slavery. Owners were not paid for their slaves. Many had died in the

---

[29] John Woolman, *The Journal and Essays of John Woolman*, edited by Phillips P. Moulton (New York: Oxford University Press, 1971), pages 185-186.

[30] *Journal of John Woolman*, edited by Amelia Mott Gummere, pages 322-323; quoted in Slaughter, *The Beautiful Soul of John Woolman*, page 377.

[31] Slaughter, *The Beautiful Soul of John Woolman*, page 325. Slaughter's book also explains how Pennsylvania's restrictions on the import and keeping of slaves increased in the preceding decades.

[32] See Slave Trade Act of 1794.

[33] See Act Prohibiting the Importation of Slaves of 1807.

[34] See Slave Trade Act of 1807.

war, which killed about 655,000 people, more U.S. losses than any other war.[35]

How did John Woolman make the spark fly? By love. Michael Birkel explains:

> Although he keenly believed that slavekeeping "deprave[s] the mind in like manner and with as great certainty as prevailing cold congeals water" and therefore can "shut up the mind against the gentle movings of uncreated purity, which bear witness against the oppressive practice of slavery," there is yet a "witness" in others (i.e. the Seed) which one can reach. In fact, one is more likely to reach this witness if one manifests a "spirit of true charity" when confronting the oppressor. John Woolman therefore writes that Friends must "be kindly affectioned" toward slavekeeping Friends. His own descriptions of some of his visits to slavekeepers shows that he practiced what he preached. His *Journal* notes that "divine love and true sympathizing tenderness of heart prevailed at times in this service." On another occasion we learn that "through the strength of that love which is stronger than death, tenderness of heart was felt amongst us in our visits." This is remarkable, when one considers that Woolman not only spoke to the slaveholders on a very difficult issue but also insisted frequently on paying the slaves for their services to him.
>
> While traveling on foot to visit slavekeepers in Maryland, Woolman mentions that one of his motivations was to "set an example of lowliness before the eyes of their [*i.e.* the slaves'] sufferings of Christ and his tasting death for every man...was livingly revived in me" seems to indicate that he saw these labors in redemptive terms.[36]

John Woolman was a suffering servant, and he did his work through love.

The World's hatred (15:18-16:4)

The symbol of the vine is timeless so it is easy to forget now that we are in the final days of Jesus's life.

> [18]If the World hates you, Know that it hated me first. [19]If you were of the World, the World would Love you as its own. However, because you are not of the World but rather I chose you out of the World, that is why the the World hates you. [20]Remember what I told you: a servant is no greater than his master.[a] If they persecuted me, they will persecute you. If they kept my word, they will also keep yours. [21]But in reality, they will do all these things to you because of my name, because they do not Know who sent me. [22]If I had not come and spoken to them,

---

[35] Wikipedia reports an estimated 655,000 "military deaths" in the American Civil War. The next deadliest war for the USA was World War II, which killed 405,399. See United States Military Casualties of War, retrieved 2 May 2023.

[36] "John Woolman on the Cross", in *The Lamb's War: Quaker Essays to Honor Hugh Barbour*, edited by Michael L. Birkel and John W. Newman (Earlham College Press, 1992) pages 99-100. Original footnotes omitted.

they would not be Wrong, but now they have no excuse for their Wrong. [23]Whoever hates me also hates the Father. [24]If I had not done the works among them that no one else did, they would have no Wrong, but now they have seen and hated both me and my Father. [25]It was to fulfil the word written in their law, "They hated me without a cause."[b]

[26]When the Counsellor comes, whom I shall send from the Father, the spirit of Truth that comes from the Father, he will Testify of me.[c] [27]You too are to be Witnesses because you have been with me from the beginning.

[1]I have told you these things so you will not be ensnared. [2]They will put you out of synagogues.[d] Indeed, the time is coming when whoever kills you will think they have done God a service. [3]They will do these things because they did not Know the Father or me. [4]But I have told you these things so that, when the time comes, you may remember that I told you of them.

Meaning and resonance

a. **"a servant is no greater than his master"** (15:20): This is an echo of John 13:16. It also contradicts 15:15, "I am not calling you servants any longer". Contradictions expose paradoxes: friends may also serve.

b. **"They hated me without a cause."** (15:25): This recalls two psalms, first 35:19:

> Do not let my treacherous enemies rejoice over me,
> or those who hate me without cause wink the eye.

The other psalm is 69:4:

> More in number than the hairs of my head
> are those who hate me without cause.

c. **"he will Testify about me"** (15:26): Grammatically, the "he" refers to the "Counsellor" not the nearer "Spirit" because "Spirit" would have required an "it" here ("Spirit" is neuter in Greek). "That the Spirit is personal is strongly implied here."[37]

d. **"out of the synagogues"** (16:1): See the Reflection above on "excluded from synagogue". Note also in verse 15:25 that the allusion is to "their" law.

Jesus will go, the Counsellor will come (16:4-15)

"I did not tell you these things from the beginning because I was with you. [5]But now I am going to the one who sent me, but none of you asks me 'Where are you going?' [6]But because I have told you these things, sorrow has filled your heart. [7]But I tell you the Truth, it is better for you that I go away, for unless I go away, the Counsellor will not come to you. If I go, I will send him to you. [8]And when he comes, he will convince the World[a] of Wrongfulness, of what is right,[b] and of judgment. [9]First of Wrongfulness, because they do not Trust in me; [10]second of what is right,[b] because I go to the Father and you will no longer see me; [11]and third of judgment, because the ruler of the World has been judged.

[12]I still have many things to tell you, but you can't bear them yet. [13]When he comes, the spirit of Truth, he will guide you into all Truth,[c] for he will not speak of himself, but he will speak what he hears, and he will tell you what is coming. [14]He

---

[37] Brown, *The Gospel According to John*, volume 29A, page 689.

will glorify me because he will take from me and tell it to you. ¹⁵All that the Father has is mine; that is why I told you that he takes from me and will tell you.

Meaning and resonance

a. **"he will convince the World…"** (16:8): The word translated "convince" is ἐλέγχω, which has a range of meanings. Raymond Brown:

> The verb means both "to bring to light, expose" and "to convict someone of something" (also "to correct, punish," but such a meaning is not apropos here).

I chose "convince" as a word in between the two meanings but also used in old Quaker writings to mean something more like "convict" or "correct". Isaac Penington:

> *The first way of meeting with the Spirit of God, is as a convincer of sin.* Here is the true entrance…. It is not by soaring aloft into high imaginations and forms of worship; but by coming down to this low thing. This is the first and most proper work of the Spirit of God toward fallen man, whereby he makes way toward the writing of God's law in the heart; namely, to convince of sin. And where should man look first to meet with him, but in his first work upon him? When Christ promised the Comforter, the Spirit of truth, he said this concerning him, "that he should convince the world of sin." John 16:8.[38]

A more psychological view would note that the way to individuation is not usually simple and direct. We each have our complexes blocking the Light, so we may see nothing or only a glimmer. "It is fair to say that most people come through a far less-than-ideal childhood and youth. Individuation takes place, therefore, within a troubled mind and a complex-ridden context."[39]

b. **"of what is right"** (16:8, 16:10): This word, δικαιοσύνη, essentially means "what is right". It is also often translated as "righteousness" or justice. It is the opposite of Wrongfulness. The word is very common in Matthew and Paul, but in John, it appears only in these two verses.

c. **"he will guide you into all Truth"** (16:13): The oldest manuscripts are divided on whether this says "into all Truth" or "in all Truth".[40]

Reflection

"Unless I go away, the Counsellor will not come to you." (16:7)

This section marks a transition in the human perception of God that has never been reversed: "Unless I go away, the Counsellor will not come to you." (16:7) The physical Presence is leaving so that the inward Presence will come. Our conscious minds prefer what we can see, hear, touch and even measure. Such perception is subject to distortion by the mind, but not to the same degree as inward perception, which is far more subjective and harder to verify and correct

---

[38] *The Way of Life and Death Made Manifest*, in *Works*, volume 1, page 64. Italics in original.

[39] Stein, *The Principle of Individuation*, page 105.

[40] Brown, *The Gospel According to John*, volume 29A, page 707.

because complexes can block or distort the Light. However, with the physical presence now gone, the inward option is the only one still available. The situation is not hopeless, however, because 16:8-11 says the spirit of Truth will clear our minds. "[T]he Holy Spirit represents the aspect or function of the Self that becomes a mediating structure between the ego and the Self."[41]

Jung used the word "incarnation" to describe the entry of the Holy Spirit into the human ego and into the body. It is this incarnation of the Holy Spirit in humanity—not the incarnation of Jesus, despite his suffering—that redresses the wrong done Job.

> As stated in the first chapter of St John, Jesus represented a light which, though it shone in the darkness, was not comprehended by the darkness. He remained outside and above mankind. Job, on the other hand, was an ordinary human being, and therefore the wrong done him, and through him to mankind, can, according to divine justice, only be repaired by an incarnation of God in an empirical human being. This act of expiation is performed by the [Counsellor]; for, just as man must suffer from God, so God must suffer from man. Otherwise, there can be no reconciliation between the two.[42]

One unavoidable impression Jesus gives in John is that he is aloof from most people. Possibly not from the Beloved Disciple, Mary Magdalene, and his mother, but from most people, he maintains a certain distance. His disciples address him with titles such as "rabbi" or "teacher". John's emphasis falls on Jesus's divinity rather than his humanity. To Jung, Jesus's divine detachment from ordinary humanity makes him unsuitable for service in repairing the wrong done Job. He is too much a God. The job must be done by someone as human as Job.

"In his Answer to Job ... Jung interprets Yahweh as a representation of an archaic form of the Self, Job as the ego, and Satan as the [principle of individuation]."[43] In the story of Job, as in Eden, Satan is the entity that moves the story along; God becomes more conscious because his opposite becomes conscious and tempts God to reveal himself. God does so but does not like what he sees—but at least he now sees it. That sight enables God to make a moral choice for once, instead of torturing Job out of unconscious envy. Jack Wallis again:

> [Some people] all too easily think that morality attaches to feelings, that hateful, hostile, cruel or greedy feelings are immoral. They do not, perhaps, realise that the feelings that arise in us are neither moral nor immoral, but neutral. The supreme importance of morality is how we choose to act on

[41] Stein, "C.G. Jung, Psychologist and Theologian", in Collected Writings of Murray Stein, volume 5, page 269.

[42] Jung, Answer to Job, in Collected Works, volume 22, paragraph 257.

[43] Stein, "C.G. Jung, Psychologist and Theologian", in Collected Writings of Murray Stein, volume 5, page 268.

our feelings. And we shall not be free to choose if we do not know what they are.[44]

God becomes capable of moral choice when God becomes conscious. The God-given suffering of Job forces God into a measure of consciousness, which enables God himself to be convinced of his own Wrongfulness. "Now my eye sees you; therefore I despise myself and repent in dust and ashes," said the Lord in Job 42:6.

God is conventionally seen as perfect, incapable of Wrongdoing, but that is not the God we encounter in the book of Job, which demands that we see God as learning and changing (Job 42:1-7). God is an archetype evolving and becoming more and more conscious and complete in human minds. Jung never let on whether he thought God existed apart from in the mind.[45] However, because inwardness is all we have now—God is no longer physically present—inwardness is where we experience God, even though the inward experience does not answer the question whether God exists beyond inwardness. The inward experience is all we have, and Isaac declared many times that it is enough.

It is enough, but it is also fraught. The inward experience is easy to ignore or deny because it does not appear with the power expected for God's appearance, which may also be blocked from human awareness by complexes, our inward antagonists. It begins as "little weak stirrings of life in the heart", stirring despite the "corruption in him" (his complexes), and even though something more like a spectacle on the road to Damascus (Acts 9) would seem more powerfully persuasive:

> [B]eing touched, being quickened by the eternal power, being turned by a secret virtue and stirring of the life in his heart, then he can turn towards that which turneth him. Being drawn by the life, by the power; he can follow after the life, and after the power. Finding the sweetness of the living vine, and his soul made alive by the sap of the vine, his heart can now cleave to, and abide in, the vine....
>
> I confess the power doth not so flow forth to man, as man expects it; but the power of life works man out of death in a mystery, and begins in him as weakness. There is all the strength, all the power of the enemy, against the work of God in the heart. There is but a little thing (like a grain of mustard-seed), a weak thing, a foolish thing, even that which is not (to man's eye) [able] to overcome all this; and yet in this is the power. And here is the great deceit of man; he looks for a great, manifest power in or upon him to begin with, and doth not see how the power is in the little weak stirrings of life in the heart, in the rising up ... against the mighty strength of corruption in him; which he returning towards, cleaving to, and waiting upon the Lord in, the strength of the Lord will be made manifest in its season, and he will be drawn nearer and

---

[44] Wallis, *Jung and the Quaker Way*, page 24; also in Britain Yearly Meeting, *Quaker Faith and Practice*, paragraph 21.11.

[45] Stein, "On C.G. Jung's Psychology of Religion", in *Collected Works of Murray Stein*, volume 5, page 288.

nearer to the Lord, and his enemies be overcome and fall he
knows not how.[46]

Those "enemies" are inward (complexes); all he speaks of there is inward. The "great deceit of man" is a self-deception, looking for a big voice the better to ignore the still small one (1 Kings 19:11-12). Complexes put us at cross-purposes with ourselves and with the self in each of us, the inward Divine seeking consciousness but conflicted. Jung again:

> God acts out of the unconscious of man and forces him to harmonize and unite the opposing influences to which his mind is exposed from the unconscious. The unconscious wants both: to divide and to unite. In his striving for unity, therefore, man may always count on the help of a metaphysical advocate, as Job clearly recognized. The unconscious wants to flow into consciousness in order to reach the light, but at the same time it continually thwarts itself, because it would rather remain unconscious. That is to say, God wants to become man, but not quite. This conflict in his nature is so great that the incarnation [of the Holy Spirit in humanity] can only be bought by an expiatory self-sacrifice offered up to the wrath of God's dark side.[47]

Jesus did not die for our sins. He died for God's, according to Jung. Amazingly, Job always remained faithful to God, because he knew inwardly that his vindicator was alive *in God*, even though God seems completely unaware of what Job saw in him. Speaking to his "friends", Job said:

> How long will you torment me,
> and break me in pieces with words?
> These ten times you have cast reproach upon me;
> are you not ashamed to wrong me?
> And even if it is true that I have erred,
> my error remains with me.

> If indeed you magnify yourselves against me,
> and make my humiliation an argument against me,
> know that God has put me in the wrong,
> and closed his net around me.
> Even when I cry out, "Violence!" I am not answered;
> I call aloud, but there is no justice.
> ....

> O that my words were written down!
> O that they were inscribed in a book!
> O that with an iron pen and with lead
> they were engraved on a rock for ever!
> For I know that my Vindicator lives,
> and that at the last he will stand upon the earth;
> and after my skin has been thus destroyed,
> then in my flesh shall I see God,

---

[46] *To Such as Complain that They Want Power*, in *Works*, volume 2, page 287-289.

[47] *Answer to Job*, in *Collected Works*, volume 11, paragraph 740.

> whom I shall see on my side,
> and my eyes shall behold, and not another. [48]

Sorrow will turn to joy (16:16-33)

[16]"In a short time you will see me no longer, and again after a short time you will see me." [17]Then some of his disciples said to each other,[a] "What is this he is saying to us, 'in a short time you will see me no longer, and again after a short time you will see me', and 'I am going to the Father'?" [18]So they were saying, "What does he mean by saying 'in a short time'? We do not Know what he is talking about."

[19]Jesus Knew that they wanted to ask him, and he said to them, "You are trying to find out from each other what I meant, 'in a short time you will see me no longer, and again after a short time you will see me'. [20]Very truly I tell you that you will weep and mourn, but the World will rejoice; you will be sorrowful, but your sorrow will turn to joy. [21]When a woman is giving birth she has sorrow because her Hour has come, but when she has given birth to a child, she no longer remembers the distress for joy that a person has been born into the World. [22]So you have sorrow now,[b] but I will see you again, and your heart will rejoice, and no one will take your joy from you.

[23]"On that day you will ask nothing of me. Very truly I tell you, whatever you ask the Father for in my name, he will give you.[c] [24]Until now you have not asked for anything in my name. Ask and you will receive, so that your joy may be fulfilled.

[25]"I have been speaking to you in metaphors.[d] The Hour is coming when I will no longer speak in metaphors to you but will tell you plainly about the Father. [26]On that day you will ask in my name, and I do not say that I will ask the Father for you, [27]for the Father himself Loves you because you have Loved me and Trusted that I came from God. [28]I came from the Father and have come into the World. Again, I am leaving the World and going to the Father."

[29]His disciples said, "Yes, now you are speaking plainly and not in metaphors. [30]Now we Know that you Know all things and you have no need for anyone to ask you. By this we Trust that you came from God." [31]Jesus answered them, "Do you now Trust?[e] [32]The Hour is coming and has come for you to be scattered, each to his own, and you will leave me alone. But I am not alone because the Father is with me. [33]I have told you these things so that you may have peace in me. In the World you have trouble, but take courage, I have conquered the World."

Meaning and resonance

a. **"Then some of his disciples said to each other"** (16:17): The last time someone other than Jesus spoke was in John 14:22.

b. **"you have sorrow now"** (16:22): Some early manuscripts read "now you will have sorrow". Likewise, "no one will take your joy from you" also appears in present tense in some manuscripts, "no one takes your joy". This section has half a dozen small textual issues like these.

---

[48] Job 19:2-8 and 23-27. In the New Revised Standard Version, "Vindicator" is given as an alternative reading; the other option is "Redeemer". To me, "Vindicator" better suits the context of Job speaking of his suffering.

   c. **"whatever you ask the Father for in my name, he will give you"** (16:23): Another textual issue; the early manuscripts are divided on whether this reads as I translated it, or whether it says, "whatever you ask of the Father, he will give you in my name".

   d. **"I have been speaking to you in metaphors"** (16:25, 16:29): The word translated "metaphors" is the Greek word παροιμία. In classical Greek, it meant a maxim or proverb, but in John and the wisdom books of the Old Testament, it means a metaphor or analogy.[49] The other gospels use the word "παραβολή" (parable) instead. Parables have plot lines; the image of childbirth here is more a simple metaphor. The analogy of the sheep and the good shepherd of John 10 is also said to be a metaphor in John 10:6.

   e. **"Do you now Trust?"** (16:31): This could just as well be a statement: "Now you Trust."

Jesus speaking with his Father (17:1-26)

[1]Jesus said those things. Then he looked up to heaven and said, "Father, the Hour has come. Glorify your son,[a] so that your son may glorify you, [2]since you gave him power over all flesh to give eternal Life to all[b] you gave him. [3]This is eternal Life, to Know you, the only True God, and the one you sent, Jesus Christ.[c] [4]I glorified you on earth by completing the work you gave me to do. [5]Now glorify me, Father, at your side, with the glory that I had beside you[d] before the World was.

[6]"I revealed your name[e] to the people you gave me from the World. They were yours, you gave them to me, and they have kept your word. [7]Now they have Realised that all you gave me is from your side, [8]because the words that you gave me, I have given them, and they accepted them and Realised Truly that I came from beside you. They also Trusted that you sent me. [9]I am asking for their sake;[f] I am not asking for the sake of the World but for the sake of those you have given me, because they are yours. [10]All that is mine is yours, and I have been glorified in them. [11]And I am no longer in the World, but they are in the World, and I go to your side. Holy Father, keep them in your name,[g] which you have given me, so that they may be one[h] like us. [12]When I was with them, I kept them in your name, which you have given me, and I have been keeping them, and none of them was ruined except the son of ruin,[i] so that the scripture may be fulfilled. [13]But now I am coming to you, and I say these things in the World so that they may have my joy fulfilled in them. [14]I have given them your word and the World hated them because they are not of the World just as I am not of the World. [15]I am not asking you to take them out of the World but to keep them from evil.[j] [16]They are not of the World just as I am not of the World. [17]Make them holy in the Truth; your word is Truth. [18]Just as you sent me into the World, I sent them into the World, [19]and for their sake I make myself holy, so that they too may be made holy in Truth.

[20]"I do not ask only for their sake, but for the sake of all who Trust in me through their word, [21]so that they all may be one, just as you, Father, are in me and I in you; may they too be in us so that the World may Trust that you sent me. [22]The glory that you have given me I have given them, so that they may be one just as we are one, [23]I in them and you in me, so that they may be completed into one,

---

[49] Bauer, Arndt, Gingrich & Danker, *A Greek-English Lexicon of the New Testament*, page 629; Brown, *The Gospel According to John*, volume 29A, page 723.

so that the World may know that you sent me and you Loved them just as you Loved me.

²⁴"Father, what you have given me, I want that they too are where I am with you, so that they may see my glory, which you gave me because you Loved me before the creation of the world. ²⁵Righteous Father, the World did not Recognise you, but I Recognised you, and they Realised that you sent me. ²⁶I made your name Known to them and I will make it Known, so that the Love with which you Loved me may be in them and so I will be in them."

Meaning and resonance

a. **"Glorify your son"** (17:1): In much of this prayer, Jesus speaks of himself in the third person, as if he had detached from himself, stepped back, and is now observing himself objectively. It is a psychological accomplishment to see oneself as one actually is, rather than as a persona created by the ego to get by in the World,[50] or as an all too virtuous victim suffering at the hands of others whose faults are projections of my own unacknowledged ones.

b. **"eternal Life to all"** (17:2): "All" is neuter, so it is not limited to people and includes things.

c. **"This is eternal Life..."** (17:3): Verse 17:3 interrupts the flow. This sentence is an insertion by our ever helpful narrator.[51] Note also the verb tenses in this section; they also suggest a later view of events, the narrator's time, not Jesus's. For example, in 17:11 Jesus says "I am no longer in the World".

d. **"beside you"** (17:5 and throughout): This section frequently mentions that Jesus is at his Father's side. The word παρά used uniformly and frequently in John 17 to describe the spatial relationship between Father and son. The son is portrayed as the Father's equal, at his side not kneeling before him. They are a unity that we are to share.

e. **"I revealed your name"** (17:6, 17:11-12, 17:26): This statement is literally true; Jesus has used God's name ("I am") repeatedly; see "I am" in John's key words below.

However, other uses of "your name" in this section make less sense literally, such as "Holy Father, keep them in your name" (17:11). Normally a name and the thing named are different; as Jung said, "The name of the Tao is not the Tao."[52] However, that view does not take account of Jewish usage; as Mary Coloe explains:

> To avoid saying "God," parts of the [Old Testament], particularly the Deuteronomistic History, use "the name," as

---

[50] "Persona" was Jung's term for the part of the mind that is best adapted to survival in the external world, the part that holds down a job, gets an education, participates in a community, makes its way in the world. A persona is a necessary for survival but must ultimately be set aside in seeking wholeness. See Stein, *The Principle of Individuation*, pages 13-16.

[51] Brown, *The Gospel According to John*, volume 29A, page 741; Moloney, *Love in the Gospel of John*, page 125.

[52] Jung, *Letters*, volume 2, page 62; quoted in Stein, *Jung on Christianity*, page 61.

is the case in modern Judaism where *ha Shem* is a reverential alternative to the word "God."[53]

From that perspective, "keep them in your name" seems close to the modern Quaker phrase, "hold them in the Light".

f. **"I am asking for their sake"** (17:9): The simplest explanation for this intercession is that it is motivated by concern about what is about to come; Jesus will soon be killed but the disciples do not know that yet. He is not asking that people's sins be forgiven, or put on him to atone for; this is not about Wrongs but about Jesus their friend acting out of concern for their well-being in the trouble he knows is coming.

g. **"keep them in your name"** (17:11 and elsewhere in this section): The word translated "keep" (τηρέω) in this section is also used of commandments (14:15, 14:21, 15:10). Its basic meaning is to watch over or protect. It could well be read as meaning "protect" here; Jesus is asking the Father to protect his disciples in the coming crackdown and confusion. The same word is also translated "keep" in 17:6, "they have kept your word", and in 17:15, "keep them from evil", where "protect" would also be an apt translation.

h. **"so that they may be one"** (17:11; 17:21-23): Literally, "so that they may be one thing". "One" is simply the neuter form of the word that means "one" (ἕν). It appears 36 times in John.[54]

i. **"none of them was ruined except the son of ruin"** (17:12): The words translated "ruin" imply violent destruction of what was lost. It cannot have been a happy man who handed Jesus over to the authorities; happy people do not send someone off to be killed. Deeply unhappy people end up destroyed by their shadow sides and take others down with them.

j. **"keep them from evil"** (17:15): This could also be read as "keep them from the evil one", but I see no need to personify evil. The evil one would actually be a person's shadow, and it makes no sense to keep away from what is a part of oneself.

Reflection

"that they may be one just as we are one, I in them and you in me" (17:22)

The vine (15:1-17) gives us the image of unity, but Jesus was the vine and his disciples the branches (15:1). This prayer now draws the Father and the faithful of the future into that unity:

> I do not ask only for [the disciples'] sake, but for the sake of all who Trust in me through their word, so that they all may be one, just as you, Father, are in me and I in you; may they too be in us so that the World may Trust that you sent me. The glory that you have given me I have given them, so that they

---

[53] *Wisdom Bible Commentary*, volume 44B, page 462.

[54] Charlesworth, *Jesus as Mirrored in John*, pages 103-104.

may be one just as we are one, I in them and you in me, so
that they may be completed into one.... (17:20-22)

Unity among people is achieved by being drawn together by the Divine within them:, "just as you, Father, are in me and I in you, may they too be in us" (17:21).[55] Isaac knew this from experience, and he also knew that when unity is lacking, we fake it:

In the Spirit ... is the true unity. Feeling that in one another,
is that which unites us to one another. Every one keeping to
that in his own particular, is kept to that which unites; ... but
departing from that, there is a departing from the true unity
into the error and ground of division. And then that which
hath erred and departed from the true unity, strives to set up
a false image of unity, and blames that which abides in the
truth, because it cannot thus unite; for that which abides in
the Spirit, and in that which the Spirit hath begotten and
formed, cannot unite according to the flesh....[56]

This "false image of unity" abounds in traditional Christianity, in which human authority figures strive to maintain a sense of coherence, and reject as heretics those who will not cohere. The Light within is the authority that will draw all people into unity, but "tribal [Christian] traditions have fixed revelation in the past: 'Our fathers said...'. After the words of the authoritative figures have been recorded and codified, the resultant tradition may add only commentary and clarification."[57] This situation left poor Isaac to wail, "Alas, alas! Babylon has prevailed.... This has been the state of the apostasy since the days of the apostles".[58] He experienced it himself and described how he relied on the authority of "words formerly spoken", leaving his ego consciousness as his only guide:

The deep sense of this [apostasy] hath afflicted my soul from
my tender years ... the eternal light manifesting the darkness
all along unto me; though I knew not that it was the light, but
went about to measure its appearances in me by words which
[it] had formerly spoken to others, and so set up my own
understanding and comprehension as the measure, although
I did not then perceive or think that I did so.[59]

He also experienced the remedy:

[T]he Lord drew his sword upon me, and smote me in the very
inmost of my soul; by which stroke (lying still a while under
it) my eyes came to be opened; and then I saw the blindness
of that eye which was able to see so far, and the narrowness
of that heart and spirit which was so large and vast in

---

[55] This indwelling of Christ and God in humanity is a frequent theme in John. See Remain in "John's key words" below.

[56] *The Way of Life and Death Made Manifest*, in *Works*, volume 2, page 23.

[57] Stein, "Jung's Green Christ", page 9.

[58] Penington, *The Scattered Sheep Sought After*, in *Works*, volume 1, pages 105-107.

[59] *Ibid.*, page 106.

> comprehending: and my soul bowed down to the Lord to slay
> this, to starve this....[60]

Modern people find themselves in the same position as Isaac before he saw the Light:

> The traditional religious symbols no longer mediate the
> transcendent factors they once did; they are no longer alive.
> The modern person reveals an empty space at the center,
> which was formerly occupied by a God image. Traditional
> religions no longer adequately represent or contain the souls
> of modern men and women.[61]

To fill the void in the centre of their souls, modern people pursue pseudo-religions, causes to which they are religiously devoted. These ersatz religions are tribes devoted to "making America great again," making Britain great again through Brexit, or simply making loads of money and being top dog at the company tribe. However,

> God is not bound to tribe. The study and appreciation of
> world religions, in the full sense of the word *religion*, have
> dealt an enormous blow to the comforts of Christian
> orthodoxy in the West. The now widespread and still growing
> awareness that other people and tribes also have genuine
> religions has inflicted a deep narcissistic injury as well. So
> long as one could say, "yes but..."—"yes they have religious
> practices, but they do not know about the one true God as we
> do"; "yes, they have certain beliefs and superstitions, but
> those are false and only partially true, as we know with our
> full revelation"; "yes, they have come close and are genuinely
> struggling, but the poor benighted devils won't ever get there
> unless we teach them to read our Bible"—one could maintain
> the ... illusion that God is our father and has no other children
> but us. In our times, consciousness has shifted to the point
> where tribalism in religion is no longer tenable with good
> conscience.[62]

Isaac experienced Christian tribalism—he was born a Puritan, divided by zeal from the Church of England—but he came through it by discovering the Light within himself. The unconscious God in his soul broke through into consciousness. Now that is needed on a larger scale:

> The message to Christianity would be: Open yourself to the
> unconscious. Honor the dream. Allow the unconscious to
> smash the cathedral and to show you a larger image of God,
> because your God is too small and too confined in the boxes
> of dogma and habit. Recognize that your tribalism is based

---

[60] *Ibid.*, page 107.

[61] Stein, "Jung's Green Christ", page 3.

[62] Stein, "Jung's Green Christ", page 4.

on wish and projection and is very distorted, having very little
to do with reality.[63]

Opening to the unconscious lets God into our conscious minds, and God then leads us into unity. It is the unity of the vine, that paradoxical unity in diversity with a sense that diversity is good and unity is good. People don't all need to believe and do the same things. Isaac again:

> OH! how sweet and pleasant is it to the truly spiritual eye, to
> see several sorts of believers, several forms of Christians in
> the school of Christ, every one learning their own lesson, ...
> and knowing, owning, and loving one another in their several
> places, and different performances to their Master, to whom
> they are to give an account, and not to quarrel one with
> another about their different practices! This is the true
> ground of love and unity, not that such a man walks and does
> just as I do, but because I feel the same Spirit of life in him,
> and that he walks in his rank, in his own order, in his proper
> way and place of subjection to that. And this is far more
> pleasing to me, than if he walked just in the track wherein I
> walk; nay (so far as I am spiritual), I cannot so much as desire
> that he should do so, until he be particularly led thereto, by
> the same Spirit that led me.[64]

Or in Murray Stein's words, again addressed to Christianity, with notes of caution:

> Allow yourself to consider all the other paths to God as
> equally valid and legitimate, and possibly equally tribal and
> limited, but do not abandon your history, and do not think the
> other traditions can bail you out if you will just learn some
> new ideas from them. Instead, concentrate yourself on your
> own symbols and on your own history, and let your
> unconscious respond, trusting that the God who revealed
> himself in the beginning will respond with symbols of
> transformation and renewal. But you must be prepared to
> take responsibility for these new revelations, to test them by
> your very best means of interpretation and discernment, not
> according to what you have already known, but according to
> what you know you need and have not yet found. And be
> ready to be surprised. Above all, be prepared to let God be
> whole. This is a great risk, but your life depends on it.[65]

Kathleen Lonsdale, a modern Friend, explains how this happened for her:

> The character of Jesus Christ, the tone of his voice over the
> centuries, so to speak, has made a tremendous appeal to me.
> I think it very likely that a great deal of legend has gathered
> round the story of his life; and yet many of his sayings ring so
> true today that they — to use an old-fashioned Quaker phrase

---

[63] Stein, *The Principle of Individuation*, page 185.

[64] *Some Misrepresentations of Church Government Cleared*, in *Works*, volume 4, page 315.

[65] *The Principle of Individuation*, page 185.

— they speak to my condition. I rejected a good deal of my religious upbringing during the process of thinking for myself in my teens and later; I found it impossible to accept as true much that I had been told I must believe about Jesus; but thinking for myself brought me closer to Jesus, for he had the simplicity of approach that I wanted. He didn't just talk about God, he talked with God; and he taught his friends to do the same.[66]

---

[66] Pacific Yearly Meeting, *Faith and Practice*, number 44, page 79.

John's key words

We seem to communicate spiritual truth in words, but it actually goes deeper:

> The Lord gives grace and knowledge for another end than for men to take it upon them to be great, or rule over others because of it. And he that, because of this, thinks himself fit to rule over men's consciences, and to make them bow to what he knows or thinks to be truth, he loseth his own life hereby. For it is not so much speaking true things that doth good, but speaking them out from what is pure, and conveying them unto what is pure, for the life runs along from the vessel of life in one into the vessel of life in another. But the words, though ever so true, cannot convey life to another, but only as the living vessel opens in the one, and is opened in the other.

Isaac Penington[1]

Melvin Keiser, Isaac's biographer, described Isaac's use of language: "Religious language for Penington is doing something very different from defining a conceivable thing. It is not trying to identify God as an Object nor to define that Object's nature. Rather it is trying to bring us to experience God's mysterious reality."[2] In Isaac's own words, "the end of words is to bring men to the knowledge of things, beyond what words can utter."[3] Given that end, it is best not to "fix or stay upon words concerning the thing, but ... sink in spirit into the feeling of the life itself".[4] That experience will be a bit different for each soul.

Perhaps words never fully communicate one person's idea to another because meaning for the hearer must be found in her own experience. Words are, however, all we have of John and of Isaac, and the aim is not communication of dictionary meanings but rather words from the speaker's "vessel of life" will resonate in the reader's "vessel of life" so a deeper communication of more than just words occurs, possibly unconsciously. Some truths we know "ere we are aware", as Isaac said.[5] Still, understanding the conscious meaning can be a starting point for deepening our grasp of the underlying spiritual reality.

John uses over a dozen words repetitively to convey deeply spiritual concepts, and many are metaphorical. "Light" and "Life", for example, occur more often in John than in all the other gospels put together. One reason why John has such a poetic quality is that its key metaphors echo all through the text. Many of the words Quakers use to describe their spiritual life are taken from John, and that is particularly true of Isaac Penington.

---

[1] *An Examination of the Grounds*, in *Works*, volume 1, pages 378-379. Isaac is reacting to the hanging of Quaker Mary Dyer on Boston Common in the Massachusetts Bay Colony, which was dominated by Puritans.

[2] *Knowing the Mystery of God Within*, page 217.

[3] Letter to _____ (name left blank in original), in *Works*, volume 3, page 258.

[4] Penington, *Some of the Mysteries*, in *Works*, volume 2, page 343, quoted in Keiser and Moore, *Knowing the Mystery of God Within*, page 218.

[5] *A Treatise Concerning God's Teaching*, in *Works* volume 4, page 259. *See also* Melvin Keiser, "Felt Reality in Practical Living", pages 198-202.

The key words in John have meanings and connotations that are not in an English dictionary; John "has his own pervasive idiom".[6] Dictionaries are too superficial, for one thing; in succession, character after character misses what Jesus means because his meaning is deeper than their thinking. "The misunderstandings warn the reader not to mistake superficial for real meanings."[7] The reason for this section is that ordinary meanings of words do not apply in John or apply only at the surface level; Nicodemus thinks being born again must mean going back into the womb, but it does not (John 3:4).

For that same reason, the deconstruction of vocabulary, I often prefer unconventional translations for words because I am avoiding as best I can the theological baggage that comes with words like "faith" or "salvation". That theology came much later than John so it does not belong in John, and now many people including many Quakers are disillusioned with conventional theology. Quakers have always had a radical, fresh view.

However, to avoid redefining absolutely everything, I have stuck with some conventional terms such as "New/Old Testament", and "heaven", though not without some reservations. Wouldn't it be wonderful to hear the entire gospel in fresh, untheological terms, as John's audience did? There are also a few traditional words that seem all right. "Disciple" I don't mind because books of Quaker faith and practice used to be called "disciplines", which I take to mean what makes one a disciple.

In this book, John's repeating key words appear capitalised in sans serif type and are examined below. This is not an exhaustive list.

Counsellor

John employs a synonym for the Holy Spirit, παράκλητος, that only appears in John.[8] Παράκλητος is someone beside you whom you can call on for help. In a legal context, it was the word for an advocate; in court, your lawyer would be a παράκλητος, an adviser on your side to help you. I translate παράκλητος as "Counsellor".

In the Jewish tradition, the forensic defender before God is Moses, but Jesus reverses this role for Moses when in John 5:45 Jesus tells his Jewish audience that their *accuser* is none other than Moses, whom they think will defend them.[9] For John, that advocacy role falls to the Counsellor.

Several times in John 14 through 16, Jesus promises the Counsellor to his disciples when his Hour is over. Jesus calls the Counsellor the "spirit of Truth" in John 14:17, and "Holy Spirit" in 14:26. It is not Jesus's suffering and death that ultimately Rescues humanity from its Wrongs and leads it on to God; Jesus's death leaves his disciples in shock and confusion. Finding one's way to God is ultimately an inward process that happens in the mind and soul, and the helper in it is the Counsellor, the inner Light, as Quakers call it. Yes, God sent his son into the World, not to condemn it, but so that it would be Rescued through him (John 3:16),

---

[6] Keener, *The Gospel of John*, volume 1, page 53.

[7] Culpepper, *Anatomy of the Fourth Gospel*, page 199.

[8] John 14:15-16 equates παράκλητος and the Holy Spirit. 1 John 2:1 uses παράκλητος redefined to mean Jesus Christ.

[9] Meeks, *The Prophet-King*, pages 195 and 307.

but in John, Jesus's public life of about three years (three Passovers) was spent mostly in teaching people who rejected his message. As Jesus is about to die, he promises the Counsellor to continue his unfinished work with his disciples, the only people then willing to listen to the Counsellor.

The Counsellor arrives when Jesus breathes on his disciples in John 20:22, and it remains with them after John ends. Reinhartz notes that the effect of this is to "open the chronology of the narrative to include the time of the reader and beyond. This open-endedness allows succeeding generations of Christians to see themselves as addressed directly by Jesus and by the Beloved Disciple."[10]

Darkness

See "Light" below.

Father

'Father' appears 64 times in Matthew, 18 times in Mark, 56 times in Luke, and 136 times in John. Almost always it is Jesus who speaks of his Father in John.

The Father seems in John to be a separate being from Jesus, except that they are not separate because they are repeatedly said to be "one" (ἕν, literally "one [thing]"), a single entity (John 17). That presents us with a paradox.

Rather than create complicated rational theories about the Father/Son distinction such as the Trinity, Quakers accept a certain fluidity and interchangeability in the words we use for the Divine. John does as well; for example, "Word", "Light", and "son of man" all refer to Jesus. "While Isaac spoke of Father, Son and Spirit, these are metaphorical expressions of inward experience of divinity."[11] Light and Seed are other metaphors Isaac uses often. Each of the metaphors for God focuses on one aspect of God because a metaphor is usually based on a single image. All the metaphors we have do not add up to a complete picture; our conscious image of God is only ever partial. "Words grasp aspects, but never the whole, of reality. .... Religious words grasp aspects of an unsayable whole of reality, and carry us back into feeling originating mystery."[12]

> The finiteness of any symbol, however rich, restricts the number of aspects of an archetype it can convey. For example, Homer's Helen can convey only the erotic and seductive aspects of the anima archetype; the Virgin Mary, only the motherly, compassionate ones.[13]

In John, it is almost always Jesus who speaks of his Father. The Father is portrayed as only kind and good, a far cry from the God of Job. For Jung, the Father as presented in John is too good to be true; what has become of his dark side?

> God ... begot a good and helpful son and thus created an image of himself as the good father, unfortunately, as we must admit, again without considering that there existed in him a

---

[10] *Befriending the Beloved Disciple*, page 102.

[11] Keiser, *Felt Reality in Practical Living*, page 203. Keiser examines metaphor in greater detail in *Seeds of Silence* pages 179-194.

[12] Keiser, *Felt Reality in Practical Living*, page 201-202.

[13] Segal, *Jung on Mythology*, page 42.

> knowledge that spoke a very different truth. Had he only
> given an account of his action to himself, he would have seen
> what a fearful dissociation he had got into through his
> incarnation.[14]

In other words, God (as the human mind sees God) has split his personality. Job's God/Satan is one whole that is both good and unconsciously evil in one, with the unconscious out of control and dominant.[15] In Jesus's time, Satan has become a separate being, not internal and unconscious. Satan takes up residence in the World; in Luke, Jesus says, "I watched Satan fall from the sky like a flash of lightning".[16] Evil is not necessarily unconscious; rather, it is compensatory, and to the extent we are aware of the evil that we are, our unconscious is free of that evil.[17] If we are aware of it, we can do something about it.

Jung says the result of the split in God's personality (as seen by people) is an "enantiodromia in the grand style".[18] "Enantiodromia" is a Jungian term (borrowed from Herodotus) that literally means running between opposites; it "occurs when an extreme, one-sided tendency dominates conscious life; in time an equally powerful [unconscious] counterposition is built up, which first inhibits the conscious performance and subsequently breaks through the conscious control."[19]

Hour

The Greek word ὥρα can mean almost any period of time, but its most common usage was to mark off fractions of a day. From sunrise to sundown was 12 hours, whatever the time of year, and without clocks, the reckoning of hours was approximate. John says Jesus asked rhetorically, "Are there not twelve hours of daylight?"[20] His next words foreshadow his death: "Someone who walks during the day does not stumble, because he sees the Light of this World. But someone who walks at night stumbles, because the Light is not in him" (John 9:10).

One twelfth of all daylight hours is not a long time. In John, Jesus speaks of his last days and his death as his ὥρα, his hour. He uses only that word for that day or two of actual time. Other Greek words were available such as καιρός, a crucial

---

[14] Jung, *Answer to Job*, in *Collected Works*, volume 11, paragraph 694. Jung explained dissociation:

> If you are unconscious about certain things that ought to be conscious, you are dissociated. Then you are a man whose left hand never knows what the right is doing and counteracts or interferes with the right hand. Such a man is hampered all over the place.

"The Houston Films", in McGuire & Hull, editors, *Jung Speaking*, page 302.

[15] See "Jung's view of God's relationship with humanity" above.

[16] Luke 10:18.

[17] Stein, *Jung on Evil*, pages 6-7.

[18] *Answer To Job*, in *Collected Works,* volume 11, paragraph 694.

[19] *Jung Lexicon* (last retrieved June 2022). The quote is from Jung, and Daryl Sharp, author of the *Jung Lexicon*, adds, "Enantiodromia is typically experienced in conjunction with symptoms associated with acute neurosis, and often foreshadows a rebirth of the personality."

[20] John 11:9.

time period, but in John, Jesus almost[21] always calls his last moments his "Hour". He knew precisely when it began; see John 12:23.

Before Jesus's Hour comes and the disciples receive the Counsellor, the many references to scripture in John are introduced with words like "they remembered that it was written" (2:17) or "it is written in your law" (10:34). After Jesus's Hour comes, scripture is introduced with words like "so that the scripture may be fulfilled".[22] Noting the fulfilment of scripture helped overcome first impressions of what could easily be seen as the ignominious death of a thwarted man.

I am

In John, Jesus says "I am" (ἐγώ εἰμι) 26 times, compared to only 5 times in the other gospels.[23]

In spoken English, "I am" usually contracts to "I'm"; speaking both words is a little emphatic. If someone asks, "You're not in Preston already, are you?", the answer could be "I am", clear enough to counter the incredulity of the question, but we'd simply say "I'm" in most contexts. Similarly, in Greek, "I'm" would normally be just εἰμι, but ἐγώ εἰμι is slightly but significantly emphatic.

For Jesus's Jewish audience, "ἐγώ εἰμι" stands out enough to allude to the name that God calls himself in response to Moses's question in Exodus 3:14. In view of the third commandment, use of the name of God is blasphemous, particularly to Jews, who took care to avoid ever speaking the four letters of the divine name (see the section above on antisemitism.)[24] Rudolf Schnackenburg remarked that in saying "ἐγώ εἰμι", Jesus "borrows the voice of God himself".[25] The author of John might question the word "borrow" because in John, Jesus *is* God (John 1:1) and would not have to borrow his own voice.

Schackenburg and Brown differentiate two kinds of usage of "ἐγώ εἰμι":

- **With predicate**, in which I am is followed by something that Jesus is, express or implied. Brown says some examples may simply be ordinary usage, such as when Jesus is walking to his disciples on the water and says to his terrified disciples, "Don't worry, it's me". However, very little in John has only a surface meaning; there is more underneath, and John is full of intended ambiguity and biblical allusion.[26]

  However, often there is no such open-ended ambiguity, and instead I am begins a metaphor, such as:

  > "I am the bread of life" (6:35, 48, 51), or "I am bread come down from heaven" (6:41)

---

[21] Except in 7:6, where Jesus uses καιρός, but also applies the same word to his faithless siblings, who have no Hour coming in which they will sacrifice their lives.

[22] Evans, *Word and Glory*, pages 174-180.

[23] Schnackenburg, *Das Johannesevangelium*, volume 4:2, page 59.

[24] *Anchor Bible*, volume 1, pages 533-535.

[25] *Das Johannesevangelium*, volume 4:1, page 106.

[26] "Don't worry it's me" could also be translated, "Fear not, I am." "Fear not" is what God often says when appearing to mortals (*e.g.* Genesis 151 (Abraham), 26:24 (Isaac)). When Jesus's first disciples ask him, "where are you staying?", their question could also be translated, "where do you Remain?" "In you, I hope" is ultimately the answer to the second translation (John 15:4), but Jesus actually answers, "Come and see", which works on both levels (John 1:38-39).

"I am the light of the world" (8:12)

"I am the gate" (of the sheepfold) (10:7, 9)

"I am the good shepherd" (10:11, 14)

"I am the resurrection and the Life" (11:25)

"I am the way, the Truth, and the Life" (14:6)

"I am the vine" (15:1, 5).

In these cases, "ἐγώ εἰμι" still stands out, twice as many syllables as are necessary, and recalling the name of God.

- **Without predicate**: More striking is where "ἐγώ εἰμι" appears in absolute form, without saying that Jesus is anything in particular. There are four clear cases of this in John:

  "Unless you begin to Trust that I am, you will die in your Wrongfulness" (8:24)

  "When you lift up the Son of Man, you will Realise that I am" (8:28)

  "Before Abraham was, I am" (8:58)

  "So that when that happens, you will Trust that I am" (13:19).

  One case is ambiguous. When the soldiers come to arrest Jesus, Jesus asks them, "Who are you looking for?" They answer, "Jesus the Nazarene." Jesus replies, "I am." The surface meaning is the answer to their question (*i.e.* the predicate is implied), but the words "I am" have no express predicate. The soldiers grasp the deeper meaning because they step back and fall to the ground (John 18:5). Jesus repeats his answer "I am" in 18:8.

After showing how the phrase "ἐγώ εἰμι" does not have Greek roots but rather goes back to the Old Testament, Raymond Brown concludes, "Against this background [John's] absolute use of εγώ εἰμι becomes quite intelligible. Jesus is presented as speaking in the same manner in which Yahweh speaks".[27] More than the other gospels, John portrays Jesus as God, and it does so forthrightly. The repeated use of "ἐγώ εἰμι" is one aspect of that.

In John 17, Jesus speaks with his Father about his use of the divine name. "I revealed your name to the people," he reports, and asks, "Holy Father, keep them in your name". What does it mean to be kept in God's name? In one sense, the name of God is not God, but from John's very Jewish perspective, it is; see "I revealed your name" above. To be kept in God's name is to be kept in God. Knowing the divine name leads to God's Love and Remaining in us:

I made your name Known to them and I will make it Known, so
that the Love with which you Loved me may be in them and
so I will be in them.

John 17:26

Jews

John occasionally refers to specific categories of Jews, such as Pharisees, scribes, etc., but most often, John simply refers to "οἱ Ἰουδαῖοι" which is literally and

---

[27] *Anchor Bible*, volume 1, pages 535; see also Coloe, *God Dwells with Us*, pages 136-138.

conventionally translated "the Jews". "Οἱ Ἰουδαῖοι" appears only 16 times in all the other gospels, but over 70 times in John.[28]

I don't translate οἱ Ἰουδᾶοι as "the Jews"; I use the generic noun "Jews" instead. In Greek, generic nouns take the definite article but not in English.[29] The difference in English is subtle; "the Jews" would mean the entire category, the religion and ethnic group, which is a concept on the threshold of ethnic and religious discrimination. The generic noun is not so categorical; it refers to Jews in general, as in this example:

> The Jews rejected Jesus.

> Jews rejected Jesus.

The implication in the second example, where the noun is generic, means that Jews rejected Jesus, not necessarily all of them but a significant part; whereas the first example implies that all Jews rejected Jesus. That is not true; some Jews were not involved.[30] Nicodemus, for example, seems to have had more sympathy than the categorical "the Jews" would allow.[31] In contrast, the second example is roughly as true as any generalisation can be for its place and time.

The term οἱ Ἰουδᾶιοι has justifiably evoked much scholarly discomfort. Charlesworth prefers to translate it "Judeans",[32] but οἱ Ἰουδαῖοι indicates a religion, not just a nationality of that time.[33] Coloe, citing Ashton and Bultmann, generalises the object of John's polemic and says "οἱ Ἰουδαῖοι" is a "caricature of the unbelieving world that rejects Jesus".[34] That does not quite eliminate all my discomfort, however. A caricature distorts and mocks, and Jews, not the world, are the stated objects. Jews do not deserve to be singled out because many people, not just Jews, rejected Christianity, especially at first. Because Jesus lived in a country populated mostly by Jews, Jews were simply the part of the unbelieving world that was in range for Jesus to teach and be rejected by.

Although I share the discomfort when John singles out Jews for criticism and condemnation, it would be too much of a break with meaning and history to translate οἱ Ἰουδαῖοι as "unbelievers" or a similarly vague generalisation. The

---

[28] Yee, *Jewish Feasts and the Gospel of John*, page 14.

[29] Daniel B. Wallace, *Greek Grammar Beyond the Basics: An Exegetical Syntax of the New Testament*, pages 227-231 (Grand Rapids, Michigan: Zondervan 1996); Herbert Weir Smyth, *Greek Grammar*, sections 1122-1124 (Cambridge, Massachusetts: Harvard University Press, 1920). Perhaps the best example of a plural generic noun is Ephesians 5:25, "Husbands, love your wives"; "husbands" is 'οι ἄνδρες in Greek, *i.e.* with the definite article.

[30] Charlesworth notes some limits (*Jesus as Mirrored in John*, page 97). Of Jews (besides those believing in Jesus), only the Pharisees survived the destruction of the Temple in 70 C.E.; John was written about 20 years later. The usage of the term ὁι Ἰουδαῖοι in John is so uniform that it is probably the result of redaction that may well have come late in the writing process, when only Jews were allowed to attend synagogue.

Charlesworth also criticises the use of a single term to translate οι Ἰουδαίοι (*ibid.*, page 46), but I disagree. I think it is better to keep the uniformity that is in John but explain some of its complexity in this definition. I also agree with Reinhartz that ὁι Ἰουδαίοι cannot have meant merely "Judeans", for example, because after the destruction of Judea, Jews were scattered and lost their geographic identity until Zionism revived it in the 19th century.

[31] See the above commentary on John 3:1.

[32] Charlesworth, *Jesus as Mirrored in John*, pages 4-5.

[33] Reinhartz, *Befriending the Beloved Disciple*, page. 73; Reinhartz, "The Gospel of John", page 113.

[34] Coloe, *God Dwells with Us*, page 138-139.

best I reckon that I can do in translating the text, without taking liberties, is to translate οἱ Ἰουδαῖοι as generic rather than a categorical "the Jews". I agree with Adele Reinhartz, a Jewish scholar of John:

> There is no perfect solution to the translation conundrum. As Tina Pippin has said:
>
> > If one changes the literal meaning of Ἰουδαῖοι to refer to Judeans or Jewish religious authorities [as some scholars advocate], then one dilutes the force of the ethnic and verbal warfare, and ignores that it was a warfare that turned into so much more than a first-century dispute. If one keeps the literal "the Jews" in the English translation, then one is perpetuating hateful polemic.[35]
>
> One option is to use the Greek term without translating. But in most cases, some sort of translation is called for. If so, "Jews" remains the most appropriate translation of Ἰουδαῖοι, as it reflects a complex construction of identity that parallels, even if it cannot precisely mirror, the ethnic-political, social, religious, and emotional identity to which the ancient term *Ioudaios* refers.[36]

I also see John as angry and polemical toward Jews, for psychologically understandable but morally unjustifiable reasons (see "Is John antisemitic?" above), but I do not see John as racist. The community of John was being expelled from synagogues they had attended their entire lives, but their anger at that rejection was not racially motivated. Their extended families and friends, of the same racial stock, still attended synagogues. The community's problem with the synagogue authorities was not racist hatred but rejection as members of Judaism, which was redefining itself in the aftermath of the destruction of Judea and the Temple. As Jews lost much of their diversity and became Pharisees, Reinhartz sees John as helping to forge a new identity for Jews who Trusted in Jesus. John pushes them to see separation from other Jews as "essential to their own developing self-identification as children of God".[37]

The effect on John of so much polemic is difficult to assess but has been limiting. Brown notes that John "was written in a struggle with outsiders [Jews] and therefore emphasizes only those parts of [John's] tradition questioned by outsiders."[38] In John, Jesus speaks far more about himself than in the other gospels, and a reason for that may be that Jews rejected him, so he tried all the harder to convince them. What might John have covered if polemic had not narrowed its point of view?

Know, Recognise, Realise

Two Greek words in John are both translated "Know", but they have a subtle distinction: οἶδα means "to know", and γινώσκω means "to come to know, to

---

[35] Reinhartz cites here Tina Pippin, "'For Fear of the Jews': Lying and Truth-Telling in Translating the Gospel of John," *Semeia* 76 (1996), p. 93.

[36] Reinhartz, *Cast out of the Covenant*, page 103.

[37] *Ibid.*, page 162; see also Coloe, *Wisdom Commentary*, volume 44A, page liii; Reinhartz, "The Gospel of John", page 115.

[38] Brown, *The Epistles of John*, page 97.

realise, or recognise". The distinction in meaning is not always sharp and may be more a matter of emphasis or somewhat trodden-down nuance, rather than a clear distinction in meaning.[39] John never uses the nouns "knowledge" or "realisation"; he just uses the verbs.

For Isaac Penington, spiritual knowing begins as an inward process in which, beneath all words and forms, he experienced a reality that he called Mystery, Spirit, Life, and inward Light. Knowing occurs as that inward experience surfaces into consciousness.[40] Melvin Keiser explains:

> While principally talking about knowing God, all knowing for Isaac involved connecting beneath consciousness. By participating in the mystery, we know "ere we [are] aware". At the same time that Descartes is originating modern philosophy, grounding true knowing in reason without prethinking awareness, and denigrating feeling as merely subjective, Isaac and other Friends are grounding knowing in feeling and sensing. Knowing is affectional. To know something in its mysterious depths is to be affected, moved emotionally, to be changed. Detached, unemotional knowing is an illusion. Knowing is emergent. Waiting in silence, knowing arises though sense and feeling into patterns of thought, not, as in modernity, through imposing frameworks on phenomena.[41]

Perhaps, when Jesus was physically present in conscious life but the Counsellor was not yet present,[42] Knowing then was more immediately conscious than for Isaac Penington and the rest of us in later centuries, whose Knowing comes by experiencing the Counsellor. The Beloved Disciple would have known both because he outlived Jesus; his real-world Knowing of Jesus would have transitioned into his experience of the Counsellor, an experience presumably resembling Isaac's, as the living Jesus became a memory and the Counsellor became his present connection with the Divine. See "unless I go" above. It must have been an immense consolation to the Beloved Disciple, after losing Jesus who had Loved him, still to Know Christ through the Counsellor, and to feel Loved even after Jesus was physically gone.

Carl Jung was once asked if he believed in God. He replied that he didn't believe, he *knew* God existed.[43] This is, however, a somewhat different kind of knowing from Isaac Penington's knowing. Jung was fundamentally an empirical scientist, and God within was for him a part of human psychology, an archetype in the personal and collective unconscious that could be observed, up to a point. Jung knew empirically that God existed because he had often observed the archetype at work in the human psyche, perhaps by methods of sensing not all that different from Isaac Penington's sensing.[44]

---

[39] Keener, *The Gospel of John*, volume 1, page 244-246; Brown, *Anchor Bible* volume 29, page 514.

[40] Keiser, "Felt Reality in Practical Living," page 199.

[41] *Ibid.* page 200.

[42] John 16:7.

[43] C.G. Jung, *Letters*, selected and edited by Gerard Adler and Aniela Jaffe, volume 2, page 155-156 (Princeton: Princeton University Press).

[44] Keiser & Moore, *Knowing the Mystery of God Within*, pages 178-198.

Life, Live

"Life" (ζωή) appears 36 times in John, compared to 16 times in all the other gospels, and that does not count the incidence of the verb "to live" (ζάω). Brown notes that ζωή is not used in John to refer to natural life; instead, "soul" (ψυχή) is used for natural life.[45] Ζωή has only a spiritual sense in John.

Ζωή often comes with the adjective αἰώνιός, which is how the Greek Old Testament translates the Hebrew word `ōlām, meaning "without end".[46] In the Old Testament, ζωὴ αἰώνιός appears most often in the book of Wisdom (5:15, 6:18, 8:17 and 8:21), where it describes "the quality of life that Sophia offers the righteous".[47] Sophia is divine wisdom personified.

Looking for the meaning of "eternal Life" from context in John is interesting, and frustrating if clarity is the aim. Adele Reinhartz:

> What exactly constitutes eternal life is more difficult to discern. The passages cited above associate eternal life with resurrection (6:40), passing from death to life (5:24), and having the light of life (8:12). In 10:28, eternal life is equated with not perishing: "I give them eternal life, and they will never perish. No one will snatch them out of my hand." But other passages suggest that eternal life does not simply mean evading physical death. A paradox is suggested by 12:25: "Those who love their life lose it, and those who hate their life in this world will keep it for eternal life." Elsewhere eternal life is equated with knowledge of God: "And this is eternal life, that they may know you, the only true God, and Jesus Christ whom you have sent" (17:3). [48]

Knowing God in Jung's terms means that the unconscious self gradually becomes conscious, part of our awareness. The self comes to awareness with a "feeling of eternity";[49] "the experience of the self is nearly always connected with the feeling of timelessness, 'eternity' or immortality".[50]

The usage of ζωή alone (without "eternal") also has many facets:

- Jesus says he is the gate through which his sheep pass to go to pasture, and he has come so that his sheep may have Life abundantly (10:10).

- "Whoever hears my words and Trusts him who sent me, has eternal Life ... and has gone from death to Life" (5:24).

- Life is what the Father has and has given Jesus (5:26, 6:57).

- Jesus is the bread of Life (6:31-59)

- It is the Spirit that gives Life (6:63).

---

[45] *Anchor Bible*, page 506-507.

[46] Brown, *Anchor Bible*, volume 29, page 506. The Greek word actually relates to aeon, an age in history, but John very likely uses it with the meaning from scripture and Jewish discourse.

[47] Coloe *Wisdom Commentary*, volume 44A, page xlviii.

[48] Reinhartz, *Befriending the Beloved Disciple*, pages 114-115.

[49] Jung, "The Psychology of the Transference", in *The Practice of Psychotherapy*, in *Collected Works*, volume 16, paragraph 313.

[50] Jung, *The Symbolic Life: Miscellaneous Writings*, in *Collected Works*, volume 18, paragraph 694.

- Trusting in Jesus, once he has been lifted up, lets us have Life (3:15).
- Jesus is also Life (11:25, 14:6).
- Jesus's words are Life (6:63).
- Life is in the Word, and it is the Light of humanity (1:4).

Isaac Penington also has a certain looseness in his usage of metaphors such as "life" and "light", but that is not because he is confused or does not know what he is talking about. Each metaphor paints an aspect of the fuller picture. As Life demonstrates, it can be hard to narrow a metaphor down to a single definition.

Life, and its opposite, Death (or "out of the life", as Isaac often puts it) are among Isaac's most frequently used words. Melvin Keiser:

> The metaphor of life weaves together the multiple metaphors of Penington's thought. He takes it from the Gospel of John where it is presented as a divine characteristic. Jesus says: "I am the way; I am the Truth, and I am the life" (John 14:6 NEB). Yet "life" at the same time means being fully human, as when Jesus says: "I have come that men may have life, and may have it in all its fullness" (John 10:10). Likewise, Penington uses "life" in the same way as either divine or human, or as simultaneously both. Often it is confusing; you cannot tell which he means. This is intentional. .... Divinity and humanity are not separate realities but are intimately involved with one another. God is not simply outside us but dwells deep in our self. At that depth, we cannot distinguish the mystery that is God from the mystery that I am, that we are.[51]

Jung would agree, according to Dourley: "A living organism, individual or societal, will 'perish' when removed from the sustenance that a depth connectedness with the ground of the psyche can alone provide."[52]

Light

"Light" (φῶς) appears 23 times in John, compared to 15 times in all the other gospels.

For John and for Quakers, "light" is a common synonym for God. Many Quakers are more comfortable saying "Light" than "God" because "God" comes freighted with traditional connotations, assumptions and implications that do not fit their experience of the Light.

"Light", as used in John, is a remarkable fit for Quaker experience generally:

- John uses "Light" to describe Jesus in John (1:4-5, 8:12, 9:5, 12:35-36, 12:46)
- Light also enlightens everyone (John 1:9) and even the World (8:12, 11:9, 12:46). However, not everyone sees the Light, though a person who does what is True comes to the Light (3:19-21).

---

[51] *Knowing the Mystery of God Within*, page 133.

[52] *Jung and his Mystics*, page 17.

In John, "Light" is sometimes paired with its opposite, darkness (σκοτία in John, rather than the more common σκότος). "Darkness" appears over twice as many times in John as in the other gospels. Darkness is associated with evil, as here: "But this is the judgment: although the Light came into the world, people loved darkness rather than the Light because their deeds were evil" (John 3:19). Light and darkness in John are one of several pairs of opposites; see Opposites in John and Jung below.

"Night" (νύξ) is also used in contrast with Light. "Those who walk at night stumble because the Light is not in them" (John 11:10). As Judas leaves the last supper, John ends the paragraph with the unforgettable words, "and it was night" (13:30).

Jung noted the role of light/darkness in hero myths, a type of myth reflected in the life of Christ:

> The hero's main feat is to overcome the monster of darkness: it is the long-hoped-for and expected triumph of consciousness over the unconscious. Day and light are synonyms for consciousness, night and dark for the unconscious.[53]

Love

Greek has two words translated as love, ἀγαπάω and φιλέω, both verbs. John also has a third word for love, a noun, ἀγάπη, from the same root as ἀγαπάω. Both the verbs are far more common in John than the noun, and of the verbs, αγαπάω appears three times more than φιλέω. Ἀγαπάω appears 36 times in John, compared to 26 times in the other gospels, while φιλέω appears 13 times in John and 8 times in the other gospels.[54]

Scholars disagree on whether the two verbs have significantly different meanings or connotations in John. I agree with Raymond Brown that the two verbs seem interchangeable when all instances of their usage in John are examined.[55] They also appear synonymous in the Greek Old Testament and in secular Greek writing.

Recognise

See Know above.

Remain

"Remain" (μένω) appears 40 times in John and only 12 times in the other gospels. Sometimes μένω may have its ordinary, physical meaning as in John 1:38-39 ("where are you staying?"), although John is so full of symbolism that I doubt if anything in John is ever really just ordinary or physical. Besides "Remain", μένω could also be translated as Mary Coloe did: "Make your home in me, as I make mine in you" (John 15;4).[56] I choose "Remain" because "make your home" can be wordy in some contexts.

---

[53] *The Archetypes and the Collective Unconscious*, in *Collected Works*, volume 9, part 1, paragraph 284, quoted in Segal, *Jung on Myth*, page 132.

[54] These word counts, and the others in this section, have been calculated by Raymond Brown in *The Gospel According to John*, volume 29, pages 497-518.

[55] *Ibid.* page 498.

[56] Coloe, *God Dwells with Us*, page vii.

As in John 15:4, μένω often appears with ἐν (in). Raymond Brown notes that the concept he calls "indwelling" (μένω ἐν) is a frequent theme in John:

> [Μένω ἐν] introduces us to the whole problem of [John's] theology of immanence, *i.e.* a remaining in one another that binds together Father, Son, and the Christian believer. We hear in John that just as the Son is in the Father, and the Father is in the Son (John 14:10-11), so is the Son to be in men, and men are to be in the Father and the Son (John 17:21, 23).
>
> ....
>
> Indwelling, life and love are but different facets of the basic unity binding Father, Son and believer (John 17:11, 21, 23). Divine indwelling is an intimate union that expresses itself in a way of life lived in love.[57]

The analogy of the vine in John 15 illustrates diversity as well as "Remaining in". Different branches grow in their own ways, and that is all right as long as they "Remain in" Jesus, the vine.

Brown also notes that the incidence of "Remaining in" is high in 1, 2 and 3 John,[58] in which the author is struggling to keep the community that gave us John from slipping into false notions such as that Jesus's earthly existence was only apparent, not real and physical. See the section on the Fate of the community below. In John 17:21, Jesus prays, "As you, Father, are in me and I am in you, may they also be in us." In 1 John 2:24, faced with "antichrists",[59] "be in us" becomes "Remain" as the elder writing the letter pleads, "Let what you heard from the beginning Remain in you. If what you heard from the beginning Remains in you, then you will Remain in the Son and in the Father" (1 John 2:24).

Remaining is also at the heart of another frequent word in John, ἕν, meaning "one [thing]", which appears 36 times in John.[60] It is the word for the state of Remaining in: the Father, son and people are one when they Remain in each other.

The Remaining-in of the Father and the son in a soul is effected by the Holy Spirit: "By this means we Know that we Remain in him and he in us, that he has given us of his Spirit" (1 John 4:13, 3:24). Love as well as God Remains-in; "God is Love, and those who Remain in Love Remain in God" (1 John 4:16).

Isaac Penington, in an echo to John's words, calls us to remain in the "seed", which for him was synonymous with Christ and the Light:

> He that will come to life eternal must be translated out of his dead understanding, and all his dead ways and worships, into a living seed, and remain in that seed. Then he shall know life indeed, and the true food of that life, and the true worship

---

[57] *The Gospel According to John*, volume 29, pages 510-511.

[58] *Ibid.*

[59] "Anti" in Greek (αντί) means not just opposition but replacement. An antichrist replaces the real Christ.

[60] Charlesworth, *Jesus as Mirrored in John*, pages 103-104.

and service out from that life, and the reward belonging to all.[61]

Rescue, Rescuer

This word is actually used a little less in John than in each of the other gospels, but it comes theologically loaded in ways I don't wish to imply so I feel compelled to clarify it. Interpolating Christian theology into a text of about 95 C.E is anachronistic and a case of later projection impeding understanding. It also leaves a disagreeable aftertaste that makes Rescue seem unappealing when it is actually the opposite. In psychological terms, Rescue means getting well, the great hope for us flawed mortals.

The conventional translations of σῴζω/σωτήρ are "save" and "saviour". The Greek word σῴζω simply means to save someone or something from grave danger of death or destruction. "Rescue" is well within the range of meanings where the objects are people, as they always are for σῴζω in John.

Perhaps most memorable usage of σῴζω in John is 3:17:

> God did not send his son into the World to judge the World but that the World would be Rescued through him.

The World is not an unambiguously good thing in John (see definition below), but Jesus came to Rescue it none the less, and the World includes everyone alive. However, the Rescue of everyone requires everyone to let the inner Light do its work. Isaac Penington explains:

> *Question:* How will this [Light] save me?
>
> *Answer:* By this means: that which destroys you, and separates you from the living God, will be daily wrought out, and the heart daily changed into the image of him who is light. And you will be brought into unity and fellowship with the light, possessing it, and being possessed by it. This is your salvation.[62]

"Salvation" is a paradoxical word. It is at once our great hope but also the process that Isaac described with the words "Come to that hammer" (see above). Salvation is not done for us by Jesus and some magic that doesn't actually work because it leaves us the same people, unredeemed in reality. Salvation is a process of development led by the inner Light. Jung would say it comes from getting to know the unconscious, where the God archetype is to be found. see Opposites in John and Jung.

Sign

The word "sign" (σημεῖον) appears 10 times in John, and only 3 times in all the other gospels. John uses the word "miracle" (τεράς) only once, in 4:48, where it appears after "Signs", with the two words joined by an "and". The other gospels tell of more miracles than John, and the other gospels rarely call them Signs.

A "Sign" signifies something, but "miracle" (τεράς) not necessarily. A miracle could be taken as a portent or omen, but a miracle is not assumed to have meaning. A Sign always has meaning. However, Jesus never calls his miracles

---

[61] *The Way of Life and Death Made Manifest,* in *Works*, volume 1, pages 27-28.

[62] *The Scattered Sheep Sought After,* in *Works*, volume 1, page 126.

"Signs"; he calls his actions his "works". The natrrator calls Jesus's miracles "Signs".

Jung drew a distinction between a "sign" (or metaphor) and a "symbol":

> A sign is always less than the thing it points to, and a symbol is always more than we can understand at first sight. Therefore we never stop at the sign but go on to the goal it indicates; but we remain with the symbol because it promises more than it reveals.[63]

In Jung's terms, "signs" or metaphors have linear meanings in that they point to their significance and can be understood by conscious thinking, like the black marks on this page and the words they form represent what each word means.[64]

> As Jung understands and employs the term symbol, it is different from a metaphor in that what it is communicating or presenting to consciousness is utterly untranslatable into any other terms, at least for the time being. Symbols are opaque and often bring thinking to a standstill. Metaphors are transparent and must be so if they are to do their job. They help us think in creative ways "outside the box."[65]

Jung is making a functional distinction between symbols, which are how a conscious mind "sees" the archetypes in its unconscious core. "Because archetypes are innately unconscious, they can express themselves only obliquely, through symbols."[66] An archetype emerging into consciousness will do so through a symbol such as a mythic figure, a fairy tale character, or, in the case of the self, in a God-image such as Jesus. "Understood symbolically, Christ serves as a model for Christians seeking to cultivate their relation to the self."[67]

John does not use σημεῖον in same sense as Jung uses "sign" or metaphor. In John, a σημεῖον often says something about Jesus, and Jesus has a strong archetypal meaning because he is a symbol of the self. Often in John Jesus explains the significance of his amazing actions, such as by following the feeding miracle with the teaching about the bread of life (John 6), a metaphor pointing to a God-image. Sometimes in John, however, the symbol is not explained, such as when the man born blind is healed, but in that case, the ensuing investigation of the healing by Pharisees dramatises the symbolic meaning of blindness (John 9). In any case, as Jung noted, the meaning of the symbol underlying a Sign is greater than any single interpretation of that symbol. Often a symbol points to unconscious content so its meaning is largely unknown.

The purpose of Signs in John "is to point to Jesus' identity, though they also serve to show the fulfilment of expectations associated with Moses and the prophets (Elijah and Elisha)."[68] Jesus's extraordinary identity was threatening to the authorities. The raising of Lazarus proves too much and leaves them looking to

---

[63] "Approaching the Unconscious" in *Man and His Symbols*, (1964).*

[64] Stein, "The Reality of the Soul" in *Collected Writings of Murray Stein*, volume 6, page 215.

[65] Stein, "Symbols and the Transformation of the Psyche", published online at Symbols and the Transformation of the Psyche – Murray Stein (last retrieved July 2023).

[66] Segal, *Jung on Mythology*, page 9.

[67] Segal, *Jung on Mythology*, page 37.

[68] Culpepper, *The Gospel and Letters of John*, page 21.

apprehend Jesus (John 11:45-54) because they can't allow a miracle worker to develop a power base among the people. Psychologically, their response seems motivated by fear, not of God and his miracle worker but of Rome. Miracles can be denied or explained away by rebranding the miracle worker as a charlatan. Consequently, John seems to be of two minds about Signs; "signs confirm that Jesus is sent from God (3:2, 9:16), [but] despite seeing signs, some refuse to believe."[69]

Our human minds miss much if not most of reality. Who knows how many wonders happen that we never notice because we weren't looking for them? Isaac knew that the mysteries of God can be hidden in plain sight, in peripheral vision as it were, in a place where we don't look so they remain unconscious. We lack the eyes to see them:

> Under the old covenant, though the Lord did great things before the eyes of that people in Egypt, and exercised them with signs, miracles, and trials also in the wilderness; yet the Lord did not give them a heart to perceive, and eyes to see, and ears to hear, unto that day; as mentioned in Deut. 29:2-4. The veil was over their hearts. But the other covenant contains the giving of the new heart, the opening of the blind eye, the unstopping of the deaf ear, the writing the law in the heart, the putting the pure fear in the inward parts, the putting God's Spirit within them, and so causing them to walk in his statutes, and to keep his judgments and do them.[70]

"The new covenant" describes the relationship between God and a person who has found the inward Light, a person who is becoming a new person. The new person sees more than the old one could.

One reason we don't look for Signs nowadays is that we don't think they really happen. Penington and other early Friends believed in miracles, but we in our materialist age have an aversion to thinking of Signs as events that actually happen. However, Carl Jung had no such difficulty. His concept of synchronicity is based on the idea that some things happen with meaningful connections to reality but without a cause ascertainable by humans. There is a deeper ordering of the physical world than causation explains. That deeper ordering can be seen in the simultaneous occurrence of a certain psychic state with one or more external events which appear as meaningful parallels to the momentary psychic state.[71]

A couple of examples illustrate that definition of synchronicity:

- "Jung reports an incident he once witnessed during a therapy session... The patient was relating a dream in which she was given a golden scarab,[72] an important archetypal symbol of [regeneration]. As she was recounting the dream, an insect began knocking against the window

---

[69] Anderson, *The Riddles of the Fourth Gospel*, page 31.

[70] *Life and Immortality Brought To Light*, in *Works*, volume 4, page 151.

[71] C.G. Jung, *Synchronicity: An Acausal Connecting Principle*, (London: Routledge 1985), page 36; quoted in Kastrup, *Decoding Jung's Metaphysics*, page 61.

[72] A dung-eating beetle sacred to ancient Egyptians. Scarabs collect balls of dung many times their size and lay their eggs in them.

behind Jung. He opened the window and a rose chafer beetle—an insect very much like a scarab—flew in. It was as if the *physical world itself* were echoing the archetypal symbolism of the dream...."[73]

- "A few years ago, I was on vacation with my girlfriend in a small village in the German countryside. We had been out of touch with friends and family for about a week at that point. One morning my girlfriend woke up and immediately told me a dream she had just had, and which for some reason had made an unusually strong emotional impression on her. In the dream, her old grandmother—who, in real life, was alive and well the last time we had been in touch—appeared with a bandage of gauze wrapped around her head. She was in a hospital, flanked by two of her daughters (my girlfriend's aunts). None of the three said a word, although my girlfriend felt distinctly that her grandmother was telling her, mentally, that she was still okay, despite the head injury.

  "We thought we should call my girlfriend's father and inquire about her grandmother, just in case. And so we did. The first thing her father said was that his mother—i.e. my girlfriend's grandmother—had just had a *brain stroke* and was *hospitalized. Two of her daughters were with her in the hospital.* The first medical assessment was that *she wasn't in immediate danger anymore.* Yet, as it turns out, she would die six months later of directly related causes."[74]

Jungian philosopher Bernardo Kastrup explains that synchronicity is not as fantastical as it may at first seem. Newton's laws of physics, for example, rely on "induction—the theoretical inference of a general law from repeated instances of conjoint events—which goes beyond empirical observation."[75] In other words, the fact that a given cause has had a given effect in every observed case says nothing about cases that were not observed, or what makes the apparent cause the cause.

At the particle level of quantum mechanics, where nothing is actually observed:

> cause and effect ... and the associated necessity [the "law" implied from cause and effect] applies *only at a statistical level*; individual quantum events unfold seemingly randomly but, when taken together in large numbers, the events lawfully comply with predictable probabilistic distributions [from which Newton's 'laws' and other generalisations can be inferred].[76]

At the macro level, cause-and-effect generalisations are possible, but at the micro, quantum level, such generalisations are not possible because events seem random.

Kastrup notes further, "As a matter of fact, cosmology today states that tiny, acausal quantum fluctuations ... are what led—after amplification by gravity—to

---

[73] Kastrup, *Decoding Jung's Metaphysics*, pages 53-54 (emphasis in original). For an amazing case, see also Stein, "Not Just a Butterfly", in *Minding the Self* pages 48-53.

[74] *Ibid.*, page 56 (emphasis in original).

[75] *Ibid.*, page 49.

[76] *Ibid.*

the formation of everything, from microbial life to galaxies."[77] He then quotes Seth Lloyd, professor of quantum systems at Massachusetts Institute of Technology:

> Counterintuitive as it may seem, quantum mechanics produces detail and structure because it is inherently uncertain. ... Every galaxy, star, and planet owes its mass and position to quantum accidents of the early universe. But there's more: these accidents are also the source of the universe's minute details. ... Every roll of the quantum dice injects a few more bits of detail into the world. As these details accumulate, they form the seeds of all the variety of the universe. Every tree, branch, leaf, cell and strand of DNA owes its particular form to some past toss of the quantum dice.[78]

What Lloyd calls "accidents" are not really accidents according to Jung. Synchronicity is ordered according to the archetypes of the collective unconscious. "Next to causality, the physical world organizes itself along *archetypal correspondences of meaning*, which break down the barrier between world and psyche."[79] In Jung's words:

> It is perfectly possible, psychologically, for the unconscious or an archetype to take complete possession of a [person] and to determine his fate down to the smallest detail. At the same time, objective, non-psychic parallel phenomena can occur which also represent the archetype. It not only seems so, it simply is so, that the archetype fulfils itself not only psychically in the individual but objectively outside the individual.[80]

As noted earlier, the Signs in John have a deeper meaning than just what happened. It is as if they are events of synchronicity, occurrences in the physical world that correspond (without ascertainable causal relation) to spiritual realities in the world of the collective unconscious. Jesus is the bread of life and can create physical bread in a way I do not understand (John 6). Perhaps "the divine" is another word for the ordering force that Jung saw in the collective unconscious. If so, God determines the quantum mechanics at the base of all matter, which would make God almighty indeed. And green, according to Jung's dream see "I am the vine" above).

In any case, what is certainly true is that there are more things in heaven and earth than are dreamt of in my philosophy. A materialist demands proof, and in much of life, where we must know the accuracy of a fact, proof is a good thing to have. However, it has its limits. Beyond it, there is a world of wonder, a world we do not fully understand, but it is no less real for that. Not even scientists understand everything there is; if they did, they'd have no research to do. Because I understand only in part, I do not rule out that some phenomena in the

---

[77] *Ibid.*, page 51.

[78] Quoted in *ibid.*

[79] *Ibid.*, page 53.

[80] *Answer to Job*, in *Collected Works*, volume 11, paragraph 648.

universe happen but are beyond my (or perhaps anyone's) ability to explain why they happen.

That is also true for the Signs in John, among other things. Given the limits of my understanding, I cannot say that they did not happen, or that I fully grasp their meaning or why they did happen.

> We find that the most deep and mysterious writings of the prophets and apostles are often couched in allegorical similes; therefore, it requires our coming to the same experience, rightly to comprehend or understand them; and hence, when I meet with parts or passages of scripture that I do not understand, I leave them until I may arrive at a state of deeper experience, by which means I have come clearly to comprehend and understand some things that, at a previous time, seemed mysterious to me.
>
> Elias Hicks[81]

Testify, Testimony

See Witness below.

Trust

> Take heed, dear Friends, to the promptings of love and truth in your hearts. Trust them as the leadings of God whose Light shows us our darkness and brings us to new life.
>
> Advices and Queries no. 1[82]

The verb πιστεύω, which I translate "Trust", appears 11 times in Matthew, 14 in Mark, 9 in Luke, but 98 times in John, where it is the stated purpose (20:31).[83] No noun for Trust appears in John.

The Greek word πιστεύω is usually translated in terms of "having faith" or "believing", but both those words come with theological baggage that I prefer to avoid. Traditional Christianity emphasises a "leap" of faith (from uncertainty to authority in the form of church and doctrine), and the necessity for such a leap, but those are anachronistic theological interpolations in understanding John, which was written when there was neither church nor its doctrine. Πιστεύω essentially means to trust or have confidence, in someone or something, or that something is the case. I translate it as Trust.

Carl Jung pointed out that the faith required by conventional Christianity has become a tall order for modern Christians:

> The Churches stand for traditional and collective convictions which in the case of many of their adherents are no longer based on their own inner experience but on *unreflecting belief*, which is notoriously apt to disappear as soon as one begins thinking about it. The content of belief then comes into collision with knowledge, and it often turns out that the

---

[81] Quoted in Pacific Yearly Meeting, *Faith and Practice* no. 58, page 82.

[82] Britain Yearly Meeting, *Quaker Faith and Practice*.

[83] Charlesworth, *Jesus as Mirrored in John*, page 437.

> irrationality of the former is no match for the ratiocinations
> of the latter. Belief is no adequate substitute for inner
> experience, and where this is absent even a strong faith which
> came miraculously as a gift of grace may depart equally
> miraculously.[84]

Quakerism does not demand such "unreflecting belief". It focuses on letting people have an "inner experience" that convinces. Here Melvin Keiser describes how Isaac Penington knew things:

> Rooted in our bodily contact with reality, ideas always
> present only an aspect of truth. The whole of a mysterious
> reality exceeds our partial grasp through ideas emerging from
> our spiritually sensitized senses working from our angle of
> experience. .... Isaac's grasp of aspects of reality through his
> angle of experience of mystery did not achieve the absolute
> certainty that modernity since Descartes has sought, and
> never found, but did, nevertheless, result in confidence and
> power to live in the world.[85]

That "confidence and power" is Trust. Our minds, and our words, only ever grasp *some* of a truth, and a large part of what we can grasp is unconscious. Knowing only in part leaves us in uncertainty about what we do not consciously know. Complete certainty about anything is impossible, including about things we must do to live in the world. Trust enables us to live and function in the world despite our uncertainties about everything in it.

What to Trust as true is a theological question. For most Christians, belief in God, the church, and its doctrines is the aim. In John, the aim of Trust is more precise: the whole point of John is for the reader "to come to Trust that Jesus is the Christ, the son of God," and by so Trusting, we have Life (20:31). For Quakers including particularly Isaac Penington, "Christ" is another word for the inner Light, so the statement "Jesus is the Christ" equates Jesus with the Light, the Seed, that of God in each soul. For a Quaker reading John, the Trust we are to have is that Jesus, the son of God, is for us now a light within each of us, a light we can each find. If we Trust that there is a Light there, we go looking for it.

That Trust is not blind faith because Quakers expect to confirm it in actual experience. The only leap required is enough Trust to seek an inward experience that confirms that that Light also shines in one's own soul. Seeking that Light is the purpose of Quaker worship, which is expectant waiting in shared silence, peaceful yet attentive to what may arise from the stillness. We wait together to receive a sense, an image or idea, some input to the soul (mind or body). Melvin Keiser explains the Trust that this requires:

> To reach this level of waiting we have already undergone a
> change. The obstacle to reaching this level is our own ego
> which must be overcome—or slipped loose from. Our
> individual inclination, supported in major ways by modern
> culture, is always to control what is going on within and

---

[84] *The Undiscovered Self*, in *Collected Works*, volume 10, paragraph 521.

[85] Keiser, "Felt Reality in Practical Living", page 201. Keiser illustrates the process with a story from the life of George Fox in *Seeds of Silence* pages 9-10.

without. Yet our descent to the level of waiting detaches us from our structuring activities—both intellectually making things cohere and morally making things conform. We detach from our active thinking, willing, and imagining and from our conscious commitments and obligations. This then requires a trust to be in a structureless state that we will not ourselves disintegrate or be overwhelmed by destructive psychic forces. To reach for this level can be disorienting if not downright terrifying. To be waiting in silence is, therefore, an act (which is simultaneously a gift) of faith as a reliance upon the unknown, being patient amidst mystery.[86]

That Trust gives us the courage to seek the inner Light in conscious experience. The more we experience the Light, the more conscious it becomes, so we gradually Trust less and know more from our conscious experience.[87] As the Light grows, we find ourselves transformed. Ultimately "one never *possesses* a metaphysical belief but is *possessed* by it."[88]

Psychologically, Trust also requires courage because the unconscious mind is scary; it has "destructive psychic forces" as Keiser put it. Jung wrote:

> Can man stand a further increase in consciousness? .... I confess that I submitted to the divine power of this apparently insurmountable problem and I consciously and intentionally made my life miserable because I wanted God to be alive and free from the suffering man has put on him by loving his own reason more than God's secret intentions.[89]

Truth, True

"Truth" (ἀλήθεια) appears 20 times in John but only 8 times in the other gospels. "True" (ἀληθής) appears nine times in John. Ἀλήθεια, when said of a factual representation, means truth in contrast to a lie or appearance. "True", when said of a person, means truthful and honest.[90]

Truth is often paradoxical in John, which presents Jesus as the messiah, the great hero of Jews and successor to David. Yet, as Blumhofer shows, Jesus is never more Davidic than in his suffering and death.[91] "The very acts that would disprove Jesus' position as 'king of the [Jews]' are, in fact, ironic validations of it."[92]

Irony, a characteristic of paradox, abounds in John. For example, it is John's Pilate who has his soldiers dress Jesus in a crown of thorns and a royal purple robe, then acclaim him "Hail, King of Jews!" The irony (on top of the irony in

---

[86] Keiser, *Seeds of Silence*, page 79.

[87] Jung's approach to religion was also experience-based: "The charisma of faith was denied me. .... The only way open to me was the experience of religious realities." Jung, *Letters*, volume 2, pages 257-276.

[88] Jung, *Answer to Job*, in *Collected* Works, volume 11, paragraph 735.

[89] Quoted in Gerhard Adler, "Aspects of Jung's Personality and Work," in *Psychological Perspectives*, volume 6, page 12 (1975); see also Edinger, *The Creation of Consciousness*, page 107.

[90] Bauer, Arndt, Gingrich & Danker, *A Greek-English Dictionary of the New Testament*, page 34-36.

[91] Blumhofer, *The Gospel of John and the Future of Israel*, pages 178-211.

[92] *Ibid.*, page 207.

Pilate's sarcasm) is that Jesus *is* in Truth exactly who the soldiers say he is (19:1-5). Truth is not straightforward in John; it comes layered and often with a paradoxical twist. Paradox, for Jung, was an aspect of the self, the inner Light: "The self ... is absolutely paradoxical in that it represents in every respect thesis and antithesis, and at the same time, synthesis."[93]

Irony is a psychological principle. An inward reality that makes its way to consciousness often appears at first in tricky or misleading clothing, as a paradox, something that can't be true. Yet it is. One reason we mortals can be spiritually slow is that we ignore Truth when it violates our dress code for reality.

Unique Son

Traditionally translated as "only begotten Son" (μονογενὴς υἱὸς in John 3:16), this phrase appears only four times in John, and, although μονογενὴς only refers to Jesus in John,[94] the words it applies to are not uniform. John 3:16 and 3:18 have the complete phrase "Unique Son". The phrase is "Unique God" (μονογενὴς θεὸς) in 1:18. Earlier, he was just Unique, and I say "he" because the word μονογενὴς only fits a male (1:14). "His [God's] Unique Son" appears in 1 John 4:9.

Μονογενὴς is defined as the "only member of a kin or kind",[95] so μονογενὴς υἱὸς would be an only son or a unique (one of a kind) son. Examples in Luke 7:12, 9:38, and Hebrews 11:17, plus half a dozen spots in the Greek version of the Old Testament, show that μονογενὴς can mean an only child. However, in a sense, God has more than one child because of John 1:12 ("To all who accepted him and Trusted him, he gave power to become children of God.") Keener points out that μονογενὴς includes a connotation of particular affection; the only or Unique Son is a special son, like Abraham's Isaac, who was his "only son whom you love", as God put it when telling Abraham to sacrifice his son (Genesis 22:2).[96]

I opt to translate μονογενὴς υἱὸς as "Unique Son" because, though not his mother's only child, Jesus was a special son. John shows in Jesus's frequent mention of his Father (see Father above) that they had an extraordinarily close relationship. In the wider, deeper sense of John 1:12, however, perhaps each child of God is special in having her own place to Remain in the house of the Father (John 14:2) and being his own leaf on a branch of the vine (John 15:5).

Very truly I tell you

All of the gospels use the phrase "truly I tell you"(ἀμὴν λέγω σοι), but only John doubles the first word: "Truly, truly I tell you" (ἀμὴν ἀμὴν λέγω σοι). John always doubles that first word. I translate John's version as "Very truly I tell you".

Ἀμὴν is a Hebrew word meaning "truly" and borrowed into Greek. In the Old Testament, it appears occasionally, but only as a one-word direct quotation that is an audience response confirming something said by someone else, as if to say "so be it".[97] It never appears in the Greek version of the Old Testament in the phrase "truly I tell you".

---

[93] *Psychology and Alchemy*, in *Collected Works*, volume 12, paragraph 22.

[94] Bauer, Arndt and Gingrich, page 527.

[95] Liddell, Scott & James, *Greek-English Lexicon*, entry μονογενὴς..

[96] *The Gospel of John*, volume 1, pages 412-416.

[97] *E.g.* 1 Chronicles 16:36; 1 Ezra/Esdras 9:47.

Only Jesus uses the phrase "truly I tell you" (or in John, "Very truly I tell you"). It is as if it is a marker for an important statement from him.

Witness, Testimony, Testify

The word Witness (μάρτυς), Testimony (μαρτυρία), and the verb Testify (μαρτυρέω) appear 64 times in John and the letters of John,[98] compared to 20 times in all the other gospels.

The English word "martyr" comes from the Greek word for witness, μάρτυς, the root of which is μάρτυρ-. The English word means "a person who is killed for their religious or other beliefs",[99] and no element of "witness" remains, although that was the original meaning. Jesus foretells that Peter will die a martyr (John 19:35, 21:18-19), but in John, Peter is hardly a witness. That role falls to the Beloved Disciple (John 21:24).

We do not know how the Beloved Disciple died. It seems he took his role as a witness seriously, if only because of the beautiful gospel he left us. Even for a holy man and literary genius, it took some time to compose. The end of his gospel leaves me thinking that he did live long and perfected his stories by many years of retelling.

I doubt the Beloved Disciple was a martyr because it was rumoured that he would not die (John 21: 22-23). A premature death would have scotched that rumour out of disappointment, and made it not worth mentioning in John 21. The rumour arose from something Jesus had said to Peter: "If I want him to Remain until I come, what's that to you?" (John 21:22). That question has levels of meaning thanks to Remain, and it can be read as telling Peter to keep his nose out of a personal matter between Jesus and his Beloved.

John 21 appears to be a late, or perhaps the last, addition to the text, and it appears that by then, the Beloved Disciple has died (John 21:24). Being a witness for Jesus was his life's work. His gospel ends by declaring itself to be his Testimony and averring that it is True (21:24).

A few years after the death of this great Witness, his Spirit-led movement disintegrated; see "Fate of the community" below.

A Spirit-led movement depends on Witnesses for its continuation because it is not possible for a person to convey the Spirit to another. "The Spirit blows where it will" (John 3:8); we don't control it. The most we can impart to another person is a Testimony, so for that reason:

> We are also to be witnesses for God, and to propagate his life
> in this world; to be instruments in his hand, to bring others
> out of death and captivity into the true life and liberty.[100]

World

The Greek word κόσμος, translated "World", appears 78 times in John, compared to only 14 times in all the other gospels. Κόσμος can mean the entire universe,

---

[98] Braun, *The Epistles of John*, page 167.

[99] *Oxford Dictionary of English* (second edition), (Oxford: Oxford University Press), entry for "martyr".

[100] Penington, *The Way of Life and Death*, in *Works*, volume 1, page 93.

but in John, its usage suggests a more limited meaning as this world and the people in it.

As noted in defining <u>Father</u> above, Satan has descended to this world and is in charge. Jung quoted Luke, who wrote that Jesus saw "Satan fall like lightning" to earth, and Jung saw in that fall "the final separation of Yahweh from his dark son."[101] However, when Jesus's Hour comes, so does "the judgment of this World; now the ruler of this World will be thrown out."[102] The great prayer of Jesus over his disciples in John 17 asks for their continued protection: "Now I am no longer in the World, but they are in the World, and I am coming to you. Holy Father, protect them in your name that you have given me, so that they may be one."[103] Satan may be the ruler of this World, but Jesus prays that his disciples can be an enclave protected from the World.

Not an isolated enclave, however. Jesus prays in John 17:18, "As you sent me into the World, so I sent them into the World." Matthew gives the purpose, "Go make disciples of all nations" (28:19). The World may have an evil ruler, but its state is not so hopeless that carrying a message to it is futile from the start. So Isaac Penington writes:

> You must come out of the spirit of this world, if you will abide in God's spirit. And you must come out of the love of the things of this world, if you will come out of the spirit of this world. For in the love of the things of this world, the spirit of this world lodges and dwells, and you cannot touch the unclean things without also touching something of the unclean spirit. Therefore, John said from a true and deep understanding, "Love not the world, neither the things of the world," [1 John 2:15] (if you love the things of the world, you love the world), for "if any man love the world, the love of the Father is not in him [also 1 John 2:15]."[104]

John, Isaac Penington, and Carl Jung all see the World dominated by Satan. Jesus, by contrast, is so devoid of any evil, particularly in John, that the situation was "standing in need of eventual correction".[105] That came with the book of Revelation.[106] However, in John, Jesus and the Father are totally one-sided, for which the author[107] paid a high price:

> In [Revelation] I see less a metaphysical mystery than the outburst of long pent-up feelings such as can frequently be observed in people who strive for perfection. .... [He] had to shut out all negative feelings, and, thanks to a helpful lack of self-reflection, he was able to forget them. But though they disappeared from the conscious level they continued to rankle

---

[101] *Answer to Job,* in *Collected Works,* volume 11, paragraph 650.

[102] John 12:31; also 14:30 and 16:11.

[103] John 17:11. Much of Jesus's prayer is out of concern for leaving his disciples in the World.

[104] "The Everlasting Gospel", in *Works,* volume 3, page 432. The quotation is from 1 John 2:15.

[105] Dourley, *The Illness that We Are,* page. 62.

[106] Jung, *Answer to Job,* in *Collected Works,* volume 11, paragraphs 714ff.

[107] Jung assumes that John, the letters of John, and the book of Revelation all have the same author, which is the traditional view of their authorship. See *Answer to Job,* page 93 (Routledge edition).

beneath the surface, and in the course of time spun an elaborate web of resentments and vengeful thoughts which then burst upon consciousness in the form of a revelation. From this there grew up a terrifying picture that blatantly contradicts all ideas of Christian humility, tolerance and love of your neighbour and your enemies, and makes nonsense of a loving father in heaven and rescuer of mankind.[108]

Hindus and pagan Greeks were rather better served by their myths because their gods are not one-sided.

Now we face a different one-sidedness in that rational thinking has come to dominate all thinking, leaving our irrationality unconscious and our consciousness the poorer. Melvin Keiser:

> The church has objectified both life and resurrection by applying logic to scripture resulting in the fixedness of doctrine obscuring the inwardness of Jesus and ourselves, and eliminating the play of metaphors in our personal existence which can evoke experience of the divine and be transformative of self and the world.[109]

Christianity has always applied logic to understand itself, but Jung devoted the latter part of his life to a great effort to revive Christianity, which he thought had traditionally held out the possibility of real spiritual experience despite its excessive rationality. The section below, "The apocalypse of Carl Jung", summarises his thoughts.

The excessive rationality of the World calls for a "counter-poise" as Jung put it:

> It is not ethical principles however lofty or creeds however orthodox that lay the foundations for the freedom and autonomy of the individual, but simply and solely the empirical awareness, the incontrovertible experience of an intensely personal, reciprocal relationship between man and an extra-mundane authority which acts as a counter-poise to the "world" and its "reason".[110]

Wrong, Wrongdoing, Wrongfulness

> [W]hen one follows the path of individuation, when one lives one's own life, one must take mistakes into the bargain; life would not be complete without them.
>
> Carl Jung[111]

The words ἁμαρτάνω (the verb) and ἁμαρτία (the deed, or the state of being Wrongful) don't appear more in John than in other gospels, but their usual translation as "sin" is, with all its later-added connotations, such a loaded word

---

[108] Jung, *Answer to Job,* in *Collected Works,* volume 11, paragraph 708.

[109] Keiser, *Seeds of Silence* page 178.

[110] *Collected Works,* volume 10, paragraph 509.

[111] *Memories, Dreams, Reflections,* page 328.

that I feel compelled to find another one. The authors of John did not intend to heap thousands of years of Christian blame and guilt into this word.[112]

Both ἁμαρτάνω and ἁμαρτία originally meant no more than to make a mistake, such as when an arrow misses the target. Christianity has attached great opprobrium to the concept of sin and has exploited it to increase the power of the church and clergy. However, the original Greek word has no such connotations. For example, the Iliad used it for a spear that misses its target.[113] No great shame is called for when a spear thrower misses. Practice may improve his aim, or perhaps he just isn't cut out for spear throwing, but the miss was not evil or grounds for moral condemnation or shame.

By trying to leave aside the opprobrium sponsored by conventional Christianity, I am not advocating an abandonment of moral judgment. Freeing ourselves from shame and oppressive and unjustifiable blame can be a step toward greater self-understanding. Melvin Keiser defines "sin" in terms of its effect; it veils our perception of the inner Light, and he identifies it by its lack of depth:

> Sin is the barrier that veils our eyes from the depths of Light and New Creation. It is living on the surface, preoccupied with outward things. Fox calls this surface existence living in the "flesh": it is "flesh...which had veiled me," he says. Living in the flesh is "not [to] give up to the will of God." It is to be living on the surface where we have the illusion of control and full comprehension.[114]

Living only in ego-consciousness, in other words, with little understanding or sense of one's depth, including a darker side. Little morality is possible then; we think we are being moral, but we are really projecting while denying and repressing any thought of our own immorality, using defence mechanisms to block off an awareness of the real situation. Murray Stein:

> In order for consciousness to perform its function of moral discrimination adaptively and accurately, it must increase awareness of personal and collective shadow motivations, take back projections to the maximum extent possible, and test for validity. Time and again Jung cries out for people to recognize their shadow parts. Questions of morals and ethics must become the subject of serious debate, of inner and outer consideration and argument, and of continual refinement. The conscious struggle to come to a moral decision is for Jung the prerequisite for what he calls ethics, the action of the whole person, the self. If this work is left undone the individual and society as a whole will suffer.[115]

Dogmas and rules from a book lack "awareness of ... collective shadow motivations" and reflect the church's projection of its unconscious evil onto sinners.

---

[112] As used in John, the word may have had connotations from the Septuagint, the Greek translation of the Hebrew scriptures well known in Judea at the time, but it would not have had Christian connotations because there were not yet any Christians then.

[113] *Iliad*, book 2, 5.287.

[114] Keiser, *Seeds of Silence*, page 29.

[115] Stein, *Jung on Evil*, page 9-10.

"Keeping low" was Isaac's phrase[116] for keeping off my high horse, the "blindness of righteous indignation and moral outrage that [can] overwhelm consciousness."[117] I only need to make a moral judgment if the outcome actually affects me, but within that narrow scope, it is best not to duck the issue. "If the ego [morally] discriminates incorrectly for very long, reality will exact a high price."[118] The ultimate authority is the Light within, not an ecclesiastical light, but the formerly unknown self integrated into awareness. Projections and other forms of ducking responsibility must be seen for what they are, and seen through. Integration of the self brings a greater sense of empathy with others, a realisation of the suffering servant ideal in oneself. The suffering servant understands the Wrong, and without condoning it, also sees the pain it causes the Wrongdoer.

For Jung, how we relate to our Wrongfulness is crucial. Denying (and projecting) it harms relationships. The devil within was for Jung as real as the Christ within; both are archetypal.

> Christ espoused the sinner and did not condemn him. The true follower of Christ will do the same, and, since one should do unto others as one would do unto oneself, one will also take the part of the sinner who is oneself. And as little as we would accuse Christ of fraternizing with evil, so little should we reproach ourselves that to love the sinner is to make a pact with the devil. Love makes a man better, hate makes him worse—even when that man is oneself.[119]

Concepts not found in John

In visual art, the "negative space", space left empty or free of objects in the frame, is important in the composition. From the perspective of traditional Christianity in our time, some concepts are conspicuously absent in John. They include:

- **Church**. There is a clearly a community of people who know each other in John, but John never calls them an ἐκκλησία, a church.[120] Instead, he speaks of this community as "disciples". Matthew is the only gospel to use the word "church". Luke uses it in Acts, but not until well into chapter 5. Early in Acts, the community of disciples is called a κοινωνία, a community so socialist that the hold-outs Ananias and Sapphira dropped dead (Acts 5:1-11).

  In the scriptures from the community of John, only the last letter, 3 John, mentions "church", but it is addressed to a group that has gone astray under Diotrephes, who "likes being first" (3 John 9). The letters entitled "John" reflect a community torn apart by dissension; see "Fate of the community" below.

---

[116] For example, in *An Examination of the Grounds*, in *Works*, volume 1, 387: "Yet he that receives ever so great a measure of the Spirit, if he does not keep low and abide therein, but rather lifts himself up above his brethren, this one may easily err and draw aside others into his error."

[117] Stein, *Jung on Evil*, page 10.

[118] Stein, *Jung on Evil*, page 9.

[119] Jung, *Psychology and Alchemy*, in *Collected Works*, volume 12, paragraph 37.

[120] ¨Εκκλησια" originally meant an assembly called out from the general population. The exclusivity and lack of openness in that concept rub against the Quaker principles of equality and truth/integrity.

Instead of an institution, the community of John had the Counsellor, but looking inward for guidance is the first thing to go in the "rather strange intellectual exercises most theologies must go through to justify the ecclesiastical function of the institutions they serve".[121] The individual's support for the institution is won by first "showing humanity to be naturally divested of an innate access to the divine, in order to grant [to the church] the monopoly or near monopoly on the means of grace and salvation."[122] It is that premise that George Fox overthrew: "Your teacher is within you. Look not forth."[123] Jung concurred: "What one could almost call a systematic blindness is the effect of the prejudice that God is *outside of* man."[124]

- **Apostles and hierarchy**: The Greek word translated "apostle", ἀπόστολος, appears only once in John at 13:16. There it may simply refer to someone sent out, its ordinary meaning, rather than to an ecclesiastical leader. If it does refer to a leader, then 13:16 also keeps the leader in his place: "No apostle is greater than the one who sent him". "The twelve" appears in John,[125] but without implication that they have any authority; they may just be Jesus's inner circle of friends. The leading trio of disciples, Peter, James and John, is not mentioned at all. Peter, the pebble (πέτρος) on which the church was built (Matt. 16:18), comes across as rather a bumbler in John, in contrast to the Beloved Disciple, until the last (later appended) chapter 21.[126]

- **Sacraments**: The only religious ritual mentioned in John is immersion of people in water, which John the Baptist and perhaps Jesus do.[127] John's version of the last supper (John 13-14) does not mention what they ate and drank, much less any blessing of it or thanking for it, or any requirement for repetition. Other traditional Christian sacraments go unmentioned, except for immersion, which John was doing in the Jordan.

Why John immerses is not explained in John; presumably he was continuing the Jewish practice whose purpose was ritual purification. Traditional Christian theology sees baptism (usually not by immersion) as equivalent to being "born out of water" (John 3:4-5). However, "out of water" is how every human being is born. There is nothing in John to

---

[121] Dourley, *The Illness that We Are*, page 24.

[122] Dourley, *The Illness that We Are*, page 24.

[123] George Fox, *Journal*, 1694 edition, edited and transcribed by Thomas Ellwood, page 98; online at 1694 edition: page 98 (lancaster.ac.uk).

[124] *Psychology and Religion: East and West*, in *Collected Works*, volume 11, paragraph 100. Stein explains that Jung's protestantism placed the individual at the centre, not an institution, and encouraged a sense of dependency directly on God rather than on church or clergy. Stein, "Jungian Psychology and the Spirit of Protestantism", in *Collected Writings*, volume 6, pages 270-277. Quakers and John would concur.

[125] The few cases mentioning "the twelve" do not suggest power over others but rather a higher degree of Trust and closeness to Jesus. John 6:66-71 ("Will you also go away?"), 20:21.

[126] Brown, *The Community of the Beloved Disciple* page 82-83; Charlesworth, *Jesus as Mirrored in John*, page 388.

[127] John baptises according to John 1:31. Jesus baptised according to 3:22 and 26, but 4:2 contradicts them both and leaves doubt that Jesus baptised anyone; it was just a rumour.

suggest that a baptism ritual is a divine requirement at all. Paul Anderson sums up the situation:

> If all we had was the Gospel of John, there would be no biblical basis for baptism and communion, or other sacramental forms, in the life of the church. .... A meal of remembrance is totally missing. .... Disciples are invited to eat and drink the flesh and blood of Jesus after the feeding of the five thousand, but if the [author] really wanted to insist upon the Eucharist, why not include it at the Last Supper?[128]

- **Christians and Christianity**. "Christian" (χριστιανός) does not appear at all in the gospels. Its first use is in Acts 11:26, which is also the first usage of the word in all of Greek according to Liddell and Scott's dictionary.[129] "Christianity" is not to be found in the entire Bible. In the gospels, Jesus's disciples considered themselves Jews with an amazing rabbi, but not Christians.[130] In our time, being Christian is so important to some people's identity that it is remarkable that early disciples never even knew the concept of "Christian".

- **Homophobia**. Sex between males was common in the Greek-speaking world, but it was prohibited for Jews in Leviticus 20:13. That did not stop the Beloved Disciple from doing the gayest move in the entire Bible when he rests himself on the front of Jesus's body during the last supper (John 13:23). Ancient diners reclined at dinner, leaning up on one elbow to reach the food in the middle of the group. There the Beloved Disciple is both next to Jesus and in physical contact, closer than the others (Peter has to ask the Beloved to ask Jesus something 13:24). It would appear that the son of David has found his Jonathan, yet that does not appear to have come up in the subsequent conversation, which takes up five chapters out of the 21 in all of John (John 13-17).

When Jesus dies, most of his disciples abandon him, but not the Beloved Disciple, who is there at the foot of the cross. Jesus places his mother in his care then dies (John 19:25-30).

- **Trinity**: It is clearer from John than from any other gospel that God has at least three aspects: Father, Son, and Counsellor (Holy Spirit), although those three leave out other aspects mentioned in John about as much, such as Light, Life, etc. The Father-Son-Counsellor triad later came to be rationalised into the Trinity, a word not used in the entire Bible. The Trinity is a later construct from a time when institutional Christianity systematised and rationalised its doctrine. Jung and Quakers would say Christianity had lost its orientation to lived spiritual experience by that time, as is clear from the hyper rationalisation of its dogma afterwards.[131] Quaker thought does not include a Trinity.

---

[128] Anderson, *The Riddles of the Fourth Gospel*, page 40; see also pages 160-161 and 228-231.

[129] *Greek-English Lexicon*, page 895 (Oxford: Clarendon Press). Acts 11:26 says, "It was in Antioch that the disciples were first called "Christians.""

[130] Ashton, *The Gospel of John and Christian Origins*, page 9.

[131] See "Apocalypse of Carl Jung" below.

Jung saw the (traditionally conceived) Trinity as stopping short of completion and missing out the feminine and earthy/unpleasant aspects of reality. Jung thought it should be four not three in order to fill in those missing aspects.[132] However, in John and among Quakers, God has many images, not just the three comprising the Trinity.

- **Kingdom of God, kingdom of heaven**: This concept, so frequent in the other gospels, is almost absent in John. It appears only in John 3:3 and 3:5. When Pilate questions Jesus about his kingdom, Jesus answers that his kingdom is not of this world (John 18:36), but he does not say it is the kingdom *of God* or *of heaven*, and "kingdom" is Pilate's word, not Jesus's. There is a group of disciples in John, they know each other and are to love each other (John 14:12), but they never appear so organised and institutional as to be a kingdom. They are a circle of friends with a spirituality in common.

  Jesus also never calls himself a king in John, though others use the term of him (such as Nathaniel in 1:49 or Pilate in 18:33-19:3). Jesus rides a donkey into Jerusalem rather than look like the king that people of Jerusalem claimed he was (John 12:14).

It is remarkable how many of John's key words Quakers have adopted as their own. "Life" and "Light" are both very common metaphors for God in Penington's writings and those of other early Friends, and "Light" is still often used today in the same sense as ever. Some missing concepts are also still missing. Quaker meetings prefer not to call themselves churches, and none practice water baptism or a last-supper ritual with bread and wine. The absence of hierarchy fits the Quaker testimony to equality, which is also why many present-day Quakers are LGBT. One beautiful aspect of John is its conceptual map, a model of sublime simplicity for a spiritual community.

Opposites in John and Jung

> Jung developed a model of psychological change through the tension of holding together opposing attitudes or views, whether conscious or unconscious. The term he used for this was the transcendent function, as an expression of the symbol, or metaphor, which arises in dreams and fantasies, and which transcends the opposites and facilitates movement from one attitude to another.
>
> Martin Stone[133]

John is a book of sharp contrasts. Light contrasts with darkness and night, and Life with death, to give only two examples. The disciples contrast with the World and above all with Jews.[134] The use of contrast even extends to Jesus himself:

---

[132] Stein, *Jung's Treatment of Christianity*, pages 112-135.

[133] "Individuation", in *Vision and Supervision*, page 67.

[134] Culpepper notes that "The reasons for [Jews'] response are explained not in terms of their 'Jewishness' but in universally applicable characteristics: they have never heard of or seen the Father (5:37); they do not want to come to Jesus... (5:40); they do not have the love of God in themselves (5:42), and they do not receive jesus (5:43) or seek the glory of God (5:44). An even more basic reason emerges later: they are from a different world order. They live on the wrong

"Nowhere in the New Testament is Jesus presented as both more thoroughly human and more thoroughly divine than in John,"[135] to name just one contrast. That last one, the humanity/divinity of Jesus, prolonged the debates in the Christian councils that produced the Christian creeds.[136]

Jesus is associated with the positive side of each duality; "In him was Life, and the Life was the Light of all people" (John 1:6), for example. There is some fluidity in applying these metaphors to Jesus; "the Life was the Light", but also "I am the Light of the World" (John 8:12). Regrettably in view of history, "the Jews" are the villains of the piece and are associated with the negatives. Culpepper notes:

> Primarily the conflict is between Jesus, who is "from above," and those who cannot and will not recognize his identity. Some of the characters gradually recognize and move from the lower plateau of understanding to the higher. The symbols are predominantly dualistic: light and darkness, ordinary water and living water, plain bread and true bread ("which came down from heaven" [John 6:33]). These symbols are woven into the more extensive dualism of the gospel.[137]

I agree with Paul Anderson that John's dualism stems from the thinking of the authors of John, but, unlike him, I see too tenuous a relation to James W. Fowler's theory of faith development.[138] I also have doubts about Fowler's theory overall. However, I agree that John's author thought in binary terms.

But so do we all. "Opposites are indispensable preconditions of all psychic life,"[139] Jung explained. "Everything requires for its existence its own opposite, or else it fades into nothingness",[140] and "every truth turns into an antinomy if it is thought out to the end."[141] Opposites operate at a far deeper and less conscious psychological level than Fowler's theory, and Jungians have validated Jung's observations about opposites in every client they treat. Opposites become constellated in a personality when compensation occurs, such as when Christ is all good on the outside, leaving his other side dark and split off.

Explaining why contradictions were inevitable in her anthology of quotations of Jung, Jolande Jacobi explained that contradictions

---

side of John's dualism: 'You are from below, I am from above' (8:23). Thereafter they are associated with all of the negative categories and images in the gospel: the world, sin, the devil, darkness, blindness and death. In their unbelief the Jews are 'symbols, types of the universal human condition.'" *Anatomy of the Fourth Gospel*, page 129.

[135] Anderson, *The Riddles of the Fourth Gospel*, page 175.

[136] Anderson, *The Christology of the Fourth Gospel*, page 1.

[137] *Anatomy of the Fourth Gospel*, page. 200; see also Charlesworth, *Jesus as Mirrored in John*, pages 345-347; Reinhartz, "The Gospel of John: How 'the Jews' Became Part of the Plot", page 105; Culpepper, *The Gospel and Letters of John*, page 89.

[138] Explained by Anderson in "The Cognitive Origins of John's Unitive and Disunitive Christology", in J. Harold Ellens and Wayne G. Rollins, eds., *Psychology and the Bible*, volume 3, page 132-134; *The Riddles of the Fourth Gospel*, page 131; *Christology of the Fourth Gospel* pages 142-148.

[139] Jung, *Collected Works*, volume 14, paragraph 206.

[140] Jung, *Collected Works*, volume 11, paragraph 961.

[141] From Jung's foreword (page 14) to Erich Neumann's *Depth Psychology and a New Ethic* (New York: 1969); quoted in Jacobi, *Psychological Reflections*, page 189.

> are due to [the] structural antinomy which is inherent in the psyche because of the fundamental tension of opposites between consciousness and the unconscious. The recognition of this polarity forces itself irresistibly on everyone today; it depends whether man in the future will be able to find his way out of the entanglements of fate back to some kind of order, or whether, in ignorance of his own psychic foundations and those of his fellow men, he will remain at the mercy of the powers of darkness which we have already experienced with horror in this present age [1945], so puffed up with pride at its cultural and technological progress.[142]

Besides stark contrasts, there are also contradictions and paradoxes in John. I have learned not to assume that logical inconsistencies in John came about through careless editing. There is much more to them. Traditional Christianity has been extensively rationalised, smoothing over inconsistencies, though they remain there. Carl Jung noted:

> By following Christian morality one gets into the very worst collisions of duty. Only a person who habitually makes five an even number can escape them. The fact that Christian ethics leads to collisions of duty speaks in its favour. By engendering insoluble conflicts and consequently an [affliction of spirit], it brings man nearer to a knowledge of God. All opposites are of God, therefore man must bend to this burden; and in so doing he finds that God in his "oppositeness" has taken possession of him, incarnated himself in him. He becomes a vessel filled with divine conflict.[143]

There is a way out of the conflict, however, and to my mind, John's love and mastery of irony and symbol show that its author sensed that way.[144] The author likes thinking on multiple levels and seems unperturbed if his quantum level contradicts his Newtonian level—the Truth goes deeper than either and includes them all. John's irony, metaphor and wordplay probe and savour meaning in its multiple levels. Perhaps our author begins to sense through them a union of the opposites—but if he[145] does, that sense is too faint to affect his writing.

The author's thinking ultimately remained polarised, polarisation expressed in portraying his antagonists, the Jews in his gospel. Like the Judaism of his time and upbringing, and traditional Christianity after him, he "shied away from integration of the shadow,"[146] or he fled his Cross, in Isaac's words.[147] Had he

---

[142] "Preface to the First Edition" of *Psychological Reflections: An Anthology of Jung's Writings 1905-1961*, page x. Jung noted, "Everything human is relative, because everything rests on an inner polarity; for everything is a phenomenon of energy. Energy necessarily depends on a pre-existing polarity, without which there could be no energy." *Collected Works*, volume 7, paragraph 115.

[143] *Answer to Job*, in *Collected Works*, volume 11, paragraph 659.

[144] R. Alan Culpepper offers a brilliant study of irony in John in *Anatomy of the Fourth Gospel*, pages 165-180.

[145] I do not know the gender of the author, and as noted above, the author may well have been a group at the end, disciples of the Beloved Disciple who completed and disseminated his work. I call the author "he" in this section as a simplification.

[146] Stein, *Jung's Treatment of Christianity*, page 140.

[147] See the Reflection on "The cross" above.

not, he might have found a way to peace with Jews, first by withdrawing his projections. What our author saw in Jews was—not Jews as they actually were then but his own shadow, his own anger and hurt that he couldn't bear to acknowledge in himself. "[O]ur strongest prejudices and convictions get their strength and obstinacy from unconscious projection".[148] There was an alternative: integrating the author's shadow into his consciousness, so that the whole person is capable of making peace through a conversation rather than pursuing conflict. Peace he would then have left us in John, as he says Jesus did (John 14:27); but as it is, much of what he leaves is polemic.

If the opposites in the mind do not come together, they can tear a person apart like Jesus outstretched on the cross (see "The cross" above). A person can get stuck oscillating between opposites, a state that Jung called "enantiodromia" after Herodotus.[149] Nicodemus is an example of a person caught in such a struggle.

> I take this figure [Nicodemus] to be an expression of the need on the part of the biblical psyche to contain the violent tension of the opposites and to keep itself intact in the midst of what we see in the fourth Gospel as an intensely polarized situation: light vs. darkness, Jesus vs. "the Jews," love vs. hatred, and the old vs. the new. The hostility is all the more intense for the emphasis on love, the dark all the darker because the light is brighter. While John's is the Gospel of Love, it is also the story of equally intense emotional antagonism and resistance. This is a story of crisis in which the exponent of new consciousness and a transformed attitude confronts the entrenched exponents of a solidified tradition.[150]

In John, this confrontation of opposites ended in catastrophe:

> This attempt to introduce a transformative change first produces a violent crisis, as the intensity of opposition equals the intensity of the force for change. Every light bringer runs into this, and murderous rage and execution is not a surprising conclusion to the story.[151]

Resolving the tension between warring opposites is where "only the symbol helps":

> What takes place between light and darkness, what unites the opposites, has a share in both sides and can be judged just as well from the left as from the right, without becoming any the wiser? .... Here only the symbol helps, for, in accordance with

---

[148] Wallis, *Jung and the Quaker Way*, page 108.

[149] *Collected Works*, volume 7, paragraph 111.

[150] Stein, *The Bible as Dream*, page 190.

[151] *Ibid.*, pages 190-191.

its paradoxical nature, it represents the "tertium" that in logic does not exist, but which in reality is the living truth.[152]

"The symbol is the middle way along which the opposites flow together in a new movement, like a watercourse bringing fertility after a long drought."[153] As Jesus thirsted on the cross, so do we all when torn up by opposites on our own crosses. The hope is living water, the "watercourse bringing fertility after a long drought".[154] It is nothing less than the way to God:

> Only in the most extreme and most menacing conflict does the Christian experience deliverance into divinity, always provided that he does not break, but accepts the burden of being marked out by God. In this way alone can the [God-image] realize itself in him, and God become man.[155]

Deliverance from inner conflict does not come by attempting to suppress the dark side of the conflict. "Mere suppression of the shadow is as little of a remedy as beheading would be for a headache."[156] The suppression would have to be about as drastic as death because the shadow in life is not capable of being suppressed; it will out, one way or another. If we cannot consciously realise it, its only way out is unconscious, such as by projection. "How can anyone see straight when he does not even see himself and the darkness he unconsciously carries with him into all his dealings?"[157]

> People who strive to be excessively ethical, who always think, feel, and act altruistically and idealistically, avenge themselves for their intolerable ideals by a subtly planned maliciousness, of which they are naturally not conscious as such, but which leads to misunderstandings and unhappy situations. All these difficulties appear to them as "especially unfortunate circumstances," or the fault and the malice of other people, or as tragic complications. Consciously they imagine they are rid of the conflict, but it is still there, unseen, to be stumbled over at every step.[158]

When passing through a place that is irremediably dark or oscillating, a guide is helpful. A good psychotherapist will see a person's shadow before the person does.

> The encounter with the dark half of the personality, or "shadow," comes about of its own accord in any moderately thorough [psychological] treatment. ... The open conflict is unavoidable and painful. I have often been asked, "And what do you *do* about it?" I do nothing; there is nothing I can do except wait, with a certain trust in God, until, out of a conflict borne with patience and fortitude, there emerges the solution

---

152 Jung, *Collected Works*, volume 13, paragraph 199.

153 Jung, *Collected* Works, volume 13, paragraph 443.

154 *Ibid.*

155 Jung, *Answer to Job*, in *Collected Works,* volume 11, paragraph 559.

156 Jung, *Collected* Works, volume 11, paragraph 133.

157 Jung, *Collected* Works, volume 11, paragraph 140.

158 Jung, quoted in Jacobi, *Psychological Reflections*, page 219.

destined—although I cannot foresee it—for that particular person.[159]

"Here only the symbol helps," said Jung;[160] however, encountering one's shadow does not mean that the symbol to resolve conflicts there appears immediately, without ever experiencing the conflicts, painful as they may be. Murray Stein:

> In fantasy, symbols form. Symbols are images that combine two or more incommensurables. What is seen as impossible by consciousness—the joining of opposite attitudes (extraversion and introversion), or opposite functions (thinking and feeling, sensation and intuition), or the union of opposite aspects of the personality (masculine and feminine, persona and shadow)—can take place in the unconscious. This is revealed in fantasy. Because the unconscious contains the opposites in undifferentiated form, it can create monstrous hybrids in a fashion ego-consciousness would never imagine or design or even find satisfying in their unpolished, raw shapes. And yet these symbols will point ahead toward psychological healing and toward the next stage of development.

> Because symbols combine the opposites the ego needs for resolving the original conflict, they represent a healing force in the psyche. In their vicinity, the ego often finds itself strangely comforted and energized. Symbols, moreover, are rich with [psychic energy], and this is reflected in their numinosity and near hypnotic effect. A person can draw on a symbol for orientation and adaptation and subtly repattern himself or herself on it.[161]

As noted above, encountering one's shadow, finding the symbol key, using it to resolve conflicts in the unconscious—these actions in the darkness can benefit from a guide who knows the terrain and is adept at seeing what can be seen in the dark. The hoped-for end is that "consciousness has become transformed—reoriented and restructured from within—on the pattern of the symbol, which combines the opposites that had formerly been irreconcilable."[162]

In my own experience, I eventually found my transforming symbols, a myth that made sense of me. In my travails, I was helped greatly by a therapist, and Isaac Penington was my spiritual guide. He helped me not to be too fearful or despairing in the dark because there is also light deep inside it.

> Wait for and ... receive the checks of the Most High, and take heed of reasoning against them. As these (though in a low and mean and despicable way to your wisdom) draw and lead you out of any earthly [=conscious] thought, word, custom,

---

[159] Jung, *Collected* Works, volume 12, paragraph 37. "A way is only *the* way when one finds and follows it himself. There is no general prescription for 'how to do it'." Jung, "A Study in the Process of Individuation", first English version in *The Integration of the Personality*, translated by Stanley M. Dell; quoted in Jacobi, *Psychological Reflections*, page 298.

[160] Quoted above.

[161] Stein, *Jung's Treatment of Christianity*, page 66.

[162] Stein, *Jung's Treatment of Christianity*, page 66.

or practice, follow diligently, waiting to have your reasonings subdued to the smallest motions and lowest guidance of life in you. For I know that life is near you, even the life that would effectually redeem you. But now the life is bowed down and held captive under the dominion of the earthly wisdom. So it is that your redemption (which is to be wrought out by the life) is hindered.... For I certainly know the light manifests in you, but the darkness puts off the present manifestation of the light, and expects another.[163]

---

[163] Penington, Letter to Sarah Bond, in an insert to his *Works* entitled "Additional Letters of Isaac Penington", page 12.

What happened afterwards

John was written about 90 C.E. By that time, John's spiritual hero, the Beloved Disciple, had died (John 21:23). The Temple had been destroyed by the Romans in 70 C.E. The destruction of Judea at that time caused emigration, refugees fleeing Rome's war in Judea. John was completed by people who had fled Judea and resettled, perhaps in Ephesus, 20-30 years before. What happened to them?

Fate of the community that wrote John

Reconstructing the life of a community of people that existed 2,000 years ago is difficult, but the eminent scholar of John, Raymond Brown, makes a case that convinces me of its gist.[1] The community began as the group of disciples present at the end of John.

Was that community of disciples distinct from the group described in the other gospels and Acts? That other group centres around Peter and Paul, the great apostles of Acts. The best indication that the community of John was distinct from the rest is that John's gospel is so distinctive. The others share many similarities but John is different. Its people had their own disciple-hero, and he was not Peter but the Beloved Disciple. John also tells a somewhat different story of Jesus's life, with greater emphasis on Love, Trust, Truth, the Father, and the Counsellor, and less emphasis on miracles and authority. John employs a wealth of its own metaphors to describe the Divine, words like Life and Light, which Quakers also now use. Indeed, its community developed its own "highly symbolic language with numerous expressions which they would easily understand as referring to their shared history."[2] The letters of John also continue this distinctiveness, leaving me to conclude that the community of John was a separate grouping of Jesus's followers with their own gospel and idiom.

Brown explains how the community of John came together during Jesus's life. Some steps in the community's formation we can read in John. First, 1:35-51 mentions a few people who begin following Jesus. In Chapter 4, after the Samaritan woman tells everyone in her village of her encounter with Jesus, more people join the community (John 4:39-42). The community probably included some who were neither Jewish nor Samaritan because John translates some Hebrew words like "Messiah",[3] words that Jews and Samaritans would have understood. Non-Jews are mentioned in John 12:20-23 as having interest. By the end of John, a group of disciples of diverse backgrounds has formed around Jesus.

The community shrank at times. After Jesus teaches of the "bread of life", "many of his disciples turned back and no longer went about with him" (John 6:66). At the cross, only the Beloved Disciple, Jesus's mother and her sister, Mary wife of Clopas, and Mary Magdalene are mentioned as present (19:25).

When the first generation of disciples died, leadership of the Christian mainstream passed to successors whom the apostles admonished to hold on to what they had been taught without change (Acts 20:28-30, Titus 1:9, 2 Peter 1:12-

---

[1] Part of what makes him convincing is that he admits the difficulty of reconstructing an ancient community. Brown, *The Community of the Beloved Disciple*, pages 17-21.

[2] Martyn, *The Gospel of John in Christian History*, page 91.

[3] John 1:38, 1:41, 1:42.

21). However, no apostles or hierarchy are mentioned in John, and no such admonition to the next generation appears in John or the letters of John, even after the Beloved Disciple dies (John 21:23). Instead, the community of John had the Counsellor as its teacher after Jesus (John 14:15-17, 16:13), along with its collective memory of Jesus.[4]

Psychology plays a part in the preservation of memory. Our authoring group had a psychology, and the son of man did as well, but we see him only second-hand. We have seen how John demonises Jews, when they really just chose to remain traditionally Jewish. Nothing they say in John is abusive, and their statements make sense from a Jewish point of view. John paints them strikingly worse than the facts bear out because the author projects his/her shadow onto them (see "Your father the devil" in John 8). They get nothing right, when that rarely happens in reality. Jesus, on the other hand, is too good to be real in John. Because John's Jesus was too good, psychological compensation occurred, so his opposite appears in 1 John:

> The conscious identification with one side of the self through the assimilation of the Christ-symbol constellated a figure, the Antichrist, who represented the other side, and the early predictions of the Antichrist's coming followed "an inexorable psychological law whose existence, though unknown to the author of the [letters of John] brought him to a sure knowledge of the impending enantiodromia".[5] So the "intensified differentiation of the Christ-image" brought about a "corresponding accentuation of its unconscious complement", thereby increasing the tension between above and below.[6]

The word "antichrist" (ἀντίχριστος) appears only in 1 and 2 John, six chapters of the Bible. Its basic meaning is replacement (Christ is being superseded, as Jesus had superseded Judaism), but it also came to mean opposition.[7]

The letters of John appear at roughly the same time as John, but they make more sense if we see them as coming just after John and from an "elder" familiar with John. In them we find the community of John divided. In 1 John, the author's

> dominant concern is to reinforce readers against a group that is doing the work of the devil and the antichrist (2:18, 4:1-6), a group that has seceded from the community (2:19) but is still trying to win over more adherents. .... By not acknowledging Jesus Christ come in the flesh, they negate the importance of Jesus (4:2-3); and although they claim

---

[4] Brown sees in John a "warning against the dangers [of reliance on apostolic successors] by stressing what for John is truly essential, namely, the living presence of Jesus in the Christian through the [Counsellor]. No institution or structure can substitute for that." Brown, *The Community of the Beloved Disciple*, page 88.

[5] Jung's word, borrowed from Herodotus, meaning oscillation between opposites, see "Opposites in John and Jung" above. The quotation is from Jung, *Aion*, in *Collected Works*, volume 9 part 2, paragraph 77.

[6] Stein, *Jung's Treatment of Christianity*, page 151.

[7] Brown, *The Epistles of John*, pages 332-337.

communion with God ... they do not show love... (2:9-11, 3:10-24, 4:7-21).[8]

Brown finds support in the gospel of John for *both* the position of the author of 1 John and that of the secessionists whom the author opposes.[9] The "emphasis on the divinity of Jesus sharpened through polemics in John overshadows principles like the humanity of Jesus".[10] The secessionists "so stress the divine principle in Jesus that the earthly career of the divine principle is neglected".[11] John mentions, though only briefly, that the "Word became flesh" (1:14), that Jesus got tired (4:6) and wept (11:35), and gave other indications of being human. However, Jesus in John also treats food (4:32), bread (6:33ff) and water (4:7-14, 7:38, 9:7) as symbols of spiritual needs.[12] The meaning of those symbols derives in part from the fact that such things are physical necessities, but the symbolic meaning gets the focus not the physical reality.

When Jesus faces his impending death, the other three gospels have him praying that God "remove this cup from me" (Mark 14:36, Matt. 26:39, Luke 22:42). That would be a normal human reaction to the prospect of one's violent death, but the Jesus of John knows his destiny. Realising that his Hour has come (12:23), John's Jesus says, "Now my soul is troubled. What should I say? 'Father, save me from this Hour?' No, this is why I came to this Hour. Father, glorify your name!" (12:27-28). On the cross, Matthew and Mark have Jesus crying out, "My God, my God, why have you forsaken me?", but John's Jesus says no such thing. He looks after his mother (19:26-27) and then announces when "it is finished" (19:30). The physical is there, but again the spiritual predominates. Jesus deals with his horrific death as glorified son of God—paradoxically, in other words—rather than in a straightforward human way. The secessionists pushed that glorification and the divinity of Jesus to the point that they left aside the human Jesus, the son of man. That was a great loss. Then Jesus was no longer like us, a man with a human soul. He was a myth and archetypal God-image but not a real person.

Besides criticising his opponents' views of Jesus, the author of 1 John criticises them as people who think they can do no wrong (1 John 1:8-10). However, the author also says in 1 John 3:9, "Everyone who has been born of God does no Wrong because the seed of God Remains in him, and he cannot do Wrong because he has been born of God." That last sentence can, however, be used just as well by the author's opponents to refute the author's claim that his opponents' way of life shows no practical indication of spiritual conviction.[13] They particularly appear to have lacked love (1 John 2:7-9, 3:23, 4:21, 5:2-3).

---

[8] Brown, *The Community of the Beloved Disciple*, page 94. Brown also notes the "anomaly" of both stressing love and the unacceptability of the secessionist position: "No more eloquent voice is raised in the [New Testament] for love...yet that same voice is extremely bitter in condemning opponents who had been members of the community and were so no longer". *Ibid.*, page 132.

[9] Brown, *The Epistles of John*, pages 73-86.

[10] Brown, *The Community of the Beloved Disciple*, page 110; Culpepper, *The Gospel and Letters of John*, page 51 and 60; Brown, *The Epistles of John*, pages 74-79.

[11] Brown, *The Community of the Beloved Disciple*, page 112.

[12] Schnackenburg has a thorough lists of passages from John that support Jesus's humanity and others that leave it some doubt. *Das Johannesevangelium*, volume 4:1, pages 150-153.

[13] Brown, *The Epistles of John*, pages 80-82.

The author of 1 John struggles with varying interpretations of the gospel and of Jesus—often struggling with paradox, but, interestingly, the author never resorts to authority. He never says anything like "I outrank you in the church so you must do as I say." Brown explains why:

> The community [of John] differed from the Apostolic churches on this point, for in the tradition [of John] the position of the [Counsellor] as the authoritative teacher, and the gift of the [Counsellor], would have relativized the teaching office of any church official.[14]

Instead of pulling rank, the author of 1 John invites his opposition to test their leadings: "Do not believe every spirit, but test the spirits to see whether they are from God, for many false prophets have gone out into the World" (1 John 3:24-4:6, 4:13). The community depended on its members to discipline themselves rather than rely on a hierarchy to enforce discipline.

Unfortunately, the writer of 1 John seems to have lost his struggle. "Many deceitful people have gone out into the World, people who do not acknowledge Jesus Christ as coming in the flesh" (2 John 7). "The World" is listening to the secessionists (1 John 4:5). Brown sees in this and other hints that "numerically the opponents are gaining over the author's adherents".[15]

"After the [letters of John], there is no further trace of a distinct and separate community [of John]."[16] Brown explains that the secessionists probably became docetists and gnostics etc., as they are well on the way to such beliefs as seen from the letters of John.[17] Docetists believe that Jesus only *seemed* to have come to earth, but he wasn't really physically here. Gnostics have special, often individual, spiritual knowledge that is the key to salvation. Both docetism and gnosticism were declared heretical by the early church.[18] The best evidence that Brown has (apart from the New Testament) for his conclusion about the

---

[14] Brown, *The Community of the Beloved Disciple*, page 141.

[15] Brown, *The Community of the Beloved Disciple*, pages 143-44.

[16] Brown, *The Community of the Beloved Disciple* page 145; Brown, *The Epistles of John*, pages 103-104; see also Culpepper, *The Gospel and Letters of John*, page 61.

[17] Brown, *The Epistles of John*, pages 104-106. Docetism makes Jewish thinking easier for Greeks to accept; Keener comments, "That a docetic interpretation of the Jesus tradition would arise was almost inevitable once Christian teaching about Jesus' deity .... began circulating in a Hellenistic culture." *The Gospel of John*, volume 1, page 407.

[18] Heretics would have been very welcome in Jung's consulting room, however. Both orthodox and heterodox myth interested him. He thought of docetism, for example, "more as a completion of the historical event than a devaluation of it". Stein, *Jung's Treatment of Christianity*, page 137. "This Gnostic Christ," wrote Jung, "symbolises man's original unity and exalts it as the saving goal of his development." *Psychology and Religion: West and East*, in *Collected Works*, volume 11, paragraph 292. Gnosticism "symbolises man's original unity" because it did not repress evil". Stein, *Minding the Self*, pages 86-91; Stein, *Jung's Treatment of Christianity*, pages 150-151.

Besides Gnosticism, Jung also studied alchemy because he found "it spoke for the unconscious of Christianity", reconnecting the too-good-to-be-true conscious Christian tradition with its earthy, dark, material, and yes, evil side—but not entirely evil. See Stein, *Jung's Treatment of Christianity*, pages 142-146 for an explanation of why Jung was interested in alchemy.

secessionists prevailing is that John was very popular among docetists and gnostics[19] because it can be read as supporting their views, as explained above.[20]

Brown surmises that the part of the community of John that remained faithful to the position of the writer of 1 John was eventually absorbed into what he calls "the Great Church", the church based on the first three gospels and led initially by Peter.[21] Their assimilation required them to accept the authority of bishops over that of the Counsellor.

If Raymond Brown is right, and I think he may well be, then Jesus did not get what he prayed for in John 17, the unity of his disciples.[22] The community divided, one part turning docetist and/or gnostic etc., the other accepting the authority of bishops over the guidance of the Counsellor.

Both are tragic losses from a Quaker perspective. The fate of John's community is a highly cautionary tale for Quakers, who likewise organise themselves into egalitarian communities with minimal hierarchy and a resolve to follow the leadings of the Spirit, individually and collectively. Georgia Fuller noted:

> A faith community without hierarchy or ecclesial answer book has only itself and its roots of yesterday and its hopes and visions for tomorrow. It requires constant tending by members, who are also tending themselves through spiritual reflection and discipline. It requires mutual responsibility and accountability. Some branches [of John's community] neglected to tend their life together in the common vine [John 15:1-17]. Their attempt to live though a personal umbilical cord was fatal.[23]

No wonder Jesus emphasised so heavily the need to Remain in him (John 15:1-11). It is crucial for our survival as Friends that each generation experience for itself the inward Light, because it is not possible to pass it from one generation to the next, or even from one person to another. It cannot be inherited or transferred; it must be discovered for oneself. Paul Anderson:

> ...unlike institutional organisations, spirit-based movements are by definition and experience mono-generational. Each generation must be transformed by the Spirit anew.... This

---

[19] Brown, *The Epistles of John*, pages 106-115; Brown, *The Community of the Beloved Disciple*, pages 145-150; Elaine Pagels, *The Johannine Gospel in Gnostic Exegesis*, from the Society of Biblical Literature Monograph Series (Nashville: Abingdon, 1973); Carson, *The Gospel According to John*, page 25. Brown's view is contested by Charles Hill in *The Johannine Corpus in the Early Church*, (Oxford: Oxford University Press, 2004) page 58; but reaffirmed by Keefer, *The Branches of the Gospel of John: The Reception of the Fourth Gospel in the Early Church*, Library of New Testament Studies no. 332 (London: T&T Clark, 2006).

[20] The irony of this is not lost on Barrett, who quotes John 17:25-26, then notes the "familiar themes" of the ignorant world, and of the revealer who is to make God known, but the purpose of it all is "the cultivation not of gnosis but of love, which alone is the mark of true disciples (13:35)." "The Dialectical Theology of St John," *New Testament Essays*, page 55 (London: S.P.C.K., 1972).

[21] Brown, *The Community of the Beloved Disciple*, page 145, 155-159. John 21, appended after most of the rest of John had been written, seems to be preparing for this shift toward the "great church" by focusing on Peter.

[22] Brown, *The Community of the Beloved Disciple*, page 158-159.

[23] Georgia E. Fuller, "Johannine Lessons in Community, Witness, and Power", pages 98-99.

explains [both the movement's] explosiveness **and** vulnerability.[24]

I would add, "and also its diversity".

The eternal truths cannot be transmitted mechanically: in every epoch they must be born anew from the human psyche.[25]

Writing a millennium and a half after John and 1 John were written, Isaac Penington explains what happened to early Christianity from his vantage point:

There was a glorious day, and bright appearance of Truth in the times of the apostles. They had the true Comforter [Counsellor], who led them into all Truth, kept them alive in Truth, and Truth alive in them. ....

But behold! a thick night of darkness overspread the beauty of this! Some false brethren went out from the true church into the world, getting [in] the sheep's clothing, making a great outward appearance, and drew the world after them, yea, and some from the very churches themselves. .... And when they had overcome the living testimony of Jesus, and the true power and presence of the Spirit among them, then they set up their own dead form, making a cry all over the nations of the earth: "Revelation is ceased! There is no looking now for such an infallible Spirit, such immediate teachings as the Christians had in the apostles' days...," but they pointed men to traditions, to the church, as they called it ... or to searchings of the scripture, and reading expositions upon it, and bodies of divinity, formed by the understanding-part in man to instruct the understanding-part. Thus the whole course of religion, and of the knowledge of God, came to be out of that Spirit and life wherein it first came forth..., and consisted in doctrines of men, and a form of worship and knowledge which the wisdom of man had framed, in an imitation of that which formerly stood in the life.

And now men being gone from the life, from the Spirit, and his immediate teachings, into an outward form of knowledge and worship of God in the wrong nature, antichrist is got up, and the dragon sits in the temple, appearing there as if he were God, giving out laws and ordinances of worship in public, and putting men upon duties and exercises of devotion in private, and he is obeyed and bowed down to in the

---

[24] Paul Anderson, "Was the Fourth Evangelist a Quaker?", in *Quaker Religious Thought*, volume 76 page 30 (October 1991); quoted in Fuller, "Johannine Lessons in Community, Witness, and Power" page 99 (emphasis in original).

[25] Jung, "After the Catastrophe", in *Collected Works*, volume 10, page 217.

observation of these; but the true, living God is not known, nor his secret, still voice ... heard".[26]

That describes the world into which George Fox was born, a world full of churches with nothing that "spoke to his condition".[27] The churches were full of incomprehensible rational doctrines like the Trinity, the products of reasoning from scripture—from inspiration in other words—but without participation in the inspiration itself: Reasons are given for doctrines, confirmation by the Counsellor directly to the soul is seen as surplusage in traditional Christianity. We see a case study of the slide to that point in 1 John as the community slips into docetism and gnosticism, rational approaches reflecting the surrounding Greek culture, but a subtle yet profound departure from the Truth.

That slide was facilitated by the gospel of John, as Brown explains.[28] It is as if the gospel misses the real spiritual peril: about half of it is spent denouncing the errors of Jewish ways, but it was the massive influx of Greek speakers who caused the disintegration. Gnosticism fits well into the Greek mind; Judaism much less so. The fact that Greeks not Jews caused the problem meant John fought a cause against Jews that was already lost by the time the ink was dry on the first complete text of John. It thinks at the wrong scale: when John was written, Judea had been small and idiosyncratic, but it was now destroyed. The wider Greek-speaking culture had a far larger population, and was well established all over the eastern Mediterranean. John prepared its community for Jews, a tiny defeated minority in the world but the object of intense anger in John. Had John focused more on what Greek minds would bring to the community, it might have included a birth narrative, for example, to leave no question of Jesus's humanity. With different emphases, John might have helped preserve the Truth rather than facilitate the slide from it.

Carl Jung saw Christianity as fighting a lost cause of self-preservation. He looked ahead of his time, not back at past battles. With disturbing accuracy, he foresaw the consequences of Christianity becoming moribund.

The apocalypse of Carl Jung

> So much of what Christian symbolism taught has gone by the board for large numbers of people, without their ever having understood what they have lost. Civilization does not consist in progress as such and in mindless destruction of the old values, but in developing and refining the good that has been won.
>
> Carl Jung[29]

Jung thought Christianity became too outwardly focused in the century before him; its rituals and rationally expounded dogma lost touch with the depth of the soul. Consequently, the life of Christ is viewed as facts with dogmatic not symbolic or personal significance. Myth, however, portrays events at symbolic depth, but "it is evident to thoughtful people that Western society no longer has

---

[26] *Axe Laid to the Root of the Old Corrupt Tree*, in *Works*, volume 1, page 227.

[27] Britain Yearly Meeting, *Quaker Faith and Practice*, section 19:02.

[28] *The Community of the Beloved Disciple*, pages 106-144.

[29] *Psychology and Religion*, in *Collected Works*, volume 11, paragraph 292.

a viable, functioning myth".[30] In church, religious experience is reduced to ritual, and the "indwelling of the Holy Ghost is discouraged and ignored as much as possible."[31]

When the outward ritual and dogma fail to convince, faith is to fill the deficit.

> Inasmuch as the belief is real and living, it works. But inasmuch as it is mere imagination and an effort of the will without understanding, I see little merit in it. Unfortunately, this unsatisfactory condition prevails in modern times, and in so far as there is nothing beyond belief without understanding but doubt and scepticism, the whole Christian tradition goes by the board as a mere fantasy. I consider this event a tremendous loss for which we are to pay a terrible price. ....
>
> What we need is the development of the inner spiritual man, the unique individual whose treasure is hidden on the one hand in the symbols of our mythological tradition, and on the other hand in man's unconscious psyche. It is tragic that science and its philosophy discourage the individual and that theology resists every reasonable attempt to understand its symbols. Theologians call their creed a *symbolum*, but they refuse to call their truth "symbolic".[32]

The failure of Christianity to keep alive a symbolic dimension has abandoned humanity to our age, in which "the unique individual whose treasure" is within has been reduced to a speck of data in a world driven by statistics, marketing targets, and mass movements.[33] We think nothing of what we have lost, and instead, "a kind of rootless consciousness comes into being ... a consciousness which succumbs helplessly to all manner of suggestions and, in practice is susceptible to psychic epidemics".[34] Jung might not have foreseen exactly how "psychic epidemics" would happen, but now we can see the immense power of commercial marketing and how social media help mass movements swarm.

None the less, Jung was amazingly prescient because he did foresee:

- **Morality determined by mass movements**. A decline in personal responsibility comes about as individuals disappear into population masses. Instead of the individual, the state, political party or movement becomes the carrier of moral responsibility.[35] However, "the crowd does not rise to the level of the highest intelligences in it, but the qualities that everyone has become the dominant characteristics of the whole crowd."[36] For individuals without their own moral compass or spiritual anchor, consumption becomes the purpose of life and marketing the driving force behind it. Social media spawn and drive mass movements, so that the

---

[30] Edinger, *The Creation of Consciousness*, page 9.

[31] Jung, *Answer to Job*, in *Collected Works,* volume 11 paragraph 695.

[32] C.G. Jung, "Letter to Upton Sinclair", in *Letters*, volume 2, 208; reprinted in Stein, *Jung on Christianity*, page 167.

[33] Jung, *The Undiscovered Self*, in *Collected Works*, volume 10, paragraphs 488-502.

[34] *Collected Works,* volume 11, paragraph 267.

[35] Jung, *The Undiscovered Self*, in *Collected Works*, volume 10, paragraph 499.

[36] Jung, quoted in McGuire & Hull, *C.G. Jung Speaking*, page 144.

"whole of reality [is] replaced by words. [We] lack all contact with life and the breath of nature."[37]

- **Establishment of "creeds"**. Authentic spirituality hardens into what Jung calls "creeds", which are allied with the state.

  > A creed gives expression to a definite collective belief, whereas the word *religion* expresses a subjective relationship to certain metaphysical, extramundane factors. A creed is a confession of faith intended chiefly for the world at large and is thus an intramundane affair, while the meaning and purpose of religion lies in the relationship of the individual to God (Christianity, Judaism, Islam) or to the path of salvation and liberation (Buddhism).[38]

  In the end, creeds end up in service to the state, which "swallows up [the individual's] religious forces; the state has taken the place of God."[39]

- **Hollowing out of real religion**. Creeds include established churches, "whose members include not only true believers but vast numbers of people who can only be described as 'indifferent' in matters of religion and who belong simply by force of habit."[40] For that reason, a creed "does nothing to give the individual any foundation."[41] By contrast, in a real religion, "the life of the individual is not determined solely by the ego and its opinions or by social factors, but quite as much, if not more, by a transcendent authority" (God).[42]

  Hollow spirituality leaves the collective superficial, "a society currently [2014] living at a soul destroying and depressive level of superficiality. This shallowness extends to the failure of institutional religion currently to provide its constituents with a significant spiritual meaning."[43]

- **Fanaticism**. Creeds produce fanatics: "The religious function cannot be dislocated and falsified ... without giving rise to secret doubts, which are immediately repressed so as to avoid conflict with the prevailing trend towards mass-mindedness. The result, as always in such cases, is overcompensation in the form of fanaticism".[44] The fanaticism is political and societal as well as having a spiritual driver. The cause is that the loss of traditional symbols leaves a void, a "vacuum that gets filled with absurd political and social ideas, which one and all are distinguished by their spiritual bleakness."[45]

- **Tyrants**. "To compensate for its chaotic formlessness, a mass always produces a 'Leader,' who may have a mythic heyday but in the end

---

[37] Jung, *Collected Works*, volume 10, paragraph 882.

[38] Jung, *The Undiscovered Self*, in *Collected Works*, volume 10, paragraph 507.

[39] *Ibid.*, paragraph 511.

[40] *Ibid.*, paragraph 508.

[41] *Ibid.*, paragraph 509.

[42] *Ibid.*.

[43] Dourley, *Jung and his Mystics*, page 33.

[44] *Ibid.*, paragraph 511. See also Wallis, *Jung and the Quaker Way*, page 16.

[45] Jung, *Collected Works*, volume 9 part 1, paragraph 28.

becomes the victim of his own inflated ego-consciousness."[46] The state, now more powerful than ever because of the weakness of the church and disempowerment of individuals, falls into the hands of a strong man, often one looking back nostalgically to the good old days when Germany, Russia, America, or Britain was great. People with a saviour complex will be lurking in society, and a crisis is all it takes for a Hitler to rise.[47] We are coming full tilt into environmental crises now.

- **Truth suffers** under the lack of moral responsibility, fanaticism, tyranny, and the demand of a creed for blind faith. Naziism and Trumpism both demonstrate that, with the power of marketing, no lie is too big to be saleable. Because we lack "answers to the spiritual needs and troubles of a new epoch .... never before has 'eternal truth' been faced with such a hubris of will and power."[48]

- **Change occurs in the mass, not the individual**. "In accordance with the prevailing tendency of consciousness to seek the source of all ills in the outside world, the cry goes up for political and social changes which, it is hoped, would automatically solve the much deeper problem of split personality."[49] Looking to politics and society to fill the individual soul's lack of meaning and depth gives an opening to politicians.

  > Anyone who has once learned to submit absolutely to a collective belief and to renounce his eternal right to freedom and the equally eternal duty of individual responsibility will persist in this attitude, and will be able to set out with the same credulity and the same lack of criticism in the reverse direction, if another and manifestly 'better' belief is foisted upon his alleged idealism.[50]

Compared to this list, the book of Revelation is a comfort because its horrors are not half so realistic.

Jung's *The Undiscovered Self*, summarised above, was first published in 1957. His words are remarkably prophetic from the vantage point of 2024. Seeing the growth of technology in his own time, Jung also foresaw that present-day humanity "has incomparably more effective means with which to realise ... evil."[51] Those means are perhaps even more effective at present than he could foresee—the worldwide web and social media may not have been conceivable, even for the far-sighted, when Jung died in 1961.[52]

---

[46] Jung, *The Undiscovered Self*, in *Collected Works*, volume 10, paragraph 500.

[47] See "No greater than our father Jacob" in John 4 above.

[48] Jung, *Collected Works*, volume 16, paragraph 396.

[49] Jung, *The Undiscovered Self,* in *Collected Works*, volume 10, paragraph 558.

[50] *Ibid.*, paragraph 523.

[51] *Ibid.*, paragraph 514.

[52] Nearer our own time than Jung, Quaker Melvin Keiser explains our situation in terms remarkably similar to Jung's:

> For all our success in using critical reason, we are brought to our present difficulties of possible annihilation, felt meaninglessness, and anxiety of how to be fully and religiously in the world. (I wrote this in 1984.) While the Enlightenment's use of critical reason has

Jung wrote *The Undiscovered Self* in the aftermath of World War II, during which he had had a front-row seat from which to observe Germany. Before the War:

> Jung ... offered a psychological analysis of the distorting power of numinous images in the churned up political and social processes tearing apart the cultural fabric of Germany and central Europe at that time.[53] In this instance, Jung observed, the psychic force field of the manifestly constellated Wotan mythic image had taken possession of an entire nation and was driving Germany to an (at that time) unknown and irrationally determined end. .... The convincing power of the archetypal image and presence also shielded people from the awareness of guilt for their criminal behaviour. Everything could be justified, no matter how heinous. Archetypal possession of a collective group invests certain ideas and policies with absolute certainty and brooks no doubt [or] dispute. Contrary thoughts and images are savagely suppressed.[54]

"Wotan" is more commonly called Odin in English. No other passage I know of speaks more eloquently of the sanctity of doubt, dissent and dialogue.

It is tragic that a man as wise as Jung believed himself a failure in saving humanity from its undoing, not just in the War but in the years after it:

> I had to understand that I was unable to make people see what I am after. I am practically alone. There are a few who understand this and that but almost nobody sees the whole. ... I have failed in my foremost task, to open people's eyes to the fact that man has a soul, and that there is a buried treasure in the field and that our religion and philosophy is in a lamentable state.[55]

Jung died in 1961, before completing treatment of his patient, Christianity.[56]

---

liberated us in many ways, we have rather found us in a world cast adrift from its religious and moral moorings, shattered in its sense of meaning, experiencing the world no longer as real and shared but as a fragmented, dubious, solipsistic space. Heroically we name the denizen of such an existence an "autonomous individual," yet ironically and menacingly, meaninglessness and alienation have grown as the individual has autonomously increased its technological power. Just when we have acquired the technological capacity to destroy humanity, we have abrogated the human capacity for personal commitments, which alone is the basis upon which we might take responsibility for the continuance of life, and have rather given over leadership to impersonal objectivism (the expert-scientist or technocrat) and the self-interested manipulator of private desires (the politician).

Seeds of Silence, page 44-45.

[53] Note from the source text: Jung, *Wotan*, in *Collected Works*, volume 11.

[54] Stein, *Minding the Self*, page 84.

[55] Quoted in Edward F. Edinger, *Transformation of the God-Image: An Elucidation of Jung's Answer to Job*, page 25 (Toronto: Inner City Books, 1992).

[56] Stein, *Jung's Treatment of Christianity*, page 181.

The remedy for individuals

> Save yourselves from this untoward generation.
>
> Acts 2.40 (King James version).

Saving the collective requires beginning with the remedy for oneself. "Only the self-development of the individual, which I consider to be the supreme goal of all psychological endeavour, can produce consciously responsible spokesmen and leaders of the collective movement."[57]

> Individual self-reflection, return of the individual to the ground of human nature, to his own deepest being with its individual and social identity—there is the beginning of a cure for that blindness.[58]

Or as George Fox put it succinctly, "Your Teacher is within you. Look not forth."[59] Exactly Jung's point.[60]

A query for Friends in our time is what to do about our distinctive voice in Christianity. Jung saw Christianity as a sinking ship. Always empathetic with the Jobs of this world, he also thought of the people on that ship. After noting that we live in a time more secular and scientific, and less spiritual, than ever:

> The believer is then forced to catechise himself on the foundation of his beliefs. He is no longer sustained by the [general consensus], and is keenly aware of the weakening of the Church and the precariousness of its dogmatic assumptions. To counter this, the Church recommends more faith, as if that gift of grace was simply a tap that could be turned on at will. The seat of faith, however, is not consciousness but spontaneous religious experience, which brings the individual's faith into immediate relation with God.
>
> Here we must ask: Have I any religious experience and immediate relation with God, and hence, that certainty that will keep me, as an individual, from dissolving in the crowd?[61]

Friends would perhaps be inclined to let that query hang there for each soul to answer for herself. Jung, however, answers his own question:

> To this question there is a positive answer only when the individual is willing to fulfill the demands of rigorous self-examination and self-knowledge. If he follows through his intention, he .... will have set his hand, as it were, to a declaration of his own human dignity and taken the first step towards the foundations of his consciousness—that is,

---

[57] Jung quoted in McGuire & Hull, editors, *C.G. Jung Speaking*, page 77.

[58] Jung, *Collected Works*, volume 7, paragraph 5.

[59] George Fox, *Journal*, 1694 edition, edited and transcribed by Thomas Ellwood, page 98; online at 1694 edition: page 98 (lancaster.ac.uk).

[60] Jung, however, phrases it in terms of consciousness, and in the negative: "If even the smallest and most personal stirrings of the individual soul—so insignificant in themselves—remain as unconscious and unrecognized as they have hitherto, they will go on accumulating and produce mass groupings and mass movements which cannot be subjected to reasonable control or manipulated to a good end." *The Undiscovered Self*, in *Collected Works*, volume 10, paragraph 575.

[61] *The Undiscovered Self*, in *Collected Works*, volume 10, paragraph 564.

towards the unconscious, the only accessible source of religious experience.[62]

In other words, your Teacher is within you, not in the din of our time.

Back to that query for Friends in our time: what to do about our distinctive voice in Christianity? George Fox also answers that one:

> Be patterns, be examples in all countries, places, islands, nations, wherever you come, that your carriage and life may preach among all sorts of people, and to them; then you will come to walk cheerfully over the world, answering that of God in every one; whereby in them ye may be a blessing, and make the witness of God in them to bless you.[63]

Jung says it actually works and explains how:

> What does lie within our reach, however, is the change in individuals who have, or create, an opportunity to influence others of like mind in their circle of acquaintance. I do not mean by persuading or preaching—I am thinking, rather, of the well-known fact that anyone who has insight into his own actions, and has found access to the unconscious, involuntarily exercises an influence on his environment. The deepening and broadening of his consciousness produce the kind of effect which the primitives call "mana." It is an unintentional influence on the unconscious of others.[64]

Collective prospects: shards and hopes

> What does a culture do when transcendent meaning has left, when it is hollowed out and nothing is left but concerns about material comfort and entertainment?[65]

The apocalyptic horrors listed above are present symptoms of psychological ill health in western civilisation. The prognosis of that collective patient holds some hope, says Murray Stein in his book, *Jung's Treatment of Christianity*. First, however, let's recall the causes for the patient's symptoms:

> Jung's motives for engaging in this therapeutic of the Christian tradition were to some extent personal ones, as I have indicated, but they are also a deep and abiding concern on his part for the welfare of Christianity and Western culture. Beyond these, however, was his concern for the survival of the human race itself. Without access to vital religious symbols that solidly support a religious attitude and a sense of ego-transcendent reality, humans run the risk, he felt, of terrifying pathological inflation-depression cycles. At times the ego, identifying with the self, becomes godlike and grandiose, and in this inflation it overrides all ethical and rational constraints. At other times, when the ego loses

---

[62] *Ibid.*, paragraph 565.

[63] Pacific Yearly Meeting, *Faith and Practice*, paragraph 67, page 84.

[64] *The Undiscovered Self*, in *Collected Works*, volume 10, paragraph 563.

[65] Stein, *The Mystery of Transformation*, page 212.

connection with the self, it falls into despair and becomes the victim of the nihilism engendered by the absence of a psychological center and a symbolic life. Either way, for modern technological society this pathology is particularly lethal because of the awesome power of modern tools and weapons. Mankind can now destroy itself either in an act of hubris under the illusion of invulnerability or in a suicidal act of nihilistic non-caring. Even worse, should the dark side of God [Satan] incarnate itself in modern man, as Jung predicted it would, and find itself unmet by the full strength of a Christian (or Christian-like) spiritual standpoint, the annihilation of the race would be not only thinkable, it would be probable. The seeming inevitability of this outcome haunted Jung's last years.[66]

Murray Stein is not without hope, however, although:

Christianity may still be falling critically short of a deep-going transformation process, which Jung regarded as the only long-range solution for this ailing tradition. And, to my mind, it is highly dubious that traditional Christianity ever will, or could if it wanted to, voluntarily die and be reborn into the next phase of evolution as envisioned by Jung.

.... Jung's concept of Christianity's transformation is, I believe, of this magnitude: Christianity and its authoritative source book, the New Testament, would become for the transformed version of the tradition what Judaism and the Old Testament became for Christianity, a prefiguration and forerunner of the new revelation.

What this offspring of Christian tradition would look like Jung did not describe in detail. He was not that sort of visionary, and he felt the unconscious would, in its own time and manner, lead the way. The needed symbol would come together when the time was right. For the present, it was clear to Jung that an incubation process was under way in the collective unconscious.[67]

Murray Stein sees these "major stumbling blocks"[68] in the way of transforming Christianity:

- **The traditional understanding of God**. The Trinity falls short of being complete; it is three when it should be four.[69] It leaves out (and unconscious) the feminine and the darker, earthier aspects of life, whereas the self, the psychological image of God, is complete.

  The square, four-foldedness of all kinds, and all quadratic images represent two pairs of opposites held in tension. These quaternities represent a psychological state of

---

[66] Stein, *Jung's Treatment of Christianity*, page 180.

[67] Stein, *Jung's Treatment of Christianity*, page 186.

[68] Stein, *Jung's Treatment of Christianity*, pages 185-194.

[69] Stein, *Jung's Treatment of Christianity*, pages 123-135.

wholeness, in which the tension of opposites is maintained and contained rather than denied and collapsed into a false sense of peace and harmony through splitting, repression, and projection.[70]

This new understanding of God would be "inclusive of all aspects of reality, mundane and transcendent. God would be synonymous with reality".[71] Quakers often call God "Truth".

This new generation of disciples may not be numerous, however:

> Following the Jewish-early Christian model, however, it is clear that a transformation of this magnitude and depth takes place only for a small minority within a tradition, for a few persons who are gripped by the new vision. The transformation does not come about through the tradition's leadership's suddenly undergoing a conversion and leading the way. And indeed the old tradition does not itself transform: It gives birth to a new generation, and then the old and the newly developing traditions continue to exist side by side, much like a quarrelling set of parents and children. Indeed, the emergence of a new tradition and its separation from the old may itself have a revitalising effect on the parent tradition.[72]

- **Authority**. The second major stumbling block toward renewal is authority.

> Whether the locus of authority for creating theological doctrine and for regulating religious practice has been placed in tradition, in Scripture, or in the community of believers, it has invariably, since earliest times in Judaism and Christianity, lain outside the individual's experience of the divine. .... The individual's visions of God have had to square with external authority.
>
> .... For Jung, the source of religious authority rested completely in the individual's experience of the divine, in the individual's fully experienced and integrated vision of the self. Without this relation to the unconscious, Jung felt, there could be no authentic religious life for modern men and women. .... A person's own experience of the divine becomes a continuous sense of God's presence, which relates to everything from the most mundane activity to the most numinous vision of the Godhead. This sustained individual consciousness of God's guiding spirit, which in his psychology

---

[70] Stein, *Jung's Treatment of Christianity*, page 186.

[71] Stein, *Jung's Treatment of Christianity*, page 187.

[72] Stein, *Jung's Treatment of Christianity*, page 187-188.

Jung named the transcendent function, becomes the source of all religious authority.[73] ....

Such experiences of the self and of the *spiritus rector* can, of course, be shared among individuals in a community, but there would be no canon within this community, beyond the individual's own experiences, to confirm or disconfirm their validity.[74]

How does a community look when it has "no canon" to structure it? Stein knew of a "model":

In this transformed offspring of Christian tradition, there would be no normative text, no normative witness or revelation, no central figure or symbol or confession ("Jesus is Lord") to which a united community of believers would subscribe, and certainly no centralized ecclesiastical power. Perhaps a model for it on the ecclesiastical level would be the Quaker meeting, with each member searching the spirit with an "inward light," with no clerical leadership, and with minimal community constraints on the attitudes and behavior of the individual. What all members of this community would have in common would be a commitment to personal integration and psychological wholeness, to leading a religious life by maintaining a conscious dialectic with the unconscious, and to acknowledging the unconscious as the source of healing, transforming and guiding symbols.[75]

- **Emblematic lives**. Our "historic commitment to certain emblematic lives (Christ, the apostles, the saints) who embody [Christianity's] ideal of spiritual perfection"[76] is the third obstacle toward a new spiritual generation.

    Jung's recommendation of psychological wholeness as the new master image for a transformed Christianity would lift up emblematic lives that embodied the principle of maximum integration, of those who were able to maintain consciousness of the opposites within themselves and who hold them in tension rather than splitting the opposites and identifying with only some aspects of the self.[77]

Wholeness is an individual matter; the collective cannot be more whole than its members are, and its members do not become whole by imitating other people (see "Quaker experience of Christ and the inward Light" above).

    That Jung did not point to emblematic lives, or for that matter to his own as emblematic, should perhaps be ascribed to his

---

[73] Stein, *Jung's Treatment of Christianity*, page 189.

[74] Stein, *Jung's Treatment of Christianity*, pages 189-190.

[75] Stein, *Jung's Treatment of Christianity*, page 190; see also Dourley, *Jung and his Mystics*, pages 17-18.

[76] *Ibid.*

[77] Stein, *Jung's Treatment of Christianity*, pages 190-191.

therapeutic technique. In therapy, the patient is healed and made whole by integrating whatever emerges from the unconscious, and the resulting wholeness is thus tailored to that specific life. It is not governed by an external ideal of what, or how, the patient should be. Similarly, among the practitioners of a Christianity transformed, the images of wholeness would perhaps be shown forth less by emblematic historical persons who represent the ideal of wholeness for everyone than by inner symbolic figures who appear in dreams and fantasy and represent the state of wholeness that is specific to that individual.[78]

There is hope if we can heal our souls. "Jung would have placed his trust for the future in individuals, hoping that enough of them would become gripped by a psychological individuation process and would choose to pursue this path of religious life."[79]

As any change must begin somewhere, it is the single individual who will experience it and carry it through. The change must begin with an individual; it might be any one of us.

Nobody can afford to look around and wait for somebody else to do what he is loath to do himself. But since nobody seems to know what to do, it might be worthwhile for each of us to ask himself whether by any chance his or her unconscious may know something that will help us.[80]

---

[78] Stein, *Jung's Treatment of Christianity*, page 192.

[79] Stein, *Jung's Treatment of Christianity*, page 193.

[80] Jung and others, *Man and his Symbols*, page 101-102.

Bibliography

Paul N. Anderson, *The Christology of the Fourth Gospel: Its Unity and Disunity in the Light of John 6.* Valley Forge, Pennsylvania: Trinity Press, 1996.

Paul N. Anderson, *The Riddles of the Fourth Gospel: An Introduction to John.* Minneapolis: Fortress Press, 2011.

John Ashton, *The Gospel of John and Christian Origins.* Minneapolis: Fortress Press (2014).

C.K. Barrett, *The Gospel According to St John: An Introduction with Commentary and Notes on the Greek Text*, second edition. London: SPCK (1978).

Walter Bauer, William F. Arndt, F. Wilbur Gingrich, Frederick W. Danker, *A Greek-English Lexicon of the New Testament and Other Early Christian Literature*, second edition. Chicago and London: University of Chicago Press (1979).

John Behr, *John the Theologian and his Paschal Gospel.* Oxford: Oxford University Press (2019).

Michael L. Birkel & John W. Newman, editors, *The Lamb's War: Quaker Essays to Honor Hugh Barbour.* Richmond, Indiana: Earlham College Press (1992).

Christopher M. Blumhofer, *The Gospel of John and the Future of Israel.* Cambridge: Cambridge University Press (2020).

Britain Yearly Meeting, *Quaker Faith and Practice: The Book of Christian Discipline of the Yearly Meeting of the Religious Society of Friends (Quakers) in Britain*, 5th edition. London: Britain Yearly Meeting (2013).

Raymond E. Brown, *The Community of the Beloved Disciple.* New York: Paulist Press (1979).

Raymond E. Brown, *The Death of the Messiah: From Gethsemane to the Grave: A commentary on the Passion Narratives in the Four Gospels*, in two volumes, part of the *Anchor Bible Reference Library.* New York: Doubleday (1993).

Raymond E. Brown, *The Epistles of John*, volume 30 in W.F. Albright & David Noel Freedman, editors, *The Anchor Bible* (Garden City, New York: Doubleday (1982).

Raymond E. Brown, *The Gospel According to John*, in volumes 29 and 29A, W.F. Albright and D.N. Freedman, editors, *The Anchor Bible.* Garden City, New York: Doubleday (1970).

Raymond E. Brown, *An Introduction to the New Testament*, in David Noel Freedman, editor, *Anchor Bible Reference Library.* New York: Doubleday (1997).

F.F. Bruce, *The Gospel of John: Introduction, Exposition and Notes.* Grand Rapids, Michigan: Eerdmans (1983).

F.F. Bruce, *New Testament History.* Garden City, New York: Anchor Books, Doubleday (1972).

Christopher Bryant, *Jung and the Christian Way.* London: Darton, Longman and Todd Ltd (1983).

D. A. Carson, *The Gospel According to John.* Nottingham: Apollos (1991), published in the USA by Eerdmans of Grand Rapids, Michigan.

James H. Charlesworth, *Jesus as Mirrored in John: The Genius in the New Testament.* London: T&T Clark (2019).

Kenneth L. Carroll, "The Fourth Gospel and the Exclusion of Christians from the Synagogue," *Bulletin of the John Rylands Library* 40 (1957), 19-32.

Richard J. Cassidy, *John's Gospel in New Perspective: Christology and the Realities of Roman Power.* Eugene, Oregon: Wipf & Stock (1992).

Mary L. Coloe, *God Dwells with Us: Temple Symbolism in the Fourth Gospel.* Collegeville, Minnesota: The Liturgical Press (2001).

Mary L. Coloe, *John 1-10*, volume 44A in Mary Ann Beavis and Barbara E. Reid, *The Wisdom Bible Commentary.* Collegeville, Minnesota: Liturgical Press (2021).

Mary L. Coloe, *John 11-21*, volume 44B in Mary Ann Beavis and Barbara E. Reid, *The Wisdom Bible Commentary.* Collegeville, Minnesota: Liturgical Press (2021).

Philip W. Comfort and David P. Barrett, *The Complete Text of the Earliest New Testament Manuscripts.* Grand Rapids, Michigan: Baker Books (1999).

R. Alan Culpepper, *Anatomy of the Fourth Gospel: A Study in Literary Design.* Philadelphia: Fortress Press (1983).

R. Alan Culpepper, *The Gospel and Letters of John.* Nashville: Abingdon Press (1998).

John P. Dourley, *The Illness that We Are: A Jungian Critique of Christianity.* Toronto: Inner City Books (1984).

John P. Dourley, *Jung and his Mystics: In the End it All Comes to Nothing.* London and New York: Routledge (2014).

John P. Dourley, *On Behalf of the Mystical Fool: Jung on the Religious Situation.* London and New York: Routledge (2010).

Edward F. Edinger, *The New God-Image: A Study of Jung's Key Letters Concerning the Evolution of the Western God-Image*, edited by Dianne D. Cordic and Charles Yates. Wilmette, Illinois: Chiron Publications (1996).

Edward F. Edinger, *The Creation of Consciousness: Jung's Myth for Modern Man.* Toronto: Inner City Books (1984).

Edward F. Edinger, *The Christian Archetype: A Jungian Commentary on the Life of Christ.* Toronto: Inner City Books (1987).

Edward F. Edinger, *Transformation of the God-Image: An Elucidation of Jung's Answer to Job.* Toronto: Inner City Books (1992).

Thomas Ellwood, "Testimony of Thomas Ellwood Concerning Isaac Penington", in Penington, *Works*, volume 1.

Craig A. Evans, *Word and Glory: On the Exegetical and Theological Background of John's Prologue.* Sheffield: Sheffield Academic Press (1993).

Georgia E. Fuller, "Johannine Lessons in Cummunity, Witness, and Power", in Chuck Fager, editor, *The Bible, the Church and the Future of Friends: Papers from the Quaker Issues Roundtable.* Wallingford, Pennsylvania: Pendle Hill (1996).

Josephus, *Antiquities of the Jews*, online at
https://josephusonline.weebly.com/antiquities.html.

Carl Gustav Jung, Jolande Jacobi, editor, *Psychological Reflections: An Anthology of Jung's Writings 1905-1961.* London and New York: Routledge (1953), original German *Psychologische Betrachtungen: Eine Auslese aus den Schriften von C.G. Jung* (1945).

Carl Gustav Jung, *Aion: Researches into the Phenomenology of the Self*, second edition. London and New York: Routledge (1959).

Carl Gustav Jung, *Answer to Job,* in *Collected Works,* volume 11. Princeton, New Jersey: Princeton University Press (1954, first German edition *Antwort auf Hiob* 1952).

Carl Gustav Jung, *Modern Man in Search of a Soul.* London: Routledge (1933).

Carl Gustav Jung, *Memories, Dreams, Reflections*, recorded and edited by Aniela Jaffé. Hammersmith: Fonatan Press (1995).

Carl Gustav Jung, *Psychology and Religion: West and East*, in *Collected Works* volume 11. Princeton, New Jersey: Princeton University Press.

Carl Gustav Jung, *The Undiscovered Self*, in *Collected Works*, volume 10. Princeton: Princeton University Press (1958, first German edition *Gegenwart und Zukunft* 1957).

Bernardo Kastrup, *Decoding Jung's Metaphysics: The Archetypal Semantics of an Experiential Universe.* Winchester: iff Books (2021).

Craig S. Keener, *The Gospel of John: A Commentary.* Grand Rapids, Michigan: Baker Publishing Group 2012.

Raimar Keintzel, *C.G. Jung: Retter der Religion? Auseinandersetzung mit Work und Wirkung.* Mainz: Matthias-Grünewald-Verlag, and Stuttgart: Quell Verlag (1991).

J. Louis Martyn, *The Gospel of John in Christian History: Seven Glimpses into the Johannine Community*, Paul N. Anderson, editor, foreword by R. Alan Culpepper. Eugene, Oregon: Wipf & Stock (2019).

William McGuire & R.F.C. Hull, editors, *C.G. Jung Speaking: Interviews and Encounters*, London: Picador (1978).

R. Melvin Keiser, "Felt Reality in Practical Living and Innovative Thinking: Mary and Isaac Penington's Journey from Puritan Anguish to Quaker Truth", in Stephen W. Angel and Pink Dandelion, editors, *Early Quakers and their Theological Thought 1647-1723.* Cambridge: Cambridge University Press (2015).

R. Melvin Keiser & Rosemary Moore, *Knowing the Mystery of God Within: Selected Writings of Isaac Penington in their Historical and Theological Context.* London: Quaker Books (2005).

R. Melvin Keiser, *Seeds of Silence: Essays in Quaker Spirituality and Philosopical Theology.* Winchester: Christian Alternative Books (2021).

Wayne A. Meeks, *The Prophet-King: Moses Traditions and the Johannine Christology.* Eugene, Oregon: Wipf & Stock (1967).

Francis J. Moloney, *Love in the Gospel of John: An Exegetical, Theological, and Literary Study.* Grand Rapids, Michigan: Baker Academic (2013).

Pacific Yearly Meeting, *Faith and Practice: A Guide to Quaker Discipline in the Experience of Pacific Yearly Meeting of the Religious Society of Friends* (2001).

Isaac Penington, *The Axe Laid to the Root of the Old Corrupt Tree,* (1659) in *Works,* volume 1. Glenside, Pennsylvania: Quaker Heritage Press (1997).

Isaac Penington, *An Examination of the Grounds or Causes which are said to induce the Court of Boston, to make that Law of Banishment, upon Pain of Death, Against the Quakers,* (1660) in *Works*, volume 1. Glenside, Pennsylvania: Quaker Heritage Press (1997).

Isaac Penington, *A Further Testimony to Truth, Revived out of the Ruins of the Apostasy*, (published posthumously in 1680) in *Works*, volume 4. Glenside, Pennsylvania: Quaker Heritage Press (1997).

Isaac Penington, *The Jew Outward: Being a Glass for the Professors of this Age*, (1659) in *Works*, volume 1. Glenside, Pennsylvania: Quaker Heritage Press (1997).

Isaac Penington, *Life and Immortality Brought to Light through the Gospel*, (1671, posthumous) in *Works*, volume 4. Glenside, Pennsylvania: Quaker Heritage Press (1997).

Isaac Penington, *Naked Truth, or Truth Nakedly Manifesting Itself*, (1674) in *Works*, volume 3. Glenside, Pennsylvania: Quaker Heritage Press (1997).

Isaac Penington, *The New Covenant of the Gospel Distinguished from the Old Covenant of the Law etc.*, (1660) in *Works*, volume 2. Glenside, Pennsylvania: Quaker Heritage Press (1997).

Isaac Penington, *Of The Church in Its First and Pure State*, in *Works*, volume 3. Glenside, Pennsylvania: Quaker Heritage Press (1997).

Isaac Penington, *The Scattered Sheep Sought After*, (1659) in *Works*, volume 1. Glenside, Pennsylvania: Quaker Heritage Press (1997).

Isaac Penington, *Some Misrepresentations of me concerning Church Government*, (no date) in *Works*, volume 4. Glenside, Pennsylvania: Quaker Heritage Press (1997).

Isaac Penington, *Some of the Mysteries of God's Kingdom Glanced At*, (1663) in *Works*, volume 2. Glenside, Pennsylvania: Quaker Heritage Press (1997).

Isaac Penington, *Some Questions and Answers for the Opening of the Eyes of the Jews Natural*, (1661) in *Works*, volume 2. Glenside, Pennsylvania: Quaker Heritage Press (1997).

Isaac Penington, *To All such as Complain that they Want Power*, (1661) in *Works*, volume 2. Glenside, Pennsylvania: Quaker Heritage Press (1997).

Isaac Penington, *A Treatise concerning God's Teaching, and Christ's Law*, (ca. 1671) in *Works*, volume 4. Glenside, Pennsylvania: Quaker Heritage Press (1997).

Isaac Penington, *The Way of Life and Death made Manifest, and Set before Men*, (1658) in *Works*, volume 1. Glenside, Pennsylvania: Quaker Heritage Press (1997).

Adele Reinhartz, *Befriending the Beloved Disciple: A Jewish Reading of the Gospel of John*. New York and London: Continuum (2005).

Adele Reinhartz, *Caiaphas The High Priest*. Columbia, South Carolina: University of South Carolina Press (2011).

Adele Reinhartz, *Cast out of the Covenant: Jews and Anti-Judaism in the Gospel of John*. Lanham, Maryland: Lexigton Books/Fortress Academic (2018).

Adele Reinhartz, "The Gospel of John: How 'the Jews' Became Part of the Plot", in Paula Frederiksen & Adele Reinhartz, editors, *Jesus, Judaism and Christian Anti-Judaism: Reading the New Testament after the Holocaust*. Louisville, Kentucky: Westminster John Knox Press (2002).

Andrew Samuels, Bani Shorter & Fred Plaut, *A Critical Dictionary of Jungian Analysis*. London and New York: Routledge (1986).

Rudolf Schnackenburg, *Das Johannesevangelium*, volume IV, parts 1-3, of A. Wikenhauser and Anton Vögtle, Herausgeber, *Herders theologischer Kommentar zum Neuen Testament*. Freiburg, Basel, Wien: Herder (1979).

Robert A. Segal, *Jung on Mythology*. London and New York: Routledge, 1998.

Thomas P. Slaughter, *The Beautiful Soul of John Woolman, Apostle of Abolition*. New York: Hill & Wang (2008).

Murray Stein, *The Bible as Dream: A Jungian Interpretation*. Asheville, North Carolina: Chiron Publications (2018).

Murray Stein, "C.G. Jung, Psychologist and Theologian", in volume 5 of the *Collected Writings of Murray Stein*. Asheville, North Carolina: Chiron Publications (2023).

Murray Stein, *Collected Writings of Murray Stein*, volume 6. Asheville, North Carolina: Chiron Publications (2022).

Murray Stein, "The Future of Christianity", in volume 5 of the *Collected Writings of Murray Stein*. Asheville, North Carolina: Chiron Publications (2023).

Murray Stein, editor, *Jung on Christianity: Selected and Introduced by Murray Stein*. Princeton: Princeton University Press (1999).

Murray Stein, *Jung on Evil: Edited and with an Introduction by Murray Stein*. London and New York: Routledge (1995).

Murray Stein, "Jung's Green Christ: A Healing Symbol for Christianity", in Murray Stein and Robert L. Moore, editors, *Jung's Challenge to Contemporary Religion*. Wilmette, Illinois: Chiron Publications (1987). Also published in volume 5 of the *Collected Writings of Murray Stein*. Asheville, North Carolina: Chiron Publications (2023).

Murray Stein, *Jung's Treatment of Christianity: The Psychotherapy of a Religious Tradition*. Wilmette, Illinois: Chiron Publications (1985).

Murray Stein, *Minding the Self: Jungian Meditations on Contemporary Spirituality*. London and New York: Routledge (2014).

Murray Stein, *The Mystery of Transformation*. Asheville, North Carolina: Chiron Publications (2022).

Murray Stein, *The Principle of Individuation: Toward the Development of Human Consciousness*. Wilmette, Illinois: Chiron Publications (2006).

Giovanni V.R. Sorge, "The construct of the 'mana personality' in Jung's works: a historic-hermeneutic perspective: Part 1", in *Journal of Analytical Psychology*, 2020, volume 65, Issue 2.

Giovanni V.R. Sorge, "The construct of the 'mana personality' in Jung's works: a historic-hermeneutic perspective: Part 2", in *Journal of Analytical Psychology*, 2020, volume 65, Issue 3.

Daniel B. Wallace, *Greek Grammar Beyond the Basics: An Exegetical Syntax of the New Testament*. Grand Rapids, Michigan: Zondervan (1996).

Jack H. Wallis, *Jung and the Quaker Way*. London: Quaker Home Service (1988).

Patricia A. Williams, *Quakerism: A Theology for our Time* (West Conshohocken, Pennsylvania: Infinity (2008).

Gale A. Yee, *Jewish Feasts and the Gospel of John.* Eugene, Oregon: Wipf & Stock (1989).

Appendix

The woman (and text) caught in adultery (John 7:53-8:11)

The reason for removing this from the main text is that it is a later interpolation; see the note at the beginning of John 8.

However, its interpolation does not mean that the story has nothing to say. It beautifully dramatises the common human failing of judging others without seeing the fault in oneself. It does me no good to project unconscious evil onto other people and then stone them for *my evil*; better to see that I am not without my own faults. I can do little or nothing for someone else's faults, but I can hope to remediate my own.

> [53]They each went home, [1]but Jesus went to the Mount of Olives. [2]Early in the morning, he came again into the Temple. All the people came to him, and when he had sat down, he began teaching them.
>
> [3]The scribes and Pharisees bring a woman who had been caught in adultery,[a] and, after having her stand in the centre,[b] [4]they tell him, "Teacher, this woman was caught in the very act of committing adultery. [5]In the law, Moses commands us to stone such women. So what do you say?"[c] [6]They said that to test him, so that they might have a charge against him. Jesus bent down and wrote with his finger on the ground. [7]When they continued questioning him, he stood up and told them, "Let the sinless one among you throw the first stone at her." [8]Then again he bent over and wrote on the ground. [9]When they heard, they went away one by one, beginning with the older ones,[d] and Jesus was left alone again with the woman in the middle. [10]Jesus straightened up and said to her, "Woman, where are they? Does no one condemn you?" [11]She said, "No one, Lord."[e] Jesus said, "Nor do I condemn you. Go and do Wrong no more.

Meaning and resonance

a. **"adultery"** (8:3, 8:4): Mary Coloe explains what "adultery" meant in Judaism then:

> For adultery to occur, the woman must be married or betrothed. In that society it meant that she "belonged" to another man, and so the offense is against property rights. If the woman is single there is no adultery, even if the man is already married. If adultery has occurred, the both the man and the woman are condemned to death (Lev. 20:10; Deut 22:24). Leviticus does not specify the form of death, but Deuteronomy 22:24 states, "you shall bring both of them to the gate of that town and stone them to death." The laws are clearly androcentric, in that they consider only the marital status of the woman and ignore the status of the man. In this episode, a further injustice is evident in that only one party,

the woman, is paraded before Jesus and the crowd of people while the offending man is not.[1]

b. **"having her stand in the centre"** (8:3): The question and Jesus's response to it are the focus; she is left "standing there in the middle, dishevelled, embarrassed, alone, and we have ignored her all this time. The controversy of the text has blinded us to the controversy of the woman."[2]

c. **"In the law, Moses commands us to stone such women. So what do you say?"** (8:5): Roman law did not permit execution for adultery,[3] so the question to Jesus was a trick question meant to entrap him. Jesus is on trial here too.

"Such women" shows that she has been judged as a category of women; her accusers do not see her as a person in her own right or attempt to understand her on her own terms. To them, she is merely a slut, an object to be judged and stoned by men, with no thought of the man who would have been just as guilty.

d. **"When they heard, they went away one by one, beginning with the older ones..."** (8:9): This is astonishing behaviour, astonishing because of the honesty of the "scribes and Pharisees". Most people deal with their blameworthy behaviour by denying and repressing it, but here we have Jews whose honesty in acknowledging their own Wrongs is truly amazing psychologically. Inserted right in the middle of Jesus's most vehement anti-Jewish diatribe, this insertion is refreshingly positive about Jews.

e. **"No one, Lord"** (8:11): Although the "scribes and Pharisees" treat this woman as an object, Jesus does not. He engages her in a brief conversation, treating her as the human being she is.

---

[1] *Wisdom Bible Commentary*, volume 44A, pages 263-264.

[2] Peter Phillips, "The Adulterous Woman: Nameless, Partnerless, Defenseless," in Hunt, Tolmie and Zimmermann, *Character Studies in the Fourth Gospel*, page 411, quoted in Coloe, *Wisdom Bible Commentary*, volume 44A, page 264.

[3] Coloe, *Wisdom Bible Commentary*, volume 44A, page 264, note 7.

Index

Adam and Eve, 28, 108, 139
  became conscious in Eden, 84
  Penington's view, 22
  traditional Christian view, 17
Addiction, 104, 167
Antichrist, 277
Antisemitism. *See* Jews, *See* Jews
Apostasy, 236, 281
Archetypes, 22
  communicate through symbols, 49
  reduction to historical person, 50
Arrest of Jesus, 179
Atonement
  not required (Quaker view), 19
Author
  Beloved Disciple, 29
  identity of, 29
Authority, 279
  obstacle to renewing Christianity,
    291
Barrabas, 183
Basel cathedral smashed, 217
Beloved Disciple
  as a Witness, 262
  at the Last Supper, 170, 172
  author of John, 29, 209
  death of, 31, 209, 262
  eyewitness and author (19:35),
    191
  eyewitness to Jesus's life, 29
  follows Jesus after arrest, 181
  identity is unknown, 31
  knew both Jesus and Counsellor,
    247
  resurrection morning, 198
Bethesda
  healing at, 105
Bible
  difficult passages, 257
  fleshly knowledge of, 192
  guessing at what Spirit does not
    open, 110
  not needed for salvation, 12
  reading in the "Quaker way", 10
  Spirit necessary to understand,
    12, 47, 103, 110, 185
Born from above, 55

Bread of life, 111
Caiaphas
  decision to kill Jesus, 151
  fears Roman intervention, 152
  high priest, 152
  his fear came true, 155
  tormented by God's injustice, 155
Christ
  analogy of the self, 48
  green Christ, Jung's dream of, 218
  imitation of, 20, 192, 193
  inwardly met, 49
  meaning of, 15
  meaning of for Penington, 147
  Quaker usage, 15
Christianity
  Adam and Eve, 17
  apostasy of, 281
  chronic squabblers (Jung), 216
  creeds produce fanatics, 285
  disregards Holy Spirit, 283
  dominated by creeds, 284
  Holy Spirit, 17
  Jung's concern for modern, 289
  not a concept found in John, 268
  not the only way (Quakers), 12
  obstacles to its transformation,
    290
  requires transformation, 290
  superficiality of modern, 284
  symbols lack meaning, 283
  too outward, 283
  transformation of a minority only,
    290
  views of Christ, 16
  withered branch of the vine, 217
Church
  Counsellor the real authority, 279
  not found in John, 39, 266
Community of John
  existence of, 30, 276
  formation of, 276
  lost through division, 279
  transition away from Judaism, 40
  writing of John, 30
Complexes, 221, 227, 230
Compulsion to repeat, 109

Counsellor, 47, 226, 266, *See also*
    Holy Spirit
    aiding memory, 162
    authority of, 178
    comes when Jesus goes, 227
    convincing/convicting the World,
        227
    defined, 240
    Jung's view, 25
    promised (John 14-16), 176
    promised for bearing Cross, 194
    rather than church authority, 279
    when arrives, 241
Creation
    separating actions, 51
Creeds, 284
Cross (Quaker term), 19, 121, 191,
    272
    daily, 194, 196
    experienced by Mary, 196
    fleeing, 193
    ongoing, 194
Crucifixion. *See also* Cross (Quaker
    term)
Crucifixion of Jesus, 186
Darkness, 53
Dead Sea scrolls, 35
Disability, 138
Discernment, 145
Doubt and dissent. *See* also Faith
    importance of, 204, 287
    repression of causes fanaticism,
        285
    Thomas, 205
Dream the myth onwards, 218
Emotions happen to us, 155
Empirical   nature   of   Jung's
    psychology, 21
Envy
    gloating shadow of, 154
    motivating priests and Pharisees,
        154
    through the Bible, 153
Experience, religious
    basis for faith, 288
    eruption of the unconscious, 21
    final authority, 21
    in ordinary everyday life, 116
    not to know the Truth but to
        experience it, 110

only source is the unconscious,
    288
Trust based on, 116, 204
Faith, 17, 283, *See also* Doubt and
    dissent, *See also* Trust
    cannot be had to order, 116
    church demands to fix
        Christianity, 288
    fanaticism, 204
    how acquired, 116
    little required for Quakers, 103
    no experiential basis for, 204, 288
    no substitute for experience, 258
    not given to all, 54
    psychotherapist's, 118
    requiring it begs the question, 205
    trust in the Life in us, 147
Fate, 139
Father
    defined, 241
Fell, Margaret
    we're all thieves!, 12
    what canst thou say?, 47
Festival of Booths, 123
Flesh, 129, 192
Fox, George
    be patterns, 288
    Christianity at his time, 282
    speaking in church, 12, 47
    what canst thou say?, 47
    your teacher is within you, 118,
        267, 287
Galilee
    "sea", 113
    "sea" of, 207
Glory
    meaning of, 163
God
    and Satan, one psyche, 242
    archetype, 22
    becomes conscious thanks to Job,
        229
    becoming conscious of, 237
    continuity in evolving God-image,
        237
    defined by Jung, 21
    good split from evil, 242
    image evolves, 23, 220, 229, 237
    is dead (a dead belief), 21, 200
    not perfect in Job, 229

not tribal, for one sect only, 236
playing favourites, 154
synonyms for, 15
Good Shepherd, 142
Grace and truth, 56, 57
Greek
language of the eastern
Mediterranean, 35
Greeks
arrive and the Hour comes, 162,
163
Healing
illness not a manifestation of sin,
107
lame man on Sabbath, 105
man born blind on Sabbath, 135
official's son, 101
Healthy-mindedness, 158
Hephaistos, 221
Herod Agrippa, 36
Herod the Great, 37
rise to power, 36
History of John's time
sources for, 34
timeline, 35
Hitler, 285
Hogle, George, 156
Holy Spirit, 28, *See also* Counsellor
ignored by Christianity, 283
importance of, according to Jung,
54
incarnation into consciousness,
228
not under church control, 26
Homophobia, 268, 269
Hour comes, 159
I am
defined, 243
frequency in John 8, 128
Jesus's use of, 41
soldiers prostrate themselves, 180
Immersion in water, 59
purification as purpose (Jews), 59
Individuation, 26, 27, 28, 147, 167,
175, 221, 227
analysis and synthesis, 167
Christ's life a prototype, 193
comes through conflict, 194
differentiation from the collective,
178

for everyone, 53
hope for humanity, 293
Inflation, 285
inflation-depression cycles, 289
Inward not outward, 13, 49, 111, 121,
129, 131, 132, 192, 228, 267
Irony, 61, 62, 64, 125, 126, 137, 183,
199, 260
Jesus entering on a donkey, 161
Jerusalem
going up to, going down from, 65
pilgrimage require, 65
Jesus. *See also* Christ
aloof, 228
burial of, 197
carries his cross in John, 187
crucifixion, 186
death for a wrong done by God, 25
deconstructs his identity as king,
174
died for God's sins not ours
(Jung), 230
differently portrayed in John, 278
divinity over humanity in John,
278
foretells his betrayal, 170
historical Jesus reductive, 48
insurgent, treatment as, 39
Nazarene, when Hour comes, 180,
186
prays to Father, 232
projecting our problems onto, 193
rides donkey into Jerusalem, 158,
161
washes feet of disciples, 169
why he caught on, 52
Jews. *See also* Judaism
antisemitism, 47, 246
antisemitism a compensation, 277
antisemitism in John, 39
antisemitism in John 8, 133
antisemitism, authority for, 43
antisemitism, consequences for
John, 46
antisemitism, consequences of,
46, 247, 282
antisemitism, moral responsibility
for, 44
appropriation of culture by Jesus,
41

author shows shadow in
    portraying, 184
consoling Mary and Martha, 150
diversity of, before conquest, 40
euphemisms for, by scholars, 245
exclusion from synagogues, 141
John compensates for idealised
    Jesus, 184
John fights the wrong battle, 282
John's usage of the word, 245
manipulate Pilate, 184
reasons for rejecting John, 40
rejection of community of John,
    42
sects of, in ancient time, 39
slavery, 130
Job, 229
answered by Jesus, 164
turning point, 24
Job experiences, 140
Jung's view of, 23
morally superior to God, 25
remains faithful to God, 230
sees his vindicator *in God*, 230
story of, 23
wife of, 196
John
authority of, 32
critical reading of, 47
date of completion, 31
date of, manuscript evidence, 32
development of, 30
different from other gospels, 47
effect on division of community,
    278
episodic nature of, 30
manuscripts of, 32
polarised by opposites, 271
title of, 29
John (the Baptist), 59
Josephus, 35
sects of Judaism, 39
Judaism
superseded by Jesus, 41
Judea, 37, *See also* Jerusalem
culture, 37
destruction of, 35, 36, 39
political instability, 39
special privileges in Roman
    Empire, 37

Lazarus, 148
Life
defined, 248
eternal life explained, 248
two kinds of, 163
Light
authority of, 178
defined, 250
difference of the eye in seeing, 111
enlightens everyone (1:9), 53
experience of, 19, 178
meaning the Divine, 15
of the World, I am, 129
shows us our darkness, 19
Mana personality, 289
Manuscripts
Bodmer papyri, 33
oldest papyrus, 32
omission of John 5:4, 33, 107
picture of, 34
variations in text, 33
woman caught in adultery, 127
Map, 39
Mary (of Bethany) anoints Jesus, 158
Mary and Martha of Bethany, 148
Mary Magdalene, 64, 198
Messiah, 47
meaning of, 15
Morality, 44, 156, 229, 265
conflicts of, 271
determined by mass movements,
    284
requires understanding shadow,
    265
Moses
law given by, 57
testified of Jesus, 108
Mother of Jesus
at crucifixion, 195
at wedding at Cana, 62
suffering servant, 196
Narrator, 234
Nathaniel, 61
Nicodemus, 123, 125
struggling with opposites, 272
Numinous
as projection, 168
central to Jung's work, 166
glory as synonym, 163

Rudolf Otto first documented, 33, 166

Obedience, 109, 147, 177

Opposites, 26, 108, 230, 242, 269, 270, 292
conflict required for deliverance, 273
lead to crucifixion, 194

Paradox, 22, 103, 104, 220, 226, 260, 279
judgment by the son, 137
quiet humour of, 220

Passover
first one in Jesus's public life, 65
hyssop branch, 189
Jesus's last Passover begins, 151
slaughter of lambs as Jesus dies, 183
three Passovers in John, 114

Penington, Isaac
against Puritans of Boston, 117
come to that hammer, 20
Father's drawings, 116
first experience of the Light, 18
fleeing the cross, 193
give over thine own willing, 17
grafted into the vine, we are, 215
keeping low, 265
knowing below consciousness, 247
language of, 239
mistaken, 212
new creation, new covenant, 222
new creature, 18
on apostasy, 281
on blood of Christ, 121
on God's love, 222
on John's contradictions, 137, 144
on life and death, 249
on obedience, 177
on unity, 235, 237
Perrot controversy, 211
symbols, 121
veiled self, 18
vs. Thomas Hicks, 120
wait to feel the thing itself, 16
weak stirrings of life in the heart, 230, 255
words, 16, 239

Peter, 262

denials foretold, 170
denies Jesus three times, 180
goes fishing after Jesus dies, 207
meaning of name, 61
psychology of, 210
resurrection morning, 198
rise and fall, 210

Pharisees
survive destruction of Judea, 37, 40
we are, says Jung, 193

Pilate, Pontius
biography, 182
Jesus appears before him, 181
power over Jesus, 183

Primordial images
thousand voices, 119

Projection, 13, 34, 110, 266, 273
defined, 111
explains numinous experiences, 168
in John's treatment of Jews, 134
in John's treatment of Jews, 264
in portraying Jews, 272
onto Jesus, 193
undoing of, 111

Prophet like Moses
Jesus *the* prophet, 60, 125

Psychotherapy
limits of, 118
value of, 273

Quakers
authority among, 17
community requires self-care, 280
distinctive voice to dying Christianity, 287
model for renewed Christianity, 291
not the only way to God, 216
unity, 17, 178
who met Jung, 156

Quakers \t, 147

Qumran. See Dead Sea scrolls

Resurrection
history of the idea, 150
John vs. Paul, 200
morning of, 197
recognition difficulties, 201
transformation of consciousness, 201

Revelation, 15, 234
"ceased", 110, 281
nature of, hidden comes to light, 52
new, and discernment, 238
of archetypal image, 52
Sabbath
Father is still working, 107
healing lame man, 105
healing man, 136
Sacraments, 172, 267
no eucharist in John, 120
reductive, 120
Salvation. *See also* Rescue
is for all (Quaker view), 20
not open to all (Christian view), 17
Samaritans
conquered by Hasmonean Jews, 36
Sanhedrin, 152
decides to kill Jesus, 151
power of, 37
Scriptures. *See* Bible
Self, 147
inability to make conscious, 13
regression to paganism, 14
Shadow, 64
awareness of required for morality, 265
can't be suppressed, 273
integration of, 272
Signs
Book of Signs ends, 151
defined, 253
feeding 5,000, 112
healing lame man on Sabbath, 105
healing man born blind on Sabbath, 135
healing official's son, 101
raising of Lazarus, 148
water turned to wine, 62
Siloam, pool of, 136
Sin. *See also* Wrong
calls for love, 266
consciousness of, 109
cycle, 109
delivered from fear of (Jung), 26
effect of, 265
fall of Adam and Eve, 17

new creature cannot, 18
Social media, 286
Son of man, 61
Sophia, 27
eternal life her gift, 150
leads God to self-reflection, 25
sacred marriage with God, 27
steps in for Job, 25
Suffering servant, 165, 173, 177, 185, 201, 266
a healer vocation, 174
John Woolman as, 225
Symbols, 238, 253, 283
contrasted with Signs, 253
finiteness of, 241
formation of, 274
no longer work, 236
uniting opposites, 27, 272
Synagogues
consequences of exclusion from, 43
exclusion from, 40, 141, 226
exclusion from, transition to new identity, 45
Synchronicity, 255
Temple
bloody at Passover time, 190
destruction of, 36
Jesus's body, 41
Testimony
of oneself, 107
Thomas, 148, 176, 202
Transcendent function, 116, 168, 186, 222, 269
signals of transcendence, 119
signals of transcendence in Quaker worship, 116
Trinity, 282
incomplete concept (Jung), 268, 290
not a Quaker doctrine, 19, 241
not found in John, 268
Trust, 205
can't be willed, 205
defined, 258
official's, to heal his son, 103
required for Quaker worship, 259
Truth
evidence for, 111
shall set you free, 131

suffers from marketing, 285
Unconscious
    integration into ego, 164
Unity
    basis for, 237
    false image of, 235
    false, caused by judging, 117
    in diversity, vine metaphor, 215
    Jesus prays for, 233
    of Father, son, people, 235
Vine metaphor, 214, 230
Wedding at Cana, 62
    an incoherent story, 64
    who was getting married?, 64
Women in John, prominence of, 195
Woolman, John, 223
Word, the, 51

became flesh and lived among us,
    55
Words
    communication runs deeper, 239
    deconstruction of, 240
    inadequate to express God, 241
    leading to experience, 239
World
    defined, 262
    hates the faithful, 226
Worship, 147, 148
    not a passive experience, 101
    requires Trust, 259
Wrong. *See also* Sin
    calls for love, 266
    defined, 264
Zealots, 39